Mitigating the Risks of AI Deepfakes

Artificial intelligence (AI) has become deeply embedded in modern life, with autonomous systems now controlling many crucial functions in healthcare, transportation, and industry. However, the incredible power of AI also enables new forms of manipulation, deception, and harm. *Mitigating the Risks of AI Deepfakes* explores the dark side of AI and its dangerous implications for human wellbeing.

Spanning over 250 pages, this book examines how attackers can exploit AI systems to spread misinformation, steal identities, endanger lives through faulty diagnostics, and jeopardize public safety through products like self-driving cars. The chapters also dive into the national security risks posed by deepfakes and the use of AI to create compelling fake audio/video content used for political sabotage and blackmail. They explain how deepfakes could be uniquely disruptive in conservative societies that depend on reputation and visual evidence.

While increased reliance on AI delivers efficiency and insight, unchecked development poses catastrophic risks that outweigh the benefits. By assembling a comprehensive overview of the threats we face alongside potential solutions, this book sounds an alarm regarding the dark side of progress while laying out a blueprint for mitigating dangers. The chapters synthesize cutting-edge research on fighting back against AI manipulation through innovations in machine learning, deep learning, reinforcement learning, and federated learning.

Ultimately, *Mitigating the Risks of AI Deepfakes* serves as an essential call to action for consumers, companies, and governments to confront the hazards of AI proliferation head-on. If left unaddressed, the sinister potential of systems we depend on could endanger civil liberties and human life. We must work proactively to guard the public interest as intelligent algorithms grow more advanced. This book equips readers with the knowledge to meet that challenge.

Mitigating the Risks of AI Deepfakes

Edited by Tarek Moulahi, Malka N. Halgamuge, and Pascal Lorenz

CRC Press
Taylor & Francis Group
Boca Raton London New York

CRC Press is an imprint of the
Taylor & Francis Group, an **informa** business

First edition published 2026
by CRC Press
2385 NW Executive Center Drive, Suite 320, Boca Raton FL 33431

and by CRC Press
4 Park Square, Milton Park, Abingdon, Oxon, OX14 4RN

CRC Press is an imprint of Taylor & Francis Group, LLC

Library of Congress Cataloging-in-Publication Data
Names: Moulahi, Tarek editor | Halgamuge, Malka N. editor | Lorenz, Pascal, 1965– editor
Title: Mitigating the risks of AI deepfakes / edited by Tarek Moulahi, Malka N. Halgamuge, and Pascal Lorenz.
Description: First edition. | Boca Raton : CRC Press, 2026. | Includes bibliographical references and index.
Identifiers: LCCN 2025048008 (print) | LCCN 2025048009 (ebook) | ISBN 9781032823508 hbk | ISBN 9781032886756 pbk | ISBN 9781003539032 ebk
Subjects: LCSH: Computer security | Deepfakes | Digital forensic science | Information literacy | Computer literacy
Classification: LCC QA76.9.A25 M58497 2026 (print) | LCC QA76.9.A25 (ebook)
LC record available at https://lccn.loc.gov/2025048008
LC ebook record available at https://lccn.loc.gov/2025048009

ISBN: 978-1-032-82350-8 (hbk)
ISBN: 978-1-032-88675-6 (pbk)
ISBN: 978-1-003-53903-2 (ebk)

DOI: 10.1201/9781003539032

Typeset in Sabon
by Apex CoVantage, LLC

Contents

About the Editors

Tarek Moulahi is Associate Professor of Computer Science and IT at the College of Computer, Qassim University (Saudi Arabia), and at the University of Kairouan (Tunisia). He received his Ph.D. in Computer Science through a joint doctoral program between the University of Franche-Comté (France) and the National School of Engineering of Sfax (Tunisia) in 2015. He has published more than 80 peer-reviewed papers in cybersecurity, artificial intelligence, intelligent vehicular networks, blockchain, and data communications. He has served as a Guest Editor for numerous international journals and is listed among the Stanford–Elsevier Top 2% Scientists. He has led and contributed to multiple funded research projects, including work on integrating blockchain with AI, privacy-preserving federated learning, and secure blockchain consensus mechanisms, in collaboration with international partners in the United States, France, Saudi Arabia, and Tunisia. His research interests include IoT and WSN security, VANET/IVN routing and misbehavior detection, privacy-preserving AI, federated learning, and graph-based anomaly detection.

Malka N. Halgamuge is a Senior Lecturer in Cybersecurity at RMIT University, Melbourne, Australia. She currently serves as Chair of the IEEE Computational Intelligence Society (Victorian Section) and Vice Chair of the IEEE Victorian Section, Australia. From 2007–2021, Malka worked as a Researcher at the Department of Electrical and Electronic Engineering at the University of Melbourne. She obtained her PhD in the same department. She was awarded prestigious fellowships: Australia-China Young Scientist Fellow (China), Dyason Fellow (UCLA), Chinese Academy of Sciences (CAS) President's International Fellow (Beijing), Solander Fellow (Sweden), Incoming Leaders Fellow (Australia India Institute, Delhi), Next Step Initiative Fellow (China). Malka was the Keynote Speaker (ICEMI'25, ICACMVE'23, EcoSSSoil'19, EPR'18), Plenary Speaker (IEEEPowerCon'24, AIBC'24, ICBET'18), Associate Editor, Editorial Board Member, and IEEE Senior Member. She was the Program Co-Chair, Track Chair, Publication Chair, Advisory Chair, Publicity Co-Chair, Session Chair, Guest Editor, and a Member of the TPC for 300 international conferences. She has presented 60 invited/guest lectures in academia (e.g., Oxford University, Ohio State University), industry, and at 10 IEEE sections. Malka has conducted 18 media interviews, articles, radio interviews, and TV interviews (ABC News). She is passionate about research in IoT, data communications, cybersecurity, AI applications, and LLMs security and their energy efficiency. She has co-supervised 4 PhD students to completion at the University of Melbourne as the principal supervisor and currently supervises 10 PhD students at RMIT University.

Malka has been a chief investigator for multiple grants totalling over $2 million and has over 120 peer-reviewed publications in scientific journals and conference proceedings (GS Citations=6400, h-index=40). She has been consecutively listed among the top 2% of the world's most cited researchers (Stanford University database, 2020–2025).

Pascal Lorenz received his M.Sc. (1990) and Ph.D. (1994) from the University of Nancy, France. Between 1990 and 1995 he was Research Engineer at WorldFIP Europe and at Alcatel-Alsthom. He has been Professor at the University of Haute-Alsace, France, since 1995. His research interests include QoS, wireless networks and high-speed networks. He is the author/co-author of 3 books, 3 patents and 200 international publications in refereed journals and conferences. He was Technical Editor of the *IEEE Communications Magazine* Editorial Board (2000–2006), *IEEE Networks Magazine* since 2015, *IEEE Transactions on Vehicular Technology* since 2017, Chair of *IEEE ComSoc France* (2014–2020), Financial Chair of IEEE France (2017–2022), Chair of Vertical Issues in Communication Systems Technical Committee Cluster (2008–2009), Chair of the Communications Systems Integration and Modeling Technical Committee (2003–2009), Chair of the Communications Software Technical Committee (2008–2010) and Chair of the Technical Committee on Information Infrastructure and Networking (2016–2017), Chair of *IEEE/ComSoc Satellite and Space Communications Technical* (2022–2023), IEEE R8 Finance Committee (2022–2023), and IEEE R8 Conference Coordination Committee (2023). He has served as Co-Program Chair of IEEE WCNC'2012 and ICC'2004, Executive Vice-Chair of ICC'2017, TPC Vice Chair of Globecom'2018, Panel Sessions Co-chair for Globecom'16, Tutorial Chair of VTC'2013 Spring and WCNC'2010, Track Chair of PIMRC'2012 and WCNC'2014, Symposium Co-Chair at Globecom 2007–2011, Globecom'2019, ICC 2008–2010, and ICC'2014 and '2016. He has served as Co-Guest Editor for special issues of *IEEE Communications Magazine*, *Networks Magazine*, *Wireless Communications Magazine*, *Telecommunications Systems*, and *LNCS*. He is Associate Editor for the *International Journal of Communication Systems* (IJCS-Wiley), *Journal on Security and Communication Networks* (SCN-Wiley), and *International Journal of Business Data Communications and Networking*, *Journal of Network and Computer Applications* (JNCA-Elsevier). He is a senior member of the IEEE, an IARIA fellow, and a member of many international program committees. He has organized many conferences, chaired several technical sessions, and given tutorials at major international conferences. He was an IEEE ComSoc Distinguished Lecturer during 2013–2014.

Contributors

Bechir Alaya
Department of Management Information Systems, College of Business and Economics, Qassim University
Buraidah, Saudi Arabia

Boulbaba Ben Ammar
Data Engineering and Semantics Research Unit, Faculty of Sciences, University of Sfax
Sfax, Tunisia

K. Annapurani
SRM Institute of Science and Technology
Kattankulathur, India

Mohamed Ben Aouicha
Data Engineering and Semantics Research Unit, Faculty of Sciences, University of Sfax
Sfax, Tunisia

T. Balachander
SRM Institute of Science and Technology
Kattankulathur, India

Samar Bouazizi
Computer Science Department, Faculty of Sciences and Technologies of Sidi Bouzid, University of Kairouan
Sidi Bouzid, Tunisia
University of Sfax, National Engineering School of Sfax, REGIM-Lab., Research Groups in Intelligent Machines
Sfax, Tunisia

K. Deeba
School of CSA, REVA University
Bangalore, Karnataka, India

M. Fatima
Sagar Institute of Research and Technology
Bhopal, India

Malka N. Halgamuge
RMIT University
Melbourne, Australia

Alfiya Jahan
Sagar Institute of Research and Technology
Bhopal, India

Amit Jatav
Sagar Institute of Research and Technology
Bhopal, India

K. Lakshmi
School of CSA, REVA University
Bangalore, Karnataka, India

Pascal Lorenz
University of Haute Alsace—Université de Haute Alsace
Colmar, France

Hela Ltifi
Computer Science Department, Faculty of Sciences and Technologies of Sidi Bouzid, University of Kairouan
Sidi Bouzid, Tunisia
University of Sfax, National Engineering School of Sfax, REGIM-Lab., Research Groups in Intelligent Machines
Sfax, Tunisia

Parul Manchanda
Department of Management Studies, Netaji Subhas University of Technology
New Delhi, India

Afif Masmoudi
Laboratory of Probability and Statistics, Faculty of Sciences, University of Sfax
Sfax, Tunisia

Khalil Masmoudi
Laboratory of Probability and Statistics, Faculty of Sciences, University of Sfax
Sfax, Tunisia

Abir Mchergui
Faculty of Sciences of Gabès, Cité Erriadh
ZrigGabès, Tunisia
IResCoMath Laboratory, University of Gabes
Gabes, Tunisia

Tarek Moulahi
Qassim University, Saudi Arabia
University of Kairouan
Sidi Bouzid, Tunisia

Sindiso Mpenyu Nleya
Computer Science Department, University of Limpopo
Mankweng, Limpopo, South Africa

Anshu Punshi
Maharaja Surajmal Institute
New Delhi, India

Kalpana Rai
Sagar Institute of Research and Technology
Bhopal, India

Raphael Ramos Monteiro de Souza
University of Rio de Janeiro—UFRJ, Senior Attorney for Brazil—AGU
Rio de Janeiro, Brazil

Cosmina-Mihaela Rosca
Department of Automatic Control, Computers, and Electronics, Faculty of Mechanical and Electrical Engineering, Petroleum-Gas University of Ploiesti
Ploiesti, Romania

Zainab Saad Rubaidi
Data Engineering and Semantics Research Unit, Faculty of Sciences, University of Sfax
Sfax, Tunisia
College of Agriculture, Al-Muthanna University
Samawah, Iraq

Lamaa Sellami
CONPRI Laboratory, University of Gabes
Gabes, Tunisia

Nisha Solanki
Maharaja Surajmal Institute
New Delhi, India

K.A. Varunkumar
SRM Institute of Science and Technology
Kattankulathur, India

T. Anstey Vathani
Vel Tech High Tech Dr. Rangarajan Dr. Sakunthala Engineering College
Avadi, Chennai, India

Mthulisi Velempini
Computer Science Department, University of Limpopo
Mankweng, Limpopo, South Africa

K.A. Vinodhini
Vel Tech High Tech Dr. Rangarajan Dr. Sakunthala Engineering College
Avadi, Chennai, India

Harshita Yadav
Sagar Institute of Research and Technology
Bhopal, India

AI Tools Usage Statement

During the preparation and submission of the chapters for this book, we have applied Turnitin LLC (latest available version at the time of submission) to evaluate the originality of the content and to detect potential use of AI-generated or AI-paraphrased text.

The detection categories included:

- AI-generated only
- AI-generated text that was AI-paraphrased

Based on these results, we ensured that any submitted chapter with an AI-generated content score above 25% was rejected and not included in the book. Only chapters that met the originality requirements and passed the AI detection threshold were accepted for publication.

No other AI tools were used for content drafting, editing, or preparation of the chapters.

Chapter 1

Promises and Perils of AI

Understanding Its DUAL Capabilities

K. Lakshmi and K. Deeba

1.1 AI AND ITS APPLICATIONS IN VARIOUS DOMAINS

Artificial intelligence (AI) has evolved rapidly in recent years in such a way that it has become indispensable in various domains. In the domain of healthcare, integration of AI into robotic surgery has further advanced surgical precision, efficiency, and accessibility [1]. AI comes with numerous benefits like enhancing efficiency in government law and policy-making [2, 3]; information, communication, and technology (ICT) [4]; transport [5]; rapid return on investment in the field of economics and finance [6, 7]; sustainable environment [2]; knowledge acquisition, adaptive learning [8], and analytical reasoning in the field of education; innovation in production and services [9]; and more. AI is transforming nearly every sector, from healthcare to finance, education to entertainment. This chapter is aimed at providing a balanced exploration of AI's transformative potential and the challenges that accompany it in the context of its penetration into various domains. A diagram titled "Applications of Artificial Intelligence" with a central icon of a robot and multiple branches pointing to various domains where AI is applied: Healthcare, Finance, Education, Manufacturing, Transportation, Customer Service, Exploration, Legal, Security, Energy is given in Figure 1.1.

Several AI technologies have emerged as a transformative force across various industries, enhancing efficiency, accuracy, and decision-making. There is an enormous change in how we work and utilize technology for it. AI is becoming essential in medical diagnosis, drug discovery, robot surgery, and personalized medicine: AI-driven technologies such as Google's DeepMind and IBM Watson help diagnose diseases like cancer and Alzheimer's by examining medical images with high precision [10, 11]. The drug development process is expedited by applying AI to forecast molecular interactions, thereby shortening the time and expense of making new drugs [12]. AI-guided robotic devices, like the Da Vinci Surgical System, increase accuracy in minimally invasive surgeries [1]. Financial institutions employ AI systems for fraud detection, algorithmic trading, and customer support. AI models analyze market trends, forecast accurate predictions, and help customers make informed decisions about their trading [6]. Machine learning models are developed based on the behavioral patterns of the customers in real-time, and they are capable of detecting fraudulent transactions [13]. AI-driven chatbots are helpful to the customers in providing personalized banking assistance [14].

The education sector is influenced a lot by the advancement in AI [15]. Williamson investigates the use of algorithmic systems in Google Classroom, focusing on how automated feedback influences both students and teachers [16]. Adaptive learning systems customize

DOI: 10.1201/9781003539032-1

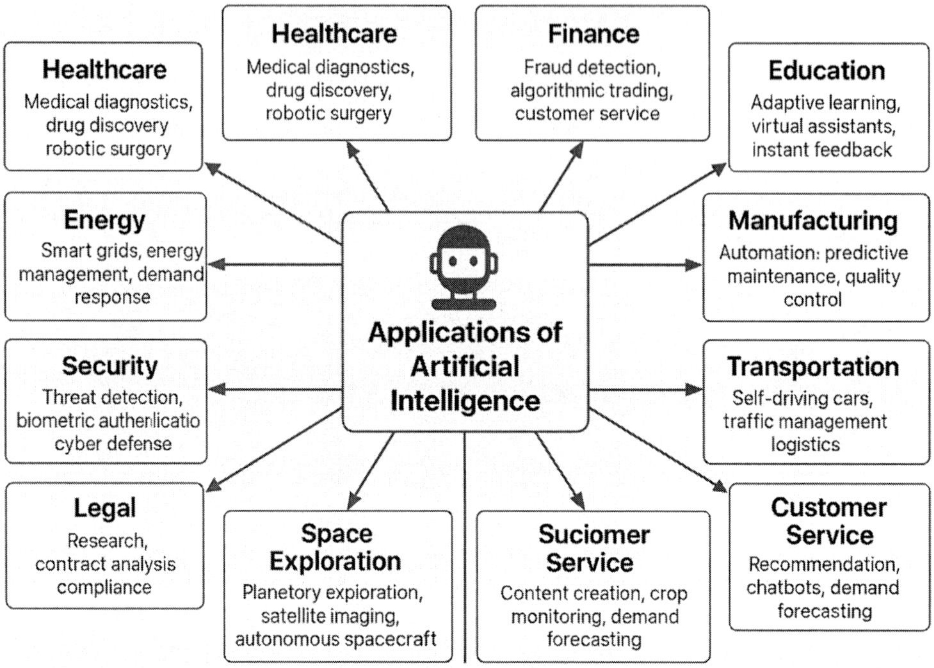

Figure 1.1 Application domains of AI.

learning experiences based on student performance [17]. AI tools help teachers in assessments and in providing instant feedback, thus reducing teachers' workload [18]. Students get assistance in problem-solving and language learning from virtual assistants [14].

In the domain of manufacturing and production, AI is helpful in enhancing automation, predictive maintenance, and quality control. AI predicts equipment failures well in advance and prevents costly downtimes [19]. Highly repetitive tasks in the assembly lines are replaced by robots, which improves efficiency [12]. Computer vision powered with AI helps ensure quality in products by detecting any defects in the products before delivery [9].

AI is revolutionizing self-driving cars, traffic management, and logistics: Companies like Tesla and Waymo use AI for self-driving technologies, enhancing road safety [5]. AI optimizes traffic flow by analyzing real-time data from sensors and cameras [20, 21]. AI improves operations management through demand forecasting, route planning, and reducing costs [22].

AI enhances customer experiences through recommendation engines and automation: AI analyzes customer behavior to suggest products [23]. AI-driven chatbots handle queries and improve engagement [14]. AI predicts demand trends, automating supply chain operations [24].

AI is transforming content creation, video editing, and deepfake technology. AI creates music, art, and stories, such as OpenAI's DALL-E and ChatGPT [25]. AI generates highly realistic synthetic media, raising ethical concerns [26]. AI-powered tools assist in film production and video summarization [27].

AI enhances digital security through threat detection and automation: AI identifies anomalies and prevents cyberattacks [13]. AI-powered biometric authentication improves security [28]. AI-driven systems mitigate cyber threats in real-time [29].

AI aids in planetary exploration, satellite imaging, and autonomous spacecraft: NASA's Perseverance rover uses AI for autonomous navigation on Mars [30]. AI processes satellite images for climate monitoring and disaster management [31]. AI assists in deep-space navigation and mission planning [32].

AI optimizes farming practices through smart analytics and automation. AI optimizes irrigation, fertilization, and pest control using real-time data [33]. AI-powered drones analyze soil and crop health, improving yields [34]. AI models forecast crop production based on weather and soil data [35].

AI streamlines legal research and contract analysis: AI detects inconsistencies and ensures compliance in legal documents [36]. AI-powered tools enhance case law analysis, improving efficiency [37]. Some judicial systems explore AI-assisted sentencing recommendations [38]. AI can assist legal professionals, careful oversight and regulatory frameworks are essential to ensure fairness and reliability [39].

1.2 PERILS OF AI IN VARIOUS DOMAINS

AI is transforming industries across domains at an exponential rate. However, alongside its benefits, it poses significant ethical, legal, and societal concerns that vary across domains but share common underlying risks—bias, lack of transparency, privacy intrusion, and security vulnerabilities.

In healthcare, if AI models are trained on biased data, they may result in incorrect diagnoses or disparities in healthcare [40]. Over-reliance on AI systems may lead to reduced clinical expertise and human oversight [41]. Handling sensitive patient data with AI raises concerns about confidentiality and security [42]. Most deep learning models used in healthcare function like black boxes, making it difficult for doctors to understand why certain recommendations are made by AI systems. The lack of explainability and traceability may result in a lack of trust among patients [43].

In finance, AI-driven trading systems can exacerbate market volatility and lead to financial crashes. AI-based lending models may unfairly disadvantage certain demographics due to biased training data [44]. AI-powered attacks pose risks to financial institutions and consumers. Existing bias in financial data used by AI systems for credit scoring, loan approvals, and risk assessment can lead to discriminatory outcomes, unfairly denying access to financial services for certain demographic groups [45]. Bias can arise from historical data reflecting societal inequalities or from flawed algorithms. AI in finance relies on vast amounts of sensitive financial data, raising concerns about data breaches, privacy violations, and the potential for misuse of personal financial information [45]. A risk impact matrix of AI in various domains is presented in Table 1.1.

In education, over-reliance on AI may reduce the importance of teacher–student relationships. AI-based learning systems collect large amounts of student data, raising security concerns [46]. AI-driven assessments may favor students from certain backgrounds, creating disparities [8]. AI in education has the risk of algorithmic bias in grading and a lack of personalized feedback [18].

In transportation, AI-driven vehicles may struggle in complex or unpredictable scenarios. AI-driven automation may replace drivers, leading to job losses [47]. AI-powered

Table 1.1 Risk impact matrix of AI in various domains

Domain	*Risk Description*	*Likelihood*	*Severity*
Healthcare	Biased diagnoses due to skewed training data	High	High
	Loss of clinical expertise from AI over-reliance	Medium	High
	Breach of patient confidentiality	High	High
	Lack of AI explainability, reducing patient/doctor trust	High	Medium
Finance	AI-driven market volatility and financial crashes	Medium	High
	Discriminatory lending due to biased algorithms	High	High
	Data breaches involving sensitive financial information	High	High
Education	Algorithmic grading bias, favoring certain student groups	Medium	Medium
	Loss of human interaction in learning	Medium	Medium
	Privacy concerns from student data collection	Medium	Medium
Transportation	Accidents due to software glitches, sensor failures, or adversarial attacks	Medium	High
	Job loss due to AI-driven automation	High	Medium
	Hacking and cybersecurity risks in smart transportation systems	Medium	High
Surveillance	Privacy violations via facial recognition and predictive policing	High	High
	Erosion of civil liberties due to mass surveillance	Medium	High

transportation systems are vulnerable to hacking and cyber threats [48]. AI systems can struggle with unpredictable situations, "edge cases," and the complexities of real-world driving. Software glitches, sensor failures, and adversarial attacks could lead to accidents with potentially serious consequences [49].

AI-powered surveillance systems, including facial recognition and predictive policing, raise serious concerns about privacy violations and the potential for mass surveillance. These technologies can be used to track individuals, monitor their behavior, and even predict their future actions, potentially eroding civil liberties [50].

1.3 ETHICAL AND LEGAL CONSIDERATIONS IN VARIOUS DOMAINS

The ethical and legal considerations with respect to healthcare, finance, justice, employment, autonomous vehicles, media, and entertainment are summarized in Table 1.2.

Responsible AI encircled around Ethical, Social, and Legal concerns that form the foundation of responsible artificial intelligence is presented in Figure 1.2.

A flowchart showing relationships between AI application domains, ethical issues, and legal considerations is presented in Figure 1.3. The flow illustrates how different domains of AI raise interconnected ethical and regulatory issues.

Table 1.2 Ethical and legal considerations of AI

S. No	*Domain*	*Ethical Issues*	*Legal Considerations*
1	**Healthcare**	- Bias in AI diagnosis [51] - Patient privacy concerns [52]	- Compliance with HIPAA and GDPR - Liability for AI-driven medical errors [53]
2	**Finance**	- Algorithmic bias in lending [54] - Lack of transparency in AI models [55]	- Fair Credit Reporting Act (FCRA) compliance—Anti-money laundering (AML) regulations
3	**Criminal Justice and Law Enforcement**	- Racial bias in predictive policing [56] - Lack of accountability in AI sentencing [57]	- Compliance with Fourth Amendment privacy laws - Regulation of AI surveillance [58]
4	**Employment and Workforce**	- Job displacement due to automation [59, 60] -Workplace surveillance concerns [46]	- Fair Labor Standards Act (FLSA) compliance—Proposed EU AI Act for high-risk AI in employment [58]
5	**Autonomous Vehicles**	- Ethical dilemmas in AI decision-making [61] - Safety and risk management	- Liability frameworks for AI-driven accidents [62] - Federal vs. state-level regulations
6	**AI in Media and Deepfake Technology**	- Misinformation and fake news - Consent and manipulation concerns [63]	- Defamation and intellectual property laws - Emerging regulations against deepfake misuse [64]

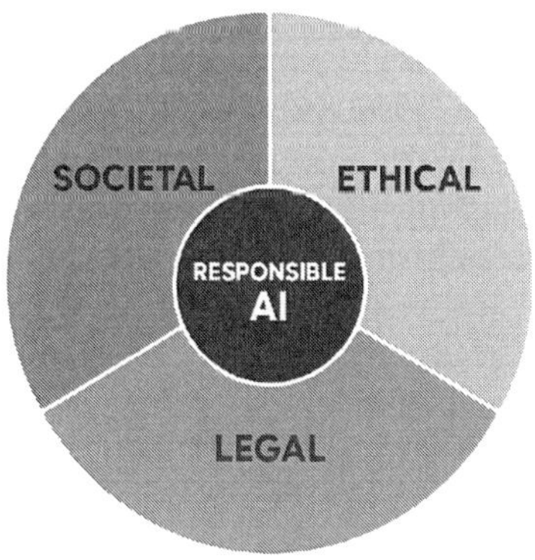

Figure 1.2 Ecosystem for responsible AI.

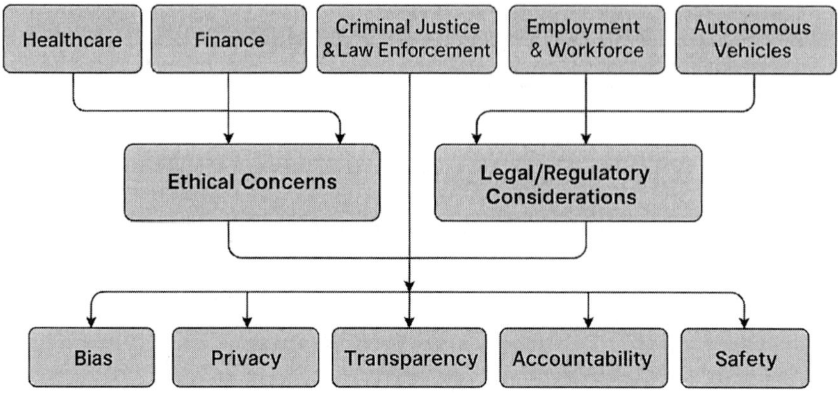

Figure 1.3 Societal, ethical, and legal concerns for responsible AI across domains.

1.4 HOW CAN WE USE AI RESPONSIBLY? RECOMMENDATIONS FOR RESEARCHERS AND POLICYMAKERS

To ensure the conscious and responsible use of AI, policymakers and researchers should consider the following recommendations:

1.4.1 Recommendations for Policymakers

To ensure AI systems in healthcare are safe and effective, robust regulatory frameworks are needed, involving rigorous testing, validation protocols, and continuous monitoring [64, 65]. Stringent data protection laws are crucial to ensure compliance with GDPR and HIPAA [66] and to safeguard sensitive user information while promoting secure data sharing practices among healthcare stakeholders [67].

AI systems should prioritize algorithm transparency, offering clear explanations for their decision-making processes, especially in critical medical contexts [68]. Healthcare professionals have to be well equipped with the required knowledge to use AI systems. This can be achieved by integrating AI and data science into the curriculum of medical education [65]. Finally, patient engagement through educational campaigns and involvement in AI development ensures that healthcare AI tools for healthcare needs are developed in alignment with public needs.

Ethical considerations are the biggest challenge for the use of AI in many domains, especially in sensitive domains like healthcare and finance. To address this challenge, AI review boards need to be established to frame and review guidelines. With clear liability frameworks and accountability mechanisms, AI systems can be ensured to provide the expected service without any bias [68–70].

Collaborative efforts among industry, academia, and policymakers must be encouraged through government funding for AI research. This can foster innovations in AI research [71].

Standardization can enhance interoperability. Standards for data formats and procedures for integrating AI tools into existing healthcare systems are mandatory [72]. AI integration policy needs continuous evaluation and updating to be in pace with the technological developments and the emerging challenges [72].

1.4.2 Recommendations for AI Researchers

AI researchers should focus on the development of ethical, responsible, and explainable AI systems. Standard frameworks such as AI ethics impact assessments and guidelines should be adopted to evaluate potential risks and societal impacts [68]. AI models must be transparent enough to provide explainable solutions. This can foster public trust and support accountability [66].

AI researchers should focus on solutions catering to diverse societal needs [71]. Partnerships between academia, industry, and government can foster interdisciplinary and multidisciplinary research that can drive inclusive innovation. Researchers and policymakers should engage together in AI development to ensure its alignment with evolving regulations, such as the EU AI Act [72].

Bias mitigation strategies must be integrated into AI systems. Researchers should design fair machine learning models by testing for discrimination without relying on sensitive data [69].

Finally, continuous monitoring and evaluation of AI technologies should be embedded into the research practices of AI systems. This can help researchers to ensure that the developed AI systems continue to be effective, safe, and ethically responsible [67, 69, 70].

1.4.3 Policies and Their Impact on Real-World Examples

The impact and need for framework and policies for responsible AI systems can be understood with the help of two real-world examples presented below.

Use Case 1: *Clearview AI Facial Recognition in the EU*

Clearview AI facial recognition system by a U.S.-based company was used by law enforcement in several countries, including some in the EU. As per the EU AI Act, such remote biometric identification systems in public spaces for law enforcement are classified as "high-risk" or even "prohibited" in real-time applications without strict safeguards. Clearview AI was fined heavily by the EU authorities, and its operations are banned under GDPR and it would be restricted further under the EU AI Act.

Use Case 2: *Microsoft's Use of NIST AI RMF in Azure OpenAI Services*

Microsoft adopted NIST's AI Risk Management Framework to govern the deployment of AI models like GPT within its Azure OpenAI Service. It incorporated safety, security, and trustworthiness benchmarks as recommended by the framework. This has enabled Microsoft to secure government contracts and enterprise trust, especially in regulated sectors like healthcare and finance, where AI risk mitigation is crucial.

1.5 BALANCING THE DUAL CAPABILITIES OF AI IN VARIOUS DOMAINS

AI presents both promises and perils across various sectors. Balancing these dual capabilities is crucial for responsible AI deployment.

1.5.1 Benefits and Risks of AI Implementation

AI and its benefits across various domains, along with its associated risks, are summarized in Table 1.3.

1.5.2 Strategies for Balancing AI Capabilities

- **Implement Ethical AI Frameworks:** Guidelines should be developed to ensure AI is used responsibly [68].
- **Enhance AI Transparency:** Explainability is required in high-risk AI applications [43].
- **Enforce Bias Mitigation Strategies:** Regular audits and diverse datasets can reduce discriminatory outcomes [81].
- **Encourage Human–AI Collaboration:** AI should complement human decision-making rather than replace it [82].
- **Promote AI Literacy:** Educating stakeholders on AI's benefits and risks fosters informed decision-making [83].

An infographic with six icons representing key aspects of ethical AI:

Transparency—represented by a document with a magnifying glass.
Fairness—represented by balanced scales.
Collaboration—represented by two people with a gear between them.
Implementing Ethical AI Frameworks—represented by a checklist and pen.
Bias Mitigation—represented by a shield with a checkmark.
AI Literacy—represented by a light bulb, symbolizing knowledge and understanding is given in Figure 1.4.

Table 1.3 Benefits and the associated risks of AI in various domains

Domain	*Benefits of AI*	*Associated Risks*
Healthcare	- Improved diagnostics and personalized medicine [73] - Enhanced Treatment outcomes [70]	Bias in AI decision-making, patient data privacy concerns [51]
Finance	Fraud detection, algorithmic trading efficiency [74]	Bias in credit scoring, lack of transparency in AI models [75]
Law Enforcement	Enhanced crime prediction, resource optimization [76]	Risk of racial bias in predictive policing, lack of accountability [39, 77]
Employment	Increased productivity, automation of repetitive tasks [77]	Job displacement, workplace surveillance concerns [78]
Autonomous Vehicles	Improved road safety, reduced human error [79]	Ethical dilemmas in accident scenarios, liability concerns [62]
Media and Deepfake Technology	Enhanced content creation, media accessibility [63]	Spread of misinformation, digital manipulation risks [80]

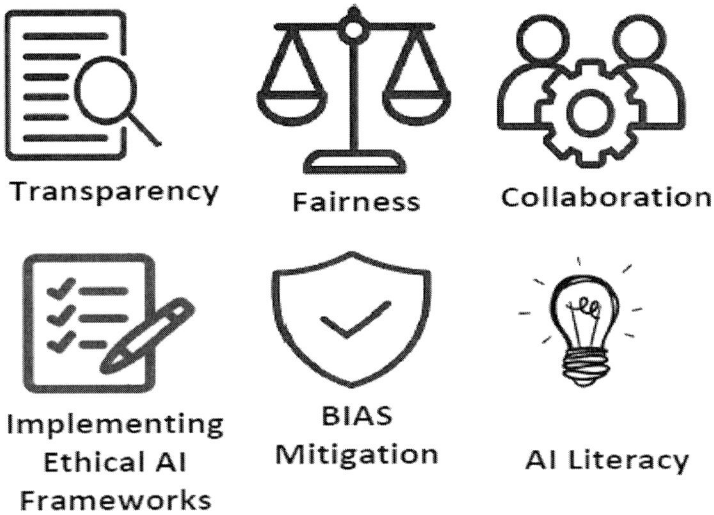

Figure 1.4 Strategies for balanced AI.

1.6 REAL-WORLD APPLICATIONS AND CASE STUDIES

Some real-world applications of AI in various domains, along with the benefits and challenges, are presented in Table 1.4.

A horizontal timeline showing key AI case studies highlighting ethical challenges from 2016 to 2020 is presented in Figure 1.5.

2016—IBM Watson for Oncology: Faced criticism for unsafe treatment recommendations due to biased training data.
2018—COMPAS: An AI risk assessment tool found to have racial bias.
2018—Uber: Uber's self-driving car accident raised concerns about AI safety and liability in autonomous vehicle crashes.
2019—Criminal Justice and Law Enforcement/Apple Card: Amazon's AI hiring tool was scrapped after being found discriminatory against women.
2020—AI in Media and Deep Fake Technology: A deep fake video of Barack Obama demonstrated the risks of AI-driven misinformation.

IBM Watson [11, 93], a cognitive computing system, was developed by IBM with the intention to assist in various domains, with its primary focus on oncology in healthcare. It is useful for recommending treatment options for cancer patients. The approach used was evidence-based treatment options; thus, it was helpful in decision-making processes and patient outcomes. But IBM Watson for Oncology was criticized for providing unsafe treatment recommendations [94]. The reason was found to be due to biased training data.

In 2019, Apple Card, a credit card issued by Goldman Sachs in partnership with Apple, faced allegations of gender bias in its credit limit decisions. The controversy began when

Table 1.4 Real-world applications of AI—benefits and challenges

Domain	*Application Area*	*Case Study/Example*	*Key Benefits*	*Key Challenges/Perils*
Healthcare	Diagnosis and Disease Detection	PathAI's AI-powered pathology platform [84] assists pathologists in diagnosing cancer more accurately.	Improved accuracy, faster diagnosis, personalized treatment	Data bias, lack of explainability, and regulatory hurdles
Finance	Fraud Detection	Feedzai's AI platform [85] detects fraudulent transactions in real-time.	Reduced fraud losses, improved customer experience	Data privacy concerns, algorithmic bias
Transportation	Autonomous Vehicles	Waymo's self-driving cars [86] navigate complex real-world environments	Increased safety, improved traffic flow, and accessibility for people with disabilities	Safety concerns, ethical dilemmas (e.g., "trolley problem"), and job displacement
Law	Legal Research	ROSS Intelligence's AI-powered legal research platform [36] helps lawyers find relevant case law and statutes.	Increased efficiency, improved access to justice	Bias in legal data, ethical considerations of AI in legal decision-making
Security	Threat Detection	Darktrace's AI platform detects cyber threats in real-time [87] by learning the "normal" behavior of a network	Improved security, faster threat detection	Potential for false positives, privacy concerns
Education	Personalized Learning	Duolingo's AI-powered language learning platform [88] adapts to individual learner's pace and style.	Personalized learning experience, improved learning outcomes	Data privacy concerns, potential for deskilling
Retail	Personalized Recommendations	Amazon's recommendation engine [89] gives product suggestions based on the browsing history and purchase patterns of users.	Increased sales, improved customer experience	Privacy concerns, filter bubbles
Manufacturing	Predictive Maintenance	GE's Predix platform [90] uses AI to predict equipment failures and optimize maintenance schedules.	Reduced downtime, improved efficiency, cost savings	Data security concerns, integration with legacy systems

Table 1.4 (Continued) Real-world applications of AI—benefits and challenges

Domain	*Application Area*	*Case Study/Example*	*Key Benefits*	*Key Challenges/Perils*
Agriculture	Precision Farming	Blue River Technology's See & Spray [91] robot uses computer vision and AI to reduce herbicide use by precisely targeting weeds for spraying.	Reduced environmental impact, increased crop yields	Cost of technology, accessibility for small farmers
Entertainment	Content Creation	OpenAI's GPT-3 generates [92] human-like text, including articles, poems, and code.	Automation of content creation, new creative possibilities	-Lack of trust -Reputation

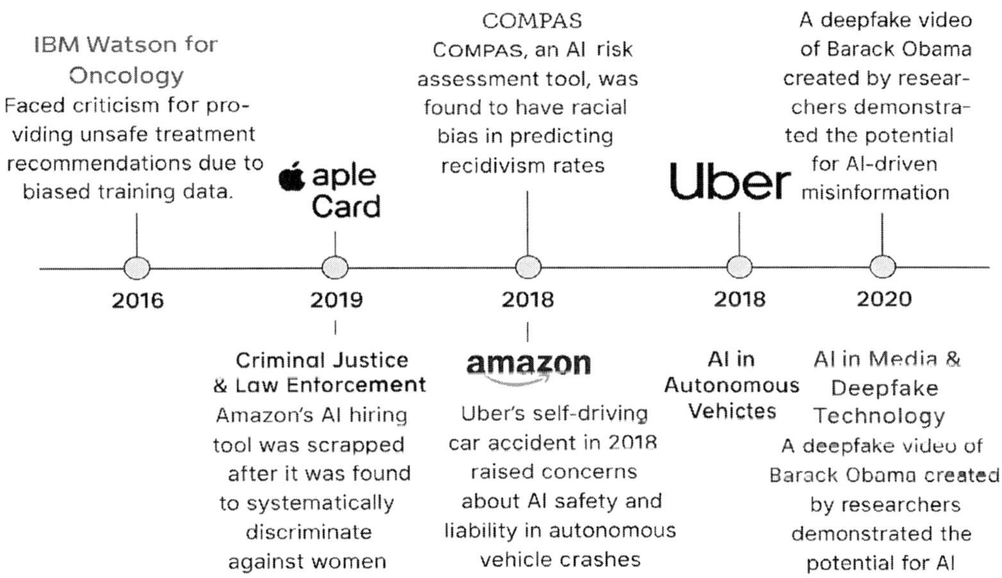

Figure 1.5 Key AI case studies—ethical challenges and lessons learned across domains.

prominent tech entrepreneur David Heinemeier Hansson publicly claimed that he was offered a credit limit 20 times higher than his wife, despite her having a better credit score. Such imbalances were experienced by numerous other users as well, Apple co-founder Steve Wozniak among them. This has created doubts regarding possible algorithmic bias when approving credit and has shed light on the issues regarding the fairness and transparency of algorithms used in financial services.

COMPAS (Correctional Offender Management Profiling for Alternative Sanctions) [35] is an AI risk assessment system utilized in the American criminal justice system. It has been largely implemented to aid judges in sentencing and parole by predicting the recidivism risk of a defendant. In a 2016 investigative report, ProPublica [56] examined COMPAS's predictions and identified strong racial bias in its risk assessments. Dressel and Farid [95] found that the COMPAS recidivism prediction algorithm performs no better than human judgment while also exhibiting racial bias, raising concerns about its reliability in criminal-justice decisions. This racial bias in COMPAS sparked ethical and legal questions regarding fairness in AI-based decision-making. Critics maintained that these biases were likely to perpetuate systemic discrimination within the criminal justice system.

Amazon AI's recruitment tool was employed to automate the recruitment process by pre-screening resumes. Nevertheless, in 2018, a Reuters investigation [3] discovered that the tool systematically discriminated against women. The bias in discrimination was discovered to have been caused by biased training data: a decade-long pool of resumes predominantly from male candidates. The model had been trained using gender-biased data, resulting in discrimination against women during recruitment in favor of male candidates. Subsequently, the project was scrapped by Amazon due to its failure to provide unbiased recommendations [96]. This also informed us of the risks of training AI models from historically biased data and the importance of transparency and human oversight in AI-powered recruitment processes.

With autonomous cars, there are serious safety and liability issues around AI. This was effectively brought about by a deadly crash with one of Uber's autonomous vehicles in Tempe, Arizona, in 2018. In a report submitted by the National Transportation Safety Board, the AI system of the car had detected a pedestrian walking across the road but could not properly identify the individual as a risk in time to brake. While there was a human backup driver on hand at the time, he was preoccupied and did not act in time. The accident generated heated debate over the suitability of AI technology for use on public roads. It also opened lots of questions about responsibility between AI systems and human operators. It called for better AI algorithms, more rigorous safety testing, and more transparent regulatory standards to control autonomous vehicle deployment [38].

Deepfake technology is based on Generative Adversarial Networks (GANs) and is helpful to produce hyper-realistic but completely artificial content. Deepfakes, although fascinating for media and entertainment, are also bringing the world immense ethical and societal issues. With deepfake technology, de-aging or bringing back actors becomes effortless, eliminating the requirement of extensive CGI work. The most famous instance includes the application of AI for de-aging characters. AI voices enable unhampered dubbing of different languages, boosting access and worldwide exposure of content [63]. News outlets in countries like China have introduced AI news anchors capable of delivering news 24/7 without breaks [80].

What can we learn from the above these cases?

⚠ Healthcare

IBM Watson for Oncology recommended unsafe treatments due to biased training data, raising concerns about clinical safety and AI reliability [93].

Finance

Apple Card was accused of gender bias in credit limits, leading to regulatory scrutiny and questions on fairness in AI-based lending [97].

Criminal Justice and Law Enforcement

The COMPAS tool showed racial bias in predicting recidivism, labeling Black defendants disproportionately as high-risk [98].

Employment and Workforce

Amazon's AI hiring tool was scrapped after it discriminated against women, showing how training data can embed workplace biases [3].

Autonomous Vehicles

An Uber self-driving car caused a fatal accident in 2018 due to sensor and AI decision failures, raising liability and safety concerns [99].

AI in Media and Deepfake Technology

A deepfake video of Barack Obama highlighted the risk of AI-generated misinformation and manipulation in digital media [63].

1.7 CONCLUSION

The promises and perils of AI are deeply intertwined across various domains, presenting both unprecedented opportunities and significant risks. While AI has the potential to revolutionize industries, improve efficiency, and enhance human capabilities, it also introduces complex ethical and legal challenges that must be addressed. Striking a balance between innovation and responsibility is essential to ensuring that AI remains a force for good. Robust governance, ethical frameworks, and continuous interdisciplinary research are necessary to mitigate risks such as bias, privacy violations, and accountability gaps. Moving forward, AI policy must be adaptive and inclusive, considering both societal needs and technological advancements to foster a future where AI is used consciously and equitably.

REFERENCES

1. Iftikhar, M., Saqib, M., Zareen, M., and Mumtaz, H. (2024). Artificial intelligence: Revolutionizing robotic surgery: Review. *Annals of Medicine and Surgery (Lond)*, 86(9), 5401–5409. https://doi.org/10.1097/MS9.0000000000002426.
2. Sharma, G. D., Yadav, A., and Chopra, R. (2020). Artificial intelligence and effective governance: A review, critique and research agenda. *Sustainable Futures*, 2, https://doi.org/10.1016/j.sftr.2019.100004.
3. Dastin, J. (2018). *Amazon Scrapped 'Sexist AI' Tool.* Reuters.
4. Chakir, A., Chergui, M., and Andry, J. F. (2020). A smart updater IT governance platform based on artificial intelligence. *Advances in Science, Technology and Engineering Systems Journal*, 5(5), 47–53. https://doi.org/10.25046/aj050507.

5. Bojarski, M., et al. (2016). End to end learning for self-driving cars. *arXiv preprint arXiv:1604.07316.*
6. Chopra, R., and Sharma, G. D. (2021). Application of artificial intelligence in stock market forecasting: A critique, review, and research agenda. *Journal of Risk and Financial Management*, 14(11), 526. https://doi.org/10.3390/jrfm14110526
7. Agrawal, A., Gans, J., and Goldfarb, A. (2018). *Prediction Machines: The Simple Economics of Artificial Intelligence*. Harvard Business Review Press.
8. Selwyn, N. (2019). *Should We Be Worried About AI in Education?* Bloomsbury Academic.
9. Anagnostou, M., et al. (2022). Characteristics and challenges in the industries towards responsible AI: A systematic literature review. *Ethics and Information Technology*, 24(3). https://doi.org/10.1007/s10676-022-09634-1.
10. Topol, E. (2019). High-performance medicine: The convergence of human and artificial intelligence. *Nature Medicine*, 25(1), 44–56.
11. Ferrucci, D., Brown, E., Chu-Carroll, J., Fan, J., Gondek, D., Kalyanpur, A., et al. (2010). Building watson: An overview of the DeepQA project. *AI Magazine*, 31(3), 59–79. https://doi.org/10.1609/aimag.v31i3.2303
12. Zhavoronkov, A., et al. (2019). Deep learning enables rapid identification of potent DDR1 kinase inhibitors. *Nature Biotechnology*, 37(9), 1038–1040.
13. Buczak, A. L., and Guven, E. (2016). A survey of data mining and machine learning methods for cybersecurity. *Journal of Information Security and Applications*, 17, 182–192.
14. Adamopoulou, E., and Moussiades, L. (2020). Chatbots: History, technology, and applications. *Machine Learning with Applications*, 2, 100006.
15. Holmes, W., Bialik, M., and Fadel, C. (2019). *Artificial Intelligence in Education*. UNESCO. https://unesdoc.unesco.org/ark:/48223/pf0000366994
16. Williamson, B. (2020). The automatic teacher? Algorithmic feedback in Google Classroom. *Learning, Media and Technology*, 45(3), 251–263. https://doi.org/10.1080/17439884.2020.1690985
17. Xu, Z. (2024). AI in education: Enhancing learning experiences and student outcomes. *Applied and Computational Engineering*, 51.
18. Luckin, R., Holmes, W., Griffiths, M., and Forcier, L. B. (2018). *Artificial Intelligence and Future of Teaching and Learning*. Center for Curriculum Redesign.
19. Borges, A. F. S., Laurindo, F. J. B., Spínola, M. M., Gonçalves, R. F., and Mattos, C. A. (2021). The strategic use of artificial intelligence in the digital era: Systematic literature review and future research directions. *International Journal of Information Management*, 57. https://doi.org/10.1016/j.ijinfomgt.2020.102225.
20. Bojarski, A., Del Testa, D., Dworak, D., Firner, B., Flepp, M., Goyal, N., . . . and Zhang, X. (2016). End to end learning for self-driving cars. *arXiv preprint arXiv:1604.07316.*
21. Genders, W., and Razavi, S. M. (2019). Using deep reinforcement learning to manage traffic signal timing. *Expert Systems with Applications*, 137, 260–270.
22. Choi, T.-M., Hui, C.-L., and Li, X. (2018). Big data analytics in operations management. *Production and Operations Management*, 27(10), 1868–1884.
23. Linden, G., Smith, B., and York, J. (2003). Amazon.com recommendations: Item-to-item collaborative filtering. *IEEE Internet Computing*, 7(1), 76–80.
24. Mishra, D., Anand, P., and Kumar, R. (2020). AI-powered supply chain management: Research agenda and implications. *Journal of Business Research*, 120, 574–585.
25. Elgammal, A., et al. (2017). CAN: Creative adversarial networks, generating art by learning about styles and deviating from style norms. *Arxiv preprint arXiv:1706.07068.*
26. Mirsky, Y., and Lee, W. (2021). The creation and detection of deepfakes: A survey. *ACM Computing Surveys*, 54(1), 1–41.
27. Song, Y., et al. (2018). Deep video compression and summarization. *Proceedings of the IEEE Conference on Computer Vision and Pattern Recognition (CVPR)*, 4786–4795. IEEE/Computer Vision Foundation.

28. Jain, A. K., Nandakumar, K., and Ross, A. (2016). 50 years of biometric research: Accomplishments, challenges, and opportunities. *Pattern Recognition Letters*, 79, 80–105.
29. Sommer, R., and Paxson, V. (2010). Outside the closed world: On using machine learning for network intrusion detection. *Proceedings of the IEEE Symposium on Security and Privacy*, 305–316. https://ieeexplore.ieee.org/document/5504795
30. Verma, V., et al. (2023). Autonomous robotics is driving Perseverance rover's progress on Mars. *Science Robotics*, 8(80).
31. Reichstein, M., et al. (2019). Deep learning predicts spatial patterns of carbon exchange from earth observation data. *Nature Communications*, 10(1), 1–12.
32. Wagstaff, K. L., et al. (2018). Machine learning for science: Investigating the impact of AI in scientific discovery. *Proceedings of the AAAI Conference on Artificial Intelligence*, 9805–9811. https://ojs.aaai.org/index.php/AAAI/article/view/11844
33. Liakos, K. G., et al. (2018). Machine learning in agriculture: A review. *Sensors*, 18(8), 2674.
34. Tsouros, D. C., Bibi, S., and Vlachos, D. G. (2019). Review of agricultural robotics: Unmanned aerial vehicles and plant phenotyping. *Computers and Electronics in Agriculture*, 156, 406–415.
35. Kamilaris, A., and Prenafeta-Boldú, F. X. (2018). Deep learning in agriculture: A survey. *Computers and Electronics in Agriculture*, 147, 70–90.
36. Surden, H. (2019). Artificial intelligence and law: An overview. *Georgia State University Law Review*, 35(4), 1305–1337.
37. Ashley, K. D. (2017). *Artificial Intelligence and Legal Analytics*. Cambridge University Press.
38. Katz, D. M., Bommarito II, M. J., and Blackman, J. (2017). A general approach for predicting the behavior of the Supreme Court of the United States. *PLoS ONE*, 12(4), e0174698.
39. Surden, H. (2019). Artificial intelligence and law: An overview. *Georgia State University Law Review*, 35(4), 1205–1264.
40. Seymour, L., and Blumenthal-Baruch, M. (2022). Algorithmic fairness in health care: A framework for evaluation. *Journal of Medical Internet Research*, 24(1), e34892.
41. Luxton, D. D. (2020). Artificial intelligence in healthcare: A primer on bias and fairness. *AMA Journal of Ethics*, 22(11), E1008–E1011.
42. Raghupathi, W., and Raghupathi, V. (2014). Big data analytics in healthcare: Promise and potential. *Health Policy and Technology*, 3(3), 215–220.
43. Lipton, Z. C. (2018). The myth of model interpretability. *Queue*, 16(3), 31–57.
44. Barocas, S., and Selbst, A. D. (2016). Big data's disparate impact. *California Law Review*, 104(3), 671–732.
45. Varian, H. R. (2014). Big data: New tricks for econometrics. *Journal of Economic Perspectives*, 28(2), 3–28.
46. Ajunwa, I. (2019). The paradox of automation as anti-bias intervention. *Cardozo Law Review*, 40(4), 1671–1717.
47. Acemoglu, D., and Restrepo, P. (2020). Robots and jobs: Evidence from US labor markets. *Journal of Political Economy*, 128(6).
48. Petit, J., and Shladover, S. E. (2015). Security of cyber-physical systems: A case study of autonomous vehicles. *Proceedings of the IEEE*, 103(8), 1151–1165.
49. Kalra, N., and Paddock, J. A. (2016). Driving to safety: How autonomous vehicles will make our roads safer. *RAND Corporation*.https://www.rand.org/pubs/research_reports/RR1478.html
50. Zuboff, S. (2019). *The Age of Surveillance Capitalism: The Fight for a Human Future at the New Frontier of Power*. PublicAffairs.
51. Obermeyer, Z., et al. (2019). Dissecting racial bias in an algorithm used to manage the health of populations. *Science*, 366(6464), 447–453.
52. Leslie, D. (2019). *Understanding Artificial Intelligence Ethics and Safety: A Guide for the Responsible Design and Implementation of AI Systems in the Public Sector*. The Alan Turing Institute.
53. Price II, W. N. (2021). Medical malpractice and AI decision-making. *Harvard Journal of Law & Technology*, 34(2), 239–281.
54. Hardt, M., Price, E., and Srebro, N. (2016). *Equality of Opportunity in Supervised Learning*. NeurIPS.

55. Brundage, M., et al. (2020). Toward trustworthy AI development: Mechanisms for supporting verifiable claims. *arXiv preprint arXiv:2004.07213*.
56. Angwin, J., Larson, J., Mattu, S., and Kirchner, L. (2016, May 23). Machine bias: There's software used across the country to predict future criminals. And it's biased against blacks. *ProPublica*. https://www.propublica.org/article/machine-bias-risk-assessments-in-criminal-sentencing
57. Huq, A. Z. (2019). Racial equity in algorithmic criminal justice. *Duke Law Journal*, 68(6), 1043–1134.
58. Binns, R. (2020). Human judgement in algorithmic loops: Individual justice and automated decision-making. *Regulation & Governance*, 14(2), 201–221.
59. Acemoglu, D., and Restrepo, P. (2017). Robots and jobs: Evidence from US labor markets. *NBER Working Paper*. National Bureau of Economic Research. https://doi.org/10.3386/w23285
60. Brynjolfsson, E., and McAfee, A. (2017). *The Second Machine Age: Work, Progress, and Prosperity in a Time of Brilliant Technologies*. W. W. Norton & Company.
61. Bonnefon, J.-F., Shariff, A., and Rahwan, I. (2016). The social dilemma of autonomous vehicles. *Science*, 352(6293), 1573–1576.
62. Gless, S., Silverman, E., and Weigend, T. (2016). If robots cause harm, who is to blame? Self-driving cars and criminal liability. *New Criminal Law Review*, 19(3), 412–436.
63. Chesney, B., and Citron, D. (2019). Deepfakes: A looming challenge for privacy, democracy, and national security. *California Law Review*, 107(6), 1753–1820.
64. Jasanoff, S. (2016). *The Ethics of Invention: Technology and the Human Future*. Princeton University Press.
65. KPMG International. (2020). AI in healthcare: Preparing for the future. *KPMG Global Report*. https://home.kpmg/xx/en/home/insights/2020/01/ai-in-healthcare-preparing-for-the-future.html
66. Wachter, S., Mittelstadt, B., and Floridi, L. (2017). Why a right to explanation of automated decision-making does not exist in the general data protection regulation. *International Data Privacy Law*, 7(2), 76–99.
67. Taddeo, M., and Floridi, L. (2018). Regulate artificial intelligence to avert cyber arms race. *Nature*, 556(7701), 296–298.
68. Floridi, L., and Leslie, D. (2020). Regulating artificial intelligence: The case for an AI ethics impact assessment. *Philosophy & Technology*, 33, 1–24.
69. Veale, M., and Binns, R. (2017). Fairer machine learning in the real world: Mitigating discrimination without collecting sensitive data. *Big Data & Society*, 4(2), 1–17.
70. IEEE. (2019). Ethically aligned design: A vision for prioritizing human well-being with autonomous and intelligent systems. *IEEE Global Initiative on Ethics of Autonomous and Intelligent Systems*. https://ethicsinaction.ieee.org/
71. Arora, S., and Stirling, A. (2017). Infrastructures for inclusive innovation: Enhancing the role of experimental spaces. *Innovation and Development*, 7(2), 257–275.
72. European Commission. (2021). *Proposal for a Regulation Laying Down Harmonized Rules on Artificial Intelligence (Artificial Intelligence Act)*. European Commission.
73. Topol, E. (2019). High-performance medicine: The convergence of human and artificial intelligence. *Nature Medicine*, 25(1), 44–56.
74. Brundage, M., et al. (2020). Toward trustworthy AI development: Mechanisms for supporting verifiable claims. *arXiv preprint arXiv:2004.07213*.
75. Hardt, M., Price, E., and Srebro, N. (2016). Equality of opportunity in supervised learning. *NeurIPS*. In *Advances in Neural Information Processing Systems 29 (NeurIPS 2016)*, 3315–3323. Curran Associates, Inc.
76. Lum, K., and Isaac, W. (2016). To predict and serve? *Significance*, 13(5), 14–19.
77. Brynjolfsson, E., and McAfee, A. (2017). *The Second Machine Age: Work, Progress, and Prosperity in a Time of Brilliant Technologies*. W. W. Norton & Company.
78. Ajunwa, I. (2019). The paradox of automation as anti-bias intervention. *Cardozo Law Review*, 40(4), 1671–1717.

79. Bonnefon, J.-F., Shariff, A., and Rahwan, I. (2016). The social dilemma of autonomous vehicles. *Science*, 352(6293), 1573–1576.
80. Vaccari, C., and Chadwick, A. (2020). Deepfakes and disinformation: Exploring the impact of synthetic political video on deception, uncertainty, and trust in news. *Social Media + Society*, 6(1), 1–13.
81. Mehrabi, N., et al. (2021). A survey on bias and fairness in machine learning. *ACM Computing Surveys*, 54(6), 1–35.
82. Doshi-Velez, F., and Kim, B. (2017). Towards a rigorous science of interpretable machine learning. *arXiv preprint arXiv:1702.08608*.
83. Mittelstadt, B. D., et al. (2016). The ethics of algorithms: Mapping the debate. *Big Data & Society*, 3(2), 1–21.
84. Esteva, A., Kuprel, B., Novoa, R. A., and Thrun, S. (2017). A dermatologist-level classification of skin cancer with deep neural networks. *Nature*, 542(7639), 115–118.
85. Bolton, R. J., Hand, D. J., and West, D. (2002). Statistical fraud detection: A review. *Statistical Science*, 17(3), 235–255.
86. Awad, E., Dsouza, S., Kim, R., and Rahwan, I. (2018). The moral machine experiment. *Nature*, 563(7729), 59–64.
87. Axelsson, J. (2000). *Intrusion Detection Systems: A Survey and Overview*. Chalmers University of Technology.
88. Holmes, W., Bialik, M., and Fadel, C. (2019). *Artificial Intelligence in Education*. UNESCO.
89. Jannach, D., Zanker, M., Felfernig, A., and Friedrich, G. (2010). *Recommender Systems: An Introduction*. Cambridge University Press.
90. Lee, J., Lapira, A., Bagheri, B., and Sung, H. A. (2016). *Cyber Physical Systems in Manufacturing*. Springer.
91. Mkhabela, M. S., and Madala, N. E. (2020). Precision agriculture: Technology and economic implications. *African Journal of Agricultural Economics*, 15(1), 1–11.
92. Brown, T. B., Mann, B., Ryder, N., and Amodei, D. (2020). Language models are few-shot learners. *Advances in Neural Information Processing Systems*, 33, 1877–1901.
93. High, R. (2012). *The Era of Cognitive Systems: An Inside Look at IBM Watson and How It Works*. IBM Redbooks.
94. Ross, C., and Swetlitz, I. (2018, July 25). IBM's watson recommended 'unsafe and incorrect' cancer treatments, internal documents show. *STAT News*. https://www.statnews.com/2018/07/25/ibm-watson-recommended-unsafe-incorrect-treatments/
95. Dressel, J., and Farid, H. (2018). The accuracy, fairness, and limits of predicting recidivism. *Science Advances*, 4(1), eaao5580. https://doi.org/10.1126/sciadv.aao5580.
96. Dastin, J. (2018, October 10). Amazon scraps secret AI recruiting tool that showed bias against women. *Reuters*. https://www.reuters.com/article/us-amazon-com-jobs-automation-insight-idUSKCN1MK08G
97. Knight, W. (2019, November 11). Apple card investigated after gender bias complaints. *MIT Technology Review*. https://www.technologyreview.com/2019/11/11/238948/apple-card-investigated-after-gender-bias-complaints/
98. Angwin, J., Larson, J., Mattu, S., & Kirchner, L. (2016). Machine bias: There's software used across the country to predict future criminals. And it's biased against blacks. *ProPublica*. https://doi.org/10.1080/17439884.2020.1690985
99. Hawkins, A. J. (2018, May 24). Uber's self-driving car saw the pedestrian but didn't brake in fatal crash, report says. *The Verge*. https://www.theverge.com/2018/5/24/17389942/uber-self-driving-car-crash-death-arizona-ntsb

Chapter 2

Policy and Governance Dimensions of AI and Deepfakes

Sindiso Mpenyu Nleya and Mthulisi Velempini

2.1 INTRODUCTION

The internet has witnessed a sharp rise in deepfake usage, with statistics showing an increase from 500,000 files in 2023 to 8 million in 2025 [1], and experts warning of an impending surge that could make deepfakes a leading enterprise threat by 2026 [2]. The term "deepfake" is itself derived from a combination of "deep" [referring to deep learning (DL)] and "fake." It is normally used to refer to the manipulation of existing media (image, video, and/or audio) or the generation of new (synthetic) media using DL-based approaches [3]. Thus, according to [4] deepfakes are characterized firstly by, image manipulation: wherein faces are altered in photographs or videos to create the illusion of another person's presence. Secondly, voice synthesis in which audio deepfakes replicate someone's voice, making it appear like they said something they never did. Thirdly, video creation whereby an entire video clip can be generated to make it seem as if someone is performing actions they never did. Common types of deepfake data include fake facial images, synthetic speech, and videos that combine both [3]. Fake facial image deepfakes, focus on face and body swapping. This specifically blends the body and the face with someone else's face or body. The result is a completely different person in the original image.

The deepfake paradigm inspired by AI is a double-edged sword with both negative and positive impacts. On the positive perspective, deepfakes are employed in creative or artistic purposes such as commentary and satire, transforming identities and exploring personas, and reviving historical figures. The negative perspective includes the use of deepfakes in deceiving individuals, such as political disinformation, internet fraud, and cybercrimes. Clearly, the double-edged nature of deepfakes renders them a crucial subject for scrutiny owing to the fake and real content.

An understanding of deepfakes is vital in view of both the potential constructive and destructive uses. Consequently, governments, enterprises, and individuals must be wary of the dangers posed by deepfakes and must thus take due diligence. Moreover, awareness of state-of-the-art protection methods encompassing digital watermarking, AI-inspired detection technologies, and strong ethical standards is important. According to [5] deepfakes raise several critical policy concerns across multiple dimensions: (i) the harm inflicted on individuals when such content is distributed without their consent; (ii) risks to data protection and privacy; (iii) questions of personality rights and intellectual property, including ownership of content generated through deep learning; (iv) the proliferation of non-consensual sexual deepfakes or those that threaten public order; and (v) the need to establish guardrails for AI development, alongside due diligence requirements governing the dissemination and

DOI: 10.1201/9781003539032-2

distribution of this content. The aim of this chapter is to critically examine the policy and governance dimensions of artificial intelligence (AI) and deepfakes, focusing on how regulatory frameworks, accountability mechanisms, and institutional capacities shape responses to the risks posed by synthetic media. The chapter seeks to highlight both the strengths and limitations of current approaches while offering actionable recommendations for building resilient governance systems.

Following this introductory section, the structure of the chapter is organized as follows: Section 2.1 outlines the methodological approach employed to conduct this research and compile the chapter. In Section 2.2, Analyze Policy Frameworks and Regulatory Responses wherein a review of global and regional instruments governing AI and deepfakes is carried out. Specifically, we examine frameworks such as the EU AI Act, NIST AI Risk Management Framework, and national deepfake laws. Furthermore, we also assess platform obligations regarding transparency, labeling, takedown protocols, and liability. Additionally, we compare how different jurisdictions converge or diverge in their regulatory approaches. In section 2.3 an evaluation of governance and accountability mechanisms is the main focus through, investigating liability structures across developers, platforms, and users, assessment of requirements for auditability, transparency, and explainability, identification of enforcement gaps and weak monitoring capacities. Furthermore, an exploration of the balance between state regulation and industry self-governance, especially in resource-limited contexts. Section 2.4 is premised on Identification of implementation Challenges and Institutional Gaps. This is achieved through, a discussion of why existing policies struggle in practice, including definitional ambiguities and limited technical capacity. This is followed by Examining compliance burdens for smaller platforms, a highlight of jurisdictional conflicts in cross-border enforcement and analysis of tensions between platform profit motives and compliance obligations. An examine of Policy-Centric Case Studies is the center of focus for section 2.5 wherein there is a presentation of case studies that emphasize governance and regulatory failures, exploration examples from the Netherlands and Spain contexts. The section wraps up by deriving lessons on governance capacity, enforcement challenges, and regulatory design. In section 2.6, a proposal of actionable policy and governance recommendations is presented through a suggestion on steps for harmonizing AI and deepfake laws regionally and globally, recommend investments in regulatory capacity building and monitoring tools, and advocating for mandatory transparency reports and independent audits. In the final analysis, an Encouragement for open datasets, research collaborations, and multistakeholder governance and provision of a roadmap for strengthening accountability and resilience in AI governance.

2.2 METHODOLOGY

This study employs a Qualitative Comparative Case Study Methodology (QCCS) to comprehensively summarize and synthesize existing research on deepfakes. Unlike in [6] our methodological approach comprises six stages as depicted in Figure 2.1, namely, research design, data sources, analytical framework, case studies, Comparative thematic analysis and recommendations.

In the first stage, research design is concerned with a qualitative, comparative approach, normative analysis and a comparative lens. The qualitative design considers policy texts, governance frameworks and case studies rather than datasets. This is also combined with a normative analysis wherein the evaluation of the adequacy of existing policies against the basic principles of accountability, transparency and resilience. The first stage finishes with a comparative view of the similarities and differences across jurisdictions (EU, U.S., China, India, Africa). The second stage constitutes the data sources which are categorized into primary and secondary sources.

The primary source category covers official policy documents (EU AI Act, NIST AI Risk Management Framework, national deepfake laws). In addition, legislative texts, regulatory guidelines, and platform transparency reports are also examined. The secondary category covers academic literature (IEEE, ACM, Springer etc.) on AI governance and synthetic media, and reports from think tanks, NGOs, and international organizations. The media coverage and expert commentary on enforcement challenges are also covered under the secondary category.

In the third stage focus is on an analytical framework which, involves analyzing policy frameworks to identify objectives, enforcement mechanisms, and stakeholder obligations, while mapping accountability structures and transparency requirements. Additionally, it assesses institutional gaps, compliance costs, and enforcement capacity, particularly in resource-limited contexts, to evaluate the effectiveness of governance systems. The fourth stage of the approach pertains to case studies involving selection of jurisdictions with notable regulatory initiatives or enforcement challenges (EU, U.S., China, Africa) to examine how policies are applied in practice. To this end, focus is on drawing lessons about institutional capacity and regulatory design from these diverse contexts. In the comparative and analysis stage we compare regulatory approaches across jurisdictions to identify areas of convergence, such as shared principles of transparency, and divergence, such as differing liability structures. Findings are then synthesized into key themes

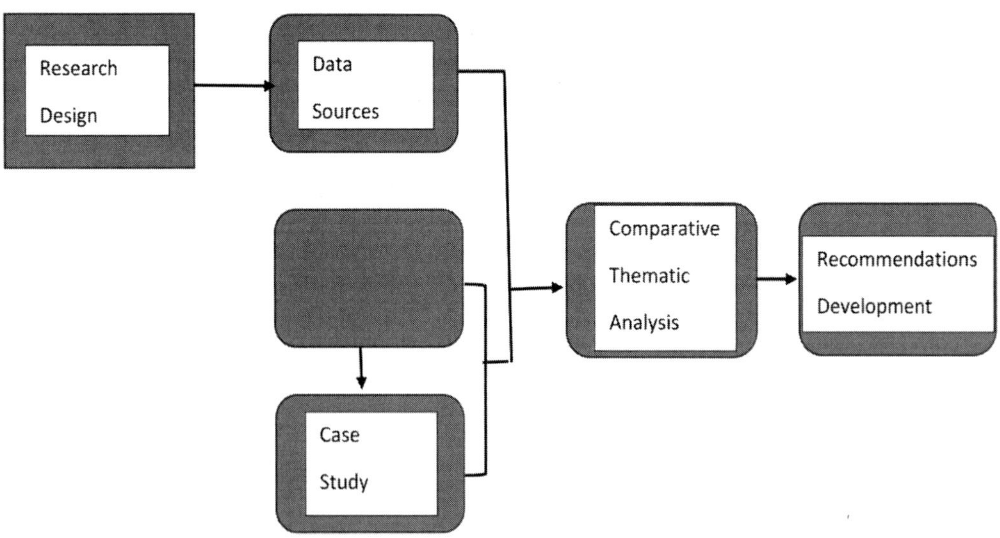

Figure 2.1 Qualitative comparative case study methodology.

including enforcement gaps, accountability challenges, and institutional capacity to provide a structured understanding of governance strengths and weaknesses. In the sixth and final stage we synthesize comparative findings and case study insights to generate actionable recommendations. It then constructs a policy roadmap that emphasizes harmonization strategies, capacity-building initiatives, and multi-stakeholder governance models for effective AI regulation.

2.3 POLICY FRAMEWORKS AND REGULATORY RESPONSES

Global and regional policy instruments addressing deepfakes and AI regulation are rapidly evolving, with the EU's AI Act (2025) setting a global benchmark, while countries like the US, China, UK, Canada, and South Korea have introduced targeted laws and guidelines to mitigate risks such as identity fraud, misinformation, and non-consensual content [6].

(i) Global policy

- EU AI Act: The EU has proposed laws mandating social media companies to remove deepfakes and other disinformation from their platforms. This act was updated in June 2022, the EU's Code of Practice on Disinformation addresses deepfakes through fines of up to 6 percent of global revenue for violators. The code was initially introduced as a voluntary self-regulatory instrument in 2018 but now has the backing of the Digital Services Act. The Digital Services Act, which came into force in November 2022, increases the monitoring of digital platforms for various kinds of misuse. Under the proposed EU AI Act, deepfake providers would be subject to transparency and disclosure requirements [7]. Rather than imposing an outright ban, the AI Act mandates transparency for those creating or using deepfakes, requiring them to disclose the artificial origin of the content and provide information on the techniques used. The Act categorizes AI systems into four risk levels: unacceptable, high, limited, and minimal. Deepfakes are generally placed in the 'limited risk' category due to their potential to mislead individuals who may struggle to recognize them as AI-generated. To mitigate this, Article 50(3) establishes transparency obligations requiring that AI-generated content be clearly labeled, ensuring users are aware when engaging with synthetic media.

However, deepfakes intended to influence elections or political processes may fall under the 'high-risk' category, as outlined in Annex III, particularly when they pose a threat to democratic integrity. The precise criteria for such classification, however, remain undefined. Critics argue that disclosure requirements alone are insufficient to address the dangers posed by deepfakes, especially given their rapid proliferation and transnational reach.

As the AI Act is still in its early implementation phase, questions remain about the effectiveness of its enforcement mechanisms. The creation of the EU AI Office in February 2024 marks an important step toward establishing enforceable rules. Nonetheless, experts stress the need for a clear liability framework within the EU, supported by robust enforcement measures—including criminal liability for individuals who produce or distribute deepfakes with the intent to manipulate, harass, or defraud

- NIST AI Risk Management Framework: The National Institute of Standards and Technology (NIST) developed the AI Risk Management Framework (AI RMF) in response to the growing complexities and risks of artificial intelligence systems. Initiated in 2021 and formally released in January 2023, it represents a collaborative effort involving stakeholders from both the public and private sectors. The framework promotes cooperation to address AI's technical, ethical, and governance challenges, aiming to ensure systems remain secure, resilient, and respectful of privacy and civil liberties [8]. At its foundation, the NIST AI Risk Management Framework (RMF) is structured around four core functions: Govern, Map, Measure, and Manage.
  a. **Govern:** This function underscores the need to cultivate a risk-aware organizational culture, stressing that effective AI risk management begins with strong leadership commitment supported by clear governance structures.
  b. **Map:** The Map function is designed to contextualize AI systems within their broader operational environments, requiring organizations to evaluate multifaceted impacts across technical, social, and ethical dimensions [8].
  c. **Measure:** This function mandates a multidimensional risk assessment, utilizing both quantitative and qualitative analysis to gauge the probability and consequences of AI-driven threats.
  d. **Manage**: This function governs the critical risk response phase, directing organizations to prioritize and mitigate identified threats [8] through an integrated application of technical controls and procedural safeguards.
- **National deepfake laws**: Across the globe, an increasing number of countries have enacted laws criminalizing non-consensual sexual deepfakes, regulating their use in political manipulation, and mandating transparency in AI-generated content. The EU's AI Act (2025) has set a global benchmark, while the United States, China, the United Kingdom, and several other nations have introduced targeted statutes to address these challenges [9] as depicted in Table 2.1. Table 2.1 depicts the regulatory approaches to deepfake challenges, starting with the USA, we note that it has the regulatory patchwork through deepfake accountability act and the protect Elections from deceptive AI. The deepfake accountability strives to protect national security by simultaneously imposing transparency requirements on AI-generated content and providing legal recourse for victims of harmful deepfakes.

Table 2.1 Regulatory responses

Country	*Approach*
United States	Regulatory Patchwork through the Deepfakes Accountability Act and the Protect Elections from Deceptive AI Act.
China	Comprehensive Control
European Union	Transparency, and Risk Management Under the AI Act
UK	Protecting Against Non-Consensual Deepfakes
Taiwan	Criminalizing Deepfake Fraud
Italy	Addressing Deepfakes Through Existing Laws

The **Protect Elections from Deceptive AI Act** bans the knowing distribution of materially deceptive AI-generated content in elections, while allowing exemptions for satire, parody, and legitimate news broadcasts with proper disclosures; violators face significant fines, and federal candidates misrepresented by deepfakes can seek legal remedies. However, outside of election contexts, the U.S. still lacks comprehensive deepfake-specific laws, leaving victims of personal abuse or fraud reliant on existing harassment and identity theft statutes, with the FTC proposing new rules to expand protections against AI-driven impersonation.

China's **Provisions on the Administration of Deep Synthesis of Internet Information Services** (January 2024) take a comprehensive approach to regulating deepfakes, requiring mandatory labelling of all AI-generated content, prohibiting unauthorized use of personal likeness, and placing responsibility on platforms to ensure ethical AI use. This regulation reflects China's broader strategy of leveraging technology companies to maintain social and political stability, compelling firms like Alibaba and Tencent to align with government mandates under the "common prosperity" agenda. Unlike the U.S., where free speech protections limit strict regulation, China's expansive framework underscores its reliance on tight control over digital content to safeguard national security and regime stability. **UK** has prioritized tackling non-consensual deepfakes, elevating the sharing of intimate AI-generated images to a "priority offence" under the Online Safety Act, requiring platforms to swiftly detect and remove such content while holding both platforms and individuals accountable.

Taiwan has criminalized deepfake fraud through amendments to its criminal law (May 2023), imposing severe penalties of up to seven years in prison and significant fines for using AI-generated media to deceive individuals.

Italy relies on existing constitutional, civil, and copyright laws to protect personal rights and privacy, allowing individuals to claim compensation for unauthorized use of their likeness, as illustrated by Prime Minister Giorgia Meloni's legal action against deepfake pornographic videos.

All in all, while national laws set the foundation for regulating deepfakes, their effectiveness ultimately depends on how platforms implement these rules, making platform obligations a critical next step in ensuring accountability and user protection.

- **Platform obligations**
  The platform obligations are described in [10] and subsequently summarized as presented in Table 2.2

For particular countries such as the USA, EU, China, UK and south Korea, specific platform obligations are as depicted in Table 2.3. This table outlines how different regions impose obligations on platforms to address deepfakes and synthetic media. It highlights measures such as labeling AI content, prompt takedown systems, user verification, watermarking, and cooperation with law enforcement. Together, these approaches show a global trend toward strengthening accountability, protecting users, and deterring misuse through varied legal frameworks.

Finally, the implication of the table is that platforms worldwide are increasingly being assigned legal responsibilities to manage deepfakes and synthetic media, but the scope and enforcement mechanisms vary across regions. It shows a global convergence toward accountability through measures like labeling, takedown systems, watermarking, and liability while also reflecting differences in emphasis, such as criminal penalties in South Korea or user verification in China. Overall, the table underscores that deepfake regulation is

Table 2.2 Platform obligations

Obligation	*Explanation*
Transparency and Disclosure Requirements	Creators and distributors of deepfakes should be legally required to label manipulated content and embed watermarks or digital signatures, ensuring transparency, credibility, and enforceability.
Enforcement Mechanisms	Clear penalties should be established for the creation and distribution of harmful deepfakes, while law enforcement agencies must be empowered with the tools and training needed to detect, investigate, and prosecute such crimes.
Victim Protection and Redress	Victims of malicious deepfakes should be granted the right to swift removal of harmful content from online platforms and the ability to seek compensation for financial, emotional, and reputational damages.
Platform Responsibilities	Online platforms should be required to implement strong content moderation to detect and remove harmful deepfakes, report them to authorities, and face penalties for non-compliance to ensure proactive accountability.
Public Awareness and Education	Public awareness campaigns and AI literacy initiatives should be implemented to educate individuals about deepfakes, their risks, and how to recognize and respond to manipulated media, thereby strengthening resilience against misinformation [10].
International Collaboration	To combat the borderless threat of synthetic media, nations must foster international collaboration and adopt unified global standards for the detection, labeling, and ethical regulation of deepfakes.
Ongoing Review and Adaptation	Deepfake regulations should be regularly reviewed and updated to keep pace with technological advances, incorporating feedback from law enforcement, industry experts, and the public to ensure continuous improvement [10].
Ethical and Legal Safeguards	Effective deepfake legislation must protect freedom of expression through exemptions for artistic and educational uses while strictly enforcing data privacy rights to ensure individuals maintain control over their personal likeness [10].

Table 2.3 Platform obligations under regional deepfake and AI laws

Region/Law	*Platform Obligations*
EU AI Act	Labelling of AI content, classify risks, cooperate with EU AI office enforcement [11]
US (TAKE IT DOWN ACT)	Platforms are expected to **promptly remove non-consensual intimate deepfakes, enforce disclosure requirements, safeguard minors, and regulate disinformation** to ensure accountability and user protection [12]
China (CAC rules)	-**Label synthetic content** clearly to indicate manipulation. -**Verify user identities** to track and hold creators accountable. -**Penalize harmful distribution** of deepfakes to deter misuse [13]
UK (Online safety	Prevent harmful synthetic media [14]
South Korea	-**Criminal liability** applies to both hosting and distributing sexual deepfakes. -Platforms and users must **enforce an ethics code** to guide responsible AI use [15].
South Africa	Prompt takedown systems, Watermarking requirements, tracing mechanisms and Cooperation with law enforcement [16]

becoming a critical part of digital governance, with platforms positioned as central actors in preventing harm and ensuring trust online.

2.4 GOVERNANCE AND ACCOUNTABILITY MECHANISMS

Deepfake technology, leveraging artificial intelligence to create hyper-realistic synthetic media, has emerged as both an innovation and a challenge to global governance. It has significant implications for privacy, misinformation, identity fraud and societal trust [9]. In general, deepfakes have been discursively framed with centrality of their harmful potential. In this context, the definition of deepfakes centers on their role as synthetic media tools for illicit purposes, specifically highlighting their potential for electoral interference and personal data exploitation [18] [10]. An important framing of deepfakes emphasizes the ethical and legal challenges they create, viewing them as violations of personal rights—particularly privacy and consent. This perspective highlights their frequent use without permission, such as in synthetic pornography or fraudulent manipulation of someone's likeness, underscoring the urgent need for legal protections to shield individuals from such abuses. By stressing governance's role in safeguarding privacy and consent, deepfakes are largely seen as threats to individual freedoms, especially the right to control one's own image and identity. In the EU, this framing is likely to shape regulatory approaches aligned with human rights protections under frameworks like the GDPR, demonstrating how governance can balance technological innovation with core societal values such as privacy, democracy, and security [18].

Liability structures: The assignment of legal responsibility for deepfakes is complicated by the intricate digital ecosystems in which they are created, disseminated, and amplified. Their lifecycle involves numerous actors, and this multiplicity challenges traditional liability models that rely on clear distinctions between creators, intermediaries, and end-users. Scholars examining intermediary liability frameworks highlight that harmful content is often produced anonymously or within decentralized environments, making accountability elusive. As a result, it becomes difficult to separate those who design the algorithms, those who manipulate audiovisual material, and those who ultimately distribute the content across social media platforms [11].

The role of distributors adds another layer of complexity to deepfake accountability. Individuals who share or repost deepfakes often play a pivotal role in amplifying harm, yet existing legal doctrines typically distinguish between primary creators and secondary disseminators. Analyses of platform governance emphasize that digital platforms act as critical conduits, shaping the visibility and reach of synthetic content. Their influence over information flows has raised pressing concerns about democratic accountability. At the same time, AI developers occupy a central position in the liability landscape, as they design the generative models that make deepfake creation possible. Critics of structural digital power argue that the concentration of technological expertise within a few corporate actors heightens questions about the responsibilities of those who build systems capable of large-scale manipulation. Finally, malicious users exploit the accessibility of these tools for fraud, extortion, or political disruption, further straining online ecosystems already challenged by harmful content and governance gaps.

Auditability and Transparency: In the European Union, deepfakes are addressed under the proposed AI Act, which opts for regulation rather than outright prohibition. Article 52(3) requires creators and distributors of deepfakes to ensure transparency by disclosing their artificial origin and providing details about the techniques used. The goal is to empower consumers with the knowledge needed to critically assess digital content and reduce susceptibility to manipulation. However, transparency alone may not fully mitigate the risks, as malicious actors could circumvent disclosure requirements. Significant uncertainties remain, particularly around legal liability and whether the current regulatory framework is robust enough to confront the evolving threats posed by deepfakes [12]. Given the significant harmful impact of deepfakes, these should be considered high risk. Clearly, the EU AI Act does not establish a clear framework for legal liability regarding developers of deepfake technology, focusing instead on preventative measures rather than punitive ones. It emphasizes technical safeguards, such as watermarking and detection algorithms, to reduce misuse, but the absence of explicit liability provisions leaves uncertainty about who is responsible when harm occurs. While the Act marks an important step in regulating AI systems, including those capable of generating deepfakes, critics argue that it falls short in addressing the unique challenges posed by malicious deepfake use [20].

Enforcement gaps: Enforcement gaps in addressing deepfakes are a consequence of rapid technological advancements not being in tandem with legislation. In some legislative frameworks that govern the use of deepfakes, there exists legislative gaps. For example, an examination of the legal framework in India concerning deepfake pornography and revealed significant gaps in existing legislation [13]. Specifically, by considering the Information Technology Act's applicability to deepfakes it is important to note that while Section 67 and 67A of the IT Act address obscene and sexually explicit content, they fail to specifically address the unique harm of deepfakes where a person's likeness is used without consent. Consequently, research points to the need for amendments in the Indian legislation to explicitly criminalize deepfake sexual content, recommending the creation of specific provisions that recognize the distinct harms of identity appropriation through AI technologies and suggesting implementation of both civil and criminal remedies for victims. South African law clearly prohibits the misuse of identity through deepfakes, but enforcement gaps leave victims exposed. Without affordable legal access, faster platform accountability, and effective international cooperation, illegal deepfakes will continue to increase [14]. The outcome has been a fragmented Legal Landscape for example in India, state legislatures have led the regulatory response, enacting 169 laws since 2022 and introducing 146 bills in 2025 alone. But the variation creates compliance complexity [15]. Furthermore, while different jurisdictions apply inconsistent rules, with some focusing on transparency (e.g., EU AI Act) while others rely on general fraud or harassment laws. The result of the mismatch in legislative rules is an enforcement gap. Platform accountability in managing deepfakes requires a blend of legislative action, technical safeguards, and corporate responsibility. Laws such as the U.S. *Deepfake Accountability Act* and the EU's *Digital Services Act* impose obligations on platforms to address harmful content. At the same time, transparency measures like labeling AI-generated material help build public trust. Together, these approaches ensure platforms are held responsible for both preventing misuse and promoting ethical AI practices [3]. Big Enterprise companies, such as IBM and Meta, are investing in the research and development of AI mechanisms for limited technical and collaboration with cybersecurity experts [16].

Public–private coordination: Public-private partnerships are also vital in addressing deepfake issues. Governments and technology companies combine and coordinate their efforts to establish regulatory frameworks, exchange threat intelligence, and promote responsible AI practices. Through a combination of resources and capabilities, stakeholders can create a more resilient digital environment. IAM's evolving role in combating deepfakes underscores the need for ongoing innovation and vigilance. With increasingly sophisticated technology, the commitment to protecting identities and securing digital environments cannot waver. Collectively, technology, legislation, and awareness can mitigate the severe threats posed by deepfake technology [17].

2.5 IMPLEMENTATION CHALLENGES AND INSTITUTIONAL GAPS

In the realm of deepfake technology, a host of ethical and legal challenges emerge, including privacy violations, the dissemination of misinformation, the destruction of personal identity, and behaviors with potential criminal implications, often occurring in the absence of clear legal recourse. This stems from the relatively underdeveloped legal frameworks, such as those governing intellectual property and consent, which struggle to keep pace with technological advancements [18].

- **Limited Technical capacity:** The spread of deepfake technology has raised significant concerns, especially in developing and underdeveloped countries where technological infrastructure is limited. These environments often lack the advanced tools, regulatory capacity, and technical expertise needed to detect and counter synthetic media effectively. As a result, societies in low-tech contexts are more vulnerable to exploitation, misinformation, and harmful uses of deepfakes. This makes the governance and accountability dimensions of AI particularly urgent in such regions [3]. Deepfakes hyper-realistic, AI-generated media pose significant risks to political stability, social trust, and economic resilience in regions where media literacy is limited and the capacity to counter such threats remains weak [16]. Furthermore, individuals with non-technical skills can create some form of deepfake and this easily, poses new challenges, and affects the media and societal interplay [19]. Specifically, the relatively low level of technical expertise and equipment needed to produce deepfakes makes it possible for such content to be created with ease and rapidly disseminated online. This accessibility lowers barriers to entry, enabling individuals without advanced skills to generate synthetic media. As a result, deepfakes can spread widely across digital platforms, amplifying risks of misinformation, exploitation, and abuse. The simplicity of production underscores the urgency of strong governance and accountability measures to mitigate harm. A case in point is that of taxi driver deepfake which requires a conventional home PCs that are equipped with gaming graphics cards for its creation.
- **High compliance costs for small platforms:** India's new AI law requires companies to establish dedicated moderation teams, following legislation that mandates the swift removal of deepfake posts containing nudity, defamatory material, or other illicit content [20]. The firms are required to remove non-consensual sexual imagery within two hours and not 24 hours and any other unlawful content should be removed within

three hours instead of 36hours. The assumption is that all companies have the capacity to scan and curb harmful content online. Experts warn that such limited timelines will make it difficult to achieve compliance. It is argued that removing the 10% watermark on AI generated content is progressive, but the limited time line is a challenge to both big and small companies. This is owing to the fact that most content monitoring algorithms are automated, taking down specific content will invariably require human oversight. Compressing these algorithms exponentially, could be at huge costs for big companies and nearly impossible for smaller companies. Beyond India and elsewhere in the world, developing and implementing sophisticated AI detection systems are costly, and smaller EU member states may face significant obstacles to deploying these technologies on a broad scale [21].

- **Cross-border enforcement:** Deepfake-related phishing and fraud have escalated dramatically, with reports indicating a 3000% surge since 2022. By 2024, attempts to generate deepfakes occurred on average every five minutes. This reflects an unprecedented rise in global deepfake activity, driven by their capacity to manipulate election outcomes, fabricate non-consensual pornographic material, and enable sextortion schemes. Criminals exploit these technologies to take advantage of gaps in cross-border legal systems. Because national laws are misaligned and international frameworks remain underdeveloped, victims of deepfake crimes face significant barriers in seeking justice [22]. A typical case of fragmented EU national criminal laws, including varying definitions of what constitutes a deepfake or different thresholds for prosecution, could hinder cross-border AI crime investigations, challenging effective detection and attribution. To this end, the lack of a clear definition necessitates examining how existing legal concepts, such as "illegal content" (Article 3(h)), are applied to deepfakes used in financial fraud or malicious impersonation. This definitional ambiguity contrasts with potentially more precise definitions in jurisdictions such as the US and China, leading to jurisdictional tensions in cross-border enforcement [23]. Moreover, differing legal standards and enforcement mechanisms across countries make criminal proceedings related to deepfake crimes difficult. On a similar note, cloud platforms and social media companies hosting deepfake content may be registered in countries with weak regulations or limited international cooperation, making it harder for authorities to remove content or obtain evidence [22]. Also in the same vein, given that each jurisdiction has developed its own distinct approach to regulating deepfakes: the EU AI Act emphasizes transparency and rights, China enforces strict labeling and identity verification, and the U.S. regulates piecemeal at the state level [20]. In contrast, many Global South countries such as Indonesia, India, and Brazil rely on broader IT or data laws rather than explicit deepfake provisions, as their frameworks are still evolving. This fragmented regulatory landscape poses serious risks for global banks, since fraud easily crosses borders and could trigger liquidity shocks, mass withdrawals, and market manipulation through synthetic press releases or fake executive videos. [24].

Cross-border enforcement mechanisms represent essential components of effective deepfake governance, as synthetic media production and distribution frequently span multiple jurisdictions. Current approaches include bilateral mutual legal assistance treaties, multilateral enforcement agreements, and international norm-setting bodies. The Budapest Convention on Cybercrime provides a potential template for coordinated responses, though significant gaps remain in addressing synthetic media specifically [25]. Thus, International cooperation and harmonization of laws are necessary to address the cross-border nature of deepfake dissemination. However, achieving consensus on legal standards and enforcement mechanisms across different jurisdictions is a significant hurdle [26].

2.6 POLICY-CENTRIC CASE STUDIES

The EU has emerged as a global pioneer in AI regulation with its groundbreaking AI Act.24 Initially proposed in 2021,25 the EU AI Act secured overwhelming approval in the European Parliament in June 2023 and entered into force on August 1, 2024.26 Designed to establish a comprehensive framework for AI governance, the Act aspires to become the global standard for regulating AI development and use.27 EU policymakers anticipate that the legislation will trigger the "Brussels effect," whereby EU regulations influence international standards, conferring long-term benefits on the Union's regulatory leadership.28 However, whether the Act is well-suited to serve as a global benchmark warrants examination. At its core, the Act seeks to ensure that AI systems are "overseen by people, are safe, transparent, traceable, non-discriminatory, and environmentally [27]. Our case studies, derived from [35], examine how the **EU AI Act** is being implemented in **the Netherlands and Spain.**

2.6.1 Netherlands

Considering the policy issues in the Netherlands, focus will be on the landscape, legal gaps, civil society engagement and cross sector working group. The Dutch supervisory authority landscape is considered a scattered landscape. This is because there are many supervisory authorities that monitor and control sub aspects of the development and use of algorithms and AI. Their activities are based on different international and national (legal) frameworks, and each organization has a different role based on their legal basis. The scattered landscape subsequently leads to inaccessibility for citizens and organizations as they do not always know which supervising authority they need to contact and how. Moreover, the existing, legal frameworks do not contain provisions that focus specifically on the development, deployment or supervision and enforcement of AI-systems and algorithms. Clearly, this legal gap is currently filled by initiatives run by relevant supervision authorities that aim to develop open norms and standards. These open norms and standards are unable to give clear guidance for intervening and sanctioning violations in the context of AI governance and enforcement [35]. The Dutch Data Protection Authority (Autoriteit Persoonsgegevens) and its Directorate of Coordination of Algorithms (DCA) play a key role, but Civil Society Organization (CSO) involvement remains informal and inconsistent.

2.6.2 Spain

In Spain, the policy issues encompass governance model, mandate, coordination issues, civil society concerns and independence challenges. Spain has established **AESIA**, the first dedicated AI supervisory authority in the EU, to enforce the forthcoming AI Act. Its mandate includes raising awareness, providing training, promoting responsible AI use, coordinating with other regulators, and setting up regulatory sandboxes to protect users and prevent bias. AESIA will also oversee the deployment and marketing of AI systems, particularly those posing risks to health, safety, or fundamental rights. However, it will operate alongside

Spain's data protection authority (AEPD), and questions remain about how the two regulators will coordinate to ensure consistent enforcement of AI regulation.

Spain's national AI governance model through AESIA reflects both ambition and complexity. The agency's **mandate** is broad, encompassing awareness-raising, training, regulatory sandboxes, and oversight of AI systems that may pose risks to health, safety, or fundamental rights. However, **coordination issues** remain unresolved, particularly in relation to the Spanish Data Protection Authority (AEPD), which continues to regulate AI applications involving personal data under the GDPR, creating potential overlaps and inconsistencies in enforcement. Civil society has voiced strong **concerns** about being excluded from AESIA's establishment process, with CSOs now organizing coalitions to demand advisory boards, transparency petitions, and algorithm registers to ensure meaningful participation. Finally, **independence challenges** arise from the outsourcing of AESIA's management contract to a private consultancy, raising fears that large consultancies and tech companies may exert disproportionate influence while civil society remains sidelined, undermining the agency's credibility and accountability.

2.7 ACTIONABLE POLICY AND GOVERNANCE RECOMMENDATIONS

Governments increasingly recognize AI's potential as a transformative tool but remain acutely aware of its susceptibility to misuse. This has driven some countries to implement regulatory frameworks, while others continue to deliberate on effective governance strategies [27].

2.7.1 Legal and Regulatory Frameworks

Over the past few years, significant groundwork has been done by both Eurojust and eu-LISA, as well as the European Commission to speed-up digital transformation and the adoption of IT solutions based on artificial intelligence (AI) in the field of Justice and Home Affairs (JHA). For example, the study on Cross-border Digital Criminal Justice, commissioned by DG JUST, performed an assessment of business needs in cross-border criminal justice cooperation and proposed a set of solutions tackling those needs. These solutions included, for example, the creation of a collaboration platform for Joint Investigation Teams (JITs) and a redesigned Eurojust Case Management System, where AI based components were suggested for both. Artificial intelligence was also defined as a priority area in the Action Plan for e-Justice 2019–2023. However, the world over there has been lack of a non-legal definition of what constitutes a deepfakes. For example, several U.S. states have enacted laws to regulate deepfakes in response to specific concerns such as election interference, non-consensual adult material, and identity theft. In California, Assembly Bill 730 prohibits the use of deepfakes in political campaigns, while Assembly Bill 602 establishes accountability for perpetrators of non-consensual pornography by granting victims legal recourse [36]. At the same time, Texas enacted Senate Bill 751 to prohibit the creation and distribution of deepfake videos intended to interfere with the electoral process. In addition, some states ban the production of sexually explicit deepfakes that impersonate individuals without consent, while others including Florida, New York, Illinois, and Virginia have introduced targeted regulations in specific areas. However, because these laws differ in scope and definition, they collectively form a fragmented, state-by-state system of protection rather than a uniform national framework [36] [28]. Clearly, an adoption of a legal definition of deepfakes such as the one in India's 2026 IT rules amendment, which classifies algorithmically altered audio/visual content under strict oversight is advisable.

(ii) Mandatory labelling: Taking a que from the China approach, China has taken a proactive stance against deepfake technology, swiftly enacting strict regulations to curb misuse. Beginning in 2023, these laws require all AI-generated content to be clearly labeled to prevent confusion among end-users [28] [36].

(iii) Swift take down protocols: he Take It Down Act aims to quickly remove deepfake images without disrupting America's AI progress [29]. This underlines the need for action. The Take It Down Act requires platforms to remove content. The law has implications on victims, content creators and platforms. As For Victims they have a right to request removal of NCII within 48 hours, while creators it unlawful to create or distribute NCII without consent. Finally, platforms must implement clear procedures to comply with takedown requests [30].

2.7.2 Governance and Oversight

(i) Independent regulatory Bodies: As deepfake technology advances, lawmakers must decide how to curb its most damaging uses without sacrificing free speech or stifling innovation [31]. It is thus imperative to establish specialized bodies that strengthen existing media/IT regulators to monitor deepfake proliferation.

(ii) **Cross-Border Collaboration:** Countries may also agree to extradite and prosecute individuals for serious deepfake crimes across borders. This means that nations would not only assist each other in investigations but also require platforms to geofence illegal content in specific jurisdictions [32]. International cooperation will play a critical role in addressing the challenge of deepfakes given the way they are widely distributed worldwide. Countries should strive towards an international agreement or treaty which would outline and standardize how the law views deepfakes, further bringing borderless-ness to enforcement. International cooperation between law enforcement agencies and platforms is needed to contain the dispersal of deepfakes around the world [33]. A Coordination among global frameworks such as the EU AI Act, OECD AI principles, and UNESCO AI Ethics to harmonize standards.

(iv) **Audit & Redress Mechanisms:** A recommendation in [34] requires institutions to have privacy and retention controls wherein there is enforcement of minimal data retention, limited access and comprehensive audit trails for biometric and liveness data. These guardrails for responsible use reduce privacy and compliance risks while maintaining detection capabilities. It also recommends governance documentation wherein there is maintenance of clear operational guidelines, thresholds and appeal mechanisms. This documentation and these operational guardrails ensure that decisions remain consistent, auditable and defensible. Clearly platforms should provide audit trails for AI-generated content and enable user redress when harmed.

2.7.3 Platform Accountability

In [43] it is argued that deepfake creators exploit gaps in regulatory frameworks and undermine accountability. Accountability speaks to issues of transparency, algorithmic audit and user empowerment tools.

(ii) **Transparency reports:** Collaborating with businesses can be beneficial as their specialized knowledge and abundant resources can contribute 15 to creating technologies, for identifying deepfakes. Furthermore, establishing and enforcing processes that encourage transparency and accountability in using deepfakes for purposes. This may involve implementing reporting obligations or setting up inspection committees [35].

(ii) **Algorithmic Audits:** AI systems are trained using large datasets that often reflect biases already present in society. For example, the Dutch government's AI-driven welfare fraud detection system, Systeem Risico Indicatie, (SyRI) was found by a Dutch court to have algorithmic risk models that targeted low-income and minority-background neighborhoods [36]. As a requirement independent audit of AI models used for content moderation and generation are a necessity.

(iii) **User Empowerment Tools:** Provide watermarking, authenticity verification, and reporting mechanisms for users.

2.7.4 Cybersecurity & Identity Protection

(i) **Criminalization of Malicious Use:** Model providers and compute providers should be held liable for negligence, with a clear obligation to demonstrate that safeguards are in place to prevent their resources from being misused for the creation of deepfakes. This responsibility entails applying techniques that ensure responsible use, including implementing reasonable measures to monitor user activity, detecting attempts to generate synthetic or harmful content, and restricting access for malicious actors [3]. By embedding these practices into their operations, providers can show due diligence in protecting against abuse and contribute to a more accountable AI ecosystem [36]. Clearly the deepfake use in fraud, theft, election interference or harassment should be penalized.

(ii) **Data Privacy Safeguards:** Researchers and developers must address the challenges posed by deepfakes with a focus on creating safeguards and detection methods. This call to action is crucial to protect individuals, especially those vulnerable to information poverty, from the harmful effects of deepfake [37]. Model developers must be required to guarantee that the datasets used to train their systems are free from illegal material, such as child sexual abuse content. A recent example illustrates the risks: researchers discovered such material within LAION-5B, a large image dataset that had been used to train several models, including Stable Diffusion. In response, the organization responsible for LAION-5B voluntarily withdrew the dataset, but this action was not mandated by law. To ensure accountability, such safeguards should be codified into legislation, making developers liable unless they apply reasonable techniques to verify that their models are not trained on datasets containing prohibited content [3].

(iii) **Secure Infrastructure:** Governments should allocate resources to fund research and development of deepfake detection technology and establish legislation to discourage malicious use. Collaboration between technology companies and social media platforms is crucial to implementing effective solutions for detecting and preventing the spread of deepfakes. Social media platforms and technology companies must take responsibility for combating deepfakes by implementing robust content moderation policies and investing in AI systems that can detect and flag potentially harmful deepfake content. A multifaceted approach combining technological advancements, policy measures, education, and collaboration is necessary to effectively combat the spread of deepfakes and mitigate their potential harm to individuals and society.

Encourage banks, governments, and media houses to adopt deepfake detection technologies.

2.7.5 Public Awareness & Education

Public awareness and education are essential in combating deepfake threats, particularly in the context of information poverty. Promoting media literacy and teaching individuals to discern between real and manipulated content can empower them to make informed decisions and mitigate the spread of deepfakes. Industry leaders and companies must establish clear guide lines and ethical standards for creating and disseminating synthetic media, contributing to a more trustworthy information environment [37].

(i) **Digital literacy campaigns:** While advancements in wireless technologies including TV White Spaces [48] [49] [50] and 5G/6G [51] [52] [53] have helped bridge the digital divide and promote digital literacy, they have also introduced new complexities in media consumption. The link between digital literacy and the ability to recognize deepfake content is crucial in an era where synthetic media threatens information integrity. Digital literacy encompasses a broad set of skills related to effectively using and understanding digital technologies, which are essential for spotting manipulated or deceptive media [47].

(ii) **Media partnerships:** RSF encourages journalists and media to maintain a clear and transparent distinction between authentic and synthetic audio-visual content. The media must favor the use of authentic footage and recordings to depict actual events, as urged by the Paris Charter on AI and Journalism [38].

(iii) **AI Literacy in Schools:** In the school context, AI literacy isn't just about teaching students how to use AI tools—it's about preparing them to live in a digital environment where appearances can be deceptive and deepfakes blur the line between truth and fabrication. Students need to learn critical thinking, source verification, and ethical awareness so they can navigate a reality where "seeing" or "hearing" something is no longer enough to confirm authenticity. This equips them not only to use technology responsibly but also to safeguard their rights, identities, and trust in information [49].

Integrate awareness into curricula to build resilience against misinformation: In today's information-driven world, misinformation and disinformation pose serious threats to democracy, public health, and social cohesion. Training teachers in Media and Information Literacy (MIL) is therefore not just advisable it is essential. By equipping educators with the skills to recognize, analyze, and counter false information, schools can foster critical thinking and help build a resilient society capable of navigating the challenges of misinformation [50].

2.8 CONCLUSION

Deepfakes represent a double-edged sword, offering both opportunities and risks. In the entertainment sector, they are used constructively in areas such as advertising and education. Yet, when applied to political disinformation, fraud, or cybercrime, they pose serious threats. Their multifaceted nature means they affect individuals, institutions, and society as a whole. Addressing these challenges requires effective governance built on balanced, risk-based approaches—such as the EU AI Act—that emphasize transparency and mandatory labeling rather than outright bans. Organizational resilience can be strengthened by adopting structured methodologies like the NIST AI Risk Management Framework, which provides tools to systematically map, measure, and manage AI-related vulnerabilities.

Nonetheless, significant obstacles remain: fragmented international regulations, complex liability issues for developers and platforms, and an enforcement gap as technology advances faster than legislation. A sustainable future for AI will depend on harmonized global standards, strong data privacy protections, and a commitment to media literacy—ensuring societies are resilient against synthetic misinformation while still benefiting from technological innovation.

REFERENCES

[1] Keepnet, "Deepfake Statistics & Trends 2026: Growth, Risks, and Future Insights," 02 February 2026. [Online]. Available: https://keepnetlabs.com/blog/deepfake-statistics-and-trends.

[2] Cogent, "Deepfake Onslaught: Why 2026 Will Demand Enterprise-Grade Defense Now," 15 December 2025. [Online]. Available: https://www.cogentinfo.com/resources/deepfake-onslaught-why-2026-will-demand-enterprise-grade-defense-now. [Accessed 02 February 2026].

[3] E. Altuncu, V. N. Franqueira and. S. Li, "Deepfake: definitions, performance metrics and standards, datasets, and a meta-review," *Frontiers in Big Data,* vol. 7, p. 1400024, 2024.

[4] B. Johannes, "Understanding Deepfakes: Characteristics, Risks, and Detection Techniques," iotmktg, 24 February 2024. [Online]. Available: https://iotmktg.com/understanding-deepfakes-characteristics-risks-and-detection-techniques/. [Accessed 06 February 2026].

[5] Data Security Council of India (DSCI), "Exploratory Note on Deepfakes and Policy Considerations," DSCI Knowledge Centre, 2023.

[6] R. Trisha and J. Sangeet, "Regulating Deepfakes: Global Approaches to Combatting AI-Driven Manipulation," Observer Research Foundation (ORF), 2023.

[7] L. Amanda, "A Look at Global Deepfake Regulation Approaches," responsible.ai, 24 Aprill 2023. [Online]. Available: https://www.responsible.ai/news/a-look-at-global-deepfake-regulation-approaches/. [Accessed 03 February 2026].

[8] Palo Alto Networks, "NIST AI Risk Management Framework (AI RMF)," paloaltonetworks, 13 June 2025. [Online]. Available: https://www.paloaltonetworks.com/cyberpedia/nist-ai-risk-management-framework. [Accessed 04 February 2026].

[9] K. Jana, "Regulating Deepfakes: Global Approaches to Combatting AI-Driven Manipulation," 2024.

[10] CYFIRMA, "DEEPFAKE DEFENSE STRATEGIC SOLUTIONS," cyfirma, 05 September 2024. [Online]. Available: https://www.cyfirma.com/research/deepfake-defense-strategic-solutions/. [Accessed 05 February 2026].

[11] European Union(EU), "Artificial Intelligence Act, Article 26: Obligations of providers of high-risk AI systems.," 2024. [Online]. Available: https://artificialintelligenceact.eu/article/26/. [Accessed 05 February 2026].

[12] B. J. Derek, "House passes legislation to criminalize nonconsensual deepfakes," cyberscoop, 25 Aprill 2025. [Online]. Available: https://cyberscoop.com/take-it-down-act-passes-house-first-amendment-encryption/. [Accessed 04 February 2026].

[13] F. Vincent, "Transparency of AI-Generated Content: China Goes Further than Europe," DDG, 13 February 2026. [Online]. Available: https://www.ddg.fr/actualite/transparency-of-ai-generated-content-china-goes-further-than-europe#:~:text=Transparency%20of%20AI%2DGenerated%20Content,virtual%20scenes%20%E2%80%94%20is%20clearly%20identified.&text=Two%20cumulative%20duties%20apply:,or%20eq. [Accessed 14 February 2026].

[14] BBC News, "What the Online Safety Act is—and how to keep children safe online," bbc, 24 July 2025. [Online]. Available: https://www.bbc.com/news/articles/c0epennv98lo. [Accessed 15 February 2026].
[15] K. Tatyana, "South Korea leads world with 1st comprehensive AI safety law," qazinform., 22 January 2026. [Online]. Available: https://qazinform.com/news/south-korea-leads-world-with-1st-comprehensive-ai-safety-law-e20189#:~:text=South%20Korea%20has%20become%20the,regulating%20artificial%20intelligence%2C%20Yonhap%20reports.&text=The%20AI%20Basic%20Act%2C%20which,were%20shaping%2. [Accessed 04 February 2026].
[16] N. Mashinini, "Deepfakes and South African law: remedies on paper, gaps in practice," theconversation, 18 September 2025. [Online]. Available: https://theconversation.com/deepfakes-and-south-african-law-remedies-on-paper-gaps-in-practice-263850. [Accessed 31 January 2026].
[17] K. G. W. Claudia, "Artificial illusion: Global governance challenges of deepfake technology," iapp, 23 Aprill 2025. [Online]. Available: https://iapp.org/news/a/artificial-illusion-global-governance-challenges-of-deepfake-technology. [Accessed 02 February 2026].
[18] M. Linda, "Framing Deepfake Technology in European Union Governance: Discursive strategies and regulatory responses to deepfake technology," University of Twente (Student Thesis), 2025.
[19] A. Nowak,. B. Tóth and A. Ionescu, "Legal Challenges of Deepfakes: Liability, Harm, and Regulatory Responses," *Legal Studies in Digital Age,* vol. 2, no. 2, pp. 49–60, 2023.
[20] V. Cristina, "Deepfake Dilemma: Balancing Regulation, Responsibility, and Rights in the AI Era," 24 February 2024. [Online]. Available: https://moderndiplomacy.eu/2024/02/24/deepfake-dilemma-balancing-regulation-responsibility-and-rights-in-the-ai-era/. [Accessed 03 February 2026].
[21] L. Narmadha, "An Analysis of Legal Gaps and Enforcement Challenges in Addressing AI-Generated Deepfake Sexual Offences in India," *nternational Journal of Advanced Research in Science, Communication and Technology,* vol. 5, no. 4, pp. 239–275, 2025.
[22] L. R. Andrew and L. M. Jason, "Deepfakes-as-a-Service Meets State Laws: Governing Synthetic Media in a Fragmented Legal Landscape," joneswalker, 15 Janauary 2026. [Online]. Available: https://www.joneswalker.com/en/insights/blogs/ai-law-blog/deepfakes-as-a-service-meets-state-laws-governing-synthetic-media-in-a-fragmente.html?id=102m20g. [Accessed 31 January 2026].
[23] A. T. Wasi,,. R. N. Priti,. M. A. Khan, and. A. Rahman, "Seeing Isn't Believing: Addressing the Societal Impact of Deepfakes in Low-Tech Environments," in *Proceedings of the 2nd International Workshop on Diffusion of Harmful Content on Online Web*, 2025.
[24] Identity Management Institute (Editorial Staff), "Deepfake Risks to Identity and Access Management," Identity Management Institute, 24 July 2025. [Online]. Available: https://identitymanagementinstitute.org/deepfake-risks-to-identity-and-access-management/. [Accessed 31 Janauary 2026].
[25] N. A. RAKHMAWATI, "ANALYZING ETHICAL CHALLENGES OF DEEPFAKE TECHNOLOGY IN MEDIA AND COMMUNICATION USING BIBLIOMETRIC RESEARCH AND VOSVIEWER VISUALIZATION," *Etika Teknologi Informasi,* vol. 1, no. 2, 25.
[26] S. Karnouskos, "Artificial intelligence in digital media: The era of deepfakes," *IEEE transactions on technology and society,* vol. 1, no. 3, pp. 138–147, 2020.
[27] Communications Today Editorial, "India's first AI law tightens deepfake takedown rules, puts Big Tech on alert," 12 February 2026. [Online]. Available: https://www.communicationstoday.co.in/indias-first-ai-law-tightens-deepfake-takedown-rules-puts-big-tech-on-alert/. [Accessed 13 February 2026].
[28] B. Elton, "The challenges of deepfake technology on the decision-making processes within," University of Malta, 2025.
[29] V. Lindsey, "Is the Take It Down Act Enough?," Washington Journal of Law, Technology & Arts (Blog), 12 February 2026. [Online]. Available: Is the Take It Down Act Enough?. [Accessed 13 February 2026].

[30] F. Romero-Moreno, "Deepfake detection in generative AI: A legal framework proposal to protect human rights," *Computer Law & Security Review,* vol. 58, p. 106162, 2025.
[31] N. Tuhu, "Cross-Border Deepfake Threats: A Systemic Risk to Global Finance," moderndiplomacy., 29 September 2025. [Online]. Available: https://moderndiplomacy.eu/2025/09/29/cross-border-deepfake-threats-a-systemic-risk-to-global-finance/. [Accessed 06 February 2026].
[32] A. Shivam, "The misinformation epidemic: combating AI-generated fake content and deepfakes," *World Journal of Advanced Research and Reviews,* vol. 26, no. 2, pp. 1632–1639, 2025.
[33] S. Anxhela, "Legal Responses to Challenges Posed by Deepfakes," SSRN?, 2025.
[34] W. ALEX, "AI Regulation Across Borders: Legal," *an Diego International Law Journal,* vol. 26, p. 317, 2024.
[35] I. Karolina and. D. Hadassah, "Case studies: national-level enforcement of the AI Act in the Netherlands," European Center for Not-for-Profit Law (ECNL), 2023.
[36] KYC Hub Editorial Team, "Deepfake Laws and Regulations: All You Need to Know in 2025," kychub, 2024. [Online]. Available: https://www.kychub.com/blog/what-are-deepfakes/. [Accessed 03 February 2026].
[37] E. McGowan, "Take It Down, Keep Moving: How to Take Down Deepfake Images Without Stalling U.S. AI Leadership," Swiss Institute of Artificial Intelligence (SIAI), 16 December 2025. [Online]. Available: https://siai.org/memo/2025/12/202512285283. [Accessed 04 February 2026].
[38] Facia.ai Editorial Team, "USA's TAKE IT DOWN Act: Deepfake Laws, Key Provisions & Penalties," Facia, 18 September 2025. [Online]. Available: https://facia.ai/knowledgebase/usas-take-it-down-act-deepfake-laws-key-provisions-penalties/. [Accessed 05 February 2026].
[39] S. Grace, L. Atinuke and. E. Woo, "Reckoning With the Rise of Deepfakes," Regulatory Review, 14 June 2025. [Online]. Available: https://www.theregreview.org/2025/06/14/seminar-reckoning-with-the-rise-of-deepfakes/#:~:text=Before%20the%20TAKE%20IT%20DOWN,platforms%20that%20fail%20to%20comply. [Accessed 04 February 2026].
[40] P. Zarema, "Deepfake Laws: Global Overview and Emerging Regulations," ondato, 2025. [Online]. Available: https://ondato.com/blog/deepfake-laws/. [Accessed 01 February 2026].
[41] N. Kamal, "Strengthening Privacy Laws to Combat Deepfakes: An Evaluation of Current Legal Protection and Future Directions, " *International Journal for Multidisciplinary Research,* vol. 7, no. 2, 2024.
[42] World Economic Forum (WEF), "Unmasking Cybercrime: Strengthening Digital Identity Verification against Deepfakes," World Economic Forum I Insight Report, 2025.
[43] S. A. Maryam, "Analyzing the Potential Future Consequences of the Widespread," Rochester Institute of Technology, Dubai, 2023.
[44] United Nations Development Programme (UNDP) and S. Emrys, "A Shared Vision for Digital Technology and Governance: The role of governance in ensuring digital technologies contribute to development and mitigate risk:Development Futures Series No. 68," United Nations, 2024.
[45] W. Matli, "Extending the theory of information poverty to deepfake technology," *International Journal of Information Management Data Insights,* vol. 4, no. 2, p. 100286, 2024.
[46] Reporters Without Borders (RSF—Reporters sans fr, "Four recommendations for combating the threat to the right to information posed by deepfakes," rsf, November 2023. [Online]. Available: https://rsf.org/en/four-recommendations-combating-threat-right-information-posed-deepfakes. [Accessed 29 January 2026].
[47] A. Miotti and A. Wasil, "Combatting deepfakes: Policies to address national security threats and rights violation," *arXiv preprint arXiv:2402.09581,* 2024.
[48] S. M. Nleya and M. Velempini, "Industrial metaverse: A comprehensive review, environmental impact, and challenges," *Applied Sciences,* vol. 14, no. 13, p. 5736, 2024.

Chapter 3

From Deepfakes to Trust

The Role of Normative Goals in Brand Authenticity and Consumer Purchase Intentions

Parul Manchanda, Nisha Solanki, and Anshu Punshi

3.1 INTRODUCTION

Deepfake technology emerged from a confluence of advancements in artificial intelligence (AI), particularly in machine learning and neural networks, with its origins tracing back to the 1990s when researchers began exploring image manipulation techniques (TechTarget, 2023; Reality Defender, 2023). The breakthrough moment for deepfake technology came in 2014 with the introduction of generative adversarial networks by Ian Goodfellow and his team, which allowed for the creation of highly realistic synthetic media (Reality Defender, 2023; TechTarget, 2023).

Hence, in the present day, deepfake technology is considered one of the most fascinating, frightening advances in AI as it continues to blur the lines of reality and fabrication. This technology is considered to be a game-changer in most sectors. The most believable applications of deepfakes could be making personalized content for marketing and education. In marketing, deepfakes allow for cost-effective video production by enabling brands to create campaigns without the need for in-person actors, thus saving time and resources (Sahota et al., 2024).

Furthermore, they facilitate hyper-personalization in advertising, allowing brands to tailor messaging based on customer demographics, which enhances inclusivity and market reach (Intelligency Group, 2022). In education, deepfakes bring history to life and allow students to communicate and engage with realistic simulations of past subjects, therefore heightening engagement and facilitating deeper understanding of historical events (Legamart, 2024).

Furthermore, deepfakes can revolutionize the film industry: Production processes become easier and faster since filmmakers can now use this technology to generate scenes featuring actors not on the sets; this saves time and resources for artists involved. Lastly, in the realm of public health communication, deepfakes have been effectively used to deliver important messages in multiple languages by well-known personalities, thereby broadening their reach and impact (Toews, 2020).

When deepfake technology is used in a thoughtful and principled manner, it has the potential to foster active participation and stimulate creativity throughout a number of industries. This is because deepfake technology applies various complex algorithms to edited footage. But researchers have also observed deepfakes as tools to present pseudo-real events, sway viewers' opinions, and weaken the political process (Chesney & Citron, 2019; Godulla et al., 2024). The use of deepfake technology to alter speeches of politicians has the opportunity to change the outcome of an election and cause severe damage to their reputation

DOI: 10.1201/9781003539032-3

(Karnouskos, 2020; Lorenzo, 2022). Even further, the creation of non-consensual sexual material with deepfake technology is an extreme invasion of privacy and can ruin one's life (Hobbs, 2024; Hartmann & Giles, 2020).

In addition, the spread of deepfakes has created general skepticism toward digital media, thus increasingly making it challenging for audiences to distinguish authentic content from manipulated ones (Godulla et al., 2024; Sahota et al., 2024). Hence, the social impacts of deepfake technology require urgent attention and effective strategies to reduce its harmful effects (Reddy et al., 2024).

As the technology of AI is improving, the future deepfakes will probably become more realistic and difficult to trace. This new development throws urgent questions related to ethics and accountability in the context of deepfakes (Legamart, 2024). So, the regulation of deepfake information becomes necessary for good innovation and restricting malicious uses. It has been discovered from the literature that the focus of studies regarding deepfake information is mostly technical in terms of the detection process (Ismail et al., 2021b). Not many studies were done on the ethical implications of deepfake information, while most of these only qualitatively described relevant issues in terms of ethical implications that may be an invasion of privacy (Öhman, 2020), online harassment, slander, identity theft, and bullying (Kietzmann et al., 2020), while responsibility becomes obscure (Dobber et al., 2021).

Hence, it has been seen that consumers have voiced ambivalence toward deepfakes. Hence, a strategic approach to guarantee its acceptance would not only be aligned with mitigating risks but also brand positioning favorably in an increasingly competitive marketplace. Hence, through this research work, we emphasize the priority of ethical considerations in the application of deepfake technology to enhance consumer acceptance and brand authenticity for driving purchase intentions. This will ensure that businesses implement policies that outline the ethical guidelines governing deepfake usage. This authenticity fosters a sense of reliability among consumers, making them more likely to engage with the brand and thus make purchase decisions (Figure 3.1).

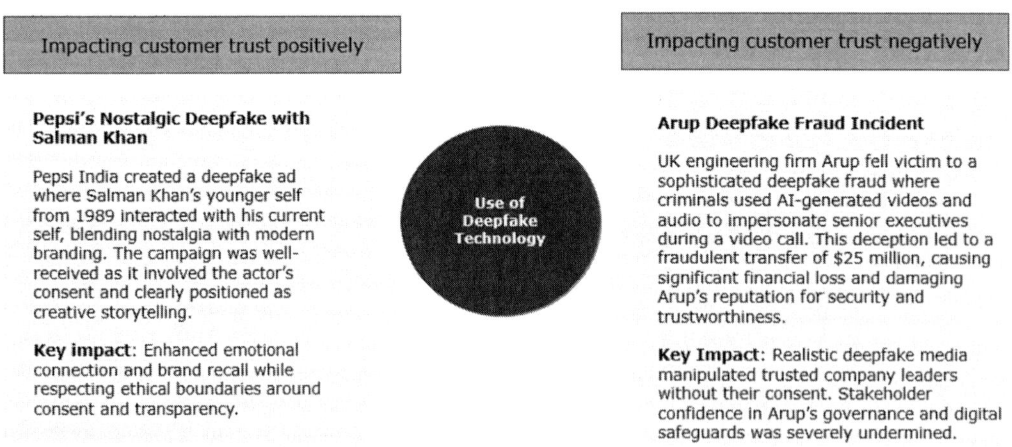

Figure 3.1 Deepfake technology affecting consumer trust positively and negatively.

Source: Authors' own creation.

Further, in this research paper, we have used the "goal-framing theory," particularly focusing on normative goals, providing a robust framework for understanding the ethical acceptability of deepfake information. This theory postulates that people's choices and actions are determined by the framing of objectives.

This framing helps navigate the complex ethical landscape which lies ahead with the advent of deepfake technology. Hence, we try to fill this gap by addressing how different types of normative goals and acceptance of deepfake information influence people and hence formulate the following research questions:

RQ1 How do the various normative goals affect the ethical acceptability of deepfake information?

RQ 2 How does the ethical acceptability of deepfake information affect brand authenticity?

RQ 3 How does brand authenticity encourage consumers toward intention to purchase?

3.2 THEORETICAL BACKGROUND

3.2.1 How Normative Goals Shape Ethical Perceptions

As a goal theorist (Modigliani & Gamson, 1979), goal-framing theory argues that human behavior and attitude are heavily framed by the attainment of goals that we see tied to an agenda in a specific context. The theory further suggests that the conquest of something as abstract as a perception—as well as the response it provokes—can be mapped simply by what "type" of information one presents, which, in the case of deepfakes, can be seen in complexity.

This chapter examines the role of normative ideals such as fair use, informed consent, privacy protection, traceability, non-deceptive practices, and other principles as ethical boundaries regarding the use of deepfake information. The normative concerns serve as a framework for the consumers' assessment of the ethics of deepfake technology and, consequently, affect brand trustworthiness and the intention to buy.

The ethical concerns surrounding deepfake technology should be understood within the broader framework of the ethical state, whose normative goals guide and structure this evaluation. For example, the principle of reasonable use states that the technology of deepfake must be used in socially acceptable and desired ways, tending to the expectation of the consumer. Informed consent, that is the consciousness and informed consent of individuals about using their likeness in deepfake content material, is critical for ethical compliance.

Privacy protection is essential in building user trust concerning deepfake systems, safeguarding records from misuse. Traceability pursuits at tracking the origin, creation, and modification of deepfake content, enhancing the responsibility and transparency, which are fundamental for ethical reputation. Non-deception fosters honesty in the portrayal of records and prevents trust manipulation, reinforcing trust. Taken together, these normative purposes strengthen the framework for evaluating the moral boundary of deepfakes on society. For clients experiencing their interactions with brands utilizing this technology, these principles assist in making assessments about discernment.

3.3 LITERATURE REVIEW AND PROPOSED HYPOTHESIS

3.3.1 Normative Goals and Ethical Acceptability of Deepfake Information

3.3.1.1 *Reasonable Use*

This speculation is that, while brands and creators observe the principle of reasonable use—when deepfake content is created and used in socially responsible and ethically sound ways—the public might be much more likely to see such content as ethically applicable. There have been previous studies, which suggest that necessity for ethical frameworks when employing deepfake technology, that reasonable use contributes to a more favorable perception among consumers (Li & Wan, 2023; Eberl et al., 2022). Therefore, this relationship is critical in understanding how normative goals can shape consumer attitudes toward emerging technologies like deepfakes.

H1: Reasonable use of deepfake technology positively influences the ethical acceptability of deepfake information.

3.3.1.2 *Informed Consent*

This hypothesis postulates that if the creators and users of deepfake technology consider the aspect of informed consent—that is, ensuring people know and consent to the use of their likenesses in deepfakes—the information becomes more ethically acceptable (Kaur et al., 2024). A report by Spair (2024) indicates that deepfakes have a strong psychological impact on people and society. The ability to make realistic videos that manipulate reality can result in mistrust and anxiety for the viewer. Deepfake technology, though it can increase creative expression and storytelling, brings along with it issues of consent. This means their privacy and dignity are respected (Zheng et al., 2025). Therefore, based on the previous discussion, we come up with the following hypothesis:

H2: Adherence to informed consent positively influences the ethical acceptability of deepfake information.

3.3.1.3 *Privacy Protection*

Deepfake technology, which uses AI to produce hyper-realistic media, poses significant threats to individual privacy by enabling unauthorized alterations of personal images and voices (Coruzant Technologies, 2023; NovoJuris Legal, 2023). This hypothesis posits that when creators and users of deepfake technology prioritize privacy protection—ensuring that individuals' personal data and likenesses are used responsibly and with consent—the ethical acceptability of such deepfake content is enhanced (Mahashreshty, 2023; Ajder et al., 2019).

H3: Adherence to privacy protection principles positively influences the ethical acceptability of deepfake information.

3.3.1.4 *Traceability*

The crucial dating between traceability and the moral acceptability of deepfake technology pertains to the ethical dilemmas that stand up in its misuse. Traceability mechanisms, which become aware of the origins and changes of deepfake content, are a pivotal tool in mitigating risks associated with incorrect information and manipulation. As deepfake generation advances, traceability can contribute to greater responsibility and transparency, therefore growing its moral role (Ismail et al., 2023). Source tracing of deepfakes, besides supporting in monitoring malicious uses, promotes media to consider enabling authenticity verification (Huang, 2022). In addition, traceability-based ethical frameworks can direct developers to design accountable AI programs that respect the rights and privacy of people (Goodwine, 2020). Ultimately, organizing a significant relationship between traceability and ethical acceptability is essential for growing a responsible digital environment that minimizes damage even as maximizing the potential blessings of deepfake generation (Abdul Hussein, 2023). This hypothesis states that when creators and customers of deepfake technology hire traceability measures—making sure that the origins and modifications of deepfake content may be tracked and validated—the ethical acceptability of such statistics is enhanced. From this discussion, we have the subsequent hypothesis:

H4: Adherence to traceability principles positively influences the ethical acceptability of deepfake information.

3.3.1.5 Non-Deception

An overarching ethical approach to deepfakes is centered on the notions of consent and truthfulness: by misrepresenting people in content without permission and knowledge, what is created would be problematic from an ethical aspect (Kaur et al., 2024; Deepak & Krishnamoorthy et al., 2024). A deeper look shows how deepfakes that were fashioned with nefarious intent, such as blackmail and misleading information, are absolutely wrong things to create. Conversely, deepfakes are considered ethically acceptable when created for legitimate purposes, such as entertainment or educational content, and all parties involved have consented to their use (Robb, 2023; JETIR, 2023). This distinction points out that the intent behind making a deepfake has a significant influence on its ethical implications (Mathews, 2014; Singh, 2008). Therefore, the hypothesis is that when creators and users of deepfake technology put non-deception first—when the content will not mislead or manipulate the viewers—the ethical acceptability of such information improves (Figure 3.2).

H5: Adherence to non-deception principles positively influences the ethical acceptability of deepfake information.

3.4 ETHICAL ACCEPTABILITY AND BRAND AUTHENTICITY

Ethical acceptability is the extent to which deepfake content adheres to established norms, including informed consent, privacy protection, traceability, and non-deception. If brands use deepfake technology ethically, consumers will trust them more because more people are aware of and concerned about the ethical implications of marketing practices (Huang & Maracic 2024). Such a trust is really important for making a brand authentically more believable, particularly when consumers get to realize that the firm operates transparently and ethically. In fact, brands with deepfakes can further dilute or remove negative attributes often associated with deepfakes, such as misinformation and manipulation, which increase their authenticity. Supporting literature, such as the studies by Arora et al. (2024) and Rather (2024), underscores the importance of ethical practices in shaping consumer

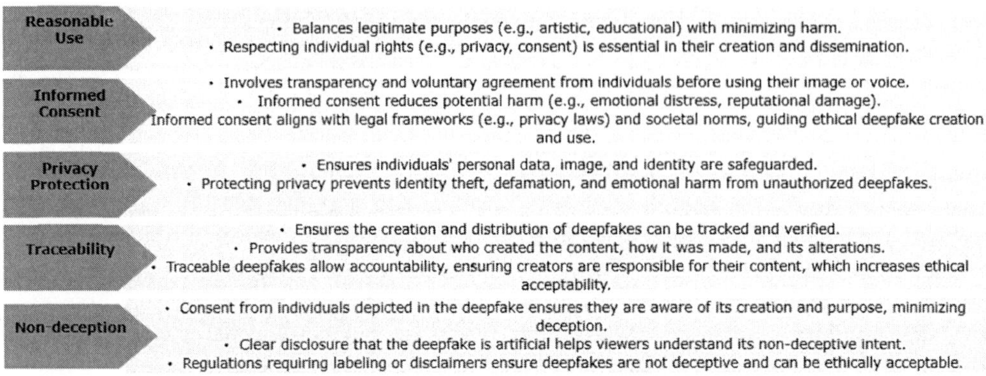

Figure 3.2 Various normative goals and their relationship with ethical acceptability.

Source: Authors' own creation.

perceptions and highlights that adherence to ethical norms not only fosters trust but also solidifies brand authenticity in an increasingly skeptical market. Hence, this hypothesis emphasizes the vital role of ethics in modern marketing strategies. As brands increasingly utilize deepfake technology for marketing and communications, the ethical standards they maintain have a more critical value in determining how to regard their authenticity.

H6: The ethical acceptability of deepfake information positively influences brand authenticity.

3.5 BRAND AUTHENTICITY AND INTENTION TO PURCHASE

Deepfake technology enables marketers to create highly realistic content, which can make stories more engaging and personalize marketing messages. However, ethical implications such as privacy violations, misrepresentation, and the possibility of deception might undermine consumer trust. When applied ethically by brands, transparency, and consent from individuals whose images are used, deepfake technology can improve the perceived authenticity of a brand (Rixom & Rixom, 2023). This is because today's consumers are becoming more sophisticated; they are looking for true engagement with brands that share their values and act ethically. In this respect, the fact that a brand uses deepfake technology responsibly can help it reap the benefits of the technology without losing authenticity, which is necessary to boost purchase intentions in a competitive market like today (Al-Meshal et al., 2020; Alhosseiny & Nabih, 2024). For example, research has indicated that consumers are more likely to trust and be loyal to brands that openly communicate their use of innovative technologies such as deepfakes while adhering to ethical standards.

H7: Brand authenticity positively influences consumers' intention to purchase.

Thus, based on the aforementioned discussion, we propose the following hypothesis, which is illustrated in Table 3.1 and the research model in Figure 3.3.

The hypotheses proposed to test the influence of the ethical acceptability of deepfake information on brand authenticity and purchase intention are summarized in Table 3.2.

Table 3.1 Hypothesis for establishing the influence of various normative goals on the acceptability of deepfake information

Normative Goals	*Hypothesis*
Reasonable Use	H1: Reasonable use of deepfake technology positively influences the ethical acceptability of deepfake information.
Informed Consent	H2: Adherence to informed consent positively influences the ethical acceptability of deepfake information.
Privacy Protection	H3: Adherence to privacy protection principles positively influences the ethical acceptability of deepfake information.
Traceability	H4: Adherence to traceability principles positively influences the ethical acceptability of deepfake information.
Non-deception	H5: Adherence to non-deception principles positively influences the ethical acceptability of deepfake information.

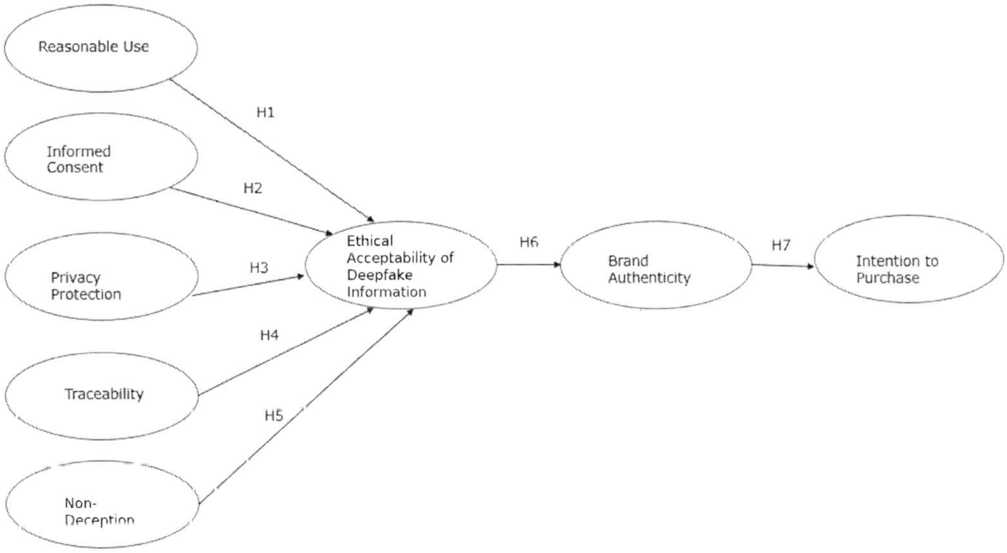

Figure 3.3 Proposed research model.

Source: Authors' own creation.

Table 3.2 Hypothesis for testing the influence of ethical acceptability of deepfake information on brand authenticity and intention to purchase

Normative Goals	*Hypothesis*
Ethical Acceptability	H6: The ethical acceptability of deepfake information positively influences brand authenticity.
Brand Authenticity	H7: Brand authenticity positively influences consumers' intention to purchase.

3.6 RESEARCH TOOLS AND TECHNIQUES ADOPTED

While conducting this research, we have approached it through the following steps as depicted in Figure 3.4.

3.6.1 Measurement Scale Adaptation

A seven-point Likert scale questionnaire was designed, consisting of three parts. The first section presents cases of deepfake information in various scenarios (like David Beckham's malaria awareness campaign; interactive experiences with historical figures aiming to enhance the interviewees' perception of deepfake information). The second part includes a question-and-answer session covering all variables. The third part collects basic information such as age and gender. Filtered items were designed to exclude participants who had no prior exposure to deepfake information.

3.6.2 Sample Characteristics and Data Collection Procedures

We removed samples with response instances that had been both too quick and too long, in addition to people who did no longer bypass, the eye take a look at (Podsakoff et al., 2012). Out of the 385 questionnaires gathered, 275 (71.4%) were valid. The characteristics of the sample are supplied in Table 3.3. The gender distribution became quite balanced, with 57% male and 43% female respondents. The majority of individuals were between 20 and 40, which aligns with the actual ratio of publicity to emerging technology. The respondents normally had better levels of training and had been exposed to numerous forms of packages.

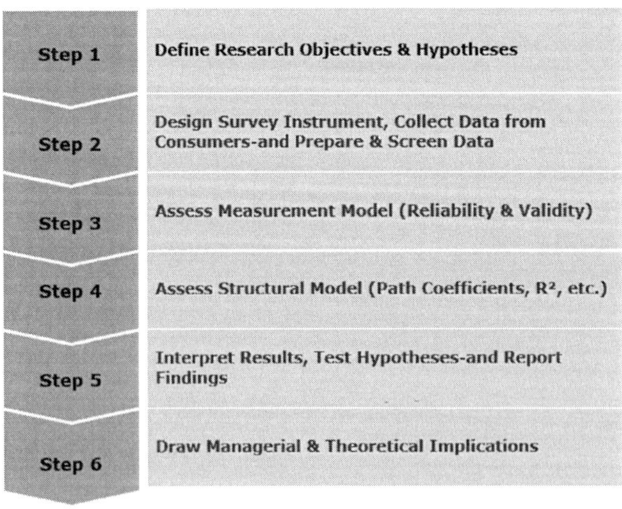

Figure 3.4 Steps adopted in the research methodology.

Source: Authors' own creation.

Table 3.3 The respondents' demographic profile

Gender	
Male	157
Female	118
Age	
20–30	114
31–40	101
41–50	60

3.6.3 Common Method Bias

The single-aspect take a look at devised by way of Harman become utilized to assess bias on Common Method Variance (Podsakoff et al., 2003). In the current paper, it changed into claimed that 40.06% of the variance is on account of a single factor. This suggests the absence of commonplace technique bias which become plenty lesser than 50% threshold (Molinillo et al., 2019).

3.6.4 PLS Results

We used SmartPLS3.3.6 to test the hypotheses because Partial Least Square Structural Equation Modeling has lower requirements for sample size and a normal distribution of data (Chin, 1998). It is particularly suitable for exploratory and theory-promoting studies, and it excels in the reliability of score construction (Shmucli et al., 2019).

3.6.5 Model Specification: Measurement Component

The reliability and validity test results are presented in Table 3.4. Composite reliability (CR) and internal consistency coefficient (Cronbach's α) exceeded 0.8 for all variables that came up, with high reliability (Ismail et al., 2021b). The variance extracted (AVE) values were greater than 0.5, and the factor loading coefficient was greater than 0.7, indicating strong convergent validity. Furthermore, the square root of the AVE of each variable is higher than its correlation coefficient, with the other latent variables indicating satisfactory discriminant integrity (Henseler et al., 2015) (Tables 3.4–3.6).

3.6.6 Structural Model Testing and Findings

Structural replica values have studied the relationship between structures and their importance for pre-inference. The simulation of the proposed concept was repeated: 5% needed a position of 5,000 lags in the simulation. Initially, the structural replica was adopted as a reflective measurement replica in the form of sylphs. For this purpose, the variance inflation factor (VIF) was determined from 3.33 (Diamantopoulos, 2008); in addition, the final mediation coefficient for the analysis of the process coefficient (R2) and the effect size (F2) was determined. All hypotheses of direct relationships are supported by a significant 5%. The total number of paths was significant based on bootstrap confidence intervals (Figure 3.5 and Table 3.7).

Table 3.4 Results of the measurement model

Construct	*Indicator*	*Factor Loading*	*Cronbach's α*	*rho_A*	*CR*	*AVE*	*VIF*
Reasonable Use	RU 1	0.750	0.878	0.857	0.860	0.676	1.448
	RU 2	0.729					1.432
	RU 3	0.730					2.524
	RU 4	0.699					2.451
Informed Consent	IC 1	0.826	0.762	0.833	0.932	0.630	2.234
	IC 2	0.834					1.741
	IC 3	0.773					2.524
Privacy Protection	PP 1	0.823	0.868	0.966	0.945	0.662	2.126
	PP 2	0.845					2.916
	PP3	0.831					2.917
	PP 4	0.780					2.451
Traceability	TR 1	0.838	0.771	0.789	0.856	0.863	1.836
	TR 2	0.752					1.789
	TR 3	0.861					1.114
Non-deception	ND 1	0.726	0.824	0.844	0.915	0.569	2.342
	ND 2	0.817					2.782
	ND 3	0.803					1.773
Ethical Acceptability of Deepfake Information	EA 1	0.825	0.869	0.858	0.952	0.673	1.667
	EA 2	0.720					2.684
	EA 3	0.714					2.665
	EA 4	0.765					2.032
Perceived Brand Authenticity	BA 1	0.716	0.877	0.823	0.829	0.566	2.618
	BA 2	0.801					1.830
	BA 3	0.782					2.656
	BA 4	0.754					2.321
	BA 5	0.796					2.121
Intention to Purchase	IP 1	0.733	0.753	0.754	0.745	0.575	2.321
	IP 2	0.679					2.126
	IP 3	0.765					2.433

3.7 RESULTS AND DISCUSSION

Creating morality policies for deepfake technology is crucial for increasing consumer confidence and maintaining brand reputation, which in turn affects purchasing decisions (Figure 3.6).

In this study, we investigated the connection between different factors influencing the ethical acceptability of deepfake statistics and their subsequent effect on logo authenticity and purchaser buying intentions. The consequences supported all proposed hypotheses, indicating that affordable use of the deepfake era (H1) substantially complements the ethical acceptability of deepfake information. Furthermore, adherence to knowledgeable

Table 3.5 DV assessment by Fornell–Larcker criterion

	Reasonable Use	*Informed Consent*	*Privacy Protection*	*Traceability*	*Non-Deception*	*Ethical Acceptability*	*Perceived Brand Authenticity*	*Intention to Purchase*
Reasonable Use	**0.832**							
Informed Consent	0.423	**0.838**						
Privacy Protection	0.446	0.340	**0.855**					
Traceability	0.524	0.366	0.359	**0.685**				
Non-deception	0.324	0.283	0.105	0.235	**0.876**			
Ethical Acceptability	0.457	0.254	0.362	0.657	0.255	**0.932**		
Perceived Brand Authenticity	0.668	0.460	0.374	0.564	0.445	0.556	**0.813**	
Intention to Purchase	0.454	0.289	0.281	0.668	0.257	0.452	0.454	**0.886**

Table 3.6 DV assessment by HTMT criterion

	Reasonable Use	*Informed Consent*	*Privacy Protection*	*Traceability*	*Non-deception*	*Ethical Acceptability*	*Brand Authenticity*	*Intention to Purchase*
Reasonable Use								
Informed Consent	0.478							
Privacy Protection	0.522	0.318						
Traceability	0.631	0.437	0.420					
Non-deception	0.423	0.323	0.234	0.593				
Ethical Acceptability (EA)	0.577	0.331	0.270	0.839	0.255			
Brand Authenticity	0.627	0.432	0.354	0.685	0.556	0.528		
Intention to Purchase	0.534	0.331	0.276	0.710	0.230	0.330	0.550	

consent (H2), privacy protection standards (H3), traceability ideas (H4), and non-deception principles (H5) has been linked to a definite impact on the ethical acceptability of deepfake content. This shows that when creators and users of the deepfake era prioritize these ethical considerations, the perceived legitimacy of such content will increase. Importantly, we additionally determined that the ethical acceptability of deepfake facts (H6) undoubtedly correlates with emblem authenticity, which in flip impacts clients' goal to buy (H7). These findings underscore the importance of organizing ethical guidelines and practices surrounding the deepfake era, as they not only beautify clients' belief in digital content but also enhance brand integrity and have an impact on buying behavior. Overall, our studies highlight the crucial role that ethical considerations play in shaping public belief and the reputation of rising technologies like deepfakes in industrial contexts.

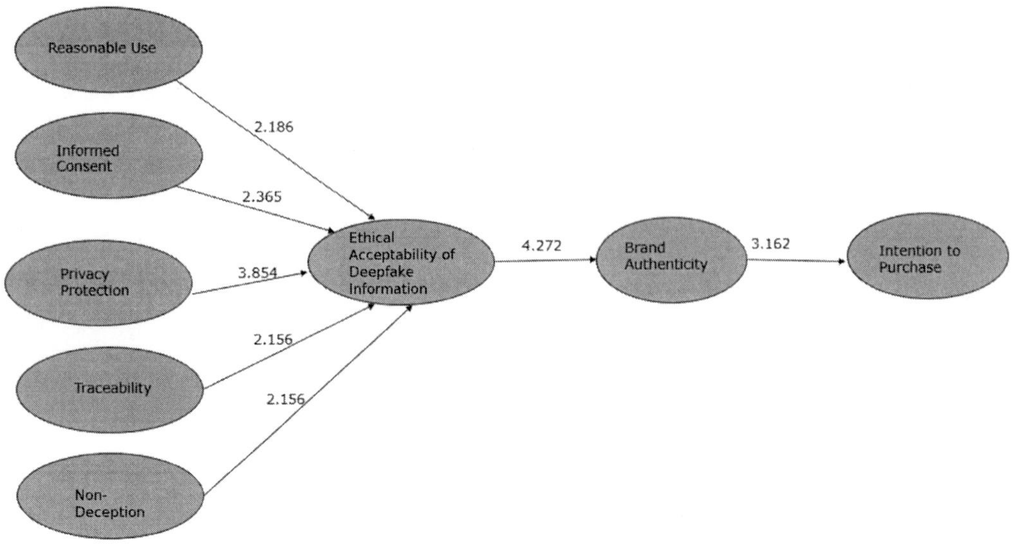

Figure 3.5 Results of the structural model (showing the t value statistics on the arrows).

Table 3.7 Path coefficients results

Hypothesis/Path	*Coefficient (Direct effects)*	*T value*	*F²*	*Confidence intervals*	*VIF*	*Inference*
Intention to Purchase						
R^2 0.189						
$Q^{2:}$ 0.284						
H1: RU→EA	0.275	2.186	—	(0.185, 0.279)	2.06	Supported
H2 IC→EA	0.298	2.365	—	(0.389, 0.473)	1.18	Supported
H3: PP→EA	0.496	3.854	—	(0.225, 0.378)	1.09	Supported
H4: TR→EA	0.493	3.253	—	(0.588, 0.564)	3.17	Supported
H5: ND→EA	0.386	2.156	—	(1.345, 2.971)	2.36	Supported
H6: EA→BA	0.382	4.272	—	(0.028, 1.178)	2.26	Supported
H7: BA→IP	0.285	3.162	—	(0.112, 0.282)	3.16	Supported

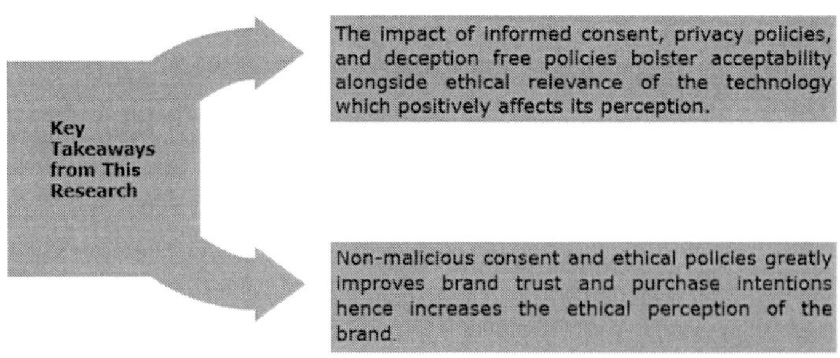

Figure 3.6 Key takeaways from this research.

Source: Authors' own creation.

3.8 RESEARCH IMPLICATIONS

3.8.1 Theoretical Implications

This chapter investigates the dynamic relationships among formal values, ethical acceptability in deepfake cases, brand authenticity, and consumer purchase intentions framed by normative goal-framing theory. This theoretical framework specifies criteria objectives—such as fair use, informed consent, privacy protection, and traceability. It provides a strong basis for understanding how it affects the ethical acceptance of deepfake throw products. The application of value-framing theory facilitates an understanding of how formally value-based policies shape consumer perceptions of complex technologies. Thus, developing in-depth information on ethical issues can have a positive effect on consumers' perceptions. The aforementioned theoretical perspective opens the way for how marketers can effectively achieve ethical commitment to engage consumers. The empirical results of the study suggest that the fulfillment of formal objectives can lead to acceptance as a source of profound ethical information. As marketing activities emphasize these goals, they can reduce concerns about deep falsehoods, which are often used to mislead and spread misinformation.

3.8.2 Managerial Implications

By the use of goal-framing theory, marketers can successfully put into effect strategies that are consistent with client expectancies and ethical standards.

Normative goals such as affordable use, knowledgeable consent, privacy safety, traceability, and non-deception must be the priority of marketers in their strategies concerning the deepfake era. This can be executed by entrepreneurs through the following ways: Brands can limit the use of deepfakes to contexts where they beautify storytelling or offer value to purchasers without deceiving them. Microsoft places a strong emphasis on user privacy as well as data protection, which is highlighted in their code of conduct, where employees are required to handle client information with care, restricting access and usage of information significantly.

Further, brands can develop easy-to-use consent forms and rent virtual platforms that permit users to withdraw their consent easily in case they change their minds. Brands must adhere to applicable data safety laws, such as GDPR, simply declaring privacy regulations for their use with the patron. The Microsoft company follows global compliance standards like the GDPR, and its privacy policies clearly outline how it collects, uses, and protects user data.

Discussing how brands should aid public communication concerning the usage of deepfakes for the violation of privacy additionally speaks volumes in safeguarding clients. In this manner, a brand ought to utilize blockchain, precise codes assigned to monitoring, which enables the tracing of its original source or ownership so easily through customers. Marketers want to craft stories that are exciting and inform authentic testimonies about their product services without overstatement or deception (Figure 3.7).

Clear articulation of such desires in marketing campaigns can enhance the ethical status of manufacturers and earn the purchaser's consideration. For instance, manufacturers can make sure that human beings appear in deepfakes with knowledgeable consent, making it transparently recognized how the content is made. Such exercise now does not best fit into the same old ethics; however, it additionally helps the emblem set up an accountable character among purchasers. Meta (Facebook, Instagram, WhatsApp) allows users to customize privacy controls, demonstrating transparency and user empowerment regarding consent and data sharing (Figure 3.8).

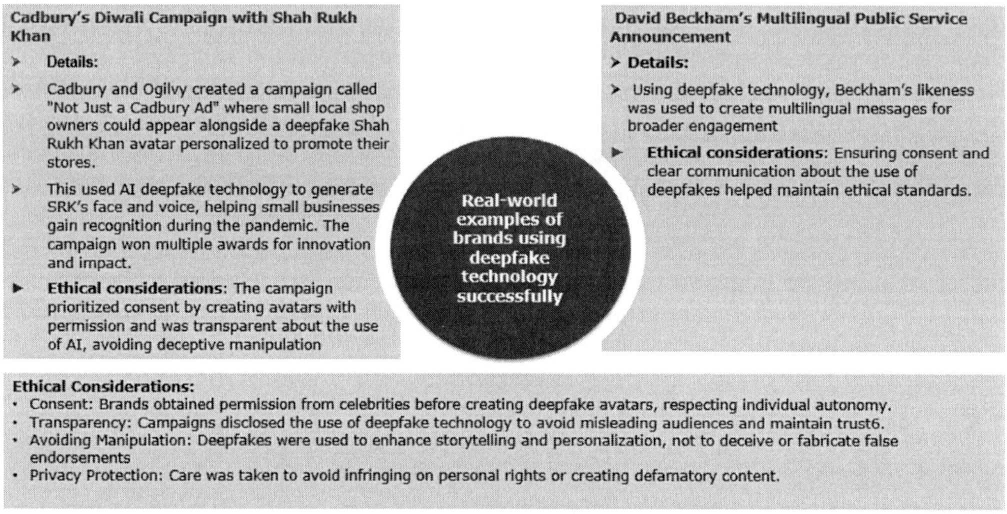

Figure 3.7 Real-world examples of brands using deepfake technology successfully.

Source: Authors' own creation.

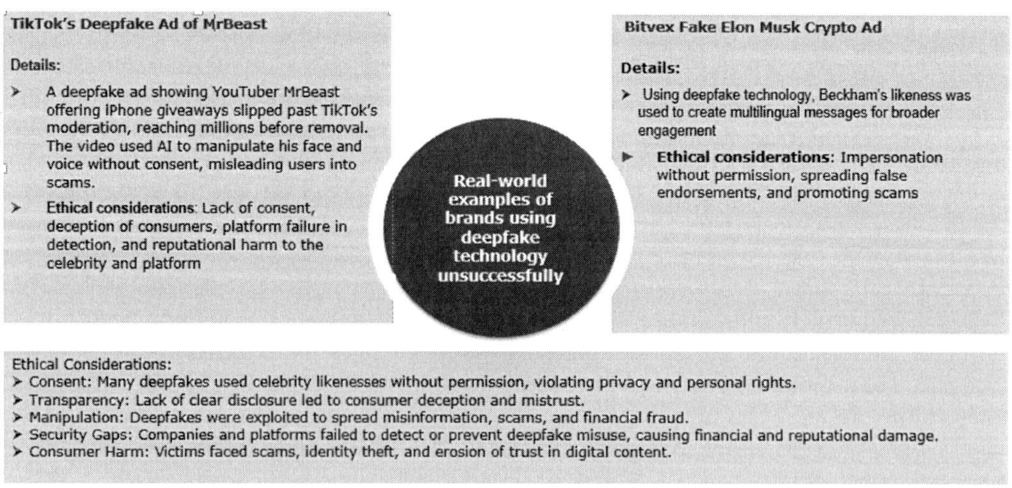

Figure 3.8 Real-world examples of brands using deepfake technology unsuccessfully.

Source: Authors' own creation.

Going forward, marketers should provide guidelines and best practices for effectively using this technology to create acceptable ethical interests for in-depth ethical issues At the very basic level, this could be an internal audit policy based on the ethical implications of deepfake content before its public release, which may also publicly discuss the ethical considerations associated with deepfake, thus demonstrating their commitment to responsible business practices. Pre-emptive steps to deal with misleading and misleading information increase consumers' perceptions of the true nature of brands.

Furthermore, marketers can use the findings of this study to develop real-world products through ethics. This requires not only pursuing deliberate objectives but also engaging and communicating the same promise to the customer in an effective manner. Brands can use history to underscore their ethical values and the authenticity of their message. For example, sharing behind-the-scenes information about in-depth ad shoots can humanize the brand and build relationships with consumers. By telling an accurate story about technology use, brands can strengthen customer trust and loyalty. Companies like Canva and Enzuzo use straightforward language and organized structures in their privacy policies, making it easy for users to understand how their data is handled.

Furthermore, to translate brand authenticity into increased purchase intentions, marketers should focus on creating campaigns that highlight the ethics of their products or services. This can be a marketing message as they will be organized around the benefits of authentic brands that adhere to high ethical standards in their operations. For example, campaigns can highlight how buying from real brands makes a difference in responsible marketing. On the other hand, positive goal framing, whereby messages focus on gains rather than losses, will be effective for motivating consumers to choose authentic brands over competitors.

REFERENCES

Abdul Hussein, Mohamed. "Social Media's Take on Deepfakes: Ethical Concerns in the Public Discourse." Bachelor thesis, Uppsala University, 2023. *DiVA Portal*. https://uu.diva-portal.org/smash/record.jsf?pid=diva2:1837417.

Aguiar, Marcos Henrique, Nicolas Felipe de Carvalho, Nicolas Oliveira Trindade, Otávio Franco da Silva Nascimento, Pedro Silva de Morais, Vinicius Augusto Fernandes Colombo, and Wilian de Sousa Lima. *Projeto Data Juris: Sistema de Gerenciamento de Dados para Advocacias*. Poá: Escola Técnica de Poá, Centro Paula Souza, 2023.

Ajder, H., G. Patrini, F. Cavalli, and L. Cullen. *The State of Deepfakes: Landscape, Threats, and Impact*. Amsterdam: Deeptrace, 2019, 27.

Alhosseiny, Hajar, and Amal Adel Nabih. "The Impact of Brand Authenticity on Purchasing Intention: The Mediating Role of Brand Trust." *Available at SSRN 4976403* (2024).

Al-Meshal, Soad Abdullah, Ghada Ahmed ALdrees, and Fozi Ali Belhaj. "Effects of Luxury Brand Authenticity on Purchase Intention: An Empirical Investigation among Saudi Arabian Customers." (2020).

Arora, Muskan, Kaushal Kishore Mishra, Mandeep Singh, Praveen Singh, and Rashmi Tripathi. "Deepfake Technology and Its Implications for Influencer Marketing." In *Navigating the World of Deepfake Technology*, pp. 66–90. IGI Global, 2024.

Azharuddin, Md, and Harish Kumar. "Deep Fake Detection for Human Face Images and Video by Using Deep Learning." *Journal of Emerging Technologies and Innovative Research* (JETIR) 10, no. 6 (June 2023).

Chesney, Bobby, and Danielle Citron. "Deep Fakes: A Looming Challenge for Privacy, Democracy, and National Security." *California Law Review* 107 (2019): 1753.

Chin, Wynne W. "Commentary: Issues and Opinion on Structural Equation Modeling." *MIS Quarterly* (1998): vii–xvi.

Chopra, Aahana, and Ananya M. A. Shukla. "Exploring the Misuse of Deepfake Technology in India: Implications for Society." *Global Media Journal – Indian Edition* 16, no. 2 (December 2024): 1–14.

Coruzant Technologies. The Invisible Threat of Deepfake Phishing. *Coruzant*, November 17, 2023. https://coruzant.com/security/the-invisible-threat-of-deepfake-phishing/.

"Deepfakes in the Wild: Understanding Their Impact on Consumer Behavior." *Consumer Psychology Review* (2024): 12–29.

Dobber, Tom, Nadia Metoui, Damian Trilling, Natali Helberger, and Claes De Vreese. "Do (Microtargeted) Deepfakes Have Real Effects on Political Attitudes?" *The International Journal of Press/Politics* 26, no. 1 (2021): 69–91.

Doherty, Camille. "The Danger of Deepfakes: Information Pollution and Epistemic Insecurity." CMC Senior theses, Claremont Colleges, 2025. https://scholarship.claremont.edu/cmc_theses/3750.

Diamantopoulos, Adamantios, Petra Riefler, and Katharina P. Roth. "Advancing Formative Measurement Models." *Journal of Business Research* 61, no.12 (2008): 1203–1218. https://doi.org/10.1016/j.jbusres.2008.01.009.

Eberl, Andreas, Juliane Kühn, and Tobias Wolbring. "Using Deepfakes for Experiments in the Social Sciences-A Pilot Study." *Frontiers in Sociology* 7 (2022): 907199.

Fornell, Claes, and David F. Larcker. "Evaluating Structural Equation Models with Unobservable Variables and Measurement Error." *Journal of Marketing Research* 18, no. 1 (1981): 39–50.

Godulla, Alexander, Daniel Seibert, and Tim Klute. "What Is Denialism? An Examination and Classification of Definitional Approaches and Relevant Actors." *Journalism and Media* 5, no. 1 (2024): 135–147.

Goodwine, Kiara. "Ethical Considerations of Deepfakes." *Prindle Institute for Ethics*, December 5, 2020. https://www.prindleinstitute.org/2020/12/ethical-considerations-of-deepfakes/.

Hartmann, Kim, and Keir Giles. "The Next Generation of Cyber-Enabled Information Warfare." In *2020 12th International Conference on Cyber Conflict (CyCon)*, vol. 1300, pp. 233–250. IEEE, 2020.

Henseler, Jörg, Christian M. Ringle, and Marko Sarstedt. "A New Criterion for Assessing Discriminant Validity in Variance-Based Structural Equation Modeling." *Journal of the Academy of Marketing Science* 43 (2015): 115–135.

Hobbs, Renee. *Media Literacy in Action: Questioning the Media*. Rowman & Littlefield, 2024.

Huang, Qirong, and Julian Maracic. "Consumer Perception of Deepfake Technology in Marketing: An Abductive Study on Consumer Attitude, Trust and Brand Authenticity." *Master's thesis, Linnaeus University*, Spring 2024. https://www.diva-portal.org/smash/get/diva2:1863794/FULLTEXT01.pdf.

Intelligency Group. *"The Pros and Cons of Deepfake Technology." Intelligency Group Blog*, June 24, 2022.

Ismail, Aya, Marwa Elpeltagy, Mervat S. Zaki, and Kamal Eldahshan. "A New Deep Learning-Based Methodology for Video Deepfake Detection Using XGBoost." *Sensors* 21, no. 16 (2021a): 5413.

Ismail, Ismail Ibrahim, Ahmed Abdelkarim, and Jasem Y. Al-Hashel. "Physicians' Attitude Towards Webinars and Online Education Amid COVID-19 Pandemic: When Less Is More." *PLoS ONE* 16, no. 4 (2021b): e0250241.

Karnouskos, Stamatis. "Artificial Intelligence in Digital Media: The Era of Deepfakes." *IEEE Transactions on Technology and Society* 1, no. 3 (2020): 138–147.

Kaur, Jaspreet, Kapil Sharma, and M. *P. Singh. "Exploring the Depth: Ethical Considerations, Privacy Concerns, and Security Measures in the Era of Deepfakes."* In *Navigating the World of Deepfake Technology*, pp. 141–165. IGI Global, 2024.

Kietzmann, Jan H., et al. "The Rise of Deepfakes: A Conceptual Framework and Research Agenda for Marketing." *Journal of Business Research* 128 (2021a): 1–10.

Kietzmann, J. H., et al. "The Role of AI in Modern Advertising Strategies." *Journal of Advertising Research* 61 (2021b): 345–360.

Kietzmann, Jan, Linda W. Lee, Ian P. McCarthy, and Tim C. *Kietzmann*. "Deepfakes: Trick or Treat?" *Business Horizons* 63, no. 2 (2020): 135–146.

Krishnamoorthy, P., R. Vasanthi, K. N. Pavithra, K. Jagadeesh, T. Vijayaraj, and Deepak Arumugam. "Internet of Things Oriented Human Body Enabled Communication Protocol Design for Health Monitoring Services." In *2024 International Conference on Intelligent Systems for Cybersecurity (ISCS)*, pp. 1–6. IEEE, 2024.

LegaMart. "Rise of DeepFake Technology." *LegaMart Knowledge Hub*, 2024.

Li, Minghui, and Yan Wan. "Norms or Fun? The Influence of Ethical Concerns and Perceived Enjoyment on the Regulation of Deepfake Information." *Internet Research* 33, no. 5 (2023): 1750–1773.

Dami, Lorenzo. 2022. "Analysis and Conceptualization of Deepfake Technology as Cyber Threat." School of Political Science "Cesare Alfieri". https://www.researchgate.net/publication/361007477_Analysis_and_conceptualization_of_deepfake_technology_as_cyber_threat

Modigliani, Andre, and William A. Gamson. "Thinking about Politics." *Political Behavior* 1 (1979): 5–30.

Molinillo, S., Y. Ekinci, and A. Japutra. "A Consumer-based Brand Performance Model for Assessing Brand Success." *International Journal of Market Research* 61, no. 1 (2019): 93–110.

NovoJuris Legal. *Deepfakes and Intellectual Property: Understanding Legal Challenges and Protections in the Artificial Intelligence Era.* NovoJuris, 2024. NovoJuris website.

Öhman, Carl. "Introducing the Pervert's Dilemma: A Contribution to the Critique of Deepfake Pornography." *Ethics and Information Technology* 22, no. 2 (2020): 133–140.

Podsakoff, Philip M., Scott B. MacKenzie, Jeong-Yeon Lee, and Nathan P. Podsakoff. "Common Method Biases in Behavioral Research: A Critical Review of the Literature and Recommended Remedies." *Journal of Applied Psychology* 88, no. 5 (2003): 879.

Rather, Raouf Ahmad. "*Conclusion: Updating Consumer-Brand Relationships and Scope for Future Research*." In *Consumer Brand Relationships in Tourism: An International Perspective*, pp. 593–606. Springer Nature Switzerland, 2024.

Reality Defender. "A Kitchen Sink Approach to Deepfake Detection." *Reality Defender* Insights, August 3, 2023.

Robb, Drew. "Deepfake Awareness Riding on Top Gun's Coattails." *JETIR* 10, no. 12 (2023).

Rixom, Jessica M., and Brett A. Rixom. "Perceived Brand Authenticity: Examining the Effects of Inferred Dedication and Anticipated Quality on Consumers' Purchase Intentions and Actual Choices." *Journal of Consumer Behaviour* 22, no. 3 (2023): 721–737.

Sahota, Shivali, Subodh Kumar, and Lidia Lombardi. "Biohythane, Biogas, and Biohydrogen Production from Food Waste: Recent Advancements, Technical Bottlenecks, and Prospects." *Energies* 17, no. 3 (2024): 666.

Shmueli, Galit, Marko Sarstedt, Joseph F. Hair, Jun-Hwa Cheah, Hiram Ting, Santha Vaithilingam, and Christian M. Ringle. "Predictive Model Assessment in PLS-SEM: Guidelines for Using PLSpredict." *European Journal of Marketing* 53, no. 11 (2019): 2322–2347.

Toews, Rob. "Deepfakes Are Going To Wreak Havoc On Society. We Are Not Prepared." *Forbes*, May 25, 2020.

Vishweshwar, Shalini Mahashreshty. Implications of Deepfake Technology on Individual Privacy and Security. *M.S.* Culminating Project, Information Assurance, St. Cloud State University, 2023. https://repository.stcloudstate.edu/msia_etds/142

Wan, Da, Manchun Cai, Shufan Peng, Wenkai Qin, and Lanting Li. "Deepfake Detection Algorithm Based on Dual-Branch Data Augmentation and Modified Attention Mechanism." *Applied Sciences* 13, no. 14 (2023): 8313.

Zheng, Guan, Jinchun Shu, and Kaigeng Li. "Regulating Deepfakes Between Lex Lata and Lex Ferenda—A Comparative Analysis of Regulatory Approaches in the US, the EU and China." *Crime, Law and Social Change* 83, no. 1 (2025): 1–23.

Chapter 4

Digital Forensics

Detecting and Authenticating AI Content

Lamaa Sellami, Abir Mchergui, and Bechir Alaya

4.1 INTRODUCTION

This chapter explores the expanding domain of digital forensics, highlighting its essential contribution to combating contemporary cyber threats through the proper handling and interpretation of digital traces. Also known as computer forensics, this field is a specialized area within forensic science that focuses on gathering, analyzing, and presenting digital evidence in a format acceptable to judicial systems [1]. While commonly employed in criminal investigations, its relevance has grown in the corporate world, particularly in addressing internal security incidents and data breaches [2]. The core mission of digital forensics is to reconstruct digital events, determine how incidents occurred, identify those responsible, and assess the impact. Achieving this requires not only technical proficiency but also a thorough understanding of the legal environment. The scope of this discipline includes, but is not limited to, computing devices, communication networks, mobile technology, and Internet of Things systems [3].

Digital forensics emerged in response to increasing digital criminal activity during the 1970s. Initially spearheaded by cybersecurity specialists and law enforcement professionals, the field adapted conventional investigative strategies to the digital context [4, 5]. Over the decades, its boundaries have widened to include subfields such as mobile forensics, network analysis, and cloud-based investigations. This growth has paralleled the rise in digital offenses like hacking, identity fraud, and phishing, which now make digital forensics a critical component of both legal and civil inquiries. By the early 2000s, standardized tools and procedural models began shaping the investigative process, driven by the need for consistent and reliable digital evidence handling [6]. Today, digital forensic processes are built around core principles such as safeguarding the integrity of evidence, accurate data recovery, and maintaining chain-of-custody protocols. Key branches of the field include computer forensics, which focuses on extracting data from computing devices; network forensics, which involves monitoring and analyzing data flows; and mobile forensics, which deals with retrieving information from smartphones and tablets. Each domain poses distinct technical and ethical challenges, particularly in relation to the quantity of data and data privacy concerns [7].

As cyber threats become more sophisticated, digital forensics must also evolve to incorporate advanced tools such as artificial intelligence (AI) and machine learning to streamline analysis. The increasing use of encrypted communications and decentralized platforms poses additional hurdles for investigators. Cross-border investigations are further complicated by jurisdictional conflicts and differing standards for digital evidence admissibility. Therefore, ongoing training and international cooperation are essential to maintain the relevance and effectiveness of digital forensic practices [8].

DOI: 10.1201/9781003539032-4

The incorporation of AI and machine learning into forensic workflows is expected to redefine the investigative process, enhancing automation, accuracy, and processing speed. Nevertheless, the use of these technologies also raises new ethical questions—particularly about algorithmic fairness, transparency, and accountability [9, 10]. To stay ahead of evolving cyber threats, investigators must continually update their expertise and foster cooperation with professionals across other disciplines. Ongoing updates to legal and compliance frameworks will also be necessary to guide responsible forensic practices. Despite the hurdles, advancements in this domain signal a promising future, where innovative tools are developed to respond more effectively to cybercrime. Simultaneously, the exponential increase in online content—including written texts, images, and videos—has brought new concerns about reliability, authenticity, and the spread of disinformation. To tackle these challenges, the development of AI-powered content verification tools has become increasingly important [11].

AI content detection, sometimes referred to as automated content verification, leverages machine learning models to evaluate digital material by analyzing linguistic, structural, and statistical markers. These systems are capable of detecting synthetic content, including AI-generated texts, copied material, and deceptive information. These detection tools offer several significant benefits. They can process and analyze large volumes of content with speed and precision, uncovering inconsistencies or anomalies that human reviewers might miss [12, 13]. This contributes to more efficient content moderation processes and enhances trust in digital information. Moreover, they are scalable for use across organizations of varying sizes. Such systems also play a crucial role in ensuring safe online environments by filtering inappropriate content and preserving intellectual property through plagiarism detection.

This chapter's objective is to design and propose comprehensive, ethically grounded methods for identifying AI-generated material. By integrating advanced digital techniques with legal and moral considerations, the research aims to safeguard the integrity of online information and protect individual rights. Encouraging cross-sector collaboration—between legal experts, data scientists, ethicists, and technologists—will be key to managing the challenges posed by the rapid growth of AI technologies.

The structure of this chapter is as follows: Section 4.2 introduces a detailed overview of digital forensics and illustrates its expanding role in addressing modern cybercrime and content verification. The next section focuses on defining digital forensics and exploring its sub-disciplines. Another part examines the importance of detecting and authenticating AI-generated content, emphasizing ethical concerns and the implications of AI. The methodologies for AI content detection are also analyzed, along with authentication techniques. Ethical challenges related to AI and privacy protection are discussed, followed by an exploration of interdisciplinary collaboration and AI regulation. Finally, the conclusion summarizes the main points and offers future perspectives for digital forensics.

4.2 DIGITAL FORENSICS

4.2.1 Modern Forensic Science

Forensic science is built upon several foundational works that have shaped its development. The postulate of [14] states that "every contact leaves a trace." This means that an interaction between two elements results in an exchange of matter and/or a modification of the environment. Traces, whether marks, signals, or objects, serve as evidence that is not always visible to the naked eye. They represent incomplete and imperfect remnants of a presence or action at a specific time and place [15]. The absence of complete traces introduces uncertainty, but the convergence of information can mitigate this gap and enhance the coherence of observed facts.

Locard's postulate is complemented by Kirk's principle [16, 17], which emphasizes the importance of identity and the processes of identifying and individualizing traces and their sources. Kirk asserts that "every object in our universe is unique," meaning that two elements, whether natural or artificial, possess distinctive characteristics that differentiate them. This focus on individualization sets forensic science apart from other scientific disciplines. While the latter typically classifies objects, forensic science aims to establish a direct link between an object and a specific source.

The main objective is to search for and demonstrate the existence of a unique origin connecting objects while explaining possible divergences. These points of convergence can manifest in various forms, such as biological characteristics of an individual, matrices, or manufacturing processes. To facilitate the identification between a trace and its source, databases are established. Some of these contain individualization data, such as DNA, fingerprints, or ballistic information, while others group technical characteristics that allow for classification by group, including narcotics, explosives, aerosol paints, or tool and footwear impressions.

However, the correlation between traces and their sources is also subject to uncertainties. Traces can be falsified or altered, and their relevance depends on the medium and environment in which they are found. A crucial aspect lies in the collection and preservation process during investigations, as numerous factors of contamination and degradation must be considered in the analysis. Probabilities play a central role in this process, integrating these biases [18, 19]. Thus, forensic science must navigate between the quest for tangible evidence and the inherent uncertainties of its field [20].

Criminal investigations also rely on the principle of abduction developed by Peirce [21, 22]. This principle involves identifying the most plausible causes for an observed event and formulating hypotheses about the crime by examining potential connections [23, 24]. For example, in a case of forcible entry, the relationship between a tool mark and the modus operandi relies on this reasoning [25].

The Bayes–Laplace theorem on cause probability, initially presented by Reverend Bayes and later expanded by Pierre-Simon Laplace, helps quantify biases and uncertainties. The study of serial elements is relevant in investigations, focusing on common properties across similar incidents. The source often serves as a point of convergence, indicated by unique methods or the use of similar objects.

Each criminal event is unique and irreversible in time and space. The observed trace is distinct from ordinary activities, and the goal of forensic analysis is to describe the case in its uniqueness. The materiality of the trace allows for the determination of its characteristics, making it comparable to known data. This primary information becomes a clue in the judicial process, establishing the circumstances surrounding the crime. Through their organization and interpretation by the judge, these elements transform into expert evidence in criminal trials.

4.2.2 Digital Forensics

Digital forensics, commonly referred to as digital forensic science, is a branch of modern forensic science focused on uncovering digital traces contained within digital media or computer infrastructures. This field is multidisciplinary, incorporating knowledge from computer science, electronics, networking, and telecommunications. It encompasses various sub-disciplines, including network forensics, memory analysis [15, 26], the recovery of deleted and fragmented data (carving) [27], and investigations involving connected devices [28, 29], mobile technology [30–32], cloud computing [33, 34], and reverse engineering, particularly in the study of malware [35–37].

The methodology of digital forensics, described in Figure 4.1, involves studying the digital scene and associated traces, starting with the identification of the incident and potential evidence. This includes the seizure, acquisition [38], and analysis [39] of digital traces and media, along with the establishment of associated traceability. This discipline encompasses both live forensics, which analyzes functioning systems, and post-mortem approaches to hardware.

Optimal acquisition involves capturing an image of volatile memory (Random Access Memory, or RAM) and creating an exact bit-by-bit copy of the media under examination. This process is ideally conducted using a write-blocking device to prevent alteration of the original data. In cases of online storage, such as cloud computing, acquisition is performed "live," creating a "logical" copy of the data. After data extraction, a hashing function is employed to ensure the accuracy and integrity of the copied data, serving as a reference for subsequent analyses.

4.3 IMPORTANCE OF DETECTION AND AUTHENTICATION OF AI-GENERATED CONTENT

4.3.1 AI: An Overview

Generative AI [40] stands among the most pivotal technologies today. It has indeed transformed numerous sectors from a professional standpoint while significantly enhancing

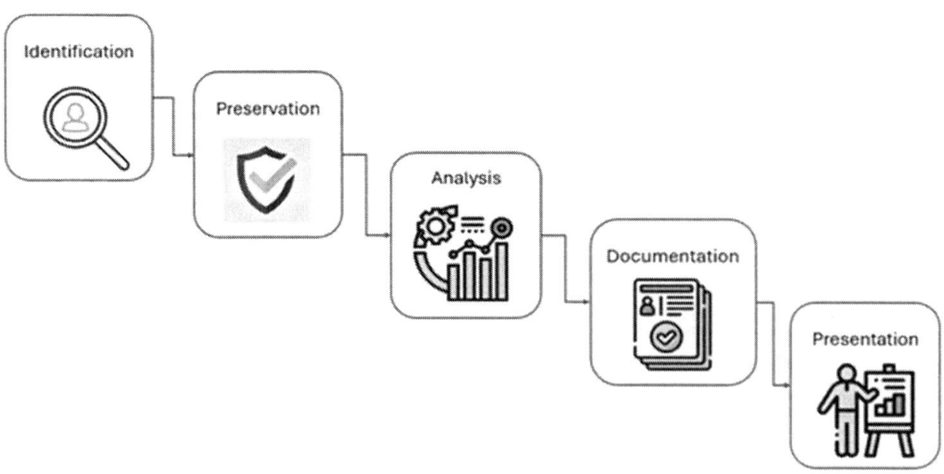

Figure 4.1 Methodology of digital forensics.

consumer convenience in daily life. This field, rooted in computer science, is capable of executing a wide range of tasks previously reserved for humans. Gradually, AI is evolving to become more sophisticated, finding applications in various professional domains, such as communication strategy development, as well as educational purposes, albeit with potential drawbacks [41].

The functions attributable to this technology encompass reasoning, image recognition, and language processing. A primary goal of AI is to emulate human cognitive functions across numerous fields.

Today, AI permeates every aspect of consumer life, even extending to medical diagnostics. However, the proliferation of AI-generated content complicates the generation of 100% authentic human content [42]. One of the most significant impacts of AI is on employment, as it induces shifts and transformations within the job market. A 2018 report from the Economic, Social, and Environmental Council estimated that between 9% and 54% of current jobs are at risk. These figures should be interpreted in the context of other evolving factors affecting the labor market, such as various policy developments. Notably, the long-term effects of AI on employment remain uncertain [43].

It is worth highlighting that while certain jobs, like translation, may be threatened or even replaced by AI, new roles are simultaneously emerging, particularly in engineering. The critical question arises: Is AI more a creator of jobs than a destroyer? The answer, however, is not straightforward. Two counterbalancing effects come into play: first, the displacement effect, which results from tasks traditionally performed by humans being transferred to technology; and second, the productivity effect, which involves increased output and the creation of new job opportunities [44].

4.3.2 Why Detect AI-Generated Content: Key Issues

The detection of content generated by AI raises critical concerns across several domains overviewed in Figure 4.2.

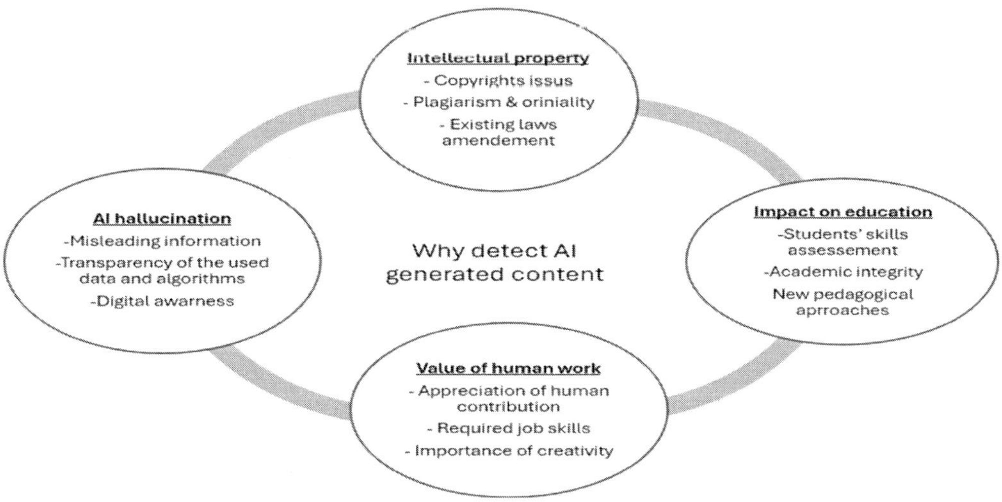

Figure 4.2 The rationale behind detecting AI-created content.

4.3.2.1 Ethics and Reliability

Addressing the ethical challenges linked to AI is essential, particularly when it comes to the trustworthiness of the information it generates. One major concern is AI's potential to contribute to the widespread circulation of false or deceptive content. Given that AI systems rely on pre-existing datasets, they may replicate inaccuracies or generate outputs that mislead readers—especially those without specialized knowledge. This dynamic threatens the integrity of online knowledge, weakens user confidence in digital platforms, and undermines constructive public dialogue by enabling the unchecked proliferation of misinformation [45].

A pressing concern in the use of AI is the phenomenon of "hallucinations," where AI systems fabricate information that seems credible but is entirely untrue [46]. These fabricated outputs can have dangerous implications, particularly in domains like healthcare, national security, and political affairs. To prevent the spread of such falsehoods, it is essential to implement systems that can identify and correct these errors before they reach the public. Equally important is the ethical challenge of determining responsibility for inaccurate or misleading content produced by AI. When an algorithm generates false information, identifying who is liable becomes difficult. To foster accountability, it is crucial to maintain transparency about how AI models are trained and the data they rely on. Users should be made aware when they are interacting with AI-generated content and informed of any potential biases within these systems that could influence the output's reliability. The widespread use of AI in content generation also has the potential to distort collective perceptions of what is real. As AI becomes capable of producing highly convincing narratives and imagery, distinguishing fact from fiction becomes more complex. This ambiguity can erode trust in traditional media and public institutions, deepening social divides and increasing the risk of misinformation [47].

In response to these risks, there is an urgent need to enhance public awareness and digital literacy. Individuals should be educated on how to critically assess online content and trained to detect signs of AI involvement. Understanding the basic principles behind AI functionality, along with adopting strategies for verifying information, will strengthen society's defenses against manipulation and disinformation [48]. Focusing on ethical integrity and the trustworthiness of AI applications is paramount. Robust frameworks must be developed to improve the quality of machine-generated content while ensuring transparency and responsibility in its deployment. Upholding these values will help us navigate the digital information space with greater confidence and clarity in an era where artificial content is becoming increasingly indistinguishable from the real.

4.3.2.2 Intellectual Property

The emergence of AI in the creative domain has sparked complex debates about intellectual property rights, particularly when it comes to copyright ownership [49]. As AI systems produce outputs that can closely resemble human-created content—often drawing from vast repositories of existing data—the question arises: who legally owns the result? Is it the developer of the AI, the individual who initiates the prompt, or does the concept of ownership become less relevant when the creator is non-human? This ambiguity presents legal complications for creators and industries concerned about unintentionally violating existing copyrights.

Another pressing issue lies in evaluating the authenticity and uniqueness of AI-generated materials. Since these systems generate content based on previously available datasets, there is a risk that the results may mirror or repeat elements of existing work [50]. This introduces potential plagiarism concerns, especially when similarities are not easily detected. Educational and legal institutions are now being challenged to revisit their standards for originality in light of this technological shift and to consider how best to uphold creative ownership without discouraging innovation.

Moreover, existing intellectual property laws are not fully equipped to handle the unique attributes of AI-generated work. Legal definitions of authorship and ownership were designed in a pre-AI context and are now being tested by advancements in machine learning and automated content creation. It is becoming increasingly necessary for lawmakers to revisit and adapt these legal frameworks to account for the distinct nature of AI-assisted outputs [51]. This may include redefining legal terminology, introducing new rights categories, or establishing hybrid authorship models that reflect the collaborative dynamic between humans and intelligent systems.

4.3.2.3 *Impact on Education*

The growing presence of AI in the educational field presents a number of pressing concerns, especially when it comes to evaluating student learning outcomes [52]. As learners increasingly turn to AI tools to complete academic tasks, educators are confronted with the difficulty of discerning genuine student effort from machine-generated assistance. This obscures the ability to accurately assess subject comprehension and individual proficiency, prompting a need to rethink current evaluation practices to suit this evolving landscape. In addition, the use of AI raises serious questions about academic ethics. The temptation for students to misuse these technologies—by avoiding independent effort and relying on AI for shortcuts—poses a threat to the integrity of the learning process. This places responsibility on educational systems to introduce clear guidelines and foster a responsible attitude toward AI use. Institutions must encourage honest learning habits and design measures to curb misuse, ensuring students develop authentic skills essential to their academic and professional growth.

Educators are also challenged to adapt their instructional strategies to meaningfully integrate AI while keeping students actively involved in their learning journey [53]. This could include team-based learning tasks where AI is used as a collaborative support rather than a tool for substitution. Such methods promote creativity and participation, allowing students to benefit from technological innovation without losing engagement or critical thinking. Ultimately, adapting pedagogy in this way equips learners with the skills and ethical grounding needed to thrive in a technology-driven world.

4.3.2.4 *Value of Human Work*

The rapid advancement of AI and the widespread use of machine-generated content are significantly reshaping how human labor is viewed—particularly in terms of authenticity and creative ownership [54]. As AI systems increasingly generate outputs that resemble human work, the line between machine-produced and human-created content is becoming more difficult to discern. This ambiguity can lead to growing skepticism regarding the originality of human efforts, potentially devaluing individual contributions in industries where AI plays a central role.

One major consequence of this shift is the need to redefine the qualifications and competencies demanded in today's job market. As automation takes over tasks once reliant on human effort, many roles are being restructured or eliminated altogether. To remain relevant, professionals must now cultivate skills that machines cannot easily emulate—such as originality, emotional intelligence, and sound judgment [55]. This reality requires educational institutions and organizations to reconsider how training and career development programs are designed, placing greater emphasis on adaptive and creative thinking. The increasing presence of AI in the workplace has also triggered widespread concerns about job security. Many workers fear being replaced by automation, which can lead to disengagement and decreased morale. These anxieties affect not only individuals but also organizational performance and culture. To counter these effects, businesses must actively support their employees through transparent communication, upskilling opportunities, and policies that reinforce the value of human capabilities in an AI-driven environment [56].

4.4 METHODOLOGIES FOR DETECTING AI-GENERATED CONTENT

The increasing prevalence of AI-generated content and misinformation presents serious challenges to the reliability of information. This section delves into advanced methodologies for identifying such content, based on the latest research and innovations in the field [57]. The primary objective is to offer a thorough overview of the most efficient strategies to tackle these emerging issues, ensuring the integrity of digital content.

4.4.1 Linguistic Analysis and Natural Language Processing

Linguistic analysis combined with natural language processing (NLP) is essential for identifying content generated by AI [58]. This method leverages advanced NLP techniques to examine text for subtle inconsistencies that may suggest it was created by a machine. Key strategies include evaluating perplexity and text discontinuity. Typically, AI-generated content demonstrates lower perplexity, meaning its word choices are more predictable, and it shows reduced sentence variation, making it structurally less diverse than human-written text. These characteristics help detection systems differentiate AI-produced material from content written by humans.

4.4.1.1 N-Gram Analysis

N-gram analysis involves studying sequences of words or characters to detect patterns that may indicate machine-generated text. This typically includes examining unigrams, bigrams, and trigrams, although higher-order n-grams can reveal deeper linguistic structures. When comparing AI-produced text to that written by humans, AI content tends to show a higher occurrence of commonly used n-grams and a lower level of linguistic variation [59]. Complementary to this, metrics such as perplexity and instability are applied to evaluate the predictability and structural consistency of the text. Lower perplexity values suggest that the language is more formulaic, while decreased instability reflects minimal shifts in sentence composition. These indicators are often calculated using language models like GPT-2 or BERT. A detailed illustration of this technique is presented in Figure 4.3.

Detecting AI generated content

1-gram	Detecting	AI	generated	content
2-gram	Detecting AI	AI generated	Generated content	
3-gram	Detecting AI generated		AI generated content	

Figure 4.3 Application of N-gram analysis.

4.4.1.2 *Perplexity and Instability*

Perplexity serves as a fundamental metric in NLP, evaluating how effectively a language model predicts a sequence of words. It gauges the model's capacity to estimate the probability of a word's occurrence within a given context. A lower perplexity indicates that the model finds the word choices relatively predictable, a characteristic often observed in AI-generated texts. This predictability can result in less variety and creativity compared to human-written content.

Conversely, instability pertains to the variation in word usage and sentence structures within a text. A text with low instability tends to employ similar grammatical constructions and vocabulary throughout, leading to a sense of monotony. In AI-generated content, this characteristic is often evident through repetitive linguistic patterns and limited diversity in the expression of ideas, resulting in a less dynamic writing style.

4.4.1.3 *Syntactic Complexity Analysis*

Syntactic complexity analysis focuses on grammatical structures, including metrics such as average sentence length, clause density, and parsing tree depth. AI generated texts often exhibit more uniform syntactic patterns, which can be analyzed using tools like Stanford CoreNLP or spaCy. Moreover, sophisticated tools like the Giant Language Model Test Room (GLTR) have been developed to analyze the likelihood of word predictions based on their context [60]. GLTR allows for a forensic inspection of a language model's visual imprint on the input text, helping to differentiate authentic text from that potentially generated by a machine.

4.4.2 Integrating Multimodal Techniques for Detecting Misinformation

Multimodal fusion strategies represent a modern approach to identifying fake news and machine-generated content by analyzing information across multiple formats—such as text, images, and metadata. As outlined in Figure 4.4, these methods significantly enhance detection accuracy by cross-referencing inconsistencies across diverse data sources. Studies have shown that models incorporating multimodal inputs can outperform text-only systems, with improvements in detection accuracy reaching up to 8.11%. This heightened effectiveness stems from the ability to better contextualize information and expose discrepancies that might go unnoticed when analyzing text in isolation.

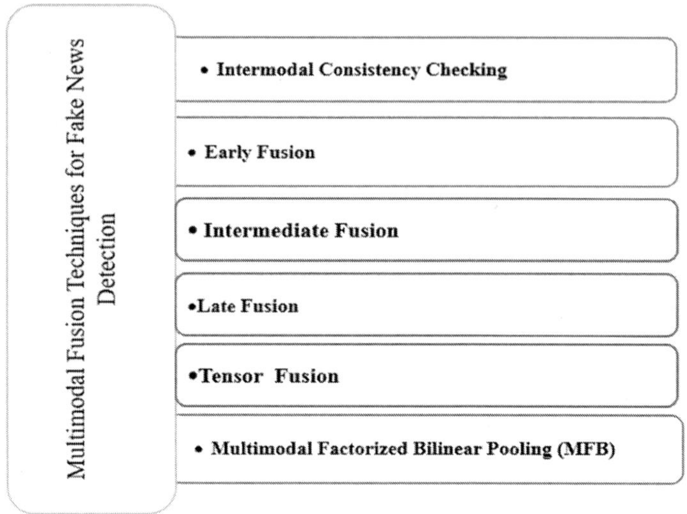

Figure 4.4 Multimodal fusion techniques.

4.4.2.1 Intermodal Consistency Checking

A promising method in this area is intermodal consistency checking. Algorithms assess the coherence between text, images, and metadata to identify manipulated or misattributed content. This technique is particularly effective for detecting deepfakes and other forms of synthetic media [61, 62].

4.4.2.2 Early Fusion

Early fusion combines features from different modalities at the input stage before passing them through a joint model [63]. Features from each modality are extracted and concatenated into a single feature vector, which is then sent to a neural network or another classifier. This allows the model to learn intermodal interactions based on raw features.

4.4.2.3 Late Fusion

Late fusion processes each modality separately and combines predictions at the decision level. Distinct models are trained for each modality, and the predictions are aggregated, often through weighted averaging. This approach allows for modality-specific architectures but may overlook some intermodal interactions [63, 64].

4.4.2.4 Intermediate Fusion

Intermediate fusion merges modalities at the intermediate layers of a neural network. Features from each modality are treated separately in the initial layers and then combined at intermediate representations, often using attention mechanisms. This balances modality-specific learning with intermodal learning [64].

4.4.2.5 *Tensor Fusion*

Tensor fusion explicitly models multiplicative interactions between modalities. It calculates the outer product of features from different modalities, capturing complex nonlinear relationships. However, this method may require significant memory for high-dimensional features [64].

4.4.2.6 *Multimodal Factorized Bilinear Pooling*

Multimodal factorized bilinear pooling efficiently approximates bilinear pooling for multimodal fusion. This method projects features from each modality into a common space, performs element-wise multiplication, and sums them up, reducing the number of parameters compared to full bilinear pooling. These fusion techniques enable multimodal fake news detection models to leverage complementary information across modalities, enhancing overall performance compared to unimodal approaches. The choice of fusion method depends on the specific task and involved modalities [64].

4.4.3 Machine Learning and Deep Learning Models

Advanced machine learning models play a crucial role in modern systems for detecting AI-generated content. By learning complex patterns that are often imperceptible to human analysts, these technologies enable more precise and effective identification of text authorship.

4.4.3.1 *Transformer-Based Models*

Transformer-based models, such as BERT and RoBERTa, excel at capturing the contextual nuances of language [65, 66]. These models are frequently fine-tuned for specific AI detection tasks, allowing them to adapt to the subtleties of generated content. Through attention mechanisms, they focus on relevant parts of the input, providing a deeper analysis of texts. Additionally, they can be combined with task-specific layers to enhance classification, maximizing their ability to identify potentially problematic content.

4.4.3.2 *Ensemble Techniques*

As illustrated in Figure 4.5, ensemble learning methods are particularly effective at boosting the accuracy of content detection systems by integrating multiple classification models. Strategies such as bagging, boosting, and stacking take advantage of the complementary strengths of diverse algorithms to yield more accurate outcomes. Widely adopted techniques like Random Forest and XGBoost are frequently employed in this framework [67]. By analyzing varied linguistic and structural features of the text, ensemble approaches outperform single-model solutions, offering improved generalization, reduced bias, and enhanced reliability in predictive tasks.

4.4.3.3 *Capsule Neural Networks*

Capsule neural networks, depicted in Figure 4.6, represent a compelling method for modeling the hierarchical structure found within textual information. Unlike conventional

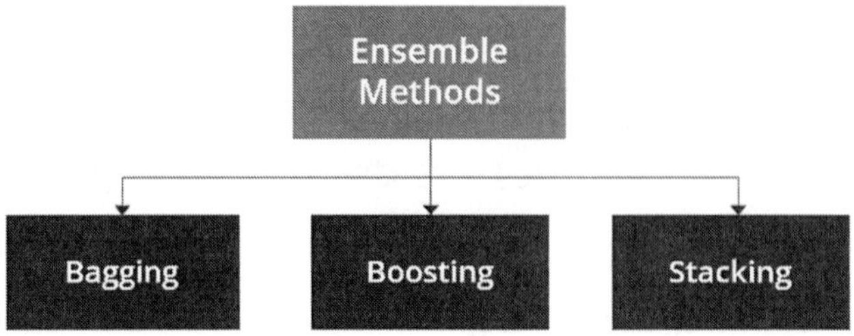

Figure 4.5 Ensemble methods.

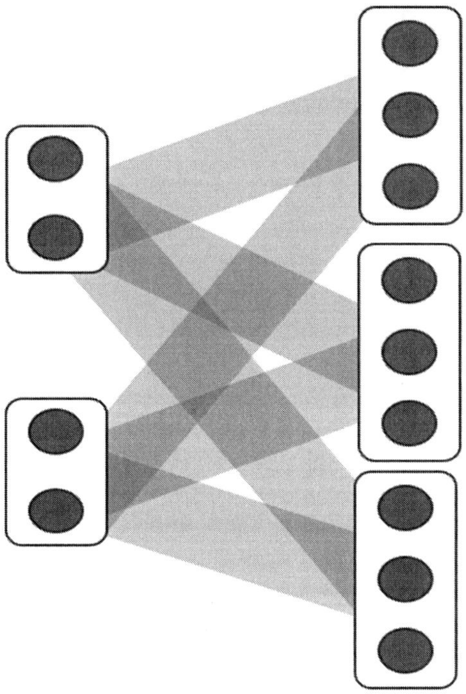

Figure 4.6 Model of capsule neural networks.

convolutional neural networks, these networks employ dynamic routing between capsules, enabling them to more accurately interpret the relationships among words and phrases—especially within shorter texts [68]. Research has demonstrated that capsule networks can surpass leading models in performance, delivering notable gains in accuracy. For example, one investigation reported a 7.8% increase in effectiveness on the ISOT dataset and a 3.1% improvement on the LIAR dataset when compared to traditional techniques.

Despite these positive outcomes, deep learning systems still face hurdles, particularly in terms of transferring their success to unfamiliar datasets. A case in point involves an ensemble model integrating a decision tree, random forest, and an extra tree classifier, which reached 99.8% accuracy during training but dropped to 44.15% when tested on the ISOT dataset, despite scoring 100% on the LIAR dataset. These disparities underscore a key limitation: While such models may perform exceptionally in controlled environments, their ability to adapt to diverse, real-world scenarios remains a critical concern in the detection of AI-generated content.

4.4.4 Temporal and Network Analysis

Analyzing the temporal dynamics and dissemination pathways of content offers critical insights into identifying AI-generated material and misinformation. These techniques focus on understanding how information circulates and changes over time, uncovering distinctive patterns commonly associated with deceptive or artificially produced content.

4.4.4.1 *Propagation Dynamics*

Graph-based methodologies are instrumental in studying how information spreads across social media platforms. By mapping user behavior and content exchanges into graphical structures, researchers gain a clearer view of how data circulates through networks [69]. Key indicators such as node centrality, clustering coefficients, and average path lengths are critical to this analysis. For instance, highly central users often exert a disproportionate influence on how information flows. Utilizing these structural attributes, machine learning algorithms can be trained to detect specific propagation trends often associated with AI-generated content or misleading narratives [70, 71].

4.4.4.2 *Temporal Features*

Temporal indicators play a vital role in uncovering unusual patterns in the spread of digital content. Monitoring the rate at which information travels across platforms can expose irregularities in user sharing behavior. In addition, assessing the timing and consistency of user engagements may reveal coordinated or deceptive activity [72]. Time-series analytical methods are particularly useful in identifying spikes and anomalies that often accompany the dissemination of deceptive content. Notably, research analyzing how misinformation circulates on Twitter (now known as X) has shown that false stories tend to spread both more rapidly and extensively than factual ones. This underscores the critical need for swift identification and responsive measures to counter the influence of misleading information.

4.4.4.3 *Detection of Coordinated Misinformation Campaigns*

Network-based investigative methods are proving highly effective in uncovering coordinated misinformation campaigns. By analyzing the flow and spread of information using graph-based models, researchers can identify irregular patterns that are commonly associated with the intentional distribution of false narratives [73]. This approach is particularly valuable for detecting systematic attempts to influence public discourse by manipulating content circulation at scale.

By mapping out interactions among various digital actors, these analyses help reveal relationship structures and engagement trends that may point to orchestrated manipulation. Tackling the challenges posed by AI-generated misinformation calls for an integrated strategy—one that unites linguistic profiling, multimodal data fusion, sophisticated machine learning techniques, and network behavior analytics.

As AI continues to advance, so must our detection frameworks. Continued innovation and interdisciplinary research are essential to safeguarding the accuracy and credibility of information in the digital sphere, ensuring that users can access trustworthy, fact-based content [74, 75].

4.5 AUTHENTICATION OF CONTENT

Ensuring the authenticity of information has become crucial in an era dominated by misinformation and AI-generated content. It is essential to maintain the integrity of content to foster trust in digital communications, whether in journalism, academia, or on social media. Various methods have been developed to validate information, protecting it from manipulation. These approaches not only enhance the credibility of the data but also assist users in distinguishing reliable sources from less credible ones. This section explores advanced strategies designed to uphold content integrity in today's digital landscape.

4.5.1 Ensuring Integrity Techniques

4.5.1.1 Hashing in Data Security

Hashing is a process, described in Figure 4.7, that converts any form of data into a unique fixed-size fingerprint known as a "hash." Regardless of the original text's length, the resulting hash will always have the same size. This feature makes hashing extremely valuable for verifying data integrity, as any alteration, no matter how minor, in the original content will produce a completely different hash [76, 77].

Among the most recognized hashing algorithms are SHA-256 and MD5. Each of these algorithms has its unique characteristics and applications; however, MD5 is now considered less secure and is not recommended for critical applications due to known vulnerabilities that can be exploited. Hashing is commonly employed to securely store passwords [78]. Instead of keeping the password itself, systems save the corresponding hash, ensuring that even in the event of a data breach, the passwords remain protected, as it is nearly impossible to retrieve the original password from its hash.

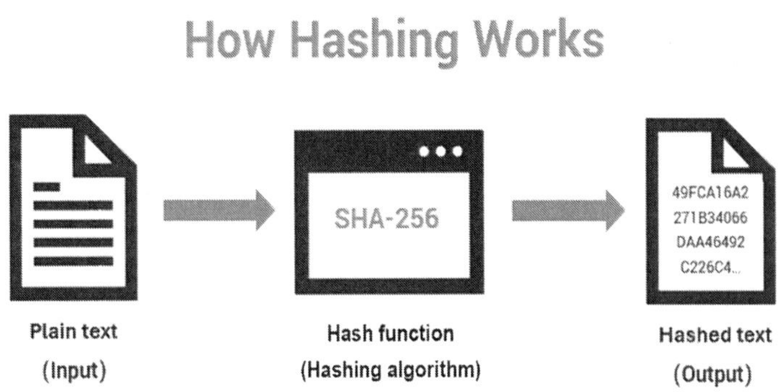

Figure 4.7 Hashing process.

4.5.1.2 Salting: Enhancing Hash Security

Salting is a technique that involves adding a unique random value, known as a "salt," to a password before hashing it. This method ensures that each hash is unique, even for identical passwords, thereby strengthening security against dictionary and brute-force attacks [79]. The process of salting is straightforward: before hashing a password, a random salt is generated and concatenated with the password. The salt is then stored alongside the hash. To verify a password, the stored salt is added to the provided password, and the resulting hash is compared to the saved hash. An example of a salting procedure is presented in Figure 4.8.

4.5.1.3 Cryptography for Data Protection

Encryption is a fundamental pillar of data security. It transforms data into an unreadable format for anyone lacking the decryption key, thereby protecting sensitive information from unauthorized access during transmission over the internet or while stored on devices or in the cloud [80, 81].

There are two main categories of encryption: symmetric and asymmetric. Symmetric encryption uses the same key for both encrypting and decrypting data. Although it is generally faster than asymmetric encryption, it poses challenges in securely managing the key, which must be shared between the sender and receiver without being compromised. Advanced Encryption Standard (AES) is one of the most widely used and recognized symmetric encryption algorithms for its security and speed.

Asymmetric encryption, or public key encryption, employs a key pair: a public key for encryption and a corresponding private key for decryption. This method addresses the secure key distribution issue inherent in symmetric encryption, as only the private key needs to remain confidential. Rivest–Shamir–Adleman (RSA) is one of the oldest and most reliable asymmetric encryption algorithms, widely used for securing online exchanges.

AES is one of the most robust and secure encryption standards available today, commonly utilized in government, financial, and personal applications to secure data. RSA is mainly used for asymmetric encryption and digital signatures, relying on the difficulty of factoring large prime numbers. Elliptic Curve Cryptography is a newer and more efficient

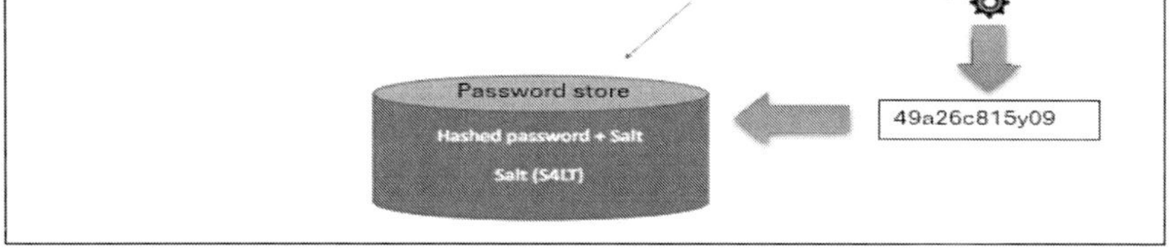

Figure 4.8 Salting hash function.

alternative to RSA, offering equivalent security levels with shorter keys, thereby reducing the load on networks and devices [82, 83].

Encryption is vital for secure communication. Protocols like HTTPS use encryption to secure communications between web browsers and servers, ensuring that transmitted data, such as credit card information, remains private. Additionally, cloud storage solutions often encrypt user data before storing it on their servers, protecting personal information against data breaches.

4.5.1.4 *Digital Signatures: Authentication and Integrity*

Digital signatures (Figure 4.9) are essential mechanisms for ensuring the authenticity and integrity of data in the digital realm. By employing encryption techniques, a digital signature attaches a cryptographic fingerprint to a document or message, confirming that the information originates from the claimed sender and has not been altered during transmission [84].

Digital signatures utilize asymmetric encryption. The sender generates a signature by applying a hashing algorithm to the original message and then encrypting the hash with their private key. The recipient, possessing the corresponding public key, can decrypt the signature to retrieve the hash, which they then compare to the hash of the received message. If the two hashes match, it confirms the message's integrity and authenticity.

Digital signatures are crucial in various fields of online interaction. They facilitate the verification of official documents like contracts and agreements without requiring handwritten signatures. In finance, banks and financial institutions implement these signatures to ensure the security of transactions and maintain the integrity of information shared. Moreover, software creators sign their applications to provide users with confidence that the software remains unaltered and comes from a reliable source.

The discussed methods for data protection—hashing, encryption, and digital signatures—each fulfill distinct yet complementary functions in safeguarding data. The choice of an appropriate method typically hinges on the specific context and the security needs at hand. Hashing is ideal for verifying data integrity and securely storing sensitive information, such as passwords, due to its irreversible nature, making it suitable when the original data should not be recoverable from its fingerprint.

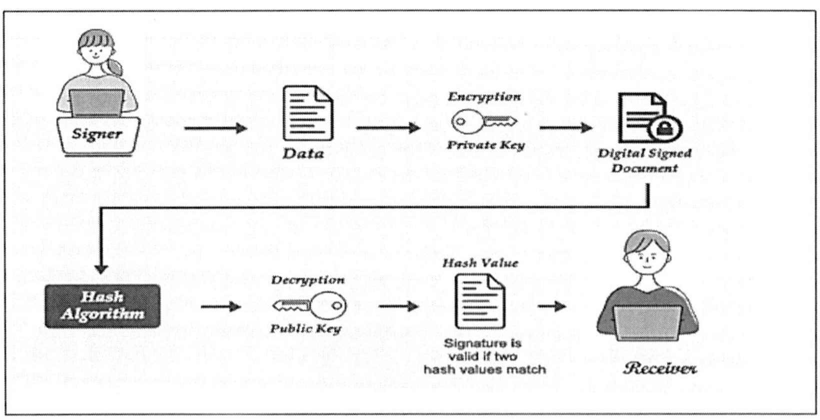

Figure 4.9 Digital signature.

Encryption is employed when data confidentiality is paramount. Whether for encrypting data-in-transit (like secure communications via HTTPS) or data-at-rest (like securely stored files), encryption ensures that only authorized parties can access the decrypted information. Digital signatures are critical for authenticating the source of data and ensuring its integrity, making them the preferred method for digital legal documents, online financial transactions, and software distribution, confirming that the data has not been altered and comes from the claimed source [85].

4.5.2 AI for Fact-Checking: Ensuring the Accuracy of AI Content

Various AI tools can perform a wide range of tasks, from creating marketing content to proofreading and planning social media posts in real-time. This enables teams to focus on strategic aspects and explore new ideas [86].

However, it is important to recognize that AI is not infallible. Approximately half of the businesses that have integrated AI into their systems reported issues with data inaccuracies. While AI can provide valuable assistance, it is essential to use it responsibly.

In this section, we will explore the most effective fact-checking techniques to leverage AI's capabilities while ensuring that your content remains accurate and reliable.

4.5.2.1 How to Fact-Check AI-Generated Content

While the use of AI is intriguing, it is crucial to understand that one cannot always rely on it for accurate information. Therefore, learning how to fact-check AI-produced content is essential.

One major reason for AI inaccuracies is the phenomenon of hallucination, which occurs when AI generates information that appears correct but is, in fact, entirely fictitious. AI can produce such inaccuracies as it primarily aims to respond to prompts.

Another risk associated with using AI is plagiarism. When AI tools create content, they may inadvertently produce text that closely resembles existing works. This raises serious concerns, especially with models like ChatGPT [87].

Although the latest version, GPT-4, claims a 40% higher probability of yielding more accurate results than its predecessors, ChatGPT is not free from errors. In the absence of appropriate fact-checking tools, there is a risk of publishing incorrect information, which could damage your credibility.

4.5.2.2 Evaluating Sources of AI-Generated Content

One of the most common ways to fact-check content produced by AI is by analyzing the sources used. This analysis helps distinguish erroneous information and validate the credibility of the cited sources. Various methods exist for this purpose, but an effective approach is the CRAAP test. The CRAAP evaluation method was developed by librarian Sarah Blakeslee at the Meriam Library of California State University, Chico (Figure 4.10). The acronym CRAAP stands for Current, Relevance, Authority, Accuracy, and Purpose. This approach provides a framework and a series of questions to assess the quality and value of the information you encounter [88].

This test helps examine the relevance, timeliness, authority, accuracy, and intent of a source in any content you evaluate.

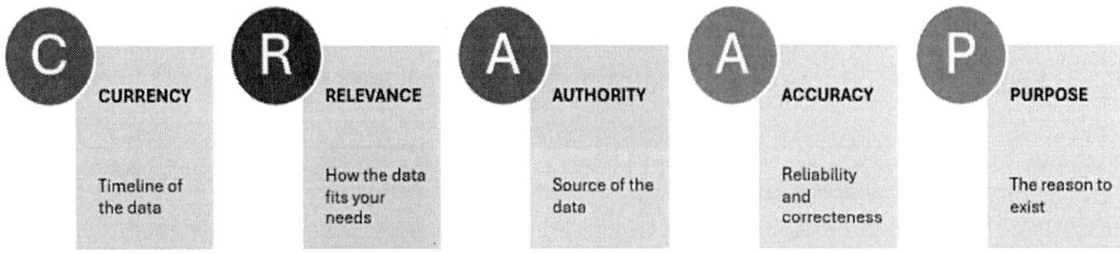

Figure 4.10 CRAAP evaluation method.

- **Current:** Ensure that the information is up-to-date. Check the publication date or the last update of the source.
- **Relevance:** Assess how relevant the information is to your needs. Is it still aligned with your topic?
- **Authority:** Analyze the credibility of the source. Who is the author or publisher, and do they have a good reputation in their field?
- **Accuracy:** Verify the reliability and correctness of the information. Does the source provide solid evidence to support its claims?
- **Purpose:** Understand the intent behind the information. Is it meant to inform, educate, sell, entertain, or persuade?

Another technique involves practicing lateral reading. This means comparing your sources with official data and other reliable references. Instead of accepting these figures at face value, it is wise to cross-reference them with data from other trustworthy sources, such as census reports [89].

These are just a few examples, but overall source evaluation allows you to determine whether a source presents data faithfully or distorts it.

4.5.2.3 Claim Detection and Contextual Analysis

Claim detection involves identifying and validating assertions within the content that require fact-checking. While generative AI can recognize linguistic patterns, it cannot assess the truthfulness of the information it produces.

This process allows for the identification and verification of statements that need validation. A claim can take the form of a statistic, a quote, or an anecdote, all of which require verification. For instance, propositional claim detection (PCD) is a task in NLP aimed at spotting statements that may be true or false [90, 91].

This tool highlights content through a PCD function, facilitating the identification, validation, and modification of potentially problematic assertions. This is especially crucial in an age where misinformation spreads easily.

Context is crucial for understanding the complexities of our content. Without it, vital information can be easily misunderstood, resulting in confusion and errors. By adding context to the fact-checking process concerning AI, you can grasp the true significance and underlying intentions of the data, leading to a more accurate analysis.

Contextual analysis involves looking at content within its historical and cultural backdrop, which enhances understanding. This method helps in interpreting the material by placing it in a wider framework, considering the roles of the creator, the target audience, and various commentators.

By doing so, you can see how different elements are linked, identify possible issues, and gain a range of perspectives. It also makes it simpler to compare this information with other trustworthy sources to find any discrepancies.

4.5.2.4 Verification Tools and Feedback Mechanisms

Verifying facts entails a careful examination of your sources, and the appropriate tools can make this task much easier. Tools designed for verification assess the reliability of information by cross-referencing a variety of trustworthy sources. They help streamline the verification process, ensuring that each claim is substantiated by credible evidence.

Notable platforms for fact-checking include FactCheck.org, Snopes, and PolitiFact, which assist users in confirming the accuracy of information on diverse topics. It is also crucial to evaluate content for signs of AI generation. A text can quickly lose its reliability if it is produced by AI. Effective detection tools, like AI Indetectable, can analyze your work as needed, checking for elements that may indicate AI involvement, thereby helping you uphold high standards of authenticity [92].

These verification resources are essential in maintaining the integrity of your content while responsibly utilizing AI capabilities. This dual approach of fact-checking and enhancing authenticity greatly improves the quality of your output.

A feedback mechanism offers a structured way to gather insights regarding the performance of your content, guiding future efforts. By automating feedback, this system reduces subjectivity and enhances objectivity. It helps mitigate the risk of feedback overload, which can arise when individuals receive too many or conflicting comments.

Rather than dwelling on past actions, these systems focus on steering future results in a positive direction. For example, a content creator might receive automated insights regarding the clarity and engagement of their writing, prompting adjustments to better capture the interest of their audience.

This forward-looking approach fosters a cycle of continuous improvement, ensuring that your content remains relevant.

4.6 CHALLENGES AND ETHICAL CONSIDERATIONS

Previous research on ethical issues related to AI has identified six types of concerns stemming from the operational parameters of decision-making algorithms and AI systems [93, 94]. The diagram in Figure 4.11 illustrates that:

1. Decision-making algorithms convert data into evidence to reach a conclusion.
2. This conclusion is then used to initiate and justify actions, which can raise ethical questions when taken alone or in combination with others.
3. This process occurs in a complex and (semi-) autonomous manner, making it challenging to attribute responsibility for the consequences of algorithmic actions.

From these characteristics, three epistemological concerns and two normative concerns can be distinguished based on how algorithms process data to generate evidence and prompt

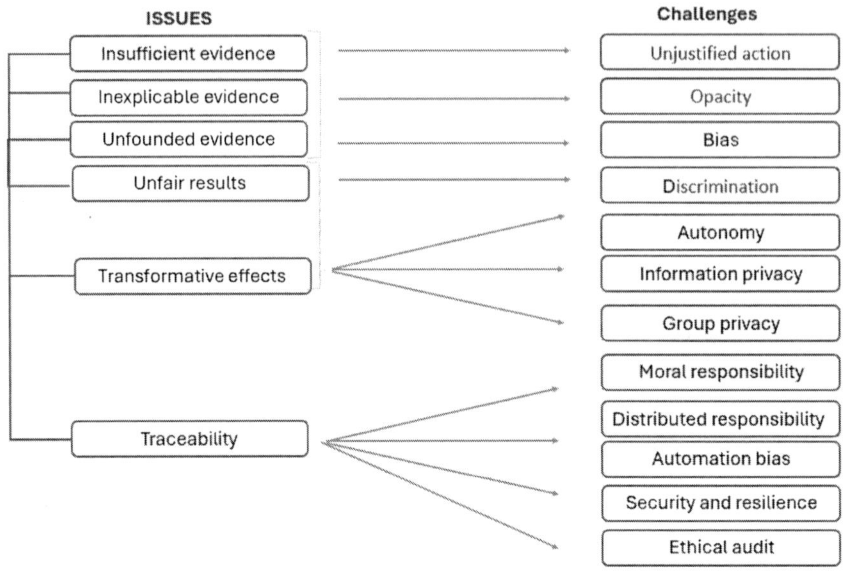

Figure 4.11 AI decision-making issues and challenges.

actions. These five categories of concerns can lead to failures involving various human, organizational, and technological actors. The interaction between humans and technologies raises delicate questions about accountability for the outcomes of AI behavior. These challenges are encapsulated in the concept of traceability, which emerges as a central and essential concern [95].

4.6.1 Rapid Advancements in AI Technologies

4.6.1.1 Intelligent Machines and Machine Learning: An Ongoing Revolution

Intelligent machines are increasingly becoming integrated into our daily lives. They learn from the data they collect and can perform tasks traditionally reserved for human intelligence. Machine learning, the field of AI that makes this possible, has seen rapid advancements in recent years. New methods, such as deep learning, are continuously employed to enable machines to better understand and interact with their environment [96].

This evolution is driven by two major forces: the vast amount of available data and constant technological advancements. These factors contribute to the ongoing improvement of learning models, enhancing the accuracy and reliability of AI systems.

4.6.1.2 AI and Energy: A Promising Partnership

AI has the potential to transform the energy sector, contributing to the creation of more efficient and sustainable systems, particularly in solar energy. Smart solar panels capable of adjusting their orientation based on the sun's position are already in development.

Additionally, AI can optimize energy distribution by predicting real-time demand and adjusting supply accordingly [97].

Nuclear fusion represents a clean and virtually boundless energy source, and AI is making notable progress in this field. Advanced neural networks are employed to simulate and forecast plasma dynamics, which are crucial for fusion processes. Thanks to AI, nuclear fusion, once considered a distant dream, is now becoming a tangible possibility.

4.6.1.3 AI in Healthcare: Revolutionizing Medical Imaging

AI is reshaping the field of medical imaging. With increasingly sophisticated algorithms, machines can analyze medical images and identify anomalies with unmatched precision [98]. AI systems are trained to recognize signs of diseases in X-rays, MRIs, or even retinal scans. These tools assist healthcare professionals in delivering quicker and more accurate diagnoses, ultimately enhancing patient survival rates [99, 100]. Additionally, AI presents exciting opportunities in medical research. Algorithms can sift through thousands of medical images to uncover new indicators of disease, paving the way for innovative treatments.

4.6.1.4 AI and Humans: A Collaboration to Explore

AI goes beyond simply replacing humans in various tasks; it holds remarkable potential to enhance human abilities. The synergy between people and machines is an emerging area that investigates how AI can collaborate with humans instead of substituting them. For instance, these systems can aid workers in making better-informed choices by offering real-time data analysis [101].

Collaborative AI platforms are being developed to help teams organize more efficiently, manage tasks, and share knowledge effectively [102]. Other uses include AI in education, where it can tailor learning experiences, and in assisting the elderly, enabling them to maintain their independence. AI is not merely a technological advancement; it embodies a human journey that continuously expands the limits of what can be achieved. It changes the ways we work, care for others, generate energy, and even think. More than just machines, they reflect our humanity, allowing us to introspect, learn, and grow.

This is an exciting time, and the coming years promise to be rich with discoveries and innovations. We should remain attentive to these advancements that, while sometimes perplexing, have the potential to positively shape our future.

4.6.2 Ethical Considerations in Data Analysis

Ethics in data analysis hinges on fundamental principles that ensure the integrity and reliability of data-driven decisions [103]. In a data-centric environment, adhering to these ethical considerations is crucial to avoid adverse consequences, such as data breaches and loss of trust [104, 105].

A major concern is data privacy, which requires respectful handling of personal information. Implementing robust protection measures is essential. Ethics in business intelligence extends beyond legal compliance; it also promotes transparency and accountability. These foster trust among stakeholders and improve decision quality. Recognizing and addressing biases in analysis is crucial for achieving fair results. By incorporating ethical standards, organizations can ensure their analyses are just and beneficial. Upholding principles like integrity, transparency, accountability, and privacy enhances credibility and the overall value of insights gained.

4.6.2.1 Ethical Data Collection Practices

When gathering data for business intelligence and analysis, it's vital to follow ethical guidelines [106]. A fundamental principle is to secure informed consent from participants, ensuring they are aware of how their data will be utilized and that they have the option to participate voluntarily. This approach fosters trust and promotes open relationships.

It's also important to ensure that the methods used for data collection are equitable and impartial, avoiding discrimination and undue influence. Ethical practices require the creation of surveys and collection tools designed to avoid favoring any particular group or outcome, thus upholding the integrity and reliability of the data. By addressing biases, organizations can derive more precise insights, which enhances decision-making quality. Another critical factor is minimizing risks during the data acquisition process. Organizations should implement strong security protocols to safeguard data from unauthorized access and breaches. Moreover, the data collected should only be employed for purposes that do not harm individuals. For additional insights on data governance, refer to our extensive guide.

By embracing these ethical practices in data collection, organizations not only comply with current regulations but also strengthen their reputation and credibility. To delve into the development of ethical strategies regarding data analysis, consult our comprehensive guide on best practices. This commitment to ethics in data handling ultimately leads to more responsible and impactful business decisions.

4.6.2.2 Data Governance and Ethical Management

Establishing robust data governance frameworks is crucial to ensure ethical management in business intelligence and data analysis [107]. Effective governance involves creating and implementing policies and procedures that govern the collection, storage, processing, and analysis of data. These frameworks help uphold data integrity and accuracy, which are essential for reliable decision-making processes.

A critical aspect of ethically managing data is the role of ethics itself. Data management officials must oversee practices and ensure compliance with ethical standards. By fostering a culture of data ethics, organizations can safeguard privacy and enhance their reputation. For more detailed information, refer to our comprehensive guide on data governance. Ensuring the integrity and accuracy of data is paramount for ethical management. This necessitates the implementation of rigorous validation processes and conducting regular audits to identify and rectify errors. By upholding high-quality standards, organizations can rely on precise information for strategic decision-making. For further insights into ethical data practices, consult our best practices guide.

Implementing strong governance and ethical data management practices is essential for sustainable and responsible business intelligence. These measures help meet legal requirements while enhancing data management capabilities and organizational reliability [108].

4.6.2.3 *Ethical Considerations of AI and Machine Learning*

The deployment of AI and machine learning technologies in data examination presents substantial moral considerations. Research indicates that while these advanced systems enhance analytical capabilities, they simultaneously introduce complex challenges regarding algorithmic fairness, data protection, and potential misapplication [109]. Contemporary organizations must therefore establish comprehensive ethical frameworks and data management protocols.

A crucial aspect concerns algorithmic fairness and operational transparency. Research demonstrates that prejudices can manifest throughout the analytical pipeline, from initial data acquisition to model development, potentially reinforcing societal disparities. Organizations seeking to address these challenges must implement sophisticated monitoring systems and embrace established principles for ethical AI deployment. Empirical investigations into machine learning applications highlight the necessity of ethically conscious implementation strategies. Such investigations provide concrete demonstrations of how moral guidelines translate into practical applications, ensuring that artificially intelligent systems produce reliable and equitable outcomes. Analysis of ethical implications across diverse industries offers valuable perspectives on optimal practices in data ethics.

The foundational elements of responsible AI utilization in data analysis encompass several key aspects: safeguarding individual privacy, maintaining transparency in automated processes, and implementing continuous bias detection mechanisms [110]. Through adherence to these foundational principles, organizations can foster stakeholder trust while achieving beneficial outcomes through ethically implemented AI systems. Examinations of successful implementations reveal that organizations prioritizing ethical considerations in their AI deployments typically achieve superior long-term outcomes compared to those focusing solely on technical capabilities. This underscores the importance of integrating ethical considerations into the core of AI strategy and implementation.

4.6.2.4 *Balancing Data Utility and Ethical Considerations*

Exploring the ethical dimension in data processing requires a balanced approach between analytical performance and confidentiality [111]. While data-driven analyses yield invaluable strategic insights, adherence to ethical principles remains crucial at every stage of the process. Organizational structures must carefully weigh the balance between leveraging information and safeguarding personal data (Figure 4.12).

In the current digital landscape, establishing an ethical framework is the cornerstone of managing a balanced approach between analytical efficiency and data protection. These strategic guidelines enable organizations to orchestrate optimal data utilization while ensuring respect for individual rights and governance standards. The application of innovative techniques, such as pseudonymization, data volume optimization, and advanced cybersecurity protocols, significantly minimizes vulnerabilities while maintaining the analytical richness of information.

Enhancing data utilization practices requires a seamless fusion of sophisticated analytical technologies and fundamental ethical principles. Modern approaches to predictive modeling and data synthesis provide valuable strategic insights while preserving the confidentiality of sensitive information [112]. Forward-thinking entities illustrate that a holistic strategy, combining technological innovation and a robust ethical framework, proves particularly effective in the current era of big data.

Figure 4.12 Ethical considerations in data analysis.

The integration of ethical practices in data analysis strengthens organizational reputation and ensures regulatory compliance. This approach fosters a culture of accountability in data usage, stimulating innovation within a defined ethical framework. Contemporary businesses recognize that data ethics represents a fundamental pillar of sustainable growth and stakeholder trust. Advancements in analytics continue to generate new challenges and opportunities in preserving this ethical balance. Experience shows that strong ethical foundations not only safeguard stakeholder interests but also catalyze innovation and enhance competitive advantage.

4.6.3 Impact on Privacy and Individuals' Rights

AI is distinguished by its capacity to replicate human behaviors like reasoning, planning, and creativity. It presents numerous possibilities for businesses, enabling better anticipation of user requirements, proactive measures, and adjustment of projects accordingly. AI also emerges as a valuable asset in addressing substantial challenges across various sectors [113, 114].

Despite these advantages, it is crucial to acknowledge that these advancements can pose negative consequences for individuals, and these risks should not be underestimated. It is essential that the development and utilization of AI uphold individual privacy and ensure the safeguarding of their personal data.

4.6.3.1 Interaction Between the General Data Protection Regulation and AI

AI supports the creation of complex systems and the development of tools that replicate certain human capabilities through the use of algorithms [115]. For instance, it can process live traffic information to suggest optimal routes and minimize delays caused by congestion.

The development of these algorithms requires a substantial amount of data, much of which is personal. The use of this data is essential for the progress of the tools. Therefore, the correlation between the General Data Protection Regulation (GDPR) and AI is evident. AI raises complex questions regarding the protection of personal data, and AI professionals must pay attention to the legal issues related to this data. These challenges must be considered from the design phase of systems to ensure a balance between legal compliance and technological innovation.

4.6.3.2 Risks Associated With AI Use

The risks associated with AI usage are varied. They can pertain to the data used to create the systems, be linked to the design of the tools themselves, or involve the data collected by these technologies [116].

AI technologies can sometimes produce unfair outcomes by reflecting underlying biases, which may result in unequal treatment of specific populations. Moreover, concerns about privacy arise when personal data is processed in ways that were not initially intended. Failure to comply with proper security protocols may expose these systems to data breaches or unauthorized modifications, including those involving highly sensitive information.

Addressing these threats presents a significant technical and ethical challenge. The CNIL's Digital Innovation Lab has emphasized that AI systems, due to their reliance on probabilistic models, are particularly susceptible to cybersecurity vulnerabilities, making their protection more difficult.

Recognizing the importance of these issues, the European Union has taken concrete steps to regulate the development and use of AI. It has introduced several policy measures, including a resolution aimed at shaping a cohesive industrial framework for AI and robotics. These regulatory efforts seek to foster innovation while ensuring that the associated dangers are effectively mitigated. As part of this initiative, the European Commission has also worked to define which AI applications should be banned outright and to set strict limitations on the conditions under which others may be deployed.

4.6.3.3 AI and GDPR

Beyond the scope of the GDPR, which already sets guidelines for AI usage, a new legal framework has been introduced: the Artificial Intelligence Act. This legislation is designed to promote the responsible creation and deployment of AI technologies, with particular emphasis on upholding individual rights and protecting personal data [117].

The regulation introduces tailored obligations for AI applications deemed high-risk—such as those involving facial recognition, user profiling, or automated decision-making processes. Developers of such systems must incorporate measures that significantly reduce potential harm to individuals.

This legal initiative reflects the European Union's commitment to an AI model rooted in "trust and excellence." The goal is to boost research and technological progress in AI, while ensuring robust safeguards for privacy and human rights.

In parallel, the French data protection authority (CNIL) has launched several initiatives to tackle the complexities linked to AI [118]. Its efforts include analyzing how AI systems operate and influence individuals, encouraging the development of data-ethical technologies, supporting innovative projects in the AI sector, and implementing supervision mechanisms to monitor and evaluate systems in order to safeguard personal freedoms.

Moreover, the CNIL has established a specialized unit focused on AI and has provided various resources aimed at guiding developers and organizations in building AI systems that adhere to regulatory standards [119]:

- A self-assessment guide for AI systems
- A dossier on AI system security
- Essential questions to consider before implementing an AI system
- Measures to ensure quality and transparency throughout the system's use
- Actions to secure data processing and prevent breaches
- Means to promote transparency and enable individuals to exercise their rights
- Key rules to follow

Given that AI technologies, particularly those based on machine learning, can be intrusive, it is crucial to ensure that they do not infringe upon individuals' rights and freedoms during their design and use. The adopted approach must consider the fundamental principles of the GDPR, as shown in Figure 4.13, such as legality, fairness, and proportionality of processing, while also aiming to reduce or prevent risks.

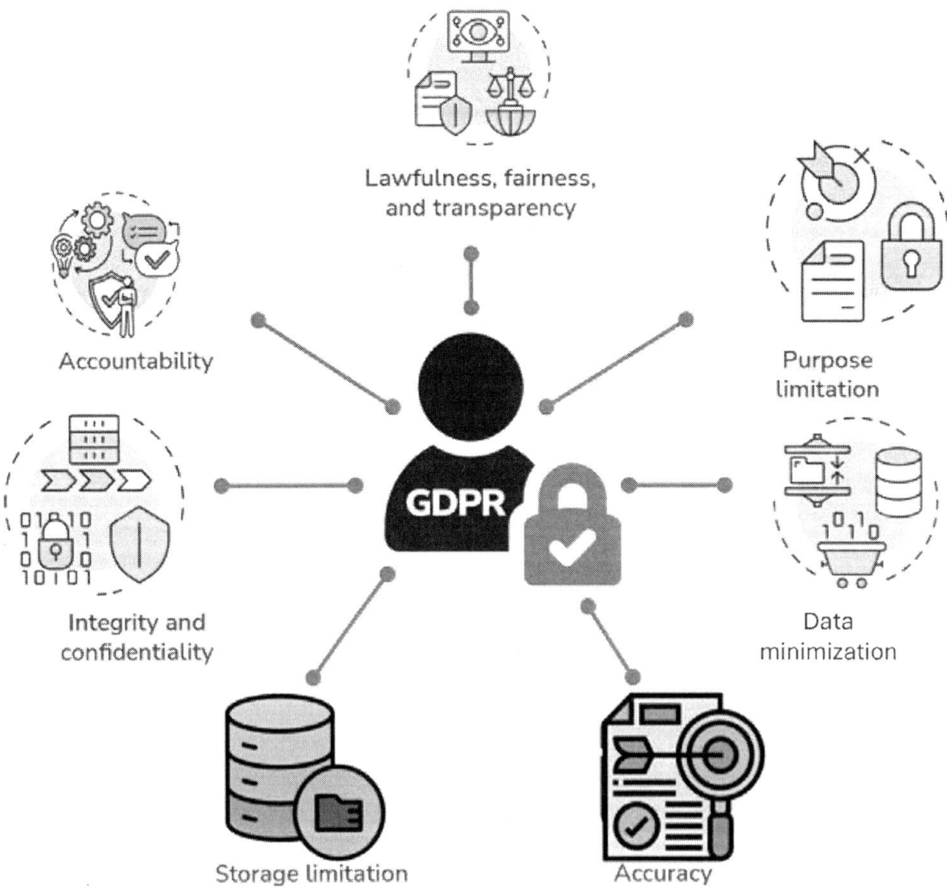

Figure 4.13 Principles of the GDPR.

4.6.4 Requirements to Fulfill

Data intended for the development of AI systems must be gathered in strict adherence to data protection regulations. This means that the data cannot be employed for any illegitimate purposes. It is the responsibility of the data controller to ensure that all data processing activities comply with relevant laws and regulations. Additionally, the controller must clearly define the specific purposes for which the data is being processed, ensuring transparency and accountability in data handling [120].

When collecting personal data for AI applications, it is essential to limit the data gathered to only what is absolutely necessary to fulfill the intended objectives. This approach is essential to avoid collecting more personal data than necessary. Frequent reviews should be carried out to monitor the volume of information used during both the development (training) and deployment phases of AI systems, ensuring that only data strictly relevant to the intended purpose is retained.

Incorporating data protection strategies from the very beginning of any AI initiative is vital. The concept of "Privacy by Design" calls for privacy considerations to be built into the system architecture and processes at every step of the project [121]. Achieving this requires coordinated efforts from various actors, including software engineers, data analysts, and organizational decision-makers, to guarantee the continuous integration of strong data protection practices.

Any personal data gathered through AI technologies must be collected in full compliance with legal data protection obligations. When required, individuals must be properly informed and their explicit consent obtained, with clear explanations provided about how their data will be processed. Moreover, such data should only be retained for as long as it serves a legitimate and defined purpose, with reliable safeguards in place to secure it during storage.

To ensure that AI systems operate transparently, data controllers are expected to put in place clear protocols that inform users about what personal data is being collected, how it will be used, and the logic behind the automated decision-making processes. When AI decisions carry substantial implications for individuals, those affected must be thoroughly informed about how these decisions are reached and what impact they may have.

To mitigate risks such as cyber intrusions or data leaks, it is crucial that organizations adopt comprehensive security measures. These protections not only guard confidential information but also help to build public trust in the AI tools being utilized. Maintaining high security standards reinforces the belief that users' data is being handled responsibly and ethically.

Ensuring adherence to these data protection obligations is a shared duty. Responsibility does not lie solely with those who supply the data but extends to all participants in the AI supply chain—this includes developers, system integrators, vendors, service providers, and hardware or software manufacturers. All parties involved must actively uphold compliance throughout the system's lifecycle, from the initial design phase to its long-term management and use.

4.7 COLLABORATION ACROSS DISCIPLINES

4.7.1 Regulation of AI

In recent years, AI has become a cornerstone in numerous industries, with a McKinsey report from June 2023 projecting that it could add as much as $13 trillion to the global economy. Despite these promising prospects, AI's rapid development raises urgent legal and ethical concerns. The establishment of comprehensive regulations is crucial to ensure responsible innovation and to mitigate risks of misuse. Legislators face the dual challenge of safeguarding individual freedoms while fostering an environment that encourages technological progress [122, 123].

Worldwide, both governments and oversight agencies are striving to strike a balance between leveraging AI's potential and limiting its associated dangers. OpenAI's Chief Technology Officer, Mira Murati, has publicly emphasized the necessity for stringent AI governance, highlighting its increasing relevance in modern society.

In Canada, the Artificial Intelligence and Data Act, embedded in Bill C-27, is currently undergoing legislative review. Though the bill would grant significant authority to governmental bodies, ongoing consultations aim to ensure Canadian policy aligns with international AI governance standards. Simultaneously, the Office of the Privacy Commissioner of Canada has launched an inquiry into OpenAI concerning potential data privacy breaches. Additionally, the Office of the Superintendent of Financial Institutions has provided guidance outlining responsible AI implementation practices within the banking and financial sectors.

Meanwhile, in the United States, the Federal Trade Commission has increased its scrutiny of AI applications, cautioning organizations against deceptive practices and unethical marketing involving AI. Alongside this, the U.S. Copyright Office has clarified its stance on intellectual property rights concerning AI-generated materials. Ongoing legislative dialogue in the U.S. Senate points to the development of a nationwide regulatory framework to oversee AI use more effectively.

Across the Atlantic, the European Union initiated legislative action on AI in 2021. Nonetheless, there is growing pressure from experts to broaden the scope of these measures to address general-purpose AI tools such as ChatGPT. The United Kingdom, in parallel, has introduced a white paper aimed at promoting ethical AI deployment. Italy, however, took a more drastic approach by temporarily banning ChatGPT, sparking further EU-level discussions about the technology's broader implications. In contrast, China has proposed rules mandating that AI-produced content must align with socialist ideology, while Japan is investigating the use of AI for administrative tasks but does not currently plan to introduce regulatory controls.

Given the pace of AI innovation, the necessity for a well-defined legal infrastructure has never been greater. Regulatory strategies around the world are continuously adapting to keep up with the transformative nature of AI technologies (see Figure 4.14).

4.7.2 Responsibility and Rule of Law in the Context of AI

The concept of individual accountability holds significant importance, as it allows each person to view themselves not only as the architect of their own life but also as an active member of a moral community. As moral agents, individuals have the capacity to make decisions that can positively or negatively impact others and the conditions necessary for harmonious coexistence. This sense of responsibility is crucial for establishing a political community founded on ethical values. Mutual respect and self-discipline are essential for ensuring social cohesion and reinforcing the rule of law [124].

Without institutional mechanisms to hold individuals accountable for their actions, a society risks losing vital protections necessary for maintaining peaceful cooperation.

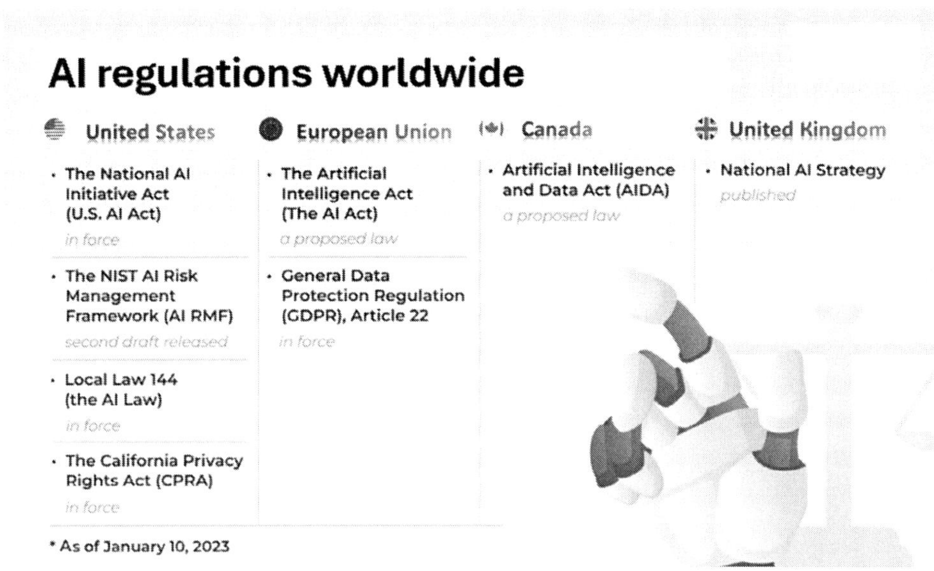

Figure 4.14 Regulation of AI.

Accountability structures are therefore critical to ensuring that law prevails over brute force. The stability of a society relies not only on the voluntary adherence of its members but also on their commitment to ethical norms.

In a society that seeks to uphold human rights, establishing formal accountability mechanisms is imperative. Accountability requires that individuals be able to justify their actions and rectify any mistakes. This process involves setting standards, uncovering relevant facts, evaluating behaviors, and assigning outcomes or responsibilities accordingly [125]. Within this framework, transparency is a cornerstone—it ensures that individuals impacted by decisions or systems can grasp the rationale behind them. In democratic societies, where public officials are meant to serve the interests of the populace, the concept of accountability gains even more importance. This same principle is increasingly relevant in the domain of AI, where the lack of clarity surrounding certain algorithmic operations can result in serious and sometimes harmful consequences for individuals and communities. Therefore, it is crucial to establish clear lines of responsibility when harm is caused by AI technologies [126].

Current legal instruments, including those that protect consumer rights and regulate personal data usage, offer a foundation for enforcing accountability in relation to algorithmic systems. Nonetheless, the discussion extends beyond these frameworks by addressing the broader consequences of emerging digital technologies, especially when they infringe on human rights. It integrates both legal obligations and ethical responsibilities, urging a comprehensive approach to managing the risks AI poses.

Given the accelerating integration of AI into daily life, there is an urgent need to implement robust accountability structures. These mechanisms are essential not only for defending individual freedoms but also for ensuring that AI technologies are developed and deployed in a manner that respects ethical principles and societal values.

4.7.3 Challenges in Regulating Algorithmic Systems

The rapid advancement of information and communication technologies (ICT) is reshaping nearly every sector, bringing with it significant challenges and potential risks. This digital evolution has redefined our interaction with computing systems, which are becoming more intricate and interconnected. At the same time, it influences how we interpret economic and social realities, often through data that may be overly simplistic or skewed. Algorithmic bias may emerge from several sources, including developers' own assumptions, limitations within the training datasets, or ongoing changes in the surrounding context [127, 128].

Focusing solely on technological innovation can lead to the neglect of core human values, making some digital developments potentially detrimental. For example, when AI is used in critical decision-making processes, it can introduce forms of discrimination that might have been avoided with proper ethical foresight. Furthermore, prolonged dependence on automated systems risks weakening interpersonal dynamics and diminishing the value of human judgment within organizational structures. This could result in less stable and equitable structures, diminishing the expected benefits of new technologies.

Additionally, ICT and AI are redefining social interactions and behaviors, leading to dependencies and new societal conflicts regarding technology's role [129]. Critiques regarding the technological impact on fundamental democratic values, such as human dignity and privacy, are crucial and must be addressed before deploying these technologies. It is vital to organize public debates that include diverse perspectives, particularly those from independent institutions, to ensure genuine consultation.

Most ICT relies on the use of vast amounts of data, often personal, raising questions about transparency, security, and control. Algorithmic governance needs to be reconceptualized from an ethical standpoint, considering both designers and society as a whole. Concerns about the societal impact of ICT and the need for greater algorithmic transparency to uphold human rights remain [130].

Establishing ethical criteria to be integrated from the design phase of algorithmic systems is essential. These principles must be adaptable and responsive to changing societal contexts. Regulation should be based on a dynamic vision that accounts for past experiences and new data to refine AI systems. Ethical analysis should not be a one-time task but rather a continuous effort, enabling society to track the influence of technological developments and respond effectively to emerging moral challenges.

The concept of "Ethics by Evolution" advocates for embedding ethical principles at every phase in the development and deployment of algorithm-driven systems [131]. This model emphasizes the importance of accountable governance, ensuring that decision-making processes remain transparent and that outcomes can be traced and verified. It also calls for the establishment of oversight structures to monitor compliance and ethical integrity.

The recommendations tied to this framework aim to foster the creation of algorithms that are not only ethically sound but also sustainable over time. It promotes collaborative governance, involving both technology developers and end-users in shaping the ethical direction of digital systems. Ultimately, the goal is to support technological innovation that aligns with human dignity, equity, and fundamental rights.

4.8 CONCLUSION

Digital forensics plays a pivotal role in bridging technology, law, and ethics, providing a crucial framework for addressing the complexities of modern cybercrime. The rapid pace of technological innovation and the increasing sophistication of cybercriminal tactics highlight the need for advanced forensic methods and practices. As digital evidence becomes an integral part of legal processes, ensuring its reliability and admissibility is essential to preserving justice.

The introduction of AI into the realm of digital forensics brings both advantages and challenges. While AI can streamline investigative tasks through automation and enhanced data analysis, it also introduces ethical dilemmas, particularly regarding accountability, transparency, and the risk of bias in algorithmic decisions. Tackling these issues is vital not only for the integrity of forensic investigations but also for maintaining public confidence in the judicial system. Furthermore, the legal and regulatory framework governing digital forensics is rapidly adapting to the rising tide of cybercrime. It is crucial for forensic professionals to stay informed about relevant laws and regulations, especially those concerning data protection and privacy, to ensure that their practices remain compliant and ethically sound. The development of clear standards and best practices will be instrumental in fostering accountability within the field.

Looking to the future, the field of digital forensics is poised for significant growth, driven by continuous technological advancements and a commitment to ethical practices. Interdisciplinary collaboration will be essential to addressing the diverse challenges posed by the digital landscape. By fostering partnerships among law enforcement, legal experts, technology professionals, and ethicists, the field can craft comprehensive solutions that enhance investigative effectiveness while safeguarding individual rights. Ultimately, the ongoing discussions around the ethical challenges of digital forensics and the influence of AI on this area will shape its future development. As we continue to navigate the complexities of the digital era, it is essential that all stakeholders remain committed to promoting ethical standards and ensuring that technological innovations contribute to, rather than compromise, the core values of justice and accountability. By prioritizing these principles, digital forensics can play a vital role in creating a safer and more just society.

REFERENCES

[1] Mohamed H., Koroniotis N., Moustafa N. 2023. Digital Forensics Based on Federated Learning in IoT Environment. In *Proceedings of the 2023 Australasian Computer Science Week (ACSW '23)*. Association for Computing Machinery, New York, 92–101. https://doi.org/10.1145/3579375.3579387

[2] Casino F., et al. 2022. Research Trends, Challenges, and Emerging Topics in Digital Forensics: A Review of Reviews. *IEEE Access*, 10, pp. 25464–25493. https://doi.org/10.1109/ACCESS.2022.3154059

[3] Shahzad F., Javed A.R., Jalil Z., Iqbal F. 2022. Cyber Forensics with Machine Learning. In: Phung D., Webb G.I., Sammut C. (eds) *Encyclopedia of Machine Learning and Data Science*. Springer, New York. https://doi.org/10.1007/978-1-4899-7502-7_987-1

[4] Solanke A.A., Biasiotti M.A. 2022. Digital Forensics AI: Evaluating, Standardizing and Optimizing Digital Evidence Mining Techniques. *Künstliche Intelligenz*, 36, pp. 143–161. https://doi.org/10.1007/s13218-022-00763-9

[5] Barmpatsalou K., Cruz T., Monteiro E., Simoes P. 2018. Current and Future Trends in Mobile Device Forensics: A Survey. *ACM Computing Surveys*, 51(3), Article 46 (May 2019), 31 pages. https://doi.org/10.1145/3177847

[6] Singano T., et al. 2025. Digital Forensics Investigations: Major Challenges in Mobile and Cloud Forensics. In: Sere A., Sie O., Saeed R.A. (eds) *Towards New e-Infrastructure and e-Services for Developing Countries*. AFRICOMM 2023. Lecture Notes of the Institute for Computer

Sciences, Social Informatics and Telecommunications Engineering, 588. Springer, Cham. https://doi.org/10.1007/978-3-031-81573-7_3
[7] AlKhanafseh M., Surakhi O. 2024. Evidence Preservation in Digital Forensics: An Approach Using Blockchain and LSTM-Based Steganography. *Electronics*, 13(18), p. 3729. https://doi.org/10.3390/electronics13183729
[8] Klasén L., Fock N., Forchheimer R. 2024. The Invisible Evidence: Digital Forensics as Key to Solving Crimes in the Digital Age. *Forensic Science International*, 362, pp. 1–7. https://doi.org/10.1016/j.forsciint.2024.112133
[9] Parambil M.M.A., Rustamov J., Ahmed S.G., Rustamov Z., Awad A.I., Zaki N., et al. 2024. Integrating AI-Based and Conventional Cybersecurity Measures into Online Higher Education Settings: Challenges, Opportunities, and Prospects. *Computers and Education: Artificial Intelligence*, 7, p. 100327. https://doi.org/10.1016/j.caeai.2024.100327
[10] Hunkenschroer A.L., Luetge C. 2022. Ethics of AI-Enabled Recruiting and Selection: A Review and Research Agenda. *Journal of Business Ethics*, 178, pp. 977–1007. https://doi.org/10.1007/s10551-022-05049-6
[11] Yu J., Shvetsov A.V., Hamood Alsamhi S. 2024. Leveraging Machine Learning for Cybersecurity Resilience in Industry 4.0: Challenges and Future Directions. *IEEE Access*, 12, pp. 159579–159596. https://doi.org/10.1109/ACCESS.2024.3482987
[12] Hashmi E., Yamin M.M., Yayilgan S.Y. 2024. Securing Tomorrow: A Comprehensive Survey on the Synergy of Artificial Intelligence and Information Security. *AI Ethics*. https://doi.org/10.1007/s43681-024-00529-z
[13] Zhao A.P., Li S., Cao Z., et al. 2024. AI for Science: Predicting Infectious Diseases. *Journal of Safety Science and Resilience*. https://doi.org/10.1016/j.jnlssr.2024.02.002
[14] Li D., Zeng X., Liu Y. 2023. Criminal Scene Investigation Image Retrieval Based on Multi-bag Multi-instance Learning Algorithm. In *Proceedings of the 2022 5th International Conference on Artificial Intelligence and Pattern Recognition (AIPR '22)*. Association for Computing Machinery, New York, 615–622. https://doi.org/10.1145/3573942.3574070
[15] Dunsin D., Ghanem M.C., Ouazzane K., Vassilev V.A. 2024. Comprehensive Analysis of the Role of Artificial Intelligence and Machine Learning in Modern Digital Forensics and Incident Response. *Forensic Science International: Digital Investigation*, 48, p. 301675.
[16] Gruber J., Humml M. 2023. A Formal Treatment of Expressiveness and Relevanceof Digital Evidence. *Digital Threats*, 4(3), Article 33, 16 pages. https://doi.org/10.1145/3608485
[17] Kirk P.L. 1963. The Ontogeny of Criminalistics. *Journal of Criminal Law, Criminology and Police Science*, 54, p. 23.
[18] Prince S., Li P., Fu Y., Mohammed U., Elder J. 2012. Probabilistic Models for Inference about Identity. *IEEE Transactions on Pattern Analysis and Machine Intelligence*, 34(1), pp. 144–157. https://doi.org/10.1109/TPAMI.2011.104
[19] Tian R., Zhu Z. 2023. Printer Source Identification Based on Graph Model. In *Proceedings of the 2023 7th International Conference on Machine Learning and Soft Computing (ICMLSC '23)*. Association for Computing Machinery, New York, 125–131. https://doi.org/10.1145/3583788.3583806
[20] Zanatta G., Caiazza G., Ferrara P., et al. 2024. Inference of Access Policies Through Static Analysis. *International Journal on Software Tools for Technology Transfer*, 26, pp. 797–821. https://doi.org/10.1007/s10009-024-00777-8
[21] Peirce C.S. 1931–1935. *Collected Papers* (Vol. 1–6, Eds. Hartshorne and Weiss). Cambridge, MA: Harvard University Press.
[22] Kadali D.K., Mohan R.N.V.J., Naik M.C. 2025. Uncertain Crime Data Analysis Using Hybrid Approach. *Discover Artificial Intelligence*, 5, p. 15. https://doi.org/10.1007/s44163-025-00234-8
[23] Alaya B., Sellami L. 2023. Toward the Design of an Efficient and Secure System based on the Software-defined Network Paradigm for Vehicular Networks. *IEEE Access*, 11, pp. 43333–43348. https://doi.org/10.1109/ACCESS.2023.3264808

[24] Aljohani T.H., Zhang N. 2023. Secure, ID Privacy and Inference Threat Prevention Mechanisms for Distributed Systems. *IEEE Access*, 11, pp. 3766–3780. https://doi.org/10.1109/ACCESS.2023.3234932

[25] Inman K., Rudin N. 2000. *Principles and Practice of Criminalistics: The Profession of Forensic Science*. CRC Press.

[26] Javed A.R., Ahmed W., Alazab M., Jalil Z., Kifayat K., Gadekallu T.R. 2022. A Comprehensive Survey on Computer Forensics: State-of-the-Art, Tools, Techniques, Challenges, and Future Directions. *IEEE Access*, 10, pp. 11065–11089. https://doi.org/10.1109/ACCESS.2022.3142508

[27] Göbel T., Baier H., Breitinger F. 2023. Data for Digital Forensics: Why a Discussion on "How Realistic Is Synthetic Data" Is Dispensable. *Digital Threats*, 4(3), Article 38, 18 p. https://doi.org/10.1145/3609863

[28] Asad M.M., Naz A., Shaikh A., et al. 2024. Investigating the Impact of IoT-Based Smart Laboratories on Students' Academic Performance in Higher Education. *Universal Access in the Information Society*, 23, pp. 1135–1149. https://doi.org/10.1007/s10209-022-00944-1

[29] Hassan S., et al. 2023. Real-Time Investigation of Cross-Technology Interference in Heterogeneous IoT Networks. *IEEE Access*, 11, pp. 112223–112235. https://doi.org/10.1109/ACCESS.2023.3321221

[30] Dobbins C., Denton P. 2017. MyWallMate: An Investigation into the Use of Mobile Technology in Enhancing Student Engagement. *TechTrends*, 61, pp. 541–549. https://doi.org/10.1007/s11528-017-0188-y

[31] Mondragón-González S.L., Burguière E., N'diaye K. 2023. Mobile Devices, Connected Objects, and Sensors. In: Colliot O. (eds) *Machine Learning for Brain Disorders. Neuromethods, 197*. Humana, New York. https://doi.org/10.1007/978-1-0716-3195-9_12

[32] Kühn R., Korzetz M., Kallenbach F., Kegel K., Aßmann U., Schlegel T. 2020. Investigating Mobile Device-Based Interaction Techniques for Collocated Merging. *In: Learning and Collaboration Technologies. Designing, Developing and Deploying Learning Experiences: 7th International Conference, LCT 2020, Held as Part of the 22nd HCI International Conference, HCII 2020*, Copenhagen, Denmark, July 19–24, 2020, Proceedings, Part I. Springer-Verlag, Berlin, Heidelberg, 92–108. https://doi.org/10.1007/978-3-030-50513-4_7

[33] Krasniqi A., Ajdari J., Zenuni X. 2021. The Cloud Computing Adoption Factors in Various Organizations: A Systematic Literature Review. *In: 2021 44th International Convention on Information, Communication and Electronic Technology (MIPRO)*, Opatija, Croatia, pp. 1364–1369. https://doi.org/10.23919/MIPRO52101.2021.9597182

[34] Alofe O.M., Fatema K. 2021. Trustworthy Cloud Computing. In: Lynn T., Mooney J.G., van der Werff L., Fox G. (eds) *Data Privacy and Trust in Cloud Computing. Palgrave Studies in Digital Business & Enabling Technologies*. Palgrave Macmillan, Cham. https://doi.org/10.1007/978-3-030-54660-1_7

[35] Aslan Ö.A., Samet R. 2020. A Comprehensive Review on Malware Detection Approaches. *IEEE Access*, 8, pp. 6249–6271.https://doi.org/10.1109/ACCESS.2019.2963724

[36] Mat S.R.T., Ab Razak M.F., Kahar M.N.M., et al. 2021. Towards a Systematic Description of the Field Using Bibliometric Analysis: Malware Evolution. *Scientometrics*, 126, pp. 2013–2055. https://doi.org/10.1007/s11192-020-03834-6

[37] Or-Meir O., Nissim N., Elovici Y., Rokach L. 2019. Dynamic Malware Analysis in the Modern Era—A State of the Art Survey. *ACM Computing Surveys*, 52(5), Article 88, 48 pages. https://doi.org/10.1145/3329786

[38] Isaac Abiodun O., Alawida M., Esther Omolara A., Alabdulatif A. 2022. Data Provenance for Cloud Forensic Investigations, Security, Challenges, Solutions and Future Perspectives: A Survey. *Journal of King Saud University Computer and Information Sciences*, 34(10), 10217–10245. https://doi.org/10.1016/j.jksuci.2022.10.018

[39] Al-Dhaqm A., Razak S.A., Ikuesan R.A., Kebande V.R., Siddique K. 2020. A Review of Mobile Forensic Investigation Process Models. *IEEE Access*, 8, pp. 173359–173375. https://doi.org/10.1109/ACCESS.2020.3014615

[40] Van der Zant T., Kouw M., Schomaker L. 2013. Generative Artificial Intelligence. In: Müller V. (eds) *Philosophy and Theory of Artificial Intelligence. Studies in Applied Philosophy, Epistemology and Rational Ethics*, 5. Springer, Berlin, Heidelberg. https://doi.org/10.1007/978-3-642-31674-6_8

[41] Asif M., Gouqing Z. 2024. Innovative Application of Artificial Intelligence in a Multi-Dimensional Communication Research Analysis: A Critical Review. *Discover Artificial Intelligence*, 4, p. 37. https://doi.org/10.1007/s44163-024-00134-3

[42] Yogesh K.D., et al. 2023. "So What If ChatGPT Wrote It?" Multidisciplinary Perspectives on Opportunities, Challenges and Implications of Generative Conversational AI for Research, Practice and Policy. *International Journal of Information Management*, 71. https://doi.org/10.1016/j.ijinfomgt.2023.102642

[43] Gustilo L., Ong E., Lapinid M.R. 2024. Algorithmically-Driven Writing and Academic Integrity: Exploring Educators' Practices, Perceptions, and Policies in AI Era. *International Journal for Educational Integrity*, 20, p. 3. https://doi.org/10.1007/s40979-024-00153-8

[44] Smith A., Anderson J. 2014. AI, Robotics, and the Future of Jobs. *Pew Research Center* [Washington], viewed 19 Feb 2025 <https://www.pewresearch.org/internet/wp-content/uploads/sites/9/2014/08/Future-of-AI-Robotics-and-Jobs.pdf>.

[45] Germani F., Spitale G., Biller-Andorno N. 2024 The Dual Nature of AI in Information Dissemination: Ethical Considerations. *JMIR AI*, 3, p. e53505. https://doi.org/10.2196/53505

[46] Williamson S.M., Prybutok V. 2024. The Era of Artificial Intelligence Deception: Unraveling the Complexities of False Realities and Emerging Threats of Misinformation. *Information*, 15(6), p. 299. https://doi.org/10.3390/info15060299

[47] Benneh Mensah G. 2023. *Artificial Intelligence and Ethics: A Comprehensive Review of Bias Mitigation, Transparency, and Accountability in AI Systems*. https://doi.org/10.13140/RG.2.2.23381.19685/1

[48] Kim J., Lee H., Cho Y.H. 2022. Learning Design to Support Student-AI Collaboration: Perspectives of Leading Teachers for AI in Education. *Education and Information Technologies*, 27, pp. 6069–6104. https://doi.org/10.1007/s10639-021-10831-6

[49] Adil S., et al. 2024. Redefining Boundaries in Innovation and Knowledge Domains: Investigating the Impact of Generative Artificial Intelligence on Copyright and Intellectual Property Rights. *Journal of Innovation & Knowledge*, 9(4). https://doi.org/10.1016/j.jik.2024.100630

[50] Sai S., Gaur A., Sai R., Chamola V., Guizani M., Rodrigues J.J.P.C. 2024. Generative AI for Transformative Healthcare: A Comprehensive Study of Emerging Models, Applications, Case Studies, and Limitations. *IEEE Access*, 12, pp. 31078–31106. https://doi.org/10.1109/ACCESS.2024.3367715

[51] Bukhari S.W.R., Hassan S. 2024. Impact of Artificial Intelligence on Copyright Law: Challenges and Prospects, 5, pp. 647–656. https://doi.org/10.52279/jlss.05.04.647656

[52] Mittal U., Sai S., Chamola V., Sangwan D. 2024. A Comprehensive Review on Generative AI for Education. *IEEE Access*, 12, pp. 142733–142759. https://doi.org/10.1109/ACCESS.2024.3468368

[53] Rane N., Shirke S., Choudhary S., Rane J. 2024. Education Strategies for Promoting Academic Integrity in the Era of Artificial Intelligence and ChatGPT: Ethical Considerations, Challenges, Policies, and Future Directions. *Journal of ELT Studies*, 1, pp. 36–59. https://doi.org/10.48185/jes.v1i1.1314

[54] Rawas S. 2024. AI: The Future of Humanity. *Discover Artificial Intelligence*, 4, p. 25. https://doi.org/10.1007/s44163-024-00118-3

[55] Tenakwah E.S., Watson C. 2025. Embracing the AI/Automation Age: Preparing Your Workforce for Humans and Machines Working Together. *Strategy & Leadership*, 53(1), pp. 32–48. https://doi.org/10.1108/SL-05-2024-0040

[56] Kim B.-J., Kim M.-J. 2024. How Artificial Intelligence-Induced Job Insecurity Shapes Knowledge Dynamics: The Mitigating Role of Artificial Intelligence Self-Efficacy. *Journal of Innovation & Knowledge*, 9(4). https://doi.org/10.1016/j.jik.2024.100590

[57] Lyu S. 2024. DeepFake the Menace: Mitigating the Negative Impacts of AI-Generated Content. *Organizational Cybersecurity Journal: Practice, Process and People*, 4(1), pp. 1–18. https://doi.org/10.1108/OCJ-08-2022-0014
[58] Verspoor K., Cohen K.B. 2013. Natural Language Processing. In: Dubitzky W., Wolkenhauer O., Cho K.H., Yokota H. (eds) *Encyclopedia of Systems Biology*. Springer, New York. https://doi.org/10.1007/978-1-4419-9863-7_158
[59] Zhao H., Chen H., Yang F., Liu N., Deng H., Cai H., Wang S., Yin D., Du M. 2024. Explainability for Large Language Models: A Survey. *ACM Transactions on Intelligent Systems and Technology*, 15(2), Article 20, 38 pages. https://doi.org/10.1145/3639372
[60] Paaß G., Giesselbach S. 2023. Pre-trained Language Models. *In: Foundation Models for Natural Language Processing. Artificial Intelligence: Foundations, Theory, and Algorithms*. Springer, Cham. https://doi.org/10.1007/978-3-031-23190-2_2
[61] Chakraborty S., Bedi A.S., Zhu S., An B., Manocha D., Huang F. 2024. Position: On the Possibilities of AI-Generated Text Detection. In *Proceedings of the 41st International Conference on Machine Learning (ICML'24)*, 235. JMLR.org, Article 235, pp. 6093–6115.
[62] Alaya B. 2021. Payoff-based Dynamic Segment Replication and Graph Classification Method with Attribute Vectors Adapted to Urban VANET. *ACM Transactions on Multimedia Computing, Communications, and Applications*. 17(3), pp. 1–22. https://doi.org/10.1145/3440018
[63] Dhawan M., Sharma S., Kadam A., et al. 2024. Game-On: Graph Attention Network Based Multimodal Fusion for Fake News Detection. *Social Network Analysis and Mining*, 14, p. 114. https://doi.org/10.1007/s13278-024-01271-4
[64] Yang Q., Zhao Y., Cheng H. 2024. MMLF: Multi-modal Multi-class Late Fusion for Object Detection with Uncertainty Estimation. https://doi.org/10.48550/arXiv.2410.08739
[65] Bebis G., et al. 2023. *Advances in Visual Computing: 18th International Symposium, ISVC 2023, Lake Tahoe, NV, USA, October 16–18, Proceedings, Part I*. Springer-Verlag, Berlin, Heidelberg.
[66] Priyanka G., Bosheng D., Chong G., Ding D. 2024. Generative AI: A Systematic Review Using Topic Modelling Techniques. *Data and Information Management*, 8(2). https://doi.org/10.1016/j.dim.2024.100066
[67] Anggrainingsih R., Hassan G.M., Datta A. 2024. Transformer-Based Models for Combating Rumours on Microblogging Platforms: A Review. *Artificial Intelligence Review*, 57, p. 212. https://doi.org/10.1007/s10462-024-10837-9
[68] Chen W., Yang K., Yu Z., et al. 2024. A Survey on Imbalanced Learning: Latest Research, Applications and Future Directions. *Artificial Intelligence Review*, 57, p. 137. https://doi.org/10.1007/s10462-024-10759-6
[69] Ni H., Sui P., Li Y., Li Y., Liang T., Yuan Y. 2024. Crowd-CapsNet: Capsule Network Based Adaptive Crowdsourcing Task Recommendation. *International Journal of Web Information Systems*. https://doi.org/10.1108/IJWIS-09-2024-0272
[70] Sellami L., Mchergui A., Alaya B. 2026. Optimizing Vehicular Networks Communications through Green Clustering and Data Aggregation. *Cluster Computing*, 29(16). https://doi.org/10.1007/s10586-025-05776-1
[71] Yanchenko E., Murata T., Holme P. 2024. Influence Maximization on Temporal Networks: A Review. *Applied Network Science*, 9, p. 16. https://doi.org/10.1007/s41109-024-00625-3
[72] Alaya B., Sellami L. 2021. Clustering Method and Symmetric/Asymmetric Cryptography Scheme Adapted to Securing Urban VANET Networks. *Journal of Information Security and Applications*, 58, pp. 1–12. https://doi.org/10.1016/j.jisa.2021.102779
[73] Ji S.-Y., Jeong B.K., Jeong D.H. 2023. An Analysis of Temporal Features in Multivariate Time Series to Forecast Network Events. *Applied Sciences*, 13(18), p. 10411. https://doi.org/10.3390/app131810411
[74] Graham T., Hames S., Alpert E. 2024. The Coordination Network Toolkit: A Framework for Detecting and Analysing Coordinated Behaviour on Social Media. *Journal of Computational Social Science*, 7, pp. 1139–1160. https://doi.org/10.1007/s42001-024-00260-z

[75] Aïmeur E., Amri S., Brassard G. 2023. Fake News, Disinformation and Misinformation in Social Media: A Review. *Social Network Analysis and Mining*, 13, p. 30. https://doi.org/10.1007/s13278-023-01028-5

[76] Kwon S., Jang B. 2025. A Comprehensive Survey of Fake Text Detection on Misinformation and LM-Generated Texts. *IEEE Access*, 13, pp. 25301–25324. https://doi.org/10.1109/ACCESS.2025.3538805

[77] Sutherland K.E. 2025. Fact Checking AI Generated Content. *In: Artificial Intelligence for Strategic Communication*. Palgrave Macmillan, Singapore. https://doi.org/10.1007/978-981-96-2575-8_9

[78] Zafir E.I., Akter A., Islam M., Hasib S.A., Islam T., Sarker S.K., Muyeen S. 2024. Enhancing Security of Internet of Robotic Things: A Review of Recent Trends, Practices, and Recommendations with Encryption and Blockchain Techniques. *Internet Things*, 28, p. 101357.

[79] Tihanyi N., Bisztray T., Borsos B., Raveau S. 2024. Privacy-Preserving Password Cracking: How a Third Party Can Crack Our Password Hash Without Learning the Hash Value or the Cleartext. *IEEE Transactions on Information Forensics and Security*, 19, pp. 2981–2996. https://doi.org/10.1109/TIFS.2024.3356162

[80] Kanta A., Coisel I., Scanlon M. 2024. A Comprehensive Evaluation on the Benefits of Context Based Password Cracking for Digital Forensics. *Journal of Information Security and Applications*, 84. https://doi.org/10.1016/j.jisa.2024.103809

[81] Pathak M., Mishra K.N., Singh S.P. 2024. Securing Data and Preserving Privacy in Cloud IoT-Based Technologies an Analysis of Assessing Threats and Developing Effective Safeguard. *Artificial Intelligence Review*, 57, p. 269. https://doi.org/10.1007/s10462-024-10908-x

[82] Alaya B. 2021. Efficient Privacy-Preservation Scheme for Securing Urban P2P VANET Networks. *Egyptian Informatics Journal*, 22(3), pp. 317–328. https://doi.org/10.1016/j.eij.2020.12.002

[83] Shivaramakrishna D., Nagaratna M. 2023. A Novel Hybrid Cryptographic Framework for Secure Data Storage in Cloud Computing: Integrating AES-OTP and RSA with Adaptive Key Management and Time-Limited Access Control. *Alexandria Engineering Journal*, 84, pp. 275–284. https://doi.org/10.1016/j.aej.2023.10.054

[84] Alaya B., Laouamer L., Msilini N. 2020. Homomorphic Encryption Systems Statement: Trends and Challenges. *Computer Science Review*, 36, pp. 1–14. https://doi.org/10.1016/j.cosrev.2020.100235

[85] Albahadily H., Jabbar I., Altaay A., Ren X. 2023. Issuing Digital Signatures for Integrity and Authentication of Digital Documents. *Al-Mustansiriyah Journal of Science*, 34, pp. 50–55. https://doi.org/10.23851/mjs.v34i3.1278

[86] Aggarwal S., Kumar N. 2021. *Digital signatures. Advances in Computers, 121*. Elsevier, pp. 95–107.

[87] Sutherland K.E. 2025. Fact Checking AI Generated Content. *In: Artificial Intelligence for Strategic Communication*. Palgrave Macmillan, Singapore. https://doi.org/10.1007/978-981-96-2575-8_9

[88] Díaz-Rodríguez N., Del Ser J., Coeckelbergh M., López de Prado M., Herrera-Viedma E., Herrera F. 2023. Connecting the Dots in Trustworthy Artificial Intelligence: From AI Principles, Ethics, and Key Requirements to Responsible AI Systems and Regulation. *Information Fusion*, 99, Article 101896. https://doi.org/10.1016/j.inffus.2023.101896

[89] Zhou J., Zhang Y., Luo Q., Parker A.G., Choudhury M.D. 2023. Synthetic Lies: Understanding AI-Generated Misinformation and Evaluating Algorithmic and Human Solutions. In *Proceedings of the 2023 CHI Conference on Human Factors in Computing Systems (CHI '23), April 23–28, 2023, Hamburg, Germany*. ACM, New York, 20 Pages. https://doi.org/10.1145/3544548.3581318

[90] Lundberg E., Mozelius P. 2024. The Potential Effects of Deepfakes on News Media and Entertainment. *AI & Society*. https://doi.org/10.1007/s00146-024-02072-1

[91] Jin F., Xiangmei P., Lanfang S., Zicong S., Keyi Z., ChinHsi L. 2025. Knowledge (Co-)Construction Among Artificial Intelligence, Novice Teachers, and Experienced Teachers in an

Online Professional Learning Community. *Journal of Computer Assisted Learning*, 41. https://doi.org/10.1111/jcal.70004

[92] Saeed W., Omlin C. 2023. Explainable AI (XAI): A Systematic Meta-Survey of Current Challenges and Future Opportunities. *Knowledge-Based Systems*, 263. https://doi.org/10.1016/j.knosys.2023.110273

[93] Quelle D., Bovet A. 2024. The Perils and Promises of Fact-Checking with Large Language Models. *Frontiers in Artificial Intelligence*, 7. https://doi.org/10.3389/frai.2024.1341697

[94] Aastha P., Rashina H., Spiegler S.V., Chakkrit T., Burak T. 2024. Ethics in the Age of AI: An Analysis of AI Practitioners' Awareness and Challenges. *ACM Transactions on Software Engineering and Methodology*, 33(3), Article 80, 35 pages. https://doi.org/10.1145/3635715

[95] Abdeladhim N., Alaya B., Touati H., 2026. A Comprehensive Survey of Machine Learning-based Techniques for Anomaly Detection in Ship Behavior within Maritime Transportation Systems. *Engineering Applications of Artificial Intelligence*, 163(2). https://doi.org/10.1016/j.engappai.2025.112596.

[96] Tsamados A., Aggarwal N., Cowls J., et al. 2022. The Ethics of Algorithms: Key Problems and Solutions. *AI & Society*, 37, pp. 215–230. https://doi.org/10.1007/s00146-021-01154-8

[97] Paleyes A., Urma R.G., Lawrence N.D. 2022. Challenges in Deploying Machine Learning: A Survey of Case Studies. *ACM Computing Surveys*, 55(6), Article 114 (June 2023), 29 pages. https://doi.org/10.1145/3533378

[98] Zehner N., Ullrich A. Dreaming of AI: Environmental Sustainability and the Promise of Participation. *AI & Society*. https://doi.org/10.1007/s00146-024-02011-0

[99] Bertl M., et al. 2025. Challenges for AI in Healthcare Systems. In: Steffen B. (ed) *Bridging the Gap Between AI and Reality. AISoLA 2023. Lecture Notes in Computer Science, 14129.* Springer, Cham. https://doi.org/10.1007/978-3-031-73741-1_11

[100] Bertl M., Lamo Y., Leucker M., Margaria T., et al. 2023. Challenges for AI in Healthcare Systems. In: *Bridging the Gap Between AI and Reality: First International Conference, AISoLA 2023, Crete, Greece, October 23–28, 2023, Selected Papers.* Springer-Verlag, Berlin, Heidelberg, pp. 165–186. https://doi.org/10.1007/978-3-031-73741-1_11

[101] Javed H., Muqeet H.A., Danesh A., Rehman A.U., Javed T., Bermak A. 2024. Impact of AI and Dynamic Ensemble Techniques in Enhancing Healthcare Services: Opportunities and Ethical Challenges. *IEEE Access*, 12, pp. 141064–141087. https://doi.org/10.1109/ACCESS.2024.3443812

[102] Wang D., Weisz J.D., Muller M., et al. 2019. Human-AI Collaboration in Data Science: Exploring Data Scientists' Perceptions of Automated AI. *Proceedings of the ACM on Human-Computer Interaction*, 3, CSCW, Article 211, 24 pages. https://doi.org/10.1145/3359313

[103] Cabrero-Daniel B., Herda T., Pichler V., Eder M. 2024. Exploring Human-AI Collaboration in Agile: Customised LLM Meeting Assistants. In: Šmite D., Guerra E., Wang X., Marchesi M., Gregory P. (eds) *Agile Processes in Software Engineering and Extreme Programming. XP 2024. Lecture Notes in Business Information Processing, 512.* Springer, Cham. https://doi.org/10.1007/978-3-031-61154-4_11

[104] Zafar A. 2024. Balancing the Scale: Navigating Ethical and Practical Challenges of Artificial Intelligence (AI) Integration in Legal Practices. *Discover Artificial Intelligence*, 4, p. 27. https://doi.org/10.1007/s44163-024-00121-8

[105] Mökander J. 2023. Auditing of AI: Legal, Ethical and Technical Approaches. *DISO 2*, 49. https://doi.org/10.1007/s44206-023-00074-y

[106] Hamon R., Junklewitz H., Sanchez I., Malgieri G., De Hert P. 2022. Bridging the Gap Between AI and Explainability in the GDPR: Towards Trustworthiness-by-Design in Automated Decision-Making. *IEEE Computational Intelligence Magazine*, 17(1), pp. 72–85. https://doi.org/10.1109/MCI.2021.3129960

[107] Kisselburgh L., Beever J. 2022. The Ethics of Privacy in Research and Design: Principles, Practices, and Potential. In: Knijnenburg B.P., Page X., Wisniewski P., Lipford H.R., Proferes N.,

Romano J. (eds) *Modern Socio-Technical Perspectives on Privacy*. Springer, Cham. https://doi.org/10.1007/978-3-030-82786-1_17

[108] Abraham R., Schneider J., Brocke J.V. 2019. Data Governance: A Conceptual Framework, Structured Review, and Research Agenda. *International Journal of Information Management*. 49, pp. 424–438. https://doi.org/10.1016/j.ijinfomgt.2019.07.008

[109] Bernardo B.M.V., et al. 2024, Data Governance & Quality Management—Innovation and Breakthroughs Across Different Fields. *Journal of Innovation & Knowledge*, 9(4). https://doi.org/10.1016/j.jik.2024.100598

[110] Stahl B.C., Leach T. 2023. Assessing the Ethical and Social Concerns of Artificial Intelligence in Neuroinformatics Research: An Empirical Test of the European Union Assessment List for Trustworthy AI (ALTAI). *AI Ethics*, 3, pp. 745–767. https://doi.org/10.1007/s43681-022-00201-4

[111] Hanna M., Pantanowitz L., Jackson B., Palmer O., Visweswaran S., Pantanowitz J., et al. 2024. Ethical and Bias Considerations in Artificial Intelligence (AI)/Machine Learning. *Modern Pathology*, 100686. https://doi.org/10.1016/j.modpat.2024.100686

[112] Jerone T., Andrews A., Zhao D., Thong W., Modas A., Papakyriakopoulos O., Xiang A. 2023. Ethical Considerations for Responsible Data Curation. In *Proceedings of the 37th International Conference on Neural Information Processing Systems (NIPS '23)*. Curran Associates Inc., Red Hook, Article 2415, pp. 55320–55360.

[113] Agarwal D., Bersin J., Lahiri G., Schwartz J., Volini E. 2018. People Data: How Far Is Too Far? <https://www2.deloitte.com/za/en/pages/human-capital/articles/people-data-how-far-is-too-far.html>.

[114] Rashid A.B., Kausik A.K. 2024. AI Revolutionizing Industries Worldwide: A Comprehensive Overview of Its Diverse Applications. *Hybrid Advances Article*, 100277. https://doi.org/10.1016/j.hybadv.2024.100277

[115] Zhao J., Gómez Fariñas B. 2023. Artificial Intelligence and Sustainable Decisions. *European Business Organization Law Review*, 24, pp. 1–39. https://doi.org/10.1007/s40804-022-00262-2

[116] Meurisch C., Mühlhäuser M. 2021. Data Protection in AI Services: A Survey. *ACM Computing Surveys*, 54(2), Article 40, 38 pages. https://doi.org/10.1145/3440754

[117] Stahl B.C., Antoniou J., Bhalla N., et al. 2023. A Systematic Review of Artificial Intelligence Impact Assessments. *Artificial Intelligence Review*, 56, pp. 12799–12831. https://doi.org/10.1007/s10462-023-10420-8

[118] Butt J. 2024. The General Data Protection Regulation of 2016 (GDPR) Meets its Sibling the Artificial Intelligence Act of 2024: A Power Couple, or a Clash of Titans? *Acta Universitatis Danubius. Juridica*, 20(2), pp. 7–52. https://dj.univ-danubius.ro/index.php/AUDJ/article/view/2788.

[119] Stahl B.C., Andreou A., Brey P., Hatzakis T., Kirichenko A., Macnish K., Laulhé Shaelou S., Patel A., Ryan M., Wright D. 2021. Artificial Intelligence for Human Flourishing—Beyond Principles for Machine Learning. *Journal of Business Research*, 124, pp. 374–388. https://doi.org/10.1016/j.jbusres.2020.11.030

[120] Bekkum M.V. 2025. Using Sensitive Data to De-Bias AI Systems: Article 10(5) of the EU AI Act. *Computer Law & Security Review*, 56. https://doi.org/10.1016/j.clsr.2025.106115

[121] Danezis G., et al. 2014. Privacy and Data Protection by Design—from Policy to Engineering. https://doi.org/10.2824/38623.

[122] Collins C., Dennehy D., Conboy K., Mikalef P. 2021. Artificial Intelligence in Information Systems Research: A Systematic Literature Review and Research Agenda. *International Journal of Information Management*, 60, p. 102383.

[123] Sadek M., Kallina E., Bohné T. et al. 2025. Challenges of Responsible AI in Practice: Scoping Review and Recommended Actions. *AI & Society*, 40, pp. 199–215. https://doi.org/10.1007/s00146-024-01880-9

[124] Alaya B. 2017. EE-(m,k)-Firm: A Method to Dynamic Service Level Management in Enterprise Environment. In *19th International Conference on Enterprise Information Systems (ICEIS)*, pp. 114–122, 26–29 April.

[125] Naik N., Hameed B.M.Z., Shetty D.K., Swain D., Shah M., Paul R., Aggarwal K., Ibrahim S., Patil V., Smriti K., Shetty S., Rai B.P., Chlosta P., Somani B.K. 2022. Legal and Ethical Consideration in Artificial Intelligence in Healthcare: Who Takes Responsibility? *Frontiers in Surgery*, 9, p. 862322. https://doi.org/10.3389/fsurg.2022.862322

[126] Rodrigues R. 2020. Legal and Human Rights Issues of AI: Gaps, Challenges and Vulnerabilities. *Journal of Responsible Technology*, 4, p. 100005. https://doi.org/10.1016/j.jrt.2020.100005

[127] Alhosani K., Alhashmi S.M. 2024. Opportunities, Challenges, and Benefits of AI Innovation in Government Services: A Review. *Discover Artificial Intelligence*, 4, p. 18. https://doi.org/10.1007/s44163-024-00111-w

[128] Socol A., Iuga I.C. 2024. Addressing Brain Drain and Strengthening Governance for Advancing Government Readiness in Artificial Intelligence (AI). *Kybernetes*, 53(13), pp. 47–71. https://doi.org/10.1108/K-03-2024-0629

[129] Storey V.C., Yue W.T., Zhao J.L. et al. 2025. Generative Artificial Intelligence: Evolving Technology, Growing Societal Impact, and Opportunities for Information Systems Research. *Information Systems Frontiers*. https://doi.org/10.1007/s10796-025-10581-7

[130] Hossin M.A., Du J., Mu L., Asante I.O. 2023. Big Data-Driven Public Policy Decisions: Transformation Toward Smart Governance. *Sage Open*, 13(4). https://doi.org/10.1177/21582440231215123

[131] Jedličková A. 2024. Ethical Approaches in Designing Autonomous and Intelligent Systems: A Comprehensive Survey Towards Responsible Development. *AI & Society*. https://doi.org/10.1007/s00146-024-02040-9

Chapter 5

Legal Remedies and Regulatory Frameworks to Combat AI-Driven Deepfakes

Raphael Ramos Monteiro de Souza

5.1 INTRODUCTION

Deceptive and misleading synthetic media content generated by artificial intelligence (AI) resources is one of the most salient concerns presented by emergent technology developments. Recent political campaigning worldwide has placed this issue in the spotlight, mainly considering worries related to massive dis/misinformation—from either textual or audiovisual-based realistic and convincing deepfakes. The literature warns that these systems could increase the scale, persuasiveness, and personalization of false election advertising amid an ongoing divided and distrusted information environment (Chesney and Citron 2019; Vaccari and Chadwick 2020; Jungherr 2023).

From false endorsements and misleading statements to distorted evidence regarding polls and policies, as well as accusations against opponents and foreign influence, there are countless ways to influence the electoral debate through these deceptive techniques. Such methods not only make the material more difficult for the human eye to detect but also provide new opportunities for distribution and amplification (Gaba 2019; Howard 2020), demonstrating the urgent need for a robust legal framework.

The recent sophisticated repertoire of AI applications includes several notable examples: Robocalls featuring an AI emulation of President Biden's voice discouraging Democracts to vote (Bond 2024); a deepfake interview with the jailed former Prime Minister of Pakistan during an election rally (Ray 2023); AI-generated videos of Bollywood stars in India urging people to support the opposition (Kalra et al. 2024); instances of female candidates being targeted by deepfake pornography in Brazilian local elections (Cruz et al. 2024); and a viral AI-enabled fake video of a candidate taking narcotics in Argentina (Centenera and Criales 2023); among others. In addition to its implications for the political public sphere, this type of material poses significant threats to vulnerable groups, particularly women, who are often targets of non-consensual intimate deepfakes. This increasing phenomenon, which affects individuals ranging from celebrities as famous singers and actresses to young girls in schools (United Kingdom 2025b), reinforces various forms of gender-based violence (Kira 2024), especially considering that such applications are widely available online. The recently adopted International Convention against Cybercrime (United Nations 2024c) also emphasizes the need to eliminate gender-based offenses perpetrated through technology systems.

Such a scenario results in a perfect storm within polarized and biased societies, triggering a further debate on AI regulation and possible legal safeguards to mitigate these risks. As highlighted by Black and Murray (2019), the previous decade of the technology law and

DOI: 10.1201/9781003539032-5

policy debate was marked by some government paralysis before the limits of digital tools in general and social media in particular, cautious with a space "where freedom seemed to create both economic and civic benefits."

The situation has shifted following events that include not only the emergent affordances of digital era developments and weaponization but also the rise of public global consciousness regarding the need for protecting threatened values, such as democracy and the safety of the information environment as a whole (Benkler et al. 2018; Mounk 2018; Singer and Brooking 2018; Keane 2020).

In light of these reasons, and also in response to the apprehension related to AI tools, many international guidelines have emerged, calling for action from the public and private actors, as well as civil society, to harmonize freedom of expression and economic initiative with other fundamental rights such as access to information, privacy, and non-discrimination.

From the United Nations Global Principles for Information Integrity to the Inter-Ministerial Declaration of the G20 Digital Economy Working Group on Information Integrity, as well as the Recommendation of the Organization for Economic Co-operation and Development Council on Information Integrity and Artificial Intelligence (OECD 2024a, 2024b), guidelines are being issued in sequence. These challenges and adverse externalities arise alongside new phenomena such as coordinated inauthentic behavior, automated bots, and foreign information manipulation and interference, demanding global responses (G'sell 2024).

This has resulted in the ranking of distrust in information processes as one of the top global risks for the second consecutive year (World Economic Forum 2025). As a consequence, it is clear that this environment underscores the increasing importance of addressing disinformation, as well as safeguarding information integrity in the context of generative AI, given the associated risks to truth, equality, and non-violence (Judson et al. 2024).

Against this backdrop of multidisciplinary defenses, this chapter aims to comprehend how recent legal efforts tackle this phenomenon, from enacted legislation to proposed bills on deepfakes, in light of representative and diverse jurisdictions such as the United Kingdom, Brazil, South Korea, Australia, the European Union, Canada, and the United States—given the time frame limit of the second semester of 2024.

Departing from the spectrum of regulatory approaches from less interventionist to more coercive and liability-based (UNESCO 2024), the overview comparative analyses provide an exploratory range of frameworks and assist in understanding how different sociocultural contexts produce different legal and institutional choices (Dixon 2020) to combat this multi-layered question. Therefore, the case selection for this small-*n* qualitative study adheres to the principle of most different cases (Hirschl 2014) in terms of regulatory approaches, while considering the legal cultures of freedom of expression legal (Barendt 2005; Murray 2013). Additionally, the analyses encompass various regions, including both parliamentary and presidential systems, as well as national and regional responses.

This chapter is structured as follows. First, it presents the main categories that guide the analyses, which include the scope, type of regulatory strategies, sources of regulation, providers' obligations and liabilities, degree of intervention, and penalties. After that, the study focuses on each selected case's responses and discusses the gaps and risks posed. The investigation aims to contribute to the tech regulatory debate by highlighting how the legal landscape currently addresses the AI deepfake issues. Finally, it is argued that these contemporary challenges necessitate a holistic, multilevel, cross-platform, and collaborative human rights-based framework.

5.2 TAXONOMY

In this first section, as mentioned, the study presents a qualitative lens to analyze the legal documents collected, classifying the material according to the proposed categories. Aiming to address these new levels of harm from AI deepfakes, each nation will focus on one or another facet of the problem.

In such a way, (i) *scope* consists of examining whether the significant concern of the legislators prioritizes specific questions, for instance, women and children protection or disinformation and election issues. In other words, it identifies whether and to what extent the normative response is piecemeal-based or part of a broader horizontal regulation. Then, (ii) the *type of strategies* considers whether the regulation introduces punitive and ban provisions, informative requirements, or a mixed approach, as well as adding digital literacy measures. Third, the (iii) *source of regulation* explores each governance power, that is, whether Parliaments directly provide all the normative rules related to this issue or delegate technical matters to a specific agency or another branch.

After that, on (iv) *developers and publishers' obligations and responsibilities*, the purpose is to investigate the degree of liability or cooperation assigned to the tech companies in the matter of mitigating the risk of AI deepfake production and dissemination, if any, followed by (v) *sanctions*, such as fines, jail, or administrative and electoral consequences and finally bring a synthesis of the (vi) degree of intervention employed, based on the UNESCO guidelines.

In sum, Table 5.1 condenses the categories that guide the present exploratory analyses.

To illustrate the range of measures specifically related to the category of strategies, it is pertinent to unpack the available options as follows.

The subsequent sections will discuss how each selected context is tackling this next level of threats posed by realistic fake content, either by updating existing laws or by creating specific provisions for AI matters.

5.3 COUNTRY-SPECIFIC REGULATORY INSIGHTS

This section will explore the legal measures adopted by each selected country to address the challenges posed by AI deepfakes, considering the aforementioned variables such as scope, strategy, and sanctions. By underscoring the similarities and differences in the stages and approaches, it highlights that, despite common impacts, regulatory concerns and pace are indissociable from the specific historical, economic, and social contexts.

5.3.1 South Korea

The South Korean case is prototypical regarding the extensive scope of AI deepfake regulation. Currently, such a country encompasses provisions not only on image abuse content (Amendments to Act on Special Cases Concerning the Punishment of Sexual Crimes) but also on electoral campaigning bans (Amendments to Public Official Election Act) sided by a fresh comprehensive legislation on AI (Basic Law on the Development of Artificial Intelligence and Establishment of Trust Base)—general framework approved in December of 2024 that will be taken into force in early 2026 (South Korea 2024c).

Recently, following public outrage at increasing reports of digital sex crimes connected to AI-generated images or videos widely shared (Smith and Brake 2024), South Korean lawmakers have enacted a strict package of punishing measures regarding this issue. In this

Table 5.1 Categories of analyses—AI deepfake regulation

Variable	*Description*	*Values*
Scope	Identify to what extent the legal systems address these questions	Specific (non-consensual intimate media, dis/misinformation on elections or public policy, illegal content, scams) General (comprehensive)
Type of Strategies	Explore the main focus in terms of the sort of responses	Punitive Informative Preventive Educational
Source	Understand which authority is responsible for setting the guidelines and enforcement	Full legislative Delegated legislative (specialized technical agency, judiciary, or executive branch)
Platforms Obligations and Liabilities	Investigate whether and how developers and publishers are obligated to act and be responsible	Active and preventive or merely corrective by notice-and-takedown subsidiary or shared
Sanctions	Examine what types of penalties are established	Criminal (imprisonment) Administrative and civil (fines, content removal, profile blocking) Electoral (ineligibility, loss of mandate)
Degree of Approach	Non-mutually excluding approach (UNESCO 2024)	Principles-based Risks-based Rights-based Liability-based

Source: Own elaboration

manner, in September of 2024, Parliament amended the Act on Special Cases Concerning the Punishment of Sexual Crimes (South Korea 2024a), strengthening the criminal sanctions for deepfake technology that targets women and girls, making such offenses even more rigorous.

The criminalization approach reform raised statutory sentences for "editing and distributing false video footage" as well as for those who possess, purchase, store, or merely view "false video footage" (Article 14-2, Paragraphs 1, 2, 3, and 4 and Article 14-3). In the first case, the maximum imprisonment term for creating and sharing pornographic and sexually explicit content increased from five to seven years, and the fines can reach up to $34,000. In the last one, penalties include up to a three-year jail sentence and fines up to $22,000. Therefore, this axis of such jurisdiction is related directly to image abuse and non-consensual intimate material, as long as South Korean "society is very concerned" and demanding "responds to deepfake crimes," as stated by representatives during the debates (South Korea 2024a).

A diagram presenting different strategies and measures for AI deepfake regulation is given in Figure 5.1. The figure categorizes regulatory approaches such as legal frameworks, technological solutions, platform policies, educational initiatives, and international cooperation, showing how each contributes to addressing the risks of deepfakes.

Furthermore, a few months before, the South Korean Congress elections had already addressed AI-related concerns about electoral integrity during political campaigning, another key topic for regulation (Callejón 2023). Conceptually, it means the content of

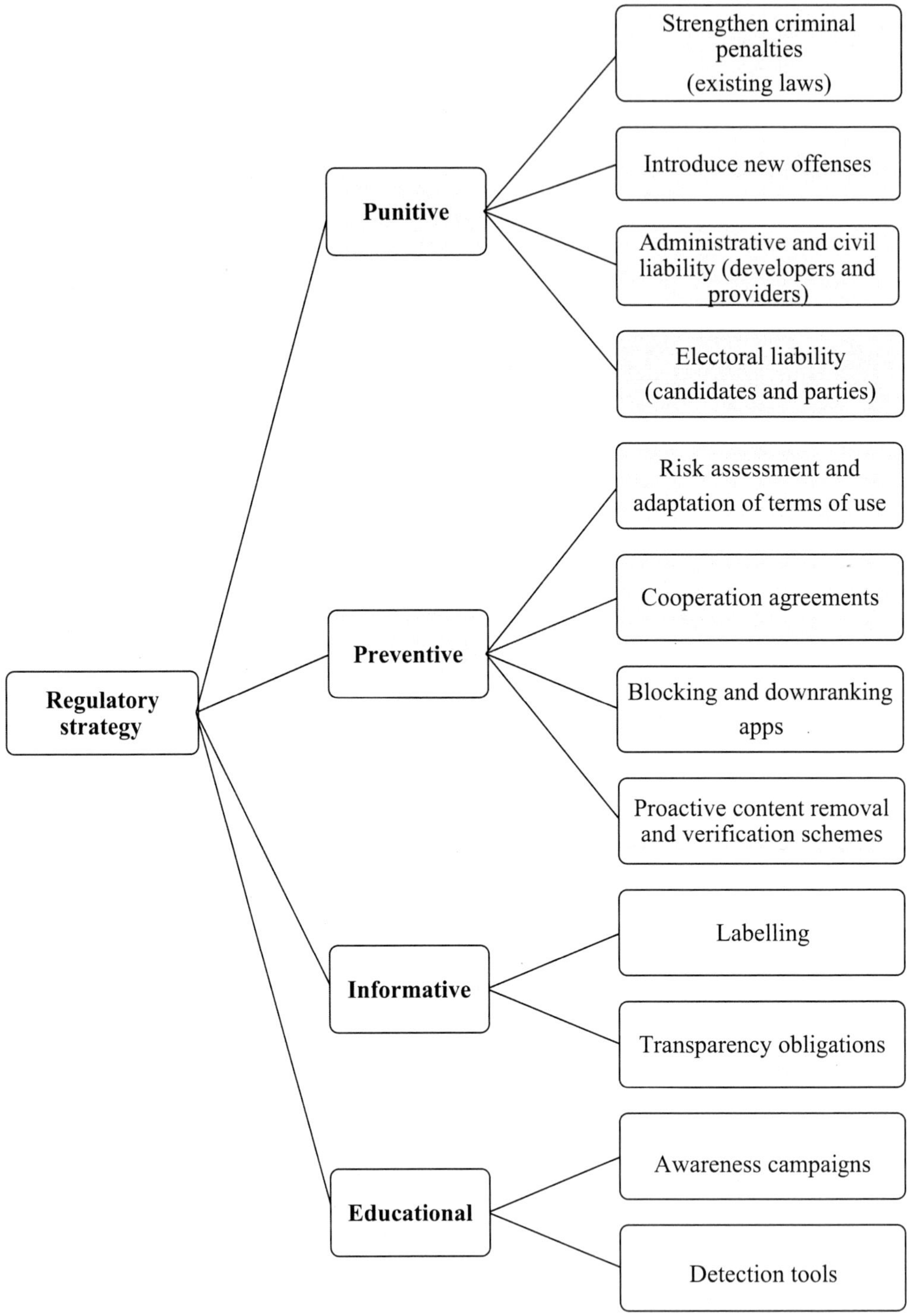

Figure 5.1 Strategies and measures—AI deepfake regulation.

sounds, images, or videos that "made virtuality difficult to distinguish from reality" created using AI technology. This way, according to the new Article 82-8, the Public Official Election Act amendment introduced (Article 82-8) a ban consisting of "no one may produce, edit, distribute, screen, or post deepfake videos for election campaigning purposes" for 90 days until the election day.

The National Election Commission will operate a special response team for false information (South Korea 2024b). In case of violation, imprisonment of up to seven years or fines can be imposed. However, outside this three-month period, deepfake material produced, edited, distributed, screened, or posted may be used as long as it clearly indicates that the information may contain AI technology in accordance with the provisions of the Central Election Management Committee Rules.

The most recently enacted AI-related package is the Basic Law on the Development of Artificial Intelligence and Establishment of Trust Base—AI Basic Act (South Korea 2024c), which establishes a comprehensive and three-fold focus, similar to the European AI Act. First, such a general initiative aims to foster innovation, research, and industry; second, it designs AI governance among public oversight bodies; and, finally, the Act sets principles and high-risk-based parameters to minimize the impact of technology.

In this way, besides concerns about energy and water supply and healthcare services, it comprises "creating a safe and reliable artificial intelligence usage environment" and, among others, introduces obligations to secure transparency and risk assessment on high-impact services (Articles 31 to 34). In cases where content is generated by an AI system, mandatory labeling is required, provided that it is clearly "notified or displayed in a manner that users can clearly recognise."

At first glance, South Korea appears to be achieving a complete score by incorporating a prohibitive and punitive approach to AI-enabled disinformation on elections alongside rules governing non-consensual intimate content. General risk-based and transparency-focused provisions from the EU AI Act-style regulation strengthened this framework. However, this new toolkit needs to be fully implemented and tested, particularly concerning its governance and the effective enforcement of obligations for service providers and developers, rather than solely focusing on provisions for end-users.

5.3.2 Brazil

The recent Brazilian experience with the AI regulation debate is also effervescent, especially considering the public attention drawn to the electoral context, which includes specific provisions currently in effect to mitigate the risks associated with deepfakes. This focus is complemented by efforts to enhance women's protection and an ongoing legislative debate regarding a comprehensive AI bill.

In the aftermath of highly polarized national electoral cycles significantly influenced by the use of social media to disseminate disinformation against opponents and public officials, criminal investigations into the deployment of digital militias before and during Bolsonaro's presidency emerged. Furthermore, the attempted coup d'état on January 8, 2023, which involved the storming of the main buildings of the Three Powers and took place within a conspiratorial and distrustful information environment among right-wing supporters, underscores the urgent need for AI regulations in the electoral context. The judicial branch was the first to address these concerns.

It is worth noting that the Brazilian Superior Electoral Court—TSE is a hybrid judicial body with constitutional status and a threefold role. It not only is responsible for managing the electoral process and resolving disputes and legal violations but also has normative powers in the electoral context, regulating topics such as online political advertisement. Since a reform introduced in 2017, the Brazilian Congress has expressly delegated this type of regulation through a clause that authorizes the update of rules "accordingly to the technological landscape and available tools" (Article 57-J, Federal Law n. 9504).

This institutional background helps to understand the responses enacted in the Brazilian context. In February of the following year, after a public consultation, the Superior Electoral Court implemented the Resolution n. 23.732/2024, which updated Resolution 23.610/2019 regarding electoral advertising for local elections (Brazil 2024). This pioneering national legal-specific response to AI and political campaigns introduced several provisions and requirements. In line with the EU AI Act, it enhanced partnerships with fact-checking agencies as verified sources and trusted flaggers (Article 9, Paragraph 1).

By the same token, it also allowed the ordinary use of AI generative content on the condition that synthetic media must be displayed (Article 9-B). Otherwise, content would be removed directly by digital providers or by judicial request. Moreover, repositories of political ads boosters and removal of content associated with electoral integrity will be shown on the official Court website—including metadata as engagement, comments, and the number of views (Articles 9-G and 27).

Chatbots that emulate candidates are banned, as is manipulated content, notoriously untrue, or severely decontextualized (Article 9-D). Specifically regarding deepfakes—image, voice, or video-based—the Resolution also banned them, regardless of whether the message is negative or positive, from a living, deceased, or fictional person (Article 9-C, Paragraph 1). The obligations for digital providers are comprehensive and include duties of adapting their terms of service, incorporating notice-and-takedown mechanisms, making recommendation systems transparent, introducing risk assessment during election years, promoting demonetization of breaching profiles or channels, publishing the right of reply, and moderating content.

Among the most significant provisions of this Resolution is Article 9-E, which goes beyond solely candidates and political parties by establishing joint civil and administrative liability for digital platforms during elections in cases of delayed content removal under five specific circumstances. It is worth noting that such a response aligns with one of the central recommendations of the Interim Report of the Australian Senate Committee on Adopting Artificial Intelligence (Australia 2024a). For the purpose of this chapter, it is important to highlight that the display or sharing of deepfake material and the failure to label AI-generated content in accordance with the regulation appropriately constitute one of these violations.

Other infringements include failing to remove content or suspend profiles that spread electoral disinformation—for example, about the electronic voting and counting process—as well as acts classified as crimes against the Democratic State of Law, racism, homophobia, Nazism, hate speech, or incitement of violence against electoral officers, judges, or prosecutors. The same framework establishes loss of electoral registry or mandates as sanctions for candidates who incur this type of abuse of means of political communication.

Additionally, since 2021, the Electoral Code has established as a criminal offense the act of spreading "in electoral advertising or during the electoral campaign period, facts that one knows to be false regarding parties or candidates and that are capable of influencing the electorate" (Article 323).

Another pillar of the Brazilian Judiciary Strategy to safeguard electoral integrity involved cooperation agreements formalized with digital platforms. These documents included all the mainstream providers, such as Meta, Google, and Twitter/X, TikTok, Kwai, Telegram, Spotify, and Telegram (Gonzales and Bragatto 2024). Such tactics are part of a Permanent Program against Disinformation introduced in 2021. This program is designed to establish expedited channels for enforcing judicial orders and disseminating official information, in addition to strengthening legal compliance and the platform's own measures according to their respective terms of service (Brazil 2024b).

Although some preliminary reports indicate that this first experience with local elections has witnessed less employment of AI deepfakes than was expected (Caballero et al. 2024; Cruz et al. 2024), similar to findings related to the British and the European Parliament's previous campaigns in 2024 (Stockwell 2024), it is still premature to draw conclusions about the effective impacts of these technologies in the coming years. Despite some criticisms regarding alleged overblown claims (Simon et al. 2023), such concerns remain remarkably consistent in view of the decreasing costs, fast-evolving applications, and growing popularization of AI-generated tools.

Finally, a National Comprehensive Bill on Artificial Intelligence (Bill 2338/2023) is currently under consideration by the Brazilian Congress (Brazil 2024c). The Federal Senate has approved it and is awaiting deliberation by the Chamber of Deputies. This EU AI Act style proposal—illustrating the so-called Brussels Effect (Bradford 2020)—adopts a risk-based approach and aims to foster innovation and competition rather than, for instance, curbing the disinformation impacts of these new applications as high-risk treatment. However, it introduces many principles that could indirectly help to protect fundamental rights (Articles 3 and 66) besides establishing a National Committee of AI Regulation and Governance, led by the National Data Protection Authority—ANPD, which has a broader mandate to enact new rules in the future (Articles 15 and 46) in cooperation with other agencies.

Regarding the protection of victims of AI-generated sexual abuse content, Brazilian Legislation has somewhat addressed this threat since the introduction of Federal Law n. 13772/2018. This law amended the Criminal Code (Article 216-B) to recognize this type of psychological violence against women. The penalties for the offense of unauthorized recording of sexual intimacy are also applied to anyone who "edits a photograph, video, audio, or any other recording with the intent of including a person in a scene of nudity or a sexual or lascivious act of an intimate nature."

Several pending bills propose increasing the maximum sentences for this crime when AI tools are utilized, currently capped at one year of imprisonment or up to three years when the victims are children. Some recent AI-enabled cases during elections have highlighted the intersection of emerging technologies and traditional gender-based biases (Cruz et al. 2024), as female candidates were targeted by deepfake pornography (so-called deep nudes), underscoring the need for specific and stringent regulations in this area.

Finally, it is relevant to point out that Brazil's Attorney General's Office filed a collective civil lawsuit against Meta, aiming to prevent the improper use of government symbols, images, and videos of public officials and lawmakers that have been manipulated by AI in scams deployed through boosted advertising (Brazil 2025). Based on the provisions of the Consumer Protection Act, this legal action aims to hold the social media platform liable for illicit enrichment and collective moral damages. In addition, it requests the improvement of the ad verification system, considering that, despite the terms and conditions, deepfakes have been increasingly spread through Facebook and Instagram—as part of the so-called celeb baits.

Such a movement reinforces a scenario in which, parallel to sluggish parliamentary debates, the real-world impacts of AI deepfakes will be addressed by existing legal provisions.

5.3.3 Australia

The Australian case is one example of how better protecting children and women has been the primary driver of the regulatory debate on online harms, in general, and AI, in particular. This focus over the last decade positions the country at the forefront of government responses in the matter, including on cyberbullying and image-based abuse schemes, especially in light of provisions of the Online Safety Act of 2021—and Criminal Code Amendment—Deepfake Sexual Material of 2024.

Reinforcing this scenario, a recent reform of its OSA (Sections 63A to 63K) made Australia the first jurisdiction in the world to require social media platforms to take reasonable steps to prevent underage children from creating accounts. In addition, the rapid growth of emerging technologies and the impacts of AI-generated tools on democracy and elections have also sparked calls for reforms in truth in political advertising laws (Australia 2024b).

First, with respect to institutional capacities, it is essential to point out the key role played by the eSafety Commissioner. Established initially as the Office of the Children's eSafety Commissioner in 2015, the Australian system expanded its mandate with the Online Safety Act of 2021, transforming the regulator into an independent administrative body responsible for promoting online safety, as well as implementing and enforcing the Act and its amendments for individuals of all ages (Australia 2021).

These functions include administering a complaints system for cyberbullying material targeting children and adults, as well as a complaints and objections system for the non-consensual sharing of intimate images (Sections 25–28) and applying civil penalties. In case of intimate, non-consent material, for instance, eSafety may give the social media or electronic service a written removal notice, requiring the provider or end-user to take down the content within 24 hours (Sections 77–78).

Additionally, these powers encompass a consistent educational approach to raise public awareness about online safety issues. The act stipulates that such a regulator must disseminate information relating to online safety and "support, encourage, conduct, accredit and evaluate educational, promotional and community awareness programs" (Section 27).

In October 2024, the Australian Parliament decided to address and update the non-consensual intimate synthetic media problem in a standalone punitive manner. In this sanctionatory vein, the passed Criminal Code Amendment—Deepfake Sexual Material (Australia 2024c) substituted Section 474.17A in the Criminal Code Act of 1995. It introduced the offense of "using a carriage service to transmit sexual material without consent."

The new criminal type defines such deepfakes as media files—images, videos, or audio—"depicting a person have been edited or entirely created using digital technology (including AI), generating a realistic but false depiction of the person" who is "engaging in a sexual pose or sexual activity" (whether or not in the presence of other persons).

These provisions encompass sexual organs and regions, as well as "the breasts of the other person if she is female." It is relevant to note that "transmitting" includes actions such as making available, publishing, distributing, advertising, and promoting and is subject to penalties of up to six years of imprisonment. Such offense is deemed aggravated if the individual who commits it is also responsible for creating or altering the material, resulting in an increased criminal sanction of up to seven years. A recent landmark ruling has resulted in a man being sentenced to jail for creating AI-generated naked images of a female teacher who was his friend. This decision has raised awareness, as it marks the first time that this type of criminal offense has been sanctioned (Turnbull 2025). On the other hand, recent events worldwide have raised concerns about the potential political harms of AI deepfakes within Australia. Although a few states passed laws on Truth in Political Advertising (TiPA) in the past (Ng 2024), there is currently no legislation addressing these issues at the federal level. Both academics and Parliament have emphasized this regulatory gap and are discussing potential strategies to address these challenges.

For instance, the Interim Report of the Australian Senate Committee on Adopting Artificial Intelligence (Australia 2024a) recommends that "mandatory guardrails for AI in high-risk settings also apply to AI systems used in an electoral or political setting." It also underscores the need for "mandatory codes applying to the developers of AI models and publishers including social media platforms." This aligns with public consultation findings suggesting that obligations "could be placed directly on the operators of AI or social media platforms." Additionally, the Committee stressed that TiPA laws "should be extended to materially deceptive AI-generated audio or visual media in carrying out an election to influence an election," excepting satirical content.

For political context enforcement, during election period, Ng (2024) indicates that the Electoral Commission is an appropriate arbiter of TiPA laws, although it "requires sufficient resourcing to carry out this task." Regarding fines, as pointed out by Hill et al. (2022) on their ideal-type regime of liabilities and remedies of false election information, "the penalty amount should be such that it cannot be easily absorbed as a routine campaign expense instrumentally or cynically incurred to gain a political advantage."

In relation to legislative measures, it is central to highlight that, in September 2024, the Government proposed the Communications Legislation Amendment—Combating Misinformation and Disinformation Bill (Australia 2024c). The primary objective of this framework is to impose

> obligations on digital communications platform providers regarding the dissemination of content on digital communication that contains information that is reasonably verifiable as false, misleading or deceptive, and is reasonably likely to cause or contribute to serious harm of a specified type (misinformation and disinformation).

The definition of disinformation tactics and techniques encompasses "impermissible manipulative behaviour" such as impersonation and malicious deepfakes (Chapter 15). If enacted, the Australian Communications and Media Authority will be responsible for enforcing its provisions, which may include pecuniary penalties of up to 5% of the annual turnover of the corporate entity over a 12-month period (Article 20), in line with European guidelines.

5.3.4 United States

As the cradle of some of the most prominent AI developers and social media publishers, such as OpenAI, Alphabet, and Meta, the American landscape must be mentioned even in the absence of federal statutes directly aimed at addressing deepfakes' associated risks—notably on the political context and disinformation harms.

It is essential to note that the radical perspective of the American First Amendment on freedom of speech is central to understanding this non-interventionist and pro-innovation approach. This doctrine paves the way for understanding a free and unrestricted marketplace of ideas as a necessary condition for autonomy (Murray 2013, 114–116). In contrast to the European tradition of balancing free speech with extensive limitations, U.S. exceptions are narrowly defined, primarily concerning situations such as imminent violence ("fighting words") or obscene material (Barendt 2005, 183–185).

As a result, this scenario could create "a virtually insurmountable obstacle to government regulation of deceptive campaign speech," which means that "any attempt to regulate false, non-defamatory statements of political speech" may be challenged as unconstitutional (Ng 2024, 19–20). The judicial order that suspended California's deepfake law during the 2024 presidential campaign, in agreement with claims of free speech violations, underscored this point (Katzenberger 2024).

According to the "AI Legislation Tracker" at the federal level, a report presented by the American Action Forum (2024), at least seven bills have been proposed to mitigate AI harms during elections. Among them are the Securing Elections from Deceptive AI Act, the AI Transparency in Elections Act of 2024, and the Preparing Election Administrators for AI Act. However, none have passed in Congress.

On the other hand, at the state level, 2024 witnessed "an explosion of state laws on AI," given that more than 100 laws were passed in 41 states on issue-specific bills related to non-consensual sexual imagery and political deepfakes. Only Colorado adopted a comprehensive regulation (Brennen and Sanderson 2024), while 18 states have passed some law regarding AI-manipulated media in elections.

The restrictions range from disclosure requirements, including watermarking and labeling and prescriptions when using synthetic material, to a restriction period of 90 days before election day (Larkin 2025). Interestingly, states like Alabama and New Mexico established that the disclaimers shall appear "in a size that is easily readable by the average viewer."

As emphasized by Larkin (2025), penalties for violating general rules vary from injunctive relief aimed at content removal—considered the most prevalent enforcement mechanism—to criminal charges (both felony and misdemeanor) and civil sanctions, such as fines. However, such financial penalties are smooth and funneled to candidates and supporters who paid for the advertising in general, varying from at least one hundred dollars to 10% of the spent (Colorado), to no more than one hundred dollars per violation (Utah), and up to ten thousand dollars (Oregon). Once again, regardless of the relatively incipient numbers of cases reported during the presidential campaign—such as the widely reported impersonation of Biden's robocalls and the false support attributed to Taylor Swift for Trump—these concerns are likely to grow, even in the face of some skepticism (Simon et al. 2023) as long as cheaper, easier, and more sophisticated tools become available.

Compounding this uncertain national regulatory environment, in early 2025, one of the first executive orders issued after President Trump's return to power was to revoke a 2023 Biden decree intended to mitigate AI's risks to consumers, minority groups, workers, and national security. At the same time, the new administration announced a $500 billion investment in AI infrastructure projects, strengthening its facilitating and enabling approach (UNESCO 2024, 27–29).

In addition, a second executive order was issued on the same day regarding "restoring freedom of speech and ending government censorship" on online platforms. By reinforcing

American doctrine on free speech and its extended boundaries, it seems highly unlikely that the country will either pass any national proposal on deepfakes—especially targeting disinformation or political speech—or engage in any international effort on this issue in the near future.

In turn, while there is currently no federal law explicitly addressing deepfake media involving non-consensual images, existing U.S. criminal laws could encompass threats related to sexual media, revenge porn, cyber harassment, and stalking. Similar to the political landscape mentioned, states are at the forefront of the debate on these issues (United States 2024b), although federal proposals are gaining traction (Elliott 2024).

In this vein, both Democratic and Republican Congress members are concerned and aim to reduce these risks. For example, the Disrupt Explicit Forged Images and Non-Consensual Edits Act—Defiance Act, presented by Alexandria Ocasio-Cortez, "improves rights to relief for individuals affected by non-consensual activities involving intimate digital forgeries" and grants up to $150,000 in civil damages (United States 2024a).

Similarly, the Take It Down Act, introduced by Ted Cruz, "would criminalise the publication of non-consensual intimate imagery, including AI-generated content, and requires social media and similar websites to have procedures in place to remove such content upon notification from a victim within 48 hours" (United States 2024b). Enforcement of this provision would be overseen by the Federal Telecommunications Commission—FTC.

Another noteworthy proposal is the Intimate Privacy Protection Act (United States 2024c). This bill establishes a duty of care and aims to eliminate the immunity granted to providers under the "safe harbor" provision of Section 230 of the Communications Decency Act. This would apply in cases where platforms fail to prevent or remove content related to cyberstalking, violations of intimate privacy, and digital forgeries. These latter are defined as any material created, manipulated, or altered to be virtually indistinguishable "from an authentic record of the speech, conduct, or appearance of an individual despite not being authentic of such speech, conduct or appearance."

Despite ongoing efforts and debates regarding the boundaries of rapidly evolving AI development, the recent alignment between the new federal administration and big tech companies does not indicate any imminent constraints or shifts in domestic regulation. In a worst-case scenario, a committee in the House of Representatives is advancing a bill proposing a ten-year freeze on state legislation regarding AI models or systems, thereby obstructing any new local enforcement initiatives (Hendrix 2025).

5.3.5 United Kingdom

Although it does not directly address general AI issues, the Online Service Act 2023 (United Kingdom 2023) is a prominent milestone in the United Kingdom regulatory landscape. This comprehensive framework, similar to the European Digital Services Act, was enacted to impose a set of duties of care on service providers to "identify, mitigate and manage the risks of harm" related to illegal content and activity, including those harmful to children's safety, such as sexual exploitation and abuse, adopting a systemic risk approach.

These obligations include prevention and transparency measures covering risk management and assessment, the design of functionalities and algorithms, the policies on terms of use, and content moderation, including taking down measures and blocking users, especially in relation to priority offenses. The Office of Communications—OFCOM is the authority responsible for enforcing and implementing the Online Services Act.

Additionally, regarding non-consent intimate material, this regulation criminalizes the intentional sharing or threat of sharing intimate photographs or film, that is, media that shows or appears to show another person in an intimate state (Sections 188–190)—by amending the Sexual Offences Act 2003. For such purpose, an interpretation clause clarifies that sharing means "by any means, gives or shows it to another person or makes it available to another person." As Kira (2024) highlights, these wide-ranging provisions overhaul previously narrow regulations—which also required the intent to cause distress or anxiety—and extend criminal liability to cover synthetic content.

Given that "one in three women have been victims of online abuse" and "the proliferation of these hyper-realistic images has grown at an alarming rate, causing devastating harm to victims" (United Kingdom 2025a), the UK government introduced new proposals to strengthen this framework against non-consensual intimate image abuse, primarily targeting adults. Currently, under the deliberation of Parliament, this initiative is part of an amendment to the Data (Use and Access) Bill. It will encompass not only the offense of sharing sexually explicit deepfakes but also the creation of such material, and will establish an unlimited fine for violations.

An additional pressing concern is related to the use of "nudification" apps, particularly due to the threats they pose to young girls. A recent report from the Children's Commissioner called not only for a legal ban on these tools but also for an immediate restriction or downranking of their access through search engines, social media sites, and app stores, as a result of risk assessment regulations (United Kingdom 2025b). The same authority recommends that providers of generative AI models be responsible for preventing and accountable for such harms.

Furthermore, concerning disinformation, it is noteworthy that the Online Service Act 2023 also introduced the false communications offense (Section 179). Under this provision, a person breaches the law by sending a message that they know to be false and, at the time of sending, intended to cause "non-trivial psychological or physical harm to a likely audience." However, given natural persons' liability for those who send a message, an exemption is made for news publishers, broadcasters, and service providers (Sections 180 and 182).

Despite the absence of general statutory regulation of AI in the UK, an extensive policy briefing from specialists (Judson et al. 2024) recommends several immediate and long-term actions to uphold democratic integrity. These measures embrace different players such as regulators, policymakers, platforms, AI companies, and political parties. For instance, "rather than create new sui generis rules for synthetic content, social media platforms should double down on the enforcement of rules against harmful speech and rules about advertising on their platforms," provided that these companies must guarantee safety by design. In addition, a report suggests that legislators should impose obligations on AI model developers, requiring them to undertake risk assessments.

In the context of effectively implementing the provisions of the Online Safety Act, Ofcom's draft codes on illegal harms and children's safety indicate that regulated tech companies—such as social media platforms, video-sharing sites, or search engines—can take robust measures to tackle illegal and harmful deepfakes. These measures include prevention, embedding, detection, and enforcement steps, such as "verification and labeling schemes, recommender algorithm design, content moderation, and user reporting and complaints" (Ofcom 2024). As stated by the core regulator, "these measures provide a strong starting point, but our ambition is always to go further," also by identifying "potential regulatory gaps in relation to deepfakes and generative AI."

5.3.6 Canada

Canadian institutions are also seeking to address the harms of deepfakes and digital threats. One of the significant legal initiatives consists of Bill 63-C—Online Harms Bill (Canada 2024a), introduced in February 2024. Among other objectives, this proposal aims to promote online safety, reduce harmful content, and ensure that the social media services operators are transparent and accountable for their duties under the Act, which includes acting responsibly, mitigating risk, and observing the duty to protect. For these purposes, it establishes the Digital Safety Commission of Canada as the authority responsible for oversight and enforcement of its provisions.

This act targets seven types of harmful content: (i) intimate content communicated without consent; (ii) content that sexually victimizes a child or revictimizes a survivor; (iii) content that induces a child to harm themselves; (iv) content used to bully a child; (v) content that foments hatred; (vi) content that incites violence; and (vii) content that incites violent extremism or terrorism. The first provision explicitly includes deepfake manipulations in the definition of intimate content shared without consent and imposes on social media services the duty to make such material inaccessible (Article 67-1) within 24 hours, either due to a user flagging it or through direct identification. Regarding the criminal consequences for individuals, publication, distribution, transmission, sale, or advertisement of an intimate image without consent currently constitutes an offense under the Canadian Criminal Code (Section 162.1). These penalties include imprisonment for a term of not more than five years.

In turn, the Canadian Elections Act (Canada 2023) has two noteworthy provisions that can be linked, to some extent, to political deepfakes. First, impersonation (Section 480) constitutes an offense when a person with the intent to mislead falsely represents themselves to be the Chief Electoral Officer, a member of the Chief Electoral Officer's staff, a party leader, a candidate, or a person who is authorized to act on a candidate's behalf. An exception is made for content intended as parody or satire. The second is misleading publications (Section 481), which consist of distributing, transmitting, or publishing, during an election period, "any material, regardless of its form, that purports to be made, distributed, transmitted or published by or under the authority of the Chief Electoral Officer, or political party, candidate or prospective candidate."

Concerning this topic, a report from the Chief Electoral Officer of Canada issued several recommendations to improve the response to emerging threats arising from AI and deepfakes (Canada 2024b). Among others, Recommendation 1.3 proposes expanding the impersonation provision in Section 480 to include misrepresentation through voice or image manipulation. This clarification aims to ensure that the provision applies to all types of misrepresentations involving the listed individuals. Additionally, Recommendation 1.4 seeks to extend the timeframe of these provisions beyond the election period. This raises an interesting point in light of the context of permanent electoral campaigning, suggesting that sectoral deepfakes regulation should cover the pre-election period and potentially the entire political process. The third suggestion to highlight is Recommendation 1.5, which proposes a transparency labeling mandate to ensure that "all paid and unpaid electoral communications (image, audio, video or text) distributed during a regulated pre-election and election period, or a contest, that have been generated or manipulated by AI should include a clear transparency marker."

Currently, there is no comprehensive AI legislation in force in Canada (G'sell 2024). However, Bill C-27, which introduced the Digital Charter Implementation Act of 2022 (Canada 2022), is worth mentioning. Once again, by adopting a risk-based approach, this proposal presents a specific part of the so-called Artificial Intelligence and Data Act—AIDA. Section 5.1 defines harm as any "a) physical or psychological harm to an individual; (b) damage to an individual's property; or (c) economic loss to an individual." Section 7.1 requires that those responsible for high-impact systems conduct risk assessments and implement measures to identify, assess, and mitigate the risks of harm or biased output that may result from the use of the system. Section 29 imposes administrative monetary penalties, and Section 33 grants the Minister of Innovation, Science, and Economic Development the authority to implement and appoint an Artificial Intelligence and Data Commissioner. Once passed, this framework will be a landmark development in the footsteps of the European AI Act, as discussed in the following text.

5.3.7 European Union

Finally, this chapter delves into the European panorama regarding deepfakes, considering the pivotal role played by the EU in shaping the debate on contemporary challenges in digital regulations, in general, and AI, in particular (Corredoira 2024). These leading efforts present a mix of complementary mandatory and voluntary measures, encompassing the EU Code of Conduct on Countering Illegal Hate Speech Online in 2016, revised in 2025 (Code of Conduct+), the General Data Protection Regulation and the revision of the Audio-visual Media Services Directive in 2018, the Cybersecurity Act (2019), the Digital Markets Act, the Digital Services Act (DSA) and the Strengthened Code of Practice on Disinformation in 2022 and, what mostly importantly, the Artificial Intelligence Act (AI Act) in 2024.

The European AI Act is a global landmark as it is the first-ever comprehensive legal framework on AI matters (European Union 2024a). Its main goal is to "promote the uptake of human-centric and trustworthy artificial intelligence while ensuring a high level of protection of health, safety, fundamental rights, including democracy [. . .] against the harmful effects of AI systems and to support innovation." In sum, AI algorithms and systems must comply with enshrined rights (Callejón 2023). Furthermore, its defines a deepfake as an "AI-generated or manipulated image, audio or video content that resembles existing persons, objects, places or other entities or events and would falsely appear to a person to be authentic or truthful," pursuant to its Article 3(60).

Given the so-called Brussels effect (Bradford 2020), regional European regulatory innovations in many areas, such as data protection, digital services, and AI, tend to be mirrored in various contexts around the globe, as inferred from the previous sections. While caution and critical thinking are essential when borrowing provisions, a seal of approval from the standards of the 27 democratic nations bloc often serves as a persuasive starting point for regulators abroad.

Longo (2024) points out that sectoral experiences in health and the environment inform the risk-based approach to the recent digital revolution. Years ago, seminal studies by Beck (1998) highlighted that society's technological developments are intrinsic to modern human life. To some extent, road traffic, rail franchises, and workplace safety (Moses 2013) have provoked similar legal debates on how to reduce or eliminate such harms. Following the internet revolution, emerging developments are just the latest chapter of this same story, although with challenges of seismic scale.

Therefore, associated risks should be managed, addressed, and prevented equitably and effectively. The AI Act adopts this approach by classifying these risks into categories: (a) minimal (as spam filters and videogames); (b) limited (general-purpose systems associated with transparency requirements such as chatbots); (c) high risk (e.g., critical infrastructure, employment, education, border control, administration of justice, and democratic processes); and (d) unacceptable (social scoring systems and person-based crime prediction).

Considering the focus of this chapter, limited and high-risk rules deserve special consideration due to their implications. Deployers and developers have obligations under the AI Act in these cases, particularly concerning transparency and risk assessment. First, deepfake applications are classified as a limited risk in general terms and for regular use. In other words, they are not prohibited as long as they do not convey any criminal offense and comply with disclosure requirements, even in the case of artistic material. Pursuant to Article 50(4), this informative approach is defined as follows:

> Deployers of an AI system that generates or manipulates image, audio or video content constituting a deep fake, shall disclose that the content has been artificially generated or manipulated. This obligation shall not apply where the use is authorised by law to detect, prevent, investigate or prosecute criminal offence. Where the content forms part of an evidently artistic, creative, satirical, fictional analogous work or programme, the transparency obligations set out in this paragraph are limited to disclosure of the existence of such generated or manipulated content in an appropriate manner that does not hamper the display or enjoyment of the work.
>
> *(European Union 2024a)*

On the other hand, electoral deepfakes are categorized as high risk due to their adverse effects on democracy and external interference in political behavior and the fundamental right to vote, as enshrined in Recital 62 of the EU AI Act. Such safeguards include an adequate and continuous process of risk assessment and mitigation, appropriate human oversight—"including the measures to facilitate the interpretation of the outputs of the AI system by the deployers"—and high-quality datasets feeding the system to reduce risks and discriminatory outcomes, as shown in Recital 65 to 72.

Additionally, in alignment with the European Commission's guidance, the Strengthened Code of Practice on Disinformation 2022 prohibits manipulative behavior through AI systems (European Commission 2022). As a self-regulatory operational measure endorsed by major online platforms, players in the advertising industry, fact-checkers, researchers, and civil society organizations, this agreement promotes a set of commitments related to harmful deepfakes and enhancing the integrity of online information. In particular, it aims to implement "more ambitious" measures than the pioneering 2018 Code, grounded in a shared understanding of unacceptable manipulative behavior and the necessity for transparency obligations and mitigation actions on deepfakes:

> Commitment 14. In order to limit impermissible manipulative behaviours and practices across their services, Relevant Signatories commit to put in place or further bolster policies to address both misinformation and disinformation across their services, and to agree on a cross-service understanding of manipulative behaviours, actors and practices not permitted on their services. Such behaviours and practices, which should periodically be reviewed in light with the latest evidence on the conducts and TTPs employed by malicious actors, such as the AMITT Disinformation Tactics, Techniques and Procedures Framework, include [. . .] Malicious deepfakes.
>
> Commitment 15. Relevant Signatories that develop or operate AI systems and that disseminate AI-generated and manipulated content through their services (e.g.,

> deepfakes) commit to take into consideration the transparency obligations and the list of manipulative practices prohibited under the proposal for Artificial Intelligence Act.
>
> *(European Commission 2022)*

In the same vein, the new regulation on Transparency and Targeting or Political Advertising—TTPA (European Union 2024b) introduced additional disclosure requirements, considering an increase in the "sophistication of disinformation, diversification of actors, the fast evolution of new technologies and intensified spread of information manipulation and interference in our democratic processes," as outlined in Recital 4. Article 19 establishes, among other things, the requirement to disclose "meaningful information on the use of artificial intelligence systems in the targeting or ad delivery of the political advertising."

Additionally, the regulation mandates keeping records of the techniques used, along with the relevant mechanisms and parameters, which somewhat resemble the requirements of Brazil's electoral ad library (Brazil 2024a). Although these obligations primarily cover official campaigns and do not encompass dark ads or third-party activities, they represent significant advances that will likely influence the debate in other jurisdictions.

With respect to pornographic deepfakes and non-consensual intimate images, it is also worth mentioning that the EU-level framework has relevant normative initiatives to combat these harms. This way, in 2024, the European Parliament passed a Directive on Combating Violence against Women and Domestic Violence (European Commission 2024). As stated by the Commission's President, "the most widespread forms of cyber-violence will be criminalized under the new rules, including the non-consensual sharing of intimate images (including deepfakes), cyberstalking, cyber harassment, misogynous hate speech, and 'cyber-flashing'."

This means that Member States that have not yet criminalized acts of "physical violence, as well as psychological, economic and sexual violence against women across the EU, both offline and online," must adapt their national laws accordingly. Ten Member States explicitly regulated this conduct. Regarding the guidelines on "Non-consensual sharing of intimate or manipulated material" (Article 5), the directive considers a criminal offense "producing, manipulating or altering and subsequently making accessible to the public, by means of ICT, images, videos or similar material that makes it appear as though a person is engaged in sexually explicit activities, without that person's consent." The penalty for this offense must include at least one year of imprisonment.

5.4 FINAL REMARKS

The objective of this chapter was to explore recent efforts in AI regulation, focusing on legal initiatives and gaps in addressing the risks posed by deepfakes. This rapidly evolving agenda is growing alongside the increasing popularity, affordability, pervasiveness, and realism of AI-generated applications.

The primary concerns of regulators relate to two issues. First, the acceleration and sophistication of dis/misinformation—encompassing the electoral process as well as a wide range of political topics such as climate change, public policy, and scams.

Second, there are significant concerns regarding non-consensual intimate images and explicit deepfakes, which often target women and girls. Beyond these specific approaches, comprehensive discussions on AI—following the European landmark framework—are also focusing on measures to mitigate the harms of deepfakes, with particular emphasis on their impacts, risk assessment, and the obligations associated with such systems.

In addition to the regulatory scopes, the study explored the primary focus of the strategies employed in each national or regional response. Specifically, it examined whether measures included criminal laws as well as informative and preventive duties. Although the protection of women against violence through intimate deepfakes was often the initial focus of response and criminalization, in light of the spread of individual perpetrations, disclosure obligations, and risk assessments have become essential to tackle such harms on a large scale.

In other words, moving beyond a purely end-user perspective, either offenders or political actors, the chapter underscored that more recent and comprehensive regulations aim to fill this initial gap. Specifically, these regulations require companies to take proactive measures rather than relying solely on passive notice-and-takedown mechanisms and hold developers and providers accountable for their systems and their impacts. Such actions align with the UN Recommendations to ensure safe, secure, and trustworthy AI by "carrying out human rights risk assessments to proactively minimize societal risks and mitigate potential harms, including to women, children, youth and other groups in situations of vulnerability and marginalisation" (United Nations 2024a).

As deepfakes illustrate, it has become widely acknowledged that there is no silver bullet for addressing disinformation and other contemporary harms associated with emerging technologies, which resembles a complex cat-and-mouse game. From a legal and administrative perspective, in addition to strengthening penalties and fines, another preventive aspect involves fostering cooperation schemes among multiple stakeholders, as highlighted in different studies and recommendations. The EU Codes of Practice on Disinformation and Code of Conduct on Countering Illegal Hate Speech Online, built on the provisions of DSA, as well as the agreements between tech companies and the Brazilian Electoral Court, reinforce this approach.

Another pitfall relates to enforcement or national oversight authorities. At this early point, it is unclear whether a centralized model will prevail over existing sectoral agencies. Despite some overlapping risks, a general coordination body or national commission, as proposed by the South Korean AI Act and Brazilian AI Bill, seems to be emerging as a standard.

In summary, some practical recommendations for policymakers and legal practitioners regarding the AI deepfakes regulation include the following:

- Conduct regular public consultations to gather critical insights and the latest developments from the scientific community, civil society, and both private and public sectors
- Foster cooperation schemes among multiple stakeholders, encompassing voluntary agreements and cross-border collaborations
- Consider implementing transparency rules, risk assessment, preventive obligations, and shared liability for developers and providers
- Establish informative measures and develop educational awareness campaigns
- Introduce specific offenses and increase criminal and civil penalties
- Strengthen institutional capacities by ensuring the availability of technical, human, and budgetary resources for independent regulation, effective monitoring, response, and enforcement, whether through a centralized agency or a sector-specific design

To conclude, as Bijker (2017) points out, technological models and artifacts are shaped by various social factors. This non-determinist conception suggests that a contingent cyclical movement could reframe an initial approach through interaction with relevant groups, particularly in the political debate and public backlash.

Despite this, the timing of technological regulation often encounters the so-called Collingridge Dilemma, which presents a two-fold challenge and requires dynamic approaches. In the early stage, regulation could be problematic due to the lack of information about the potential impact. At a later stage, regulation may turn more difficult as the technology becomes more entrenched, "making any changes demanded by regulator expensive to implement" (Moses 2013). As G'sell (2024) emphasizes, "governments cannot wait until they have perfect and complete information before they act, because doing so may be too late."

In the midst of uncertainty regarding the extent of emerging technological capabilities and risks—directly linked to an unprecedented concentration of power—alongside ongoing political turmoil and geopolitical tensions, each legal authority strives to regulate AI in general and address the harms of deepfakes in particular. These increasing harms are mapped.

As highlighted throughout this chapter, each jurisdiction aims to protect fundamental rights and values in light of its specific historical, economic, and social context. Given the pervasive and cross-national effects of AI, establishing a global, representative, and accountable—governance body would be beneficial for setting international standards and promoting cooperation and innovation (United Nations 2024b; G´sell 2024, 405–406).

Several common legal paths are already available at this stage and could significantly play a role in enforcing, preventing, and mitigating risks associated with these services—regardless of their benefits. However, potential solutions to the impacts of deepfakes will undoubtedly require a multidisciplinary toolkit that involves legal, technical, and educational efforts holistically.

REFERENCES

American Action Forum. 2024. *AI Legislation Tracker*. https://www.americanactionforum.org/list-of-proposed-ai-bills-table/ (accessed January 19, 2025).

Australia. 2021. *Online Safety Act*. https://www.legislation.gov.au/C2021A00076/latest/text (accessed January 12, 2025).

Australia. 2024a. *Interim Report of the Select Committee on Adopting Artificial Intelligence*. The Senate. https://www.aph.gov.au/Parliamentary_Business/Committees/Senate/Adopting_Artificial_Intelligence_AI/AdoptingAI/Interim_report (accessed January 11, 2025).

Australia. 2024b. *Criminal Code Amendment (Deepfake Sexual Material) Act 2024*. https://parlinfo.aph.gov.au/parlInfo/download/legislation/bills/r7205_aspassed/toc_pdf/24071b01.pdf;fileType=application%2Fpdf (accessed January 11, 2025).

Australia. 2024c. *Communications Legislation Amendment (Combatting Misinformation and Disinformation) Bill 2024*. https://parlinfo.aph.gov.au/parlInfo/download/legislation/bills/r7239_first-reps/toc_pdf/24106b01.PDF (accessed January 25, 2025).

Barendt, E. 2005. *Freedom of Speech*. 2nd ed. Oxford: Oxford University Press.

Beck, U. 1998. *La sociedade del riesgo: hacia una nova modernidade*. Barcelona: Paidós.

Benkler, Y., R. Faris and H. Roberts. 2018. *Network Propaganda*. Oxford: Oxford University Press.

Bijker, W. 2017. Why and How Technology Matters. In *The Oxford Handbook of Contextual Political Analysis*, ed. R. Goodin and C. Tilly, 681–706. Oxford: Oxford University Press.

Black, J. and A. Murray. 2019. Regulating AI and Machine Learning: Setting the Regulatory Agenda. *European Journal of Law and Technology*, 10(3):1–21.

Bond, S. 2024. A Political Consultant Faces Charges and Fines for Biden Deepfake Robocalls. *NPR*. https://www.npr.org/2024/05/23/nx-s1-4977582/fcc-ai-deepfake-robocall-biden-new-hampshire-political-operative (accessed June 29, 2024).

Bradford, A. 2020. *The Brussels Effect: How the European Union Rules the World*. Oxford: Oxford University Press.

Brazil. 2024a. *Resolution n. 23.732/2024 on Electoral Advertising*. Superior Electoral Court. https://www.tse.jus.br/legislacao/compilada/res/2024/resolucao-no-23-732-de-27-de-fevereiro-de-2024 (accessed January 4, 2025).

Brazil. 2024b. *Local Elections 2024 and Actions Report*. Superior Electoral Court. Permanent Program against Disinformation. https://www.justicaeleitoral.jus.br/desinformacao/arquivos/programa-de-acoes-e-resultados-2024.pdf. (accessed January 4, 2025).

Brazil. 2024c. *Brazilian AI Bill—PL n. 2338/2023*. Federal Senate. https://legis.senado.leg.br/sdleg-getter/documento?dm=9881643&ts=1735605226813&disposition=inline. (accessed January 2025).

Brazil. 2025. AGU Seeks Legal Action Against Meta to Curb Social Media Scams That Use Government Symbols, Manipulated Images. *Social Communications Secretariat of the Presidency of the Republic*. https://www.gov.br/secom/en/latest-news/2025/04/agu-seeks-legal-action-against-meta-to-curb-social-media-scams-that-use-government-symbols-manipulated-images (accessed May 4, 2025).

Brennen, S. B. and Z. Sanderson. 2024. *The State of State Technology Policy: 2024 Report*. New York: Center for Social Media and Politics and NYU Center on Tech Policy.

Caballero, B. I., B. Ammon, C. Gomes et al. (eds.). 2024. *Construindo Consensos: Deep Fakes nas Eleições de 2024 Relatório das decisões dos TREs sobre Deep fakes*. Brasília: LIA-IDP-ETHICS 4AI.

Callejón, F. B. 2023. *La constitución del algoritmo*. 2nd ed. Zaragoza: Fundación Manuel Giménez Abad.

Canada. 2022. *The Digital Charter Implementation Act* (Bill C-27). https://www.parl.ca/DocumentViewer/en/44-1/bill/C-27/first-reading (accessed December 19, 2024).

Canada. 2023. *Canada Elections Act*. https://laws-lois.justice.gc.ca/PDF/E-2.01.pdf (accessed December 19, 2024).

Canada. 2024a. *Online Harms Bill* (Bill C-63). House of Commons. https://www.parl.ca/DocumentViewer/en/44-1/bill/C-63/first-reading. (accessed December 8, 2024).

Canada. 2024b. *Protecting Against Threats to the Electoral Process*. Chief Electoral Officer of Canada. https://www.elections.ca/res/rep/oth/prthr/rpt/rpt_e.pdf (accessed January 7, 2024).

Centenera M. and J. Criales. 2023. Argentina's Presidential Campaign Enters the Muck of Electoral Fraud Allegations. *El Pais*. International. https://english.elpais.com/international/2023-11-11/argentinas-presidential-campaign-enters-the-muck-of-electoral-fraud-allegations.html (accessed on April 5, 2025).

Chesney B. and D. Citron. 2019. Deep Fakes: A Looming Challenge for Privacy, Democracy, and National Security. *California Law Review*, 107:1753–1820.

Corredoira L. 2024. Democracia y desinformación, respuestas regulatorias de la Unión Europea para el fortalecimento de la democracia y câmbios de rumbo del paquete de servicios digitales. In *Democracia y desinformación: nuevas formas de polarización, discursos de odio y campañas en redes. Respuestas regulatorias de Europa y América Latina*, eds. M. Serrano and L. Corrodoira, 267–294. Madrid: Dykinson.

Cruz, M., N. Santos, R. Carreiro et al. 2024. *AI in the 2024 Brazilian Elections*. Salvador and São Paulo: Aláfia Lab & Data Privacy Brasil.

Dixon, R. 2020. How to Compare Constitutionally: An Essay in Honour of Mark Tushnet. *UNSW Law Research Paper*, No. 21. http://doi.org/10.2139/ssrn.3603683 (accessed December 1, 2024).

Elliott, V. 2024. The US Needs Deepfake Porn Laws. These States Are Leading the Way. *Wired*. https://www.wired.com/story/deepfake-ai-porn-laws/ (accessed January 25, 2025).
European Commission. 2022. *Strengthened Code of Practice on Disinformation*. https://digital-strategy.ec.europa.eu/en/library/2022-strengthened-code-practice-disinformation (accessed December 21, 2024).
European Commission. 2024. *Commission Welcomes Political Agreement on New Rules to Combat Violence Against Women and Domestic Violence*. https://ec.europa.eu/commission/presscorner/detail/es/ip_24_649 (accessed December 22, 2024).
European Union. 2024a. *Artificial Intelligence Act*. Regulation (EU) 2024/1689. https://eur-lex.europa.eu/eli/reg/2024/1689/oj/eng (accessed November 30, 2024).
European Union. 2024b. *Transparency and Targeting or Political Advertising*. Regulation (EU) 2024/900. https://eur-lex.europa.eu/eli/reg/2024/900/oj (accessed December 8, 2024).
Gaba, M. 2019. Fake News e Deep Fakes. *#DDA Desafíos de la democracia en la América latina*, 4:29–33. Buenos Aires: Transparencia Electoral.
Gonzales, A. and R. Bragatto. 2024. The Politics of Content Moderation by Digital Platforms. In *Democracy Under Attack: Social Media and Disinformation in Brazilian Elections*, eds. M. von Bülow, L. Avritzer and E. Santana, 15–33. Cham: Springer
G'sell, F. 2024. *Regulating under Uncertainty Governance Options for Generative AI*. Stanford Cyberpolicy Center. https://doi.org/10.2139ssrn.4918704 (accessed November 2, 2024).
Hendrix, J. 2025. US House Committee Advances 10-Year Moratorium on State AI Regulation. *Tech Policy Press*. https://www.techpolicy.press/us-house-committee-advances-10-year-moratorium-on-state-ai-regulation/ (accessed May 18, 2025).
Hill, L., M. Douglas and R. Baltutis. 2022. *How and Why to Regulate False Political Advertising in Australia*. Singapore: Palgrave Macmillan.
Hirschl, R. 2014. *Comparative Matters*. Oxford: Oxford University Press.
Howard, P. 2020. *Lie Machines*. New Haven: Yale University Press.
Judson, E., S. Fisher, W. Howard et al. 2024. *Synthetic Politics: Preparing Democracy for Generative AI*. London: Demos, UCL Digital Speech Lab.
Jungherr, A. 2023. Artificial Intelligence and Democracy: A Conceptual Framework. *Social Media + Society*, 9(3):1–14.
Kalra, A., M. Vengatti and D. Pandya. 2024. Deepfakes of Bollywood Stars Spark Worries of AI Meddling in India Election. *Reuters*. https://www.reuters.com/world/india/deepfakes-bollywood-stars-spark-worries-ai-meddling-india-election-2024-04-22/
Katzenberger, T. 2024. Judge Blocks California Deepfakes Law That Sparked Musk-Newsom Row. *Politico*. https://www.politico.com/news/2024/10/02/california-law-block-political-deepfakes-00182277 (accessed January 26, 2025).
Keane, J. 2020. *The New Despotism*. Cambridge, MA: Harvard University Press.
Kira, B. 2024. When Non-Consensual Intimate Deepfakes Go Viral: The Insufficiency of the UK Online Safety Act. *Computer Law & Security Review*, 54:106024.
Larkin, C. J. 2025. Regulating Election Deepfakes: A Comparison of State Laws. *Tech Policy Press*. https://www.techpolicy.press/regulating-election-deepfakes-a-comparison-of-state-laws/ (accessed on January 25, 2025).
Longo, E. 2024. La disciplina del "rischio digitale". In *La regolazione europea della società digitale*. eds. C. Simone, A. Iannuzzi, E. Longo et al., 53–72. Torino: Giappichelli.
Moses, L. B. 2013. How to Think about Law, Regulation and Technology: Problems with 'Technology' as a Regulatory Target. *Law, Innovation and Technology*, 5(1):1–20.
Mounk, Y. 2018. *The People vs. Democracy*. Cambrigde: Harvard University Press.
Murray, A. 2013. *Information Technology Law*. 2nd ed. Oxford: Oxford University Press.
Ng, Y. 2024. *Truth in Political Advertising Laws: Design, Operation, Effectiveness and Recommendations for Reform*. Final Report. Monash University.
OECD. 2024a. *Recommendation of the Council on Information Integrity*. https://legalinstruments.oecd.org/en/instruments/OECD-LEGAL-0505 (accessed on December 17, 2024).

OECD. 2024b. *Recommendation of the Council on Artificial Intelligence.* https://legalinstruments.oecd.org/en/instruments/oecd-legal-0449 (accessed on December 17, 2024).

Ofcom. 2024. *Deepfake Defences: Mitigating the Harms of Deceptive Deepfakes.* Discussion Paper. https://www.ofcom.org.uk/siteassets/resources/documents/consultations/discussion-papers/deepfake-defences/deepfake-defences.pdf?v=370754 (accessed December 18, 2025).

Ray, S. 2023. Imran Khan—Pakistan's Jailed Ex-Leader—Uses AI Deepfake to Address Online Election Rally. *Forbes.* Middle East. https://www.forbesmiddleeast.com/innovation/artificial-intelligence-machine-learning/imran-khanpakistans-jailed-ex-leaderuses-ai-deepfake-to-address-online-election-rally (accessed January 9, 2025).

Simon, F., S. Altay and H. Mercier. 2023. Misinformation Reloaded? Fears About the Impact of Generative AI on Misinformation Are Overblown. *Misinformation Review. Harvard Kennedy School*, 4(5):1–11.

Singer, P. and E. Brooking. 2018. *Like War: The Weaponization of Social Media.* Boston: Eamon Dola.

Smith, G. and J. Brake. 2024. South Korea Confronts a Deepfake Crisis. *East Asia Forum*, 19 November. https://eastasiaforum.org/2024/11/19/south-korea-confronts-a-deepfake-crisis (accessed December 1, 2024).

South Korea. 2023. *Amendments to the Public Official Election Act.* National Election Commission. https://www.nec.go.kr/site/nec/ex/bbs/View.do?cbIdx=1084&bcIdx=197195 (accessed December 23, 2024).

South Korea. 2024a. *Partial Amendment Bill to the Special Act on the Punishment of Sexual Crimes.* https://likms.assembly.go.kr/bill/billDetail.do?billId=PRC_V2K4Y0U9B2E4C2V1M0M5S2Y-0W4C3W9 (accessed November 29, 2024).

South Korea. 2024b. *90 Days Until National Assembly Elections: Election Campaigns Using Deepfake Restricted.*February https://www.nec.go.kr/site/eng/ex/bbs/View.do?cbIdx=1270&bcIdx=226657 (accessed December 3, 2024).

South Korea. 2024c. *Basic Law on the Development of Artificial Intelligence and Creation of Trust Base.* https://likms.assembly.go.kr/bill/billDetail.do?billId=PRC_R2V4H1W1T2K5M1O6E4Q9T0V7Q9S0U0 (accessed December 23, 2024).

Stockwell, S. 2024. *AI-Enabled Influence Operations: Threat Analysis of the 2024 UK and European Elections.* London: Alan Turing Institute, CEAnS.

Turnbull. T. 2025. Woman's Deepfake Betrayal By Close Friend: 'Every Moment Turned into Porn. *BBC.* https://www.bbc.com/news/articles/cm21j341m31o (accessed April 19, 2025).

UNESCO. 2024. *Consultation Paper on AI Regulation: Emerging Approaches Around the World.* Digital Transformation. CI/DIT/2024/CP/01. August. https://unesdoc.unesco.org/ark:/48223/pf0000390979 (accessed November 30, 2024).

United Kingdom. 2023. *Online Service Act.* https://www.legislation.gov.uk/ukpga/2023/50 (accessed December 8, 2024).

United Kingdom. 2025a. *Government Crackdown on Explicit Deepfakes.* https://www.gov.uk/government/news/government-crackdown-on-explicit-deepfakes (accessed January 17, 2025).

United Kingdom. 2025b. One Day This Could Happen to Me' Children, Nudification Tools and Sexually Explicit Deepfakes. *Children's Commissioner.* Report. https://www.childrenscommissioner.gov.uk/resource/children-nudification-tools-and-sexually-explicit-deepfakes/ (accessed May 3, 2025).

United Nations. 2024a. *United Nations Global Principles for Information Integrity: Recommendations for Multi-stakeholder Action.* https://www.un.org/sites/un2.un.org/files/un-global-principles-for-information-integrity-en.pdf (accessed December 1, 2024).

United Nations. 2024b. *Governing AI for humanity: Final Report.* High-level Advisory Body on Artificial Intelligence. https://www.un.org/sites/un2.un.org/files/governing_ai_for_humanity_final_report_en.pdf. (accessed December 23, 2024).

United Nations. 2024c. *United Nations Convention against Cybercrime.* Office on Drugs and Crime. https://documents.un.org/api/symbol/access?j=N2442674&t=pdf (accessed May 5, 2025).

United States. 2024a. Rep. Ocasio-Cortez Leads Bipartisan, Bicameral Introduction of DEFIANCE Act to Combat Use of Non-Consensual, Sexually-Explicit "Deepfake" Media. *House of Representatives.*

https://ocasio-cortez.house.gov/media/press-releases/rep-ocasio-cortez-leads-bipartisan-bicameral-introduction-defiance-act-combat (accessed January 18, 2025).
United States. 2024b. Sen. Cruz Leads Colleagues in Unveiling Landmark Bill to Protect Victims of Deepfake Revenge Porn. *US Senate Committee on Commerce. Science and Transportation.* https://www.commerce.senate.gov/services/files/747FB142-F25D-4BB2-83D3-50FD5D44553E. (accessed January 18, 2025).
United States. 2024c. *Intimate Privacy Protection Act.* H. R. 9187, 118th Congress. https://www.congress.gov/118/bills/hr9187/BILLS-118hr9187ih.pdf. (accessed January 19, 2025).
Vaccari, C. and A. Chadwick. 2020. Deepfakes and Disinformation: Exploring the Impact of Synthetic Political Video on Deception, Uncertainty, and Trust in News. *Social Media + Society*, January–March, 1–13.
World Economic Forum. 2025. *The Global Risks Report.* 20th ed. https://reports.weforum.org/docs/WEF_Global_Risks_Report_2025.pdf (accessed January 25, 2025).

Chapter 6

Technical Solutions

Algorithms and Systems to Identify Deepfakes

Cosmina-Mihaela Rosca

6.1 INTRODUCTION

In Romania, at the beginning of 2024, a private electricity company was promoted through video content in which prominent political figures falsely claimed the trading of the company's shares. The company was the target of disinformation due to a deepfake, issuing numerous press releases to inform customers about these smear attacks due to the deepfake [1].

Deepfake is modifying audio–video content using artificial intelligence (AI) techniques, leveraging deep learning (DL) methods. The goal of these modifications is to generate realistic content that convinces viewers that the audio or video features a specific person, although it is generated by AI techniques. These technologies imitate real people or events to persuade the audience that the new representations are authentic [2].

In the literature, I have identified that deepfakes can take various forms, each utilizing advanced but distinct AI techniques. One of the most commonly used techniques is face swapping, which employs Generative Adversarial Networks (GANs) to replace faces in images or videos. GANs combine two neural networks: the generator, which creates synthetic images, and the discriminator, which evaluates their authenticity, continually improving the realism through adversarial training [3, 4].

Another technique for generating deepfake content is voice cloning. In the study [5], I identified that this method generates synthetic audio to mimic a person's intonations and speech patterns. Additionally, deepfakes are encountered in textual content by using stylistic patterns. This type of deepfake reproduces a person's writing style, including vocabulary, tone, and sentence structure.

Among the technologies that detect deepfake content are AI-specific services. These technologies perform facial analyses, stylistic analyses, or sentiment analyses. For example, Azure AI services enable sentiment analysis and the identification of patterns in complex data, whether textual or visual [6].

Deepfakes can create fabricated events or alter existing media to manipulate perception. These manipulations may include changes to video gestures or behaviors, while multimodal deepfakes combine audio, video, and text to create convincingly fake content, complicating detection processes [3]. The paper [7] analyzes deepfake characteristics at the text level, considering that an individual's writing style involves certain unique characteristics that distinguish it from someone else's text. In this case, the issue arises of a deepfake text generated by an AI tool or written by another person and claimed by someone else.

Algorithms for detecting deepfakes have been improved through hybrid methods, such as combining convolutional neural networks (CNNs) with long-short-term memory (LSTM)

DOI: 10.1201/9781003539032-6

networks. CNNs identify visual structures in images, while LSTMs analyze long-term dependencies in sequential data. In the study [8], I found that this hybrid approach increases the accuracy of deepfake detection.

The architecture of GANs allows the creation of realistic content, raising concerns about misinformation and ethics. For example, the study [9] proposes an advanced GAN model that uses spectral normalization and self-attention mechanisms to generate high-quality synthetic images, including celebrity faces. These techniques improve the training process regarding spatiotemporal complexity and produce results that accurately reflect reality, even when the content is AI-generated [10].

I also identified several events in the literature that highlight the dual potential of deepfake technology for both positive and harmful purposes. For example, a YouTuber, Shamook, created a deepfake of a younger Luke Skywalker to illustrate the deepfake potential in the entertainment industry. At the same time, a modified video of Speaker Nancy Pelosi presents the risks of falsified media for misleading the public. Other examples involve personalities such as Barack Obama or Mark Zuckerberg, who identify privacy concerns. At the same time, these incidents raise discussions about the ethical implications of this type of technology [11].

The pandemic context has accelerated the use of online technologies. Amid the turmoil of events, the technologies used exposed vulnerabilities at various levels, including those in the category of deepfakes [12]. The increase in digital interactions led to these falsifications by creating trust among the audience. Several AI algorithms are analyzed in the specialized literature to detect visual or textual manipulations through facial recognition or user data analysis. In this way, continuous efforts are being made to prevent fraud at the level of digital interactions [13, 14].

6.1.1 Deepfake Legal Implications

Studying the article [15] from the literature, I noticed that international legislation on deepfake technology is different from one region to another. The United States considers external threats and national defense as the National Defense Authorization Act. The internal issues related to deepfakes are ignored in the United States. States like California and Texas adopted laws to prevent these issues locally. Since 2023, strict rules on consent and transparency for AI-generated content have been imposed in China while increasing censorship. In the United Kingdom, issues related to the modification of audio–video content are addressed through a dedicated law on online content, which punishes the unauthorized dissemination of non-consensual pornography. The European Union positions itself as a global leader by promoting AI in the controlled use of AI technologies. Legislation such as the General Data Protection Regulation and the Digital Services Act protects personal data and online consumers from the risks of deepfake technology and uncontrolled content usage. Although South Africa emphasizes the "right to identity," it does not have specific regulations for deepfakes, relying more on general principles of law.

In the work [16], I identified that challenges related to intellectual property are associated with Generative Artificial Intelligence (GAI) systems. This study analyzes intellectual property rights in the context of deepfakes. The copyright rules are discussed in the same paper [16] for the unauthorized use of the original content. GAI models have input and output content such as text, images, audio, and video. This output content is contaminated with AI patterns. The unauthorized use, derivative works, combined content, and plagiarism violate principles specific to the authenticity of the content. I believe legislative reforms should address these issues by considering new categories of intellectual property, establishing clear licensing frameworks, and promoting transparency in AI services.

Legislation related to deepfakes must consider all forms of content that can circulate online, including video, photography, audio, and text. Research from the work [17] recommends including terms such as "synthetic media" or "AI-generated manipulated content" to indicate their origin. Additionally, the study highlights that there should be warnings for consumers about the implications of AI in creating deepfakes, clearly separating them from authorized modifications, such as those made with Photoshop. Furthermore, it would be useful to include notions related to "false" or "manipulated" content to protect legitimate uses of AI, such as those in art or medicine.

In the judicial context, I found that introducing digitally fabricated evidence complicates the process, requiring new standards and authentication techniques to protect the original content [18, 19]. When the content is used to generate entertainment material, a new framework should clarify the methods employed in these processes. A legislative framework specifying the rules that must be respected in all states should be proposed worldwide. I believe implementing active measures by the authorities could resolve the deepfake issues.

6.1.2 Deepfake Technology

Deepfake technology creates realistic faces, modifies facial expressions, and changes individuals' identities in images and videos. According to research [20], I have identified five techniques used in content-generating deepfake technology:

- Entire face synthesis, which implements non-existent but realistic faces
- Identity swapping, which replaces a person's face with the face of another person
- Attribute manipulation, which alters facial characteristics influencing age, gender, or skin tone
- Facial expression swapping while preserving the individual's identity
- Various methods that deform the face or synchronize audio–video content

These methods are utilized by different software tools such as StyleGAN (a GAN-based model capable of generating high-resolution, photorealistic images) and FaceApp (a mobile application that uses neural networks (NNs) for realistic facial transformations). These variations are active in the entertainment sector but can also be used for malicious activities such as misinformation, fraud, and identity falsification, raising ethical and security concerns [20, 21].

In the specialized literature, I have identified three categories of generations that are distinguished by the type of datasets used in training [22]:

- **First-Generation Datasets:** They use datasets such as UADFV (98 videos), Deepfake-TIMIT (960 videos), and Fake Faces in the Wild (150 videos). These contain low-resolution videos created in controlled environments with limited diversity.
- **Second-Generation Datasets:** Deepfake Detection (3,068 fake videos) and Celeb-DF (5,639 fake videos) introduced high-resolution videos with advanced face-swapping techniques.
- **Third-Generation Datasets:** Datasets such as DeepFake Detection Challenge (DFDC) (100,000 fake videos), WildDeepfake (3,509 fake videos), and ForgeryNet (220,000 videos) include real-world scenarios, diverse manipulation techniques, and perturbations such as compression and noise.

These datasets enable model training and highlight the challenges of replicating the complexity of real-world conditions. To address the detection of deepfakes, the paper [23] proposes a dynamic model focused on individual facial parts, specifically the cornea, eyes, nose, and mouth. Specialized CNN models were developed for each facial part, achieving high F1-scores—with the cornea model excelling at 99.7%. Combining these models improved performance further, with ensembles of two models achieving F1-scores of up to 99.9%.

In the paper [24], I evaluated several AI video content generation tools for scientific purposes. The five analyzed tools were evaluated based on visual quality, content relevance, consistency, authenticity, and user experience. I assigned scores to each category to differentiate between them and noted that Invideo.ai is the most performant.

Key Insights

- Deepfake detection uses AI techniques to identify visual manipulations.
- The use of frequency and spatiotemporal features to identify specific artifacts in deepfake images.
- The vulnerabilities of facial recognition systems are based on the generation of synthetic faces capable of deceiving authentication systems through techniques such as morphing or spoofing.

Using AI tools requires a large volume of data for training phases to generate a video stream that reproduces reality with maximum fidelity. The training phase also requires a high-performance hardware infrastructure, and these implications translate into high costs [25, 26].

This chapter proposes an algorithm for detecting deepfake images without using AI-based methods that require large datasets and extensive training time. The algorithm's main hypothesis is that the normal Euclidean distances between key points of the face indicate digital forgeries.

6.1.3 GAN Models on Deepfake Generation and Detection

GANs are used at both the video and audio levels, with voice synthesis enabling the reproduction of artificial speech. Through such an approach, the public can be deceived regarding certain statements made by an individual. Coupling deepfake modifications at the audio–video level can have disastrous political implications. The biggest issues in this sector are reputation damage and the spread of false information inciting violence. For instance, a prototype deepfake detection model presented in the paper [27] achieved 70% accuracy, successfully exposing 35 out of 50 deepfake videos but misclassifying 15 due to their convincing quality.

GAN-based image generation methods often leave artifact patterns, unintended anomalies, or distortions in generated images that aid in fake detection. However, these methods become less effective if artifacts are minimized. FakePolisher, a novel approach presented in the research [28], reconstructs deepfake images using a learned linear dictionary—a mathematical model that represents images using a set of basic functions learned from data—to minimize artifacts. Evaluations indicate that FakePolisher decreases the accuracy of the three leading deepfake detection methods by as much as 93%.

The role of datasets in training and evaluating deepfake detection models cannot be overstated. The DFDC dataset, as discussed by Neekhara et al. [29], is one of the largest datasets designed explicitly for this purpose. It provides a rich resource for developing and benchmarking detection algorithms, containing thousands of deepfake videos with various manipulations. Similarly, the availability of diverse datasets such as CelebA, Celeb-DF (datasets comprising high-quality deepfake images and videos of celebrities), and FaceForensics++ (a dataset containing manipulated video sequences for forensic analysis) (FF++) has accelerated research in this field. These datasets enable the development of more sophisticated detection models by providing ample training data that captures a wide range of manipulation techniques [30].

In addition to detection methods, proactive strategies to combat deepfakes include embedding watermarks—which are invisible or visible markers embedded into media content to verify their authenticity—and utilizing GANs to create deepfake-resistant content. To prevent the spread of deepfake content, I have identified several strategies in the specialized literature. Some of these propose using GANs to embed watermarks into video frames. The paper [31] presents an accuracy of 99.7% for such an approach. This idea is perfect, as the attempt to remove the watermark will affect the quality of the frames.

Another 18-layer CNN model proposed in the paper [32] uses image classification for deepfake identification. The paper mentions an accuracy of 96.24%. Also, in the paper [32], I noticed a new metric for image recognition, which achieved an accuracy of over 95% for known models and 92% for previously unseen models.

A detection model presented in the article [33], tested on the FF++ and Celeb-DF datasets, achieves an Area Under the Curve (AUC) exceeding 99% in within-dataset evaluations. The model uses 32 frames per video and focuses on facial regions, employing EfficientNet as the backbone network. EfficientNet is a family of CNN architectures that scales depth, width, and resolution in a balanced manner to improve accuracy. Cross-dataset evaluations reveal that the model outperforms existing models. The results presented in the paper [33] illustrate an AUC of 76.5% on the Celeb-DF dataset.

In the literature, there are techniques involving manual distillation. At the same time, attention mechanisms are implemented into these techniques to increase detection performance [34]. Attention mechanisms are models focused on particular aspects of the input data. These NN models are the most popular ones in the field of features for any task. Manual distillation refers to transferring knowledge from a larger, more complex model to a smaller one, often to reduce computational requirements while maintaining performance. The paper [35] proposes a CNN-based approach that incorporates attention to target specific regions, increasing the model's ability to discern subtle artifacts indicative of deepfakes. This aligns with the findings presented in the paper [36], which utilize ensemble CNNs—combining multiple CNN models—to analyze periocular data, which is information related to the region around the eye, including the eye itself, eyelids, and surrounding skin. These studies further emphasize the potential of specialized architectures in increasing deepfake detection.

Another deepfake detection model that uses the Laplacian operator to analyze edge sharpness and consistency in video frames is presented in the paper [37]. The Laplacian operator is used in image processing to detect areas of rapid intensity change, identifying edges within an image. By comparing the Laplacian values of face frames and nearby non-face frames, the method identifies inconsistencies caused by deepfake manipulations, such as blurriness and noise at facial edges. Tested on the Kaggle DFDC dataset, which is a dataset provided by Kaggle for a competition aimed at developing algorithms to detect deepfake videos, the approach demonstrated fast detection of tampered videos with acceptable accuracy (specific values were not mentioned in the paper [37]).

6.1.4 AI Methods for Identifying and Combating Deepfakes

Deepfakes contain threats to privacy, societal security, and national stability. As mentioned in the paper, advanced methods have been developed to detect manipulated videos, images, audio, and tweets [37]. LipForensics, a deepfake detection technique, focuses on unnatural mouth movements for video detection, achieving up to 99.73% accuracy on FF++ and Celeb-DF datasets. LipForensics analyzes the synchronization between lip movements and speech, detecting discrepancies that may indicate manipulation.

Transitioning to motion analysis, the study [38] introduces a novel motion-style-based deepfake detection and identity recognition system. The approach leverages a two-stream CNN to analyze motion styles, including gestures, facial muscle movements, and subconscious head motions. These are unique to individuals and less likely to be accurately replicated in deepfake videos—a two-stream CNN processes spatial and temporal information simultaneously, capturing appearance and motion cues. The proposed system extracts points from video frames, transforming them into motion representations for analysis. The architecture includes a cross-modal transfer network (TransNet) that links motion-style identity embeddings with appearance information, allowing the system to restore original frames. At the same time, the model identifies speakers in manipulated videos. The cross-modal strategy shares information between different modalities. In this way, it increases the model's ability to recognize identities. The results presented in the paper [38] indicate a 98.9% detection rate and 98.9% identification accuracy. The strategy outperforms baselines like FF++ (96.4% detection) and MesoNet (86.3% detection). MesoNet is a DL model designed for deepfake detection, focusing on mesoscopic (intermediate-scale) features within images.

The review [39] highlights advancements in deepfake detection methods across modalities like images, videos, and audio. Techniques leveraging temporal–spatial analysis and frame forgery detection have shown substantial progress. For instance, eye-blinking detection analyzes anomalous blinking rates, achieving 98.1% accuracy for fake videos using a Long-Term Recurrent Convolutional Network (LRCN). An LRCN combines CNNs for spatial feature extraction with Recurrent Neural Networks (RNNs) for temporal sequence modeling, capturing temporal dynamics in video data. MesoNet and MesoInception-4 (extension of MesoNet that incorporates Inception modules to capture features at multiple scales, increasing detection performance) achieved detection rates of 98% on the DeepFake dataset and 95% for Face2Face (real-time facial reenactment system that transfers expressions from a source to a target video) (F2F) by analyzing mesoscopic properties.

Shifting the focus to psychological aspects, individuals perceive emotional expressions from real versus AI-generated deepfake faces, as analyzed in the paper [40]. Results revealed valence-dependent effects, where the belief in a face being real or fake influenced emotional evaluations and neural processing stages. The concept of valence refers to positive or negative emotions. The analysis of deepfake content found that negative expressions, especially angry faces, are difficult to distinguish. Happy expressions showed reduced impact when presumed to be fake. Fake smiles were rated as less optimistic and less distinct from neutral expressions, and weaker neural responses were elicited in early perceptual and emotional components [41].

In the paper [42], I have identified a proposed algorithm focusing on the Discrete Fourier Transform. The paper compares the StyleGAN and StyleGAN2 architectures with real faces extracted from the FFHQ and CelebA-HQ datasets. From the tests, an accuracy of 99% was obtained. The method was compared with the pixel-by-pixel algorithm for deepfake detection. Also, this paper highlights the importance of using frequency-based features for deepfake detection.

In the paper [43], I have identified a synthesis regarding the technologies specific to deepfake modifications in images. The first category of these technologies is facial synthesis. Research associated with this category uses GAN structures such as Wasserstein generative adversarial network (WGAN) and progressive growing of generative adversarial network (PGGAN) to generate hyper-realistic images. This category faces errors in deepfake generation, making it easy to identify them as not authentic. The second category performs facial attribute editing. The disadvantage of these methods lies in controlling attributes without affecting others. The third category is attributed to face swapping [44]. Although the paper [43] mentions that detectors have excellent performance on the first generations of datasets (AUC ~100%), they show decreases on newer datasets such as DFDC and Celeb-DF (AUC < 60%). This suggests the need for improved evaluation protocols and new identification techniques. The last category is facial reenactment. In this category, the FF++ dataset used is insufficient for performing evaluations.

The research [45] records the evaluation of the Vision Transformers (ViTs) method based on global features. The method uses a multiclass deepfake detection approach. The paper positions itself as an initial study material in the exploration of ViTs in this deepfake domain. The achieved accuracy is marked at 77% for a ResNet-50 model. For the VGG-16 model, the paper records an accuracy of 95%.

The paper [46] presents a high-accuracy framework for detecting fake audio. The model combines CNN with RNN to analyze spectral and temporal features, achieving 95% accuracy, 93% precision, 95% recall, and a balanced F1-score of 94%. The model uses advanced techniques like spectro-temporal analysis, which examines both frequency (spectral) and time (temporal) aspects of audio signals, to demonstrate resilience against various audio manipulations in datasets such as ADD2022 (dataset used for Audio Deepfake Detection research).

The works analyzed in this section revealed that no algorithm promises to identify deepfake images with an accuracy high enough to be further integrated into video content.

6.1.5 Facial Recognition Vulnerabilities in the Era of Deepfakes

One of the biggest problems caused by deepfakes is facial recognition. It is used in fields that involve money or security. Facial recognition technology is based on key facial points determining a person's uniqueness. The biggest challenge comes from combating deepfakes in facial recognition systems.

In the paper [47], I identified techniques that do not rely on deepfakes but can deceive facial recognition systems. These techniques are called spoofing and use multimedia content or masks associated with authentic users [48]. The same paper [47] also mentioned that traditional facial recognition systems were not equipped with technologies capable of identifying such fraud attempts. The paper [49] presents a series of techniques that generate deepfakes using characteristics meant to mimic real facial features. In this way, the deepfake detection process is hindered. By integrating facial landmarks—key face points, such as the eyes, nose, and mouth—into deepfake creation, attackers produce fake images that faithfully reproduce a person's real face. Therefore, these facial elements mislead recognition systems.

Another attack technology specific to deepfakes is called morphing. This technology does not produce an image associated with a specific person but combines the facial characteristics of several individuals to generate another person who appears real. The resulting content is a synthetic facial image [49]. To support the reader, I will propose, as an example of this technology, a photograph is published in the media, and a child has visibly similar features to two celebrities who have never been a couple. In this way, the news generates a lot of views but harms the integrity of the two celebrities by presenting false information generated with this deepfake technology.

According to the paper [50], morphing generates high similarity scores between morphed images and authentic identity templates—the stored biometric data used for identity verification. Such attacks have implications for security applications, such as border control and financial transactions [51].

In the specialized literature, several proposed technologies are aimed at combating the deepfake morphing process. In the paper [52], the authors analyze facial portions to evaluate the originality of the image. Through a multifactorial approach, the authors hope to perfect the system to combat morphing manipulations. The evaluation of this method was conducted in three stages. Trained models used the FF++ and Celeb-DF datasets. In this methodology, the authors defined several testing groups:

- **Baseline Group:** This group used original, unmodified facial images as input for the models. It served as a reference point to evaluate the impact of obscuring facial features.
- **Cutout 1 Group:** In this group, certain external facial features, including regions such as the forehead and jawline, were obscured or masked.
- **Face-Cutout 2 Group:** This group focused on obscuring commonly analyzed facial features. This category included the eyes, nose, and mouth while analyzing other facial features.

The results showed that the Face-Cutout 2 group outperformed the Baseline and Cutout 1 groups, achieving up to 91% accuracy compared to 88% for the Cutout 1 group. Individual tests revealed that obscuring the eyes most negatively impacted performance, with a logarithmic loss (log loss) of 0.52, while covering the nose yielded the best results, with a log loss of 0.33.

In the paper [53], fusion rules were proposed to evaluate the score of accuracy improvements when using different well-established classification methods in the deepfake domain. This study explores fusion methods for deepfake detection by combining the results of six state-of-the-art classifiers (algorithms that classify data based on learned features) in intra-dataset and cross-dataset scenarios. The first scenario, intra-dataset, evaluates models on the same dataset used for training. A second scenario, cross-dataset, tests models on different datasets to evaluate generalization capabilities [54, 55].

Research in deepfake facial recognition will continue as AI becomes increasingly efficient in generating audio–video content. Additionally, I believe that as cloud infrastructures [56, 57]. offer more facilities to support the training of large data volumes at lower costs, remarkable research will be recorded in combating deepfakes.

6.2 DEEPFAKE DETECTION USING A CUSTOM ALGORITHM

In the following, I will present an algorithm for identifying modified image content by analyzing facial landmarks and spatial relationships within detected features. The algorithm uses Google Vision API to extract facial landmarks and compute normalized distances between key points to detect inconsistencies indicative of digital alterations. This process aims to identify modified images, such as those created by AI-driven deepfake generation, where subtle distortions are introduced to manipulate visual content.

The core idea behind this algorithm, the DeepFake Detection Algorithm (DDA), is to compare facial features across reference and test images, focusing on normalized spatial relationships between key points like eyes, nose, and mouth. By utilizing advanced facial detection and analysis capabilities provided by Google Vision API, the algorithm computes proportional distances and angular orientations to detect discrepancies. The DDA has the objective to identify irregularities in facial key points. This discrepancy will suggest that digital artifacts are introduced during image manipulation.

Unlike most research in the technical literature, which uses AI models requiring large volumes of data and advanced hardware infrastructure, another traditional technique is associated with image processing. In these areas, it can be identified as pixel comparison or edge detection. The DDA analyzes facial key points within a unique geometry. This geometry represents a novelty factor and a starting point for further research and development. This approach encourages the advancement of deepfake technology.

6.2.1 The DDA Description

To classify authentic images from altered images, DDA uses a series of steps summarized here and graphically illustrated in Figure 6.1.

1. The algorithm compares two input images:
   - The reference image—A known authentic image of the subject
   - The test image—An image suspected of being altered
2. Using the Google Vision API, the algorithm detects the following points for each image:
   - Bounding Box (BB): The rectangular region that encloses the detected face
   - Facial Landmarks: Eyes, nose, mouth, eyebrows, and chin

The coordinates of these landmarks are returned relative to the image dimensions.

3. To ensure comparability between the reference and test images, the DDA normalizes the coordinates of the detected landmarks. Normalization is performed concerning the BB dimensions using equations (6.1) and (6.2). In this way, the DDA eliminates differences caused by variations in image size or facial scaling.

$$\text{Normalized}_{x_{\text{FL}}} = \frac{x}{\text{BB}_{\text{width}}} \tag{6.1}$$

$$\text{Normalized}_{y_{\text{FL}}} = \frac{y}{\text{BB}_{\text{height}}} \tag{6.2}$$

where

$\text{Normalized}_{x_{\text{FL}}}$, $\text{Normalized}_{y_{\text{FL}}}$ are the normalized coordinates of a facial landmark (FL), scaled relative to the BB of the detected face. These values range between 0 and 1, providing a consistent spatial reference across images of varying sizes or resolutions.

x, *y*—the raw coordinates of the FL detected in the image. The Google Vision API provides these as absolute pixel values relative to the image dimensions.
BB_{width}, BB_{height}—the width and height of the BB enclosing the detected face.

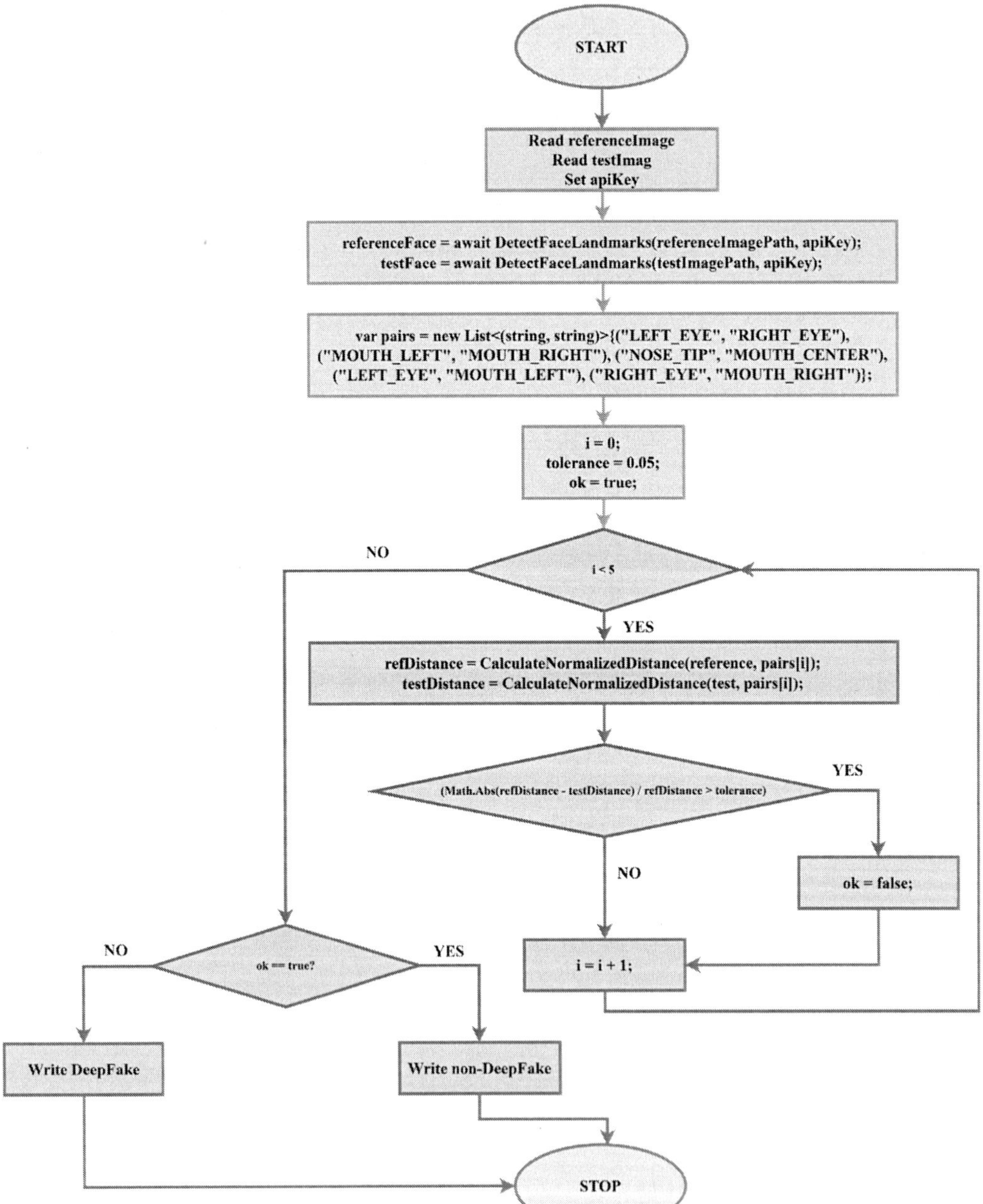

Figure 6.1 DDA logical flowchart.

4. The landmarks employed by the DDA are presented in Figure 6.2. In Figure 6.2, the landmarks specifications are:
   - Point 1 (LEFT_EYE) represents the outer corner of the left eye.
   - Point 2 (RIGHT_EYE) is the outer corner of the right eye.
   - Point 3 (NOSE_TIP) corresponds to the tip of the nose.
   - Point 4 (MOUTH_LEFT) is associated with the left corner of the mouth.
   - Point 5 (MOUTH_CENTER) is linked to the midpoint between Points 4 and 6.
   - Point 6 (MOUTH_RIGHT) has the right corner of the mouth associated.

The computed distances *d* presented in Figure 6.2 have the following meaning:

- Eye Distance between 1 and 2 markers: Measures facial symmetry and proportionality
- Mouth Width 4–6: Reflects the mouth's horizontal dimension
- Nose to Mouth Center 3–5: Evaluates vertical facial alignment
- Eye to Mouth Center 1–5 and 2–5: Measures proportions for symmetry analysis

The DDA computes normalized distances between specific pairs of FLs, such as:

- Distance between the eyes (LEFT_EYE, RIGHT_EYE)
- Distance between the corners of the mouth (MOUTH_LEFT, MOUTH_RIGHT)
- Distance between the nose tip and mouth center (NOSE_TIP, MOUTH_CENTER)
- Distance between the left eye and mouth center (LEFT_EYE, MOUTH_CENTER)
- Distance between the right eye and mouth center (RIGHT_EYE, MOUTH_CENTER)

The distances are calculated using Euclidean distances, using equation (6.3):

$$d = \sqrt{(x_2 - x_1)^2 + (y_2 - y_1)^2} \qquad (6.3)$$

where

d is the Euclidean distance between two FLs, measured in normalized units. It represents the relative spatial separation of key points on the face, such as the eyes, mouth corners, or nose.
(*x1*, *y1*)—The normalized coordinates of the reference image FL analyzed.
(*x2*, *y2*)—The normalized coordinates of the test image facial landmark were analyzed.

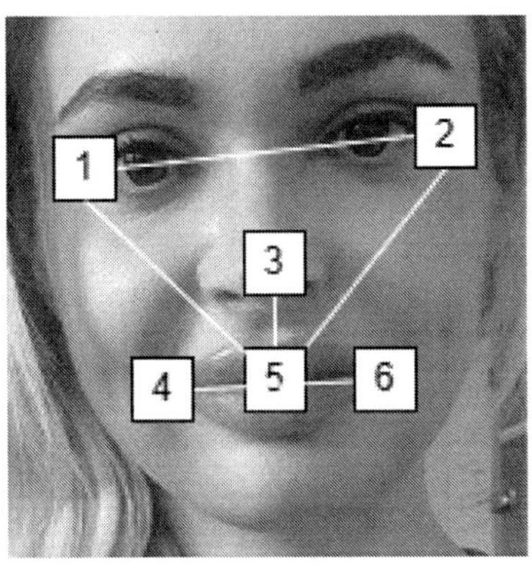

Figure 6.2 DDA analyzed landmarks.

The Google Vision API provides the raw coordinates of the landmarks.

The facial landmarks' yaw, pitch, and roll angles are extracted using the Google Vision API service. This service is advantageous because extracting key points uses a technique that does not correspond to deepfake research. Therefore, in integrating DDA, I was relieved of the task of identifying facial points and could focus on the specific algorithm. The key point extraction service is tested and pre-implemented. This is an advantage in implementing a research proposal as it significantly reduces implementation time.

5. The distances computed for the reference image are compared to those of the test image, considering the yaw, pitch, and roll, which must also be similar within a very low tolerance. This research considers a tolerance of ±36 degrees for yaw, pitch, and roll acceptable for ensuring similarity. The DDA checks for proportional consistency employing equation (6.4).

If the difference ratio exceeds a predefined tolerance threshold (5%), the test image is flagged as potentially manipulated using the DeepFake label.

$$dR = \frac{|d_{\text{test}} - d_{\text{ref}}|}{d_{\text{ref}}} \tag{6.4}$$

where

dR is the difference ratio, expressed as a normalized proportion. It represents the relative difference between the test and reference distances for a specific pair of facial landmarks.
d_{test} is the Euclidean distance between two normalized landmarks in the test image.
d_{ref} is the Euclidean distance between two normalized landmarks in the reference image.

6. All normalized distances within the acceptable tolerance threshold are calculated. The test image is classified as authentic and marked as non-DeepFake if all normalized distances within the acceptable tolerance threshold are satisfied. Otherwise, it is flagged as manipulated and marked with the DeepFake label.

The flowchart presented in Figure 6.1 outlines the DDA. It begins by reading a reference and test images, followed by landmark detection using the Google Vision API. The author emphasizes that the test and reference images must have similar yaw, pitch, and roll values. A list of key landmark pairs is defined for distance comparisons. The DDA iterates over five landmark pairs, calculating normalized distances between corresponding landmarks in the reference and test images. For each pair, it computes the relative difference between the reference and test distances. The algorithm sets ok to false if this difference exceeds a tolerance threshold (0.05). If ok remains true after all iterations, the test image is classified as non-Deepfake. Otherwise, it is labeled as Deepfake.

The empirical value of 0.05 as the tolerance threshold in the DDA was determined through extensive testing on datasets. This value skips minor variations in landmark distances due to natural facial differences (expressions) being accommodated. The distortions caused by manipulations like deepfakes in generated content are accurately labeled. A higher threshold risk allows some deepfakes to pass undetected. A lower threshold could incorrectly classify authentic images as deepfakes. The 0.05 tolerance represents an optimal trade-off, ensuring high detection accuracy across varied scenarios.

The DDA evaluates spatial consistency for each pair of landmarks, helping detect tampered or altered images. One of the biggest challenges of this detection methodology lies in the large volume of test images required to ensure representativeness across all possible angles generated by variations in yaw, pitch, and roll. Since yaw, pitch, and roll represent continuous variables with numerous potential values, capturing all possible combinations demands many images. To better understand, I will propose the following scenario. If we set the yaw to –180° to 180° in 30° increments, pitch to –90° to 90° in 30° increments, and roll –180° to 180° in 30° increments, the total number of unique combinations would be 864 combinations. If we set a higher granularity, such as dividing each axis into 20 intervals, the combinations grow to 8,000. This increase demonstrates the inherent difficulty in building the reference image dataset. Thousands of images are required to cover all potential angles adequately, making it computationally expensive and time-intensive.

To compare two images using the proposal from this chapter, I used a granularity of 30°. This value reduces the computational effort required by the hardware infrastructure. Additionally, the number of test cases is reduced. Consequently, it may omit subtle variations in landmarks, which will affect the analyzed quality indicators. Increasing the granularity directly impacts improving the quality indicators used in evaluating DDA. For applications requiring high precision, such as forensic analysis, finer granularity (e.g., 10° or less) is more appropriate. However, for broader comparisons or initial screening, 30° may suffice.

6.2.2 The DDA Results

I tested the DDA algorithm on a set of 40 images (20 original and 20 modified). The results show a recall of 100% (all deepfake images were correctly identified), but a precision of only 66.67%, due to the incorrect classification of some authentic images as deepfake.

I have implemented the DDA using the Visual Studio environment and C# language. I chose this configuration because it is compatible with asynchrony, multithread processing, and the Google Vision API. The tests I have conducted use celebrity images to obtain the deepfake content. In this way, I evaluated the model's accuracy. To extract the celebrities' faces, I have used the CelebA dataset. This dataset offers numerous facial representations. This facilitates the possibility of identifying several faces with similar positions to my selfies. All tests were performed using my selfies captured in different angles and environmental conditions. In my opinion, the process of collecting test images was very time-consuming.

In Figure 6.3(a), the reference image depicts the unaltered face of the chapter's author. In contrast, Figure 6.3(b) showcases a test image where the subject has been swapped with Brenda Joyce. The test image in the ColebA dataset is 007933.jpg. The DDA compares the test image with the reference image using normalized spatial distances and facial landmark orientation analysis. Upon execution, the algorithm classified the test image as DeepFake. The execution result in C# is displayed in Figure 6.5(a), where the correct labeling of the images can be observed, confirming the DeepFake detection outcome.

The head pose values for the reference image, Figure 6.3(a), are (174.57°, –32.44°, 179.80°), and the AI-modified image—Figure 6.3(b) (174.35°, –36.52°, 179.19°), returned by Google Vision API, exhibit slight variations in yaw, pitch, and roll. The yaw and roll values are nearly identical, with a marginal difference of 0.22° and 0.61°.

Figure 6.4(a) shows the same reference image of the author, while Figure 6.4(b) presents another unmodified (another original) test image. The DDA analysis for this pair resulted in

Figure 6.3 Comparison of original and AI-modified image with deepface detection: (a) reference image; (b) AI-generated test image.

Figure 6.4 Comparison of original and unmodified images of the same person: (a) reference image; (b) unmodified image.

a non-DeepFake, as shown in Figure 6.5(b). This demonstrates the algorithm's accuracy in distinguishing authentic content from AI-generated manipulations.

For the reference image in Figure 6.4(a) (174.57°, –32.44°, 179.80°) and the unmodified image in Figure 6.4(b) (167.44°, 29.41°, 170.91°), slight differences are evident in all axes, as returned by Google Vision API. The yaw difference of 7.13° indicates a subtle shift in horizontal alignment, while the pitch variation of 61.85° reflects an upward tilt in the unmodified image. The roll difference of 8.89° suggests minor rotation discrepancies. These differences are more pronounced than those of the AI-modified image.

Figure 6.5(a) compares the reference and test images. The normalized difference for the identified landmark pairs, such as MOUTH_LEFT—MOUTH_RIGHT (dR = 0.08), exceeds the 0.05 tolerance threshold. These results suggest inconsistencies in the geometry of the test image compared to the reference, leading the DDA to classify the test image as a DeepFake. Such discrepancies, particularly in the regions around the eyes and mouth, indicate potential digital manipulation, aligning with the expected behavior of the detection of DDA.

In Figure 6.5(b), the comparison between the reference and test images reveals minimal differences in the spatial relationships of facial landmarks. The normalized difference ratios for the same key landmark pairs fall within the acceptable tolerance of 0.05 threshold. This consistency suggests that the facial geometry in the test image closely matches that of the reference image. As a result, the DDA correctly classifies the test image as non-DeepFake, indicating that no digital manipulation has occurred.

For the DDA, 40 tests were conducted, with 20 using modified images and 20 using unmodified ones. The results showed 100% accuracy, though there is room for further improvements. Of the 20 modified images, 15 were correctly identified as DeepFake (True Positives—TP), while 5 were incorrectly identified as non-modified (False Negatives—FN). For the unmodified images, 10 were correctly identified as Non-DeepFake (True Negatives—TN), while 10 were incorrectly identified as DeepFake (False Positives—FP).

Figure 6.6 presents the confusion matrix. Equation (6.5) calculates the Accuracy, Precision (equation (6.6)), Recall (equation (6.7)), and F1-score (equation (6.8)). In the results, the DDA demonstrates a high recall rate of 100%, meaning that all the actual DeepFake

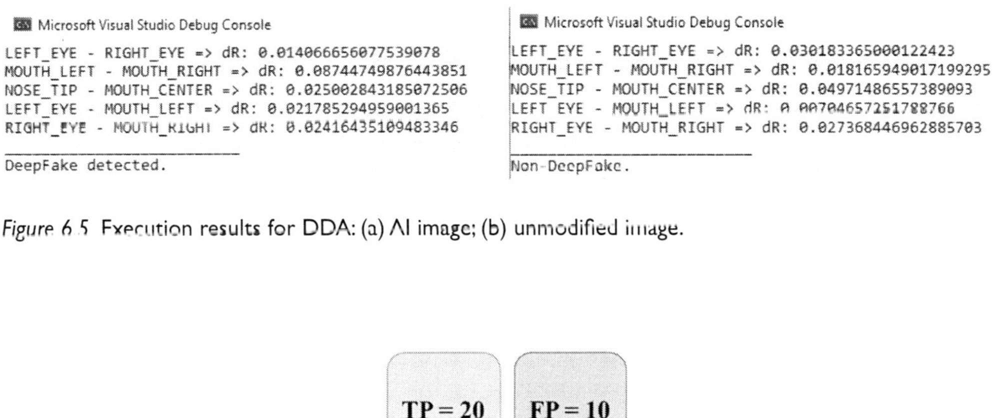

Figure 6.5 Execution results for DDA: (a) AI image; (b) unmodified image.

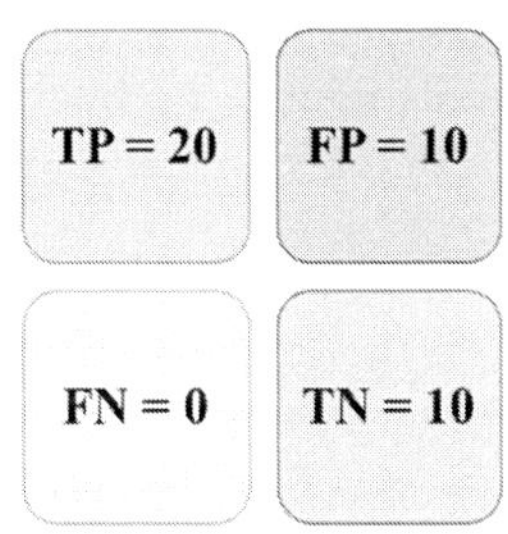

Figure 6.6 Confusion matrix.

images were correctly identified. This indicates that the system is excellent at detecting DeepFake images when they are present.

$$\text{Accuracy} = \frac{\text{TP}+\text{TN}}{\text{TP}+\text{TN}+\text{FP}+\text{FN}} \times 100 = \frac{30}{40} \times 100 = 0.75 \times 100 = 75\% \tag{6.5}$$

$$\text{Precision} = \frac{\text{TP}}{\text{TP}+\text{FP}} \times 100 = \frac{20}{30} \times 100 = 0.66 \times 100 = 66\% \tag{6.6}$$

$$\text{Recall} = \frac{\text{TP}}{\text{TP}+\text{FN}} \times 100 = \frac{20}{20} \times 100 = 1 \times 100 = 100\% \tag{6.7}$$

$$\text{F1} - \text{score} = \frac{2 \times \text{Precision} \times \text{Recall}}{\text{Precision} + \text{Recall}} \times 100 = \frac{1.33}{1.66} \times 100 = 0.8 \times 100 = 80\% \tag{6.8}$$

However, there are still challenges in terms of accuracy and F1-score. The overall accuracy of 75% suggests that DDA cannot minimize the FP. The ten unmodified images were incorrectly labeled DeepFake, affecting the algorithm's performance.

Precision, calculated using equation (6.6), measures the proportion of correctly identified DeepFake images out of all those flagged DeepFake. In this case, the precision is 66.67%.

To validate the DDA results, I calculated the F1-score using equation 6.8. The calculated value is 80%. This value shows us that the recall is perfect. At the same time, the precision needs to be improved. The first motivation for this behavior is that FP still occurs, meaning no DeepFake images are incorrectly labeled periodically. This suggests further algorithm fine-tuning, particularly to reduce the FP rates and improve precision.

Further updates, potentially leveraging advanced AI tools, could improve performance in identifying and distinguishing between DeepFake and non-DeepFake images.

6.3 CONCLUSION

The chapter proposes an algorithm for detecting deepfakes in images. The algorithm calculates the Euclidean distances between key points on the face. The results indicate a future research direction regarding the integration of AI techniques.

In this chapter, I developed an algorithm to identify images with DeepFake content. The main objective is to differentiate between non-DeepFake and DeepFake images. This objective should be obtained without large data volumes for AI methods in the training process. For this purpose, I proposed the DeepFake Algorithm (DFA). It evaluates if the analyzed image is a DeepFake by calculating the Euclidean distances between facial key points. The result is compared to a reference image with a similar head orientation. In this chapter, I emphasized the importance of a correlation between head position and facial key points represented by the Euclidean distance. I expressed this correlation using yaw, pitch, and roll for head position. In the tests performed to evaluate the proposed DFA, I observed that by increasing the number of selfies in the reference dataset, the accuracy of the DFA will increase, too.

To determine the accuracy of the DFA, I conducted a total of 40 tests. All 40 tests used my selfies, with 20 modified images and 20 unmodified ones. The results revealed certain limitations of my model, showing the need to integrate more advanced tools to improve DFA performance. The model achieved an overall accuracy of 75%, correctly identifying all 20 modified images as DeepFake. However, 50% of the authentic images were misclassified as DeepFake. This demonstrates that although the DFA detects DeepFake images, it struggles with FP rates, which affects its overall accuracy.

I also calculated the precision and obtained a value of 66.67%, meaning that while the DFA correctly identified some DeepFake images, unmodified images were misclassified. The recall was 100%, demonstrating that the DFA identified all DeepFake images. However, the F1-score was 80%, indicating good performance and the need for improvements.

For future research, I plan to replace the calculation of Euclidean distances with Mahalanobis distances and later Procrustes distances. Subsequently, I intend to integrate these distances into an anomaly detection model, as facial modifications generated by DeepFake software distort key points. In this way, I aim to identify whether an image represents an anomaly.

Finally, I want to emphasize that this chapter introduces the issue of DeepFake images and that the proposed algorithm represents a starting point for developing advanced algorithms in this field.

Funding: This research was supported by grants from the Petroleum-Gas University of Ploiesti, Romania, project number GO-GICS-30710/10.12.2024, within the Internal Grant for Scientific Research.

REFERENCES

[1] "Hidroelectrica Avertizează În Privința Videoclipurilor Deep-Fake Cu Vedete Care Promovează Tranzacții Cu Acțiuni Ale Companiei." 2024, accessed 7 May, 2025, https://www.digi24.ro/stiri/economie/companii/hidroelectrica-avertizeaza-in-privinta-videoclipurilor-deep-fake-cu-vedete-care-promoveaza-tranzactii-cu-actiuni-ale-companiei-2682325?__grsc=cookieIsUndef0&__grts=58220498&__grua=b4cf9ad024abdb0607783919b1e60921&__grrn=1.

[2] Roșca, C.-M., R.-A. Bold, and A.-E. Gerea. "A Comprehensive Patient Triage Algorithm Incorporating Chatgpt Api for Symptom-Based Healthcare Decision-Making." *Paper Presented at the Emerging Trends and Technologies on Intelligent Systems*. ETTIS 2024. Lecture Notes in Networks and Systems, Noida, India, 2025. https://doi.org/10.1007/978-981-97-5703-9_13.

[3] Gong, L. Y., and X. J. Li. "A Contemporary Survey on Deepfake Detection: Datasets, Algorithms, and Challenges." *Electronics* 13, no. 3 (2024): 585. https://doi.org/10.3390/electronics13030585.

[4] Rosca, C.-M., and A. Stancu. "A Review of Neuro-Ml Breakthroughs in Addressing Neurological Disorders." *Applied Sciences* 15, no. 10 (2025): 5442. https://doi.org/10.3390/app15105442.

[5] Shaaban, O. A., R. Yildirim, and A. A. Alguttar. "Audio Deepfake Approaches." *IEEE Access* 11 (2023): 132652–132682. https://doi.org/10.1109/access.2023.3333866.

[6] Rosca, C.-M., A. Stancu, and M. R. Tănase. "A Comparative Study of Azure Custom Vision Versus Google Vision Api Integrated into AI Custom Models Using Object Classification for Residential Waste." *Applied Sciences* 15, no. 7 (2025): 3869. https://doi.org/10.3390/app15073869.

[7] Rosca, C.-M., A. Stancu, and E. M. Iovanovici. "The New Paradigm of Deepfake Detection at the Text Level." *Applied Sciences* 15, no. 5 (2025): 2560. https://doi.org/10.3390/app15052560.

[8] Al-Dulaimi, O. A. H. H., and S. Kurnaz. "A Hybrid Cnn-Lstm Approach for Precision Deepfake Image Detection Based on Transfer Learning." *Electronics* 13, no. 9 (2024): 1662. https://doi.org/10.3390/electronics13091662.

[9] Waqas, N., S. I. Safie, K. A. Kadir, S. Khan, and M. H. Kaka Khel. "Deepfake Image Synthesis for Data Augmentation." *IEEE Access* 10 (2022): 80847–80857. https://doi.org/10.1109/access.2022.3193668.

[10] Popescu, C., M. R. Gabor, and A. Stancu. "Predictors for Green Energy vs. Fossil Fuels: The Case of Industrial Waste and Biogases in European Union Context." *Agronomy* 14, no. 7 (2024): 1459. https://doi.org/10.3390/agronomy14071459.

[11] Qureshi, K., A. Verma, H. Vachheta, A. Singh, and Z. K. Pathan. "A Multidisciplinary Threats to Emerging Cybersecurity, Legal and Ethical Threats Posed by Deepfake Technology." *International Journal for Research in Applied Science & Engineering Technology* 12, no. IX (2024): 574–580. https://doi.org/10.22214/ijraset.2024.64202.

[12] Rosca, C.-M., M. Carbureanu, and A. Stancu. "Data-Driven Approaches for Predicting and Forecasting Air Quality in Urban Areas." *Applied Sciences* 15, no. 8 (2025): 4390. https://doi.org/10.3390/app15084390.

[13] Rosca, C.-M., A. Stancu, and I.-A. Gortoescu. "Advanced Sensor Integration and AI Architectures for Next-Generation Traffic Navigation." *Applied Sciences* 15, no. 8 (2025): 4301. https://doi.org/10.3390/app15084301.

[14] Stancu, A., and C.-M. Rosca. "*Understanding the Agribusiness Model and Agricultural Value Chain with AI-Driven Technologies.*" In *Agripreneurship and the Dynamic Agribusiness Value Chain*, edited by L. Raimi, O. P. Olatidoye and T. F. H. Said, 329–344. Springer, Singapore, 2024. https://doi.org/10.1007/978-981-97-7429-6_19.

[15] Ramluckan, T. "Deepfakes: The Legal Implications." *International Conference on Cyber Warfare and Security* 19, no. 1 (2024): 282–288. https://doi.org/10.34190/iccws.19.1.2099.

[16] Sharma, A. K., and R. Sharma. "Generative Artificial Intelligence and Legal Frameworks: Identifying Challenges and Proposing Regulatory Reforms." *Kutafin Law Review* 11, no. 3 (2024): 415–451. https://doi.org/10.17803/2713-0533.2024.3.29.415-451.

[17] Meneses, J.-P. "Seeking to Define Deepfakes from U.S. State Laws." *Communication & Society* 37, no. 3 (2024): 219–235. https://doi.org/10.15581/003.37.3.219-235.

[18] Kaan Tuysuz, M., and A. Kılıç. "Analyzing the Legal and Ethical Considerations of Deepfake Technology." *Interdisciplinary Studies in Society, Law, and Politics* 2, no. 2 (2023): 4–10. https://doi.org/10.61838/kman.isslp.2.2.2.

[19] Liu, M., and X. Zhang. "Deepfake Technology and Current Legal Status of It." *Paper Presented at the 3rd International Conference on Artificial Intelligence and Education*, Chengdu, China, 24–26 June 2022. https://doi.org/10.2991/978-94-6463-040-4_194.

[20] Malik, A., M. Kuribayashi, S. M. Abdullahi, and A. N. Khan. "Deepfake Detection for Human Face Images and Videos: A Survey." *IEEE Access* 10 (2022): 18757–18775. https://doi.org/10.1109/access.2022.3151186.

[21] Rosca, C.-M., M. Popescu, C. Patrascioiu, and A. Stancu. "Comparative Analysis of pH Level Between Pasteurized and UTH Milk Using Dedicated Developed Application." *Revista de Chimie* 70, no. 11 (2019): 3917–3920. https://doi.org/10.37358/RC.70.19.11.7672.

[22] Waseem, S., S. A. R. S. Abu Bakar, B. A. Ahmed, Z. Omar, T. A. E. Eisa, and M. E. E. Dalam. "Deepfake on Face and Expression Swap: A Review." *IEEE Access* 11 (2023): 117865–117906. https://doi.org/10.1109/access.2023.3324403.

[23] Kawabe, A., R. Haga, Y. Tomioka, J. Shin, and Y. Okuyama. "A Dynamic Ensemble Selection of Deepfake Detectors Specialized for Individual Face Parts." *Electronics* 12, no. 18 (2023): 3932. https://doi.org/10.3390/electronics12183932.

[24] Rosca, C. M., I. A. Gortoescu, and M. R. Tanase. "Artificial Intelligence—Powered Video Content Generation Tools." *Romanian Journal of Petroleum & Gas Technology V (LXXVI), no.* 1 (2024): 131–144. https://doi.org/10.51865/JPGT.2024.01.10.

[25] Rosca, C.-M., G. Rădulescu, and A. Stancu. "Artificial Intelligence of Things Infrastructure for Quality Control in Cast Manufacturing Environments Shedding Light on Industry Changes." *Applied Sciences* 15, no. 4 (2025): 2068. https://doi.org/10.3390/app15042068.

[26] Rosca, C.-M., and A. Stancu. "Integration of AI in Self-Powered IoT Sensor Systems." *Applied Sciences* 15, no. 13 (2025): 7008. https://doi.org/10.3390/app15137008.

[27] Rajagopal, T., V. Chandrashekaran, and V. Ilango. "Unmasking the Deepfake Infocalypse: Debunking Manufactured Misinformation with a Prototype Model in the AI Era 'Seeing and Hearing, No Longer Believing'." *Journal of Communication and Management* 2, no. 4 (2023): 230–237. https://doi.org/10.58966/jcm2023243.

[28] Huang, Y., F. Juefei-Xu, R. Wang, Q. Guo, L. Ma, X. Xie, J. Li, W. Miao, Y. Liu, and G. Pu. "Fakepolisher: Making Deepfakes More Detection-Evasive by Shallow Reconstruction." *Paper Presented at the 28th ACM International Conference on Multimedia, Seattle WA*, 12–16 October, 2020. https://doi.org/10.1145/3394171.3413732.

[29] Neekhara, P., B. Dolhansky, J. Bitton, and C. C. Ferrer. "Adversarial Threats to Deepfake Detection: A Practical Perspective." *Paper Presented at the IEEE/CVF Conference on Computer Vision and Pattern Recognition Workshops Nashville*, TN, USA, 19–25 June 2021. https://doi.org/10.1109/cvprw53098.2021.00103.

[30] Thakral, K., H. Agarwal, K. Narayan, S. Mittal, M. Vatsa, and R. Singh. "Deephynet: Towards Detecting Phylogeny in Deepfakes." *IEEE Transactions on Biometrics, Behavior, and Identity Science* (2024). https://doi.org/10.1109/tbiom.2024.3487482.

[31] Noreen, I., M. S. Muneer, and S. Gillani. "Deepfake Attack Prevention Using Steganography Gans." *PeerJ Computer Science* 8 (2022): e1125. https://doi.org/10.7717/peerj-cs.1125.

[32] Guarnera, L., O. Giudice, M. Niesner, and S. Battiato. "On the Exploitation of Deepfake Model Recognition." *Paper Presented at the IEEE/CVF Conference on Computer Vision and Pattern Recognition Workshops*, New Orleans, LA, USA, 19–20 June 2022. https://doi.org/10.1109/cvprw56347.2022.00016.

[33] Lee, E.-G., I. Lee, and S.-B. Yoo. "Cluecatcher: Catching Domain-Wise Independent Clues for Deepfake Detection." *Mathematics* 11, no. 18 (2023): 3952. https://doi.org/10.3390/math11183952.

[34] Rosca, C. M. "*Convergence Catalysts: Exploring the Fusion of Embedded Systems, IoT, and Artificial Intelligence*." In *Engineering Applications of AI and Swarm Intelligence*, edited by X.-S. Yang, 69–87. Springer, Singapore, 2025. https://doi.org/10.1007/978-981-97-5979 8_4.

[35] Tran, V.-N., S.-H. Lee, H.-S. Le, and K.-R. Kwon. "High Performance Deepfake Video Detection on Cnn-Based with Attention Target-Specific Regions and Manual Distillation Extraction." *Applied Sciences* 11, no. 16 (2021): 7678. https://doi.org/10.3390/app11167678.

[36] Johnson, D., X. Yuan, and K. Roy. "Using Ensemble Convolutional Neural Network to Detect Deepfakes Using Periocular Data." In *Intelligent Systems and Applications. Intellisys 2023. Lecture Notes in Networks and Systems*, edited by K. Arai, 546–563. Springer, Cham, 2024. https://doi.org/10.1007/978-3-031-47724-9_36.

[37] Shahzad, H. F., F. Rustam, E. S. Flores, J. Luis Vidal Mazón, I. De La Torre Diez, and I. Ashraf. "A Review of Image Processing Techniques for Deepfakes." *Sensors* 22, no. 12 (2022): 4556. https://doi.org/10.3390/s22124556.

[38] Zhang, H., Z. M. Lu, H. Luo, and Y. P. Feng. "Restore Deepfakes Video Frames Via Identifying Individual Motion Styles." *Electronics Letters* 57, no. 4 (2021): 183–186. https://doi.org/10.1049/ell2.12015.

[39] Gupta, G., K. Raja, M. Gupta, T. Jan, S. T. Whiteside, and M. Prasad. "A Comprehensive Review of Deepfake Detection Using Advanced Machine Learning and Fusion Methods." *Electronics* 13, no. 1 (2023): 95. https://doi.org/10.3390/electronics13010095.

[40] Eiserbeck, A., M. Maier, J. Baum, and R. Abdel Rahman. "Deepfake Smiles Matter Less—the Psychological and Neural Impact of Presumed Ai-Generated Faces." *Scientific Reports* 13, no. 1 (2023): 16111. https://doi.org/10.1038/s41598-023-42802-x.

[41] Rosca, C.-M., and A. Stancu. "A Comprehensive Review of Machine Learning Models for Optimizing Wind Power Processes." *Applied Sciences* 15, no. 7 (2025): 3758. https://doi.org/10.3390/app15073758.

[42] Convertini, V. N., D. Impedovo, U. Lopez, G. Pirlo, and G. Sterlicchio. "Discrete Fourier Transform in Unmasking Deepfake Images: A Comparative Study of Stylegan Creations." *Information* 15, no. 11 (2024): 711. https://doi.org/10.3390/info15110711.

[43] Dang, M., and T. N. Nguyen. "Digital Face Manipulation Creation and Detection: A Systematic Review." *Electronics* 12, no. 16 (2023): 3407. https://doi.org/10.3390/electronics12163407.

[44] Rosca, C.-M., and A. V. Ariciu. "Unlocking Customer Sentiment Insights with Azure Sentiment Analysis: A Comprehensive Review and Analysis." *Romanian Journal of Petroleum & Gas Technology IV (LXXV), no.* 1 (2023): 173–182. https://doi.org/10.51865/JPGT.2023.01.15.

[45] Arshed, M. A., S. Mumtaz, M. Ibrahim, C. Dewi, M. Tanveer, and S. Ahmed. "Multiclass Ai-Generated Deepfake Face Detection Using Patch-Wise Deep Learning Model." *Computers* 13, no. 1 (2024): 31. https://doi.org/10.3390/computers13010031.

[46] Sunkari, V., and A. Srinagesh. "Efficient Deepfake Audio Detection Using Spectro-Temporal Analysis and Deep Learning." *Journal of Electrical Systems* 20, no. 5s (2024): 10–18. https://doi.org/10.52783/jes.1829.

[47] Ebrahimpour, N., M. A. Ayden, and B. Altay. "Liveness Control in Face Recognition with Deep Learning Methods." *The European Journal of Research and Development* 2, no. 2 (2022): 92–101. https://doi.org/10.56038/ejrnd.v2i2.36.

[48] Rosca, C.-M., and A. Stancu. "Emerging Trends in AI-Based Soil Contamination Monitoring and Prevention." *Agriculture* 15, no. 12 (2025): 1280. https://doi.org/10.3390/agriculture15121280.

[49] Masood, M., M. Nawaz, K. M. Malik, A. Javed, A. Irtaza, and H. Malik. "Deepfakes Generation and Detection: State-of-the-Art, Open Challenges, Countermeasures, and Way Forward." *Applied Intelligence* 53, no. 4 (2023): 3974–4026. https://doi.org/10.1007/s10489-022-03766-z.

[50] Scherhag, U., C. Rathgeb, and C. Busch. *"Face Morphing Attack Detection Methods." In Handbook of Digital Face Manipulation and Detection. From Deepfakes to Morphing Attacks, edited by* C. Rathgeb, R. Tolosana, R. Vera-Rodriguez and C. Busch, 331–349. Springer, Cham, 2022. https://doi.org/10.1007/978-3-030-87664-7_15.

[51] Hamza, M., S. Tehsin, H. Karamti, and N. S. Alghamdi. "Generation and Detection of Face Morphing Attacks." *IEEE Access* 10 (2022): 72557–72576. https://doi.org/10.1109/access.2022.3188668.

[52] Alanazi, F., G. Ushaw, and G. Morgan. "Improving Detection of Deepfakes through Facial Region Analysis in Images." *Electronics* 13, no. 1 (2023): 126. https://doi.org/10.3390/electronics13010126.

[53] Concas, S., S. M. La Cava, G. Orrù, C. Cuccu, J. Gao, X. Feng, G. L. Marcialis, and F. Roli. "Analysis of Score-Level Fusion Rules for Deepfake Detection." *Applied Sciences* 12, no. 15 (2022): 7365. https://doi.org/10.3390/app12157365.

[54] Rosca, C.-M., and M. Cărbureanu. "*A Comparative Analysis of Sorting Algorithms for Large-Scale Data: Performance Metrics and Language Efficiency*." *Paper Presented at the Emerging Trends and Technologies on Intelligent Systems. ETTIS 2024.* Lecture Notes in Networks and Systems, Noida, India, 2025. https://doi.org/10.1007/978-981-97-5703-9_8.

[55] Rosca, C.-M., A. Stancu, and M. Popescu. "The Impact of Cloud Versus Local Infrastructure on Automatic Iot-Driven Hydroponic Systems." *Applied Sciences* 15, no. 7 (2025): 4016. https://doi.org/10.3390/app15074016.

[56] Rosca, C.-M., A. Stancu, and A. V. Ariciu. "Algorithm for Child Adoption Process Using Artificial Intelligence and Monitoring System for Children." *Internet of Things* 26 (2024): 101170. https://doi.org/10.1016/j.iot.2024.101170.

[57] Rosca, C.-M. "*New Algorithm to Prevent Online Test Fraud Based on Cognitive Services and Input Devices Events*." In *Proceedings of Third Emerging Trends and Technologies on Intelligent Systems. Ettis 2023. Lecture Notes in Networks and Systems*, edited by A. Noor, K. Saroha, E. Pricop, A. Sen and G. Trivedi, 207–219. Springer Nature, Singapore, 2023. https://doi.org/10.1007/978-981-99-3963-3_17.

Chapter 7

Societal Resilience

Inoculating People Against Deepfake Manipulation

Malka N. Halgamuge, Tarek Moulahi, and Pascal Lorenz

7.1 INTRODUCTION: THE NEED FOR SOCIETAL IMMUNITY

7.1.1 Confronting Deepfakes Through Collective Cognitive Resilience

Artificial-intelligence-powered deepfakes represent one of the most disruptive threats of the digital era—not simply because of their technical sophistication but because of their psychological precision and social ramifications. These synthetic media artifacts do not merely falsify content—they destabilize perception, undermine trust, and fracture the shared cognitive ground upon which democratic societies depend.

At the core of this challenge is a fundamental vulnerability: the human tendency to trust what we see and hear. Deepfakes exploit this evolutionary shortcut—our reliance on sensory realism as a proxy for truth—turning it into a liability. In an environment saturated with high-fidelity visual and auditory forgeries, this instinct becomes dangerous. The result is a form of **epistemic instability**—a breakdown in society's ability to agree on what is real, credible, or worth acting upon.

Detection algorithms and platform policies, while necessary, are reactive and incomplete; they operate *downstream*, after harm has already begun to spread. What is needed is a shift *upstream*: toward a model of societal inoculation that builds psychological immunity **before** manipulation occurs.

This chapter therefore introduces the concept of **societal resilience**: a multi-layered, people-centered strategy for defending against AI-driven deception. Rather than focusing solely on detection or punishment, societal resilience aims to equip individuals and communities with cognitive defenses, emotional awareness, and civic literacy. It reframes the deepfake problem not just as a technological arms race but as a cultural and psychological struggle for truth.

7.1.2 Guiding Questions

The guiding questions for this chapter are illustrated in Figure 7.1.

DOI: 10.1201/9781003539032-7

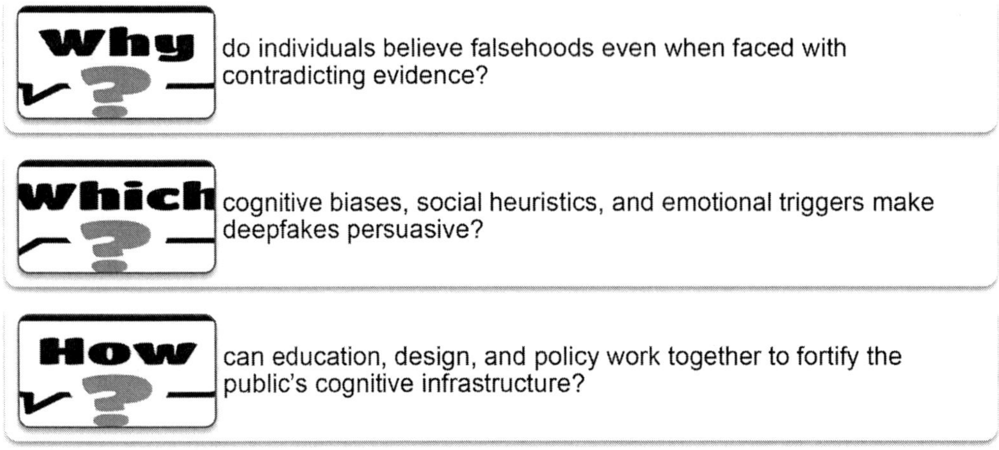

Figure 7.1 Guiding questions.

7.1.3 Core Questions Addressed in This Chapter

By answering these questions, the chapter lays a foundation for a preventive, participatory, and ethically grounded framework of deepfake resilience. Safeguarding the future of information requires more than verifying isolated facts; it requires rebuilding how people come to *trust, verify, and engage* with truth itself.

In doing so, the chapter invites a broader re-imagination of resilience—not only as defense but as cultural capacity: the ability of individuals, platforms, and institutions to act deliberately, think critically, and collaborate transparently in the face of synthetic deception.

Key Takeaway

Deepfake risk is less a technical arms race than a public health problem for trust; society needs preventive cognitive immunity, not just reactive detection.

7.2 UNDERSTANDING THE HUMAN FACTOR: WHY DEEPFAKES WORK

Treating deepfakes as a purely technical problem overlooks the central role of human psychology. Their potency stems less from code than from the ways they leverage well-known cognitive shortcuts—confirmation bias, illusory truth, authority cues, and more. Effective countermeasures must therefore be *psychologically informed*: They should anticipate how people actually process information, not how we wish they did.

Key Takeaway

Deepfakes work because they hijack automatic cognitive shortcuts—meaning effective defenses must be grounded in psychology, not engineering alone.

Figure 7.2 presents the core questions addressed in this chapter: What, Which, How, and Why.

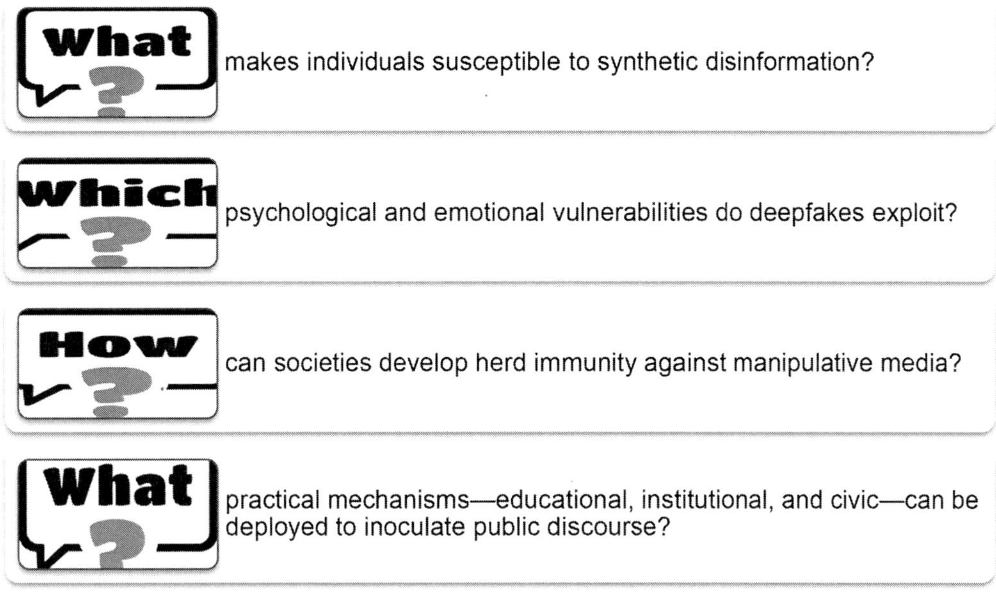

Figure 7.2 Core questions addressed in this chapter.

7.2.1 Cognitive Biases and Social Psychology

Humans rely on mental shortcuts (heuristics) to navigate a data-saturated world. These heuristics speed decision-making but leave us vulnerable to well-crafted deception. Deepfakes weaponize this vulnerability. Table 7.1 presents cognitive biases and heuristics that are commonly exploited by deepfakes.

7.2.1.1 *Implications*

Deepfakes often reach people before critical reasoning kicks in, activating automatic belief. Societal counter-strategies (prebunking, interface frictions, media-literacy drills) must therefore interrupt or slow this reflexive acceptance long enough for analysis to occur.

Key Takeaway

A small set of biases (confirmation, authority, emotion, social proof) explains most deepfake susceptibility; countermeasures must interrupt or slow these "fast-thinking" pathways.

7.2.2 The Erosion of Trust

"Seeing is no longer believing"—a phrase that captures the seismic shift in how individuals now interpret visual and auditory information. Deepfakes have not only blurred the line between real and fabricated media but fundamentally altered the cognitive contract

Table 7.1 Cognitive biases and heuristics exploited by deepfakes

Cognitive Bias/Heuristic	*How the Bias Works*	*How Deepfakes Exploit It*
Confirmation bias	We seek and accept information that aligns with pre-existing beliefs.	A partisan deepfake feels "obviously true," so viewers rarely scrutinize it.
Illusory truth effect	Repetition makes statements feel more accurate.	Viral reposts of a deepfake video boost its perceived authenticity.
Source misattribution	We forget where (or from whom) we heard something.	Stripped metadata or reposts obscure provenance, so viewers trust their eyes.
Perceptual realism	Visual/auditory realism is equated with truth.	High-fidelity face-swaps trigger a gut judgment of "real."
Authority heuristic	We grant extra credibility to perceived authority figures.	A synthetic "news anchor" or famous voice can bypass critical scrutiny.
Familiarity heuristic	Familiar formats or faces feel trustworthy.	Deepfakes mimic recognizable speakers, settings, or broadcast styles.
Emotion-driven processing	Strong emotion suppresses analytic reasoning.	Outrage- or fear-inducing fakes spread faster and evade fact-checking.
Social proof/bandwagon	Popularity is mistaken for accuracy.	Likes, shares, and comments act as persuasive "evidence."

between perception and truth. This disruption erodes the foundational trust upon which journalism, legal testimony, public institutions, and social cohesion rely.

At the core of this crisis lies the "liar's dividend" (Chesney & Citron, 2019): the strategic exploitation of deepfake awareness itself. Once individuals become aware that synthetic media exists, malicious actors can claim that authentic content is fake, thereby evading accountability. This epistemic loophole is particularly dangerous in environments of political polarization and institutional skepticism, where public willingness to believe in manipulation is already high.

7.2.2.1 *Deepfakes as Catalysts of Epistemic Instability*

In an era marked by information overload and declining trust in institutions, the knowledge that media can be convincingly forged breeds a form of *epistemic instability*—a breakdown in shared belief systems. In such conditions, individuals may fall into *two maladaptive psychological responses*:

- **Hyper-Skepticism**, where all content is viewed with doubt, even when true
- **Selective Credulity**, where only emotionally or ideologically aligned content is believed, regardless of its accuracy

This duality creates fertile ground for *belief fragmentation*, where objective facts are replaced by tribal narratives, and *truth becomes subjective*. As Marwick and Boyd (2018) argue, this results in an "attention economy" where engagement metrics outweigh accuracy, and the most emotionally provocative content—often deepfakes—garners the most visibility.

7.2.2.2 *Consequences Across Democratic and Social Domains*

The societal implications of this trust erosion are profound:

- **Democratic Processes:** When voters can no longer trust video evidence of political figures, elections shift from being issue-based to emotion-driven. A single deepfake scandal can undermine years of public diplomacy or derail a campaign, regardless of truth.
- **Legal and Personal Reputations:** Victims of deepfake abuse—especially those targeted with sexually explicit or defamatory content—face nearly insurmountable challenges in disproving falsified media. In courts of law, video was once the "gold standard" of evidence; today, it is increasingly contestable.
- **Media Credibility:** Reputable journalism faces a dual challenge: correcting deepfakes without amplifying them and proving the authenticity of real footage in a climate where audiences are conditioned to suspect manipulation.

To consolidate these insights, Table 7.2 summarizes the core psychological mechanisms and institutional vulnerabilities that enable trust erosion in the context of deepfakes. This structured view highlights how deepfakes exploit emotion, uncertainty, and media ecosystems—reinforcing the urgency of resilience-building addressed in the remainder of this chapter.

Table 7.2 Psychological and societal dimensions of trust erosion from deepfakes: summary of how deepfakes manipulate belief systems, emotional responses, and institutional trust, leading to widespread epistemic instability and societal vulnerability

Dimension of Trust Erosion	*Description*	*Mechanism or Vulnerability*	*Implications for Society*	*Scholarly References*
Liar's Dividend	Bad actors deny real content by exploiting awareness of deepfakes	Awareness of synthetic media allows plausible deniability of authentic events	Enables strategic deception; undermines accountability and evidence	Chesney and Citron (2019)
Epistemic Instability	Breakdown of consensus about what is real or true	Overexposure to disinformation triggers both hyper-skepticism and selective belief	Public becomes fractured in belief systems; facts become negotiable	Lewandowsky et al. (2017)
Hyper-Skepticism	Disbelieving all media, even accurate content	Fear of being manipulated leads to rejection of even real evidence	Weakens journalism, science communication, and institutional legitimacy	Marwick and Boyd (2018)
Selective Credulity	Believing only in ideologically consistent content	Confirmation bias reinforces false beliefs; reality is filtered by emotion or tribe	Increases polarization; truth becomes identity-dependent	Fazio et al. (2015); Kahneman (2011)
Collapse of Media Credibility	Difficulty distinguishing fake from real reduces trust in journalism	News outlets struggle to verify authenticity quickly; audience distrust grows	Weakens informed citizenship; fosters disillusionment	Tandoc et al. (2018)

(Continued)

Table 7.2 (Continued) Psychological and societal dimensions of trust erosion from deepfakes: summary of how deepfakes manipulate belief systems, emotional responses, and institutional trust, leading to widespread epistemic instability and societal vulnerability

Dimension of Trust Erosion	*Description*	*Mechanism or Vulnerability*	*Implications for Society*	*Scholarly References*
Delegitimization of Visual Evidence	Formerly reliable formats (video/audio) become suspect	Deepfakes undermine visual epistemology; courts, media, public lose trust in video proof	Legal and moral accountability is harder to establish	Citron and Chesney (2020); Stroud (2021)
Emotional Hijacking	Sensational deepfakes trigger fast emotional reactions	Emotional arousal overrides rational evaluation; moral panic ensues	Amplifies misinformation spread; weaponizes outrage	Lerner et al. (2015); Kahneman (2011)

7.2.2.3 *From Erosion to Inoculation: Reframing the Challenge*

While this erosion of trust presents a dire challenge, it also highlights the *urgent necessity of societal inoculation*—the chapter's central thesis. Recognizing the *psychological levers* that deepfakes manipulate (fear, outrage, suspicion) is the first step toward building cognitive and cultural immunity.

Resilience, in this context, means more than teaching individuals to spot forgeries; it means reinforcing *trust in legitimate institutions*, cultivating *healthy skepticism without sliding into nihilism*, and embedding *critical verification practices into digital habits*. Interventions such as *prebunking strategies*, *media literacy curricula*, and *institutional transparency standards* serve as inoculants—small doses of awareness and skepticism that prepare society to resist more virulent manipulations in the future.

In essence, deepfakes thrive in a vacuum of trust. But by identifying and addressing the *cognitive, emotional, and societal fractures* they exploit, we can begin to close that vacuum—not with censorship or panic but with informed, collective resilience. This reframing—from crisis to inoculation—is what anchors the value of this chapter. It challenges us not only to detect deception but to repair the conditions that allow deception to flourish.

Key Takeaway

Awareness of deepfakes can itself erode confidence ("liar's dividend"); resilience must rebuild credible verification channels to avoid both hyper-skepticism and blind credulity.

7.3 INOCULATION THEORY AND MEDIA LITERACY

Deepfakes exploit cognitive shortcuts, so the best defenses are *psychological*. Two complementary approaches dominate:

- **Inoculation Theory**—a "mental vaccine" delivered through short videos, games, or interactive warnings that expose people to *weakened* examples of manipulation before they meet the real thing.

Table 7.3 Inoculation theory versus media literacy 2.0

Intervention Strategy	*Core Strengths*	*Scalability*	*Key Limitations*	*Best-Fit Use Case*
Inoculation Theory	Rapid, engaging prebunking; proven short-term resistance	High—easily deployed as ads, mini-games, push notifications	Immunity wanes; less tested in low-literacy or non-Western contexts	Fast, digital-first countermeasures during elections, crises
Media Literacy 2.0	Deep, transferable understanding of AI, visuals, and emotion	Medium—needs curriculum time, teacher training	Risk of tech-jargon overload; assumes rational uptake	Long-term civic and educational resilience
Combined Approach	Marries quick resistance with deeper reflection	Strong if schools and platforms collaborate	Coordination costs; no shared success metrics (yet)	Comprehensive society-wide inoculation

- **Media Literacy 2.0**—a curriculum-level upgrade that teaches citizens how generative AI works, how to spot audio-visual forgeries, and how to regulate their own emotional responses.

A comparative overview of inoculation theory and Media Literacy 2.0 is provided in Table 7.3.

Key Takeaway

Quick hits of prebunking plus deeper Media Literacy 2.0 training offer complementary, scalable protection—rapid resistance and durable critical habits.

7.3.1 What Is Inoculation Theory?

Inoculation theory offers a psychological strategy that mirrors vaccination: by exposing individuals to weakened forms of misinformation, paired with refutations, it strengthens their resistance to future manipulation. Just as vaccines prepare the immune system to fight off a virus, this approach prepares the mind to recognize and reject misleading content.

This technique, commonly known as prebunking, involves introducing people to the tactics used in disinformation campaigns before they encounter them in real-world scenarios. For example, alerting individuals to emotional language, fake authority figures, or digitally altered media increases their ability to detect such manipulative techniques later.

Empirical research supports this method. Studies demonstrate that prebunking:

- Enhances critical thinking and skepticism toward deceptive claims
- Reduces the likelihood of sharing misinformation online
- Provides durable psychological resistance—with effects persisting weeks after initial exposure

Innovative platforms like Google's Jigsaw project have even gamified this process. Their interactive tool, *Bad News*, allows users to roleplay as creators of fake news, helping them understand how manipulation works from the inside. This experiential approach promotes deeper, more lasting comprehension than passive warnings alone.

Table 7.4 Critical evaluation of inoculation theory in deepfake contexts: review of effectiveness, limitations, and context-specific applications of inoculation-based interventions

Evaluation Dimension	*Strengths/Evidence*	*Limitations/Critique*	*Implications for Deepfake Resilience*
Empirical Effectiveness	Studies show increased resistance to misinformation post-prebunking (van der Linden et al., 2020).	Duration of resistance is not fully tested over long timescales; booster interventions may be needed.	Effective in short bursts or campaigns, especially online.
Cross-Cultural Applicability	Some evidence from Western democracies and global NGO use (e.g., Bad News in the EU).	Lacks validation in non-Western, low-literacy, or authoritarian contexts.	May require localization and cultural tailoring.
Age/Developmental Factors	Gamified tools shown to work with adolescents and young adults (Basol et al., 2020).	Limited testing in elderly or very young users; reliance on digital fluency.	Works well in youth and tech-literate groups.
Engagement Design	Interactive formats increase retention and reflection.	Can be resource-intensive to develop; effects vary with motivation.	Best deployed via gamified, mobile-friendly formats (e.g., Jigsaw, Go Viral!).

Inoculation theory is not merely an academic concept—it represents a scalable, evidence-based strategy for cultivating societal resilience against deepfake manipulation.

While inoculation theory has gained traction for its effectiveness in misinformation resistance, a closer examination reveals important limitations. **Table 7.4** evaluates the evidence supporting this approach, its performance across age and cultural groups, and the factors that shape its real-world scalability.

Key Takeaway

Brief, gamified "micro-doses" of misinformation reliably cut later susceptibility, but immunity decays—so scheduled boosters and cultural tailoring are essential.

7.3.2 Media Literacy 2.0

Traditional media literacy alone is insufficient; we need:

- AI-literate citizens who understand how generative models work
- Critical visual literacy: the ability to recognize tell-tale signs of synthetic content
- Case studies of national media-literacy initiatives (e.g., Finland, Netherlands)

While traditional media literacy has focused on evaluating sources, cross-referencing facts, and identifying bias in journalism, the era of generative AI requires a more advanced toolkit—what we might call *Media Literacy 2.0.*

To navigate the deepfake landscape, citizens need:

- **AI Literacy:** A basic understanding of how generative models, such as Generative Adversarial Networks (GANs) or large language models, operate. Awareness of how realistic media can be artificially constructed helps foster healthy skepticism without descending into blanket distrust.

- **Critical Visual Literacy:** The ability to recognize subtle indicators of manipulation in video and audio—such as unnatural blinking, mismatched lighting, irregular facial expressions, or synthetic voice patterns. This also involves understanding metadata, inconsistencies, and source reliability.
- **Emotional Literacy:** Recognizing how emotional content can override rational thought and learning to pause before reacting to sensational visuals.

Some nations have pioneered innovative approaches in this space. For example:

- **Finland** has embedded critical thinking and misinformation awareness into school curricula starting from primary education, positioning itself as a global leader in resilience against information warfare.
- **The Netherlands** has run "NewsWise" campaigns across schools, using workshops and simulation games to help students distinguish real from manipulated media.

These national initiatives highlight a crucial lesson: literacy efforts must evolve as rapidly as the technology they are designed to counter. By teaching not just what to believe, but how to evaluate what we see and hear, *Media Literacy 2.0* becomes an essential layer in the societal immune system against AI deception.

Media Literacy 2.0 proposes a comprehensive upgrade to traditional digital literacy, but it also introduces new implementation challenges and conceptual assumptions. **Table 7.5** critically assesses its core components, including AI literacy, visual analysis skills, and emotional awareness.

Media Literacy 2.0 builds *durable* resistance, but it is slower to roll out. When combined with rapid inoculation, the two layers reinforce one another—quick *and* deep protection against synthetic media.

Key Takeaway

Next-gen literacy must couple AI and visual forensics with emotion-regulation skills, turning citizens from passive consumers into active fact-check nodes.

Table 7.5 Critical analysis of media literacy 2.0 for the AI era: evaluation of objectives, limitations, and improvement strategies for next-generation media literacy programs

Pillar	*Why It Matters*	*Typical Gaps*	*Improvement Ideas*
AI Literacy	Demystifies GANs and voice-cloning; counters blind trust	Concepts too technical for many learners	Use visual demos, drag-and-drop "build a deepfake" labs
Critical Visual Literacy	Spots artifacts (lighting, lip-sync, metadata)	Forensic skills lag behind synthesis tech	Integrate crowd-sourced verification tools
Emotional Literacy	Teaches users to pause when provoked	Emotions override logic, especially in polarized topics	Embed STOP/SIFT models for self-regulation
Implementation Models	Finland's K-12 curriculum; Netherlands' NewsWise	Harder in under-resourced schools	Support grassroots clubs, teacher PD grants
Evaluation Metrics	Controlled trials show detection gains	No global benchmarks for retention	Develop cross-national assessment rubrics

7.4 THE DEEPFAKE THREAT AND THE NEED FOR RESILIENCE

7.4.1 A Threat That Is Scaling Exponentially

- **Volume Growth:** Commercial trackers estimate a 550% surge in deepfake videos, images, and voice clones posted online between 2019 and 2023 (Molins, 2025).
- **Mainstream Availability:** One-click apps now let non-experts produce photorealistic video or voice spoofs in minutes; adversaries no longer need specialized GPUs or coding skills.
- **Risk Ranking:** The World Economic Forum lists "AI-fuelled disinformation & deepfakes" among its top-10 global risks for 2024, besides climate and cyber crime.

7.4.2 High-Profile Wake-Up Calls (2023–2024)

Table 7.6 provides examples of recent deepfake incidents and their associated consequences.

7.4.3 Vectors of Harm

1. **Democratic Disruption:** Fake speeches, robocalls, or last-minute "October surprise" videos aimed at swing voters
2. **Security & Geopolitics:** Covert ops that fake surrender messages (e.g., Hwang & Solis, 2022), foment panic, or spoof military commands
3. **Personal Reputation and Harassment:** Non-consensual sexual imagery, CEO-fraud voice calls, "evidence" planted in custody battles

Historically, technical exploits—such as those leveraging USB storage devices for malware delivery (Pham et al., 2010)—have often combined with social engineering; deepfakes represent a new generation of such blended threats.

4. **Economic Crime:** Synthetic-voice approvals for wire transfers; market manipulation via forged CEO statements

The healthcare sector, for example, is already grappling with substantial security and privacy risks from Internet of Medical Things devices and emerging AI-driven threats (Nanayakkara

Table 7.6 Examples of recent deepfake incidents and their consequences

Month/Year	*Deepfake Incident*	*Impact Signal*
March 2023	Pope Francis pictured in an oversized Balenciaga-style coat	Showed how benign "lols" can still erode visual trust in newsfeeds
January 2024	Explicit AI images of a global pop star go viral	Demonstrated reputational and mental-health harms of non-consensual content
January 2024	Robocall in New Hampshire mimics the U.S. President, telling voters not to vote	First large-scale attempt to suppress turnout via synthetic audio
April 2024	AI voice clone scams Hong Kong CFO, wires $25 M	Proof that financial fraud losses can eclipse prior phishing tactics

Pattern: incidents are cross-domain (politics, reputation, finance), require almost no budget, and spread faster than platforms can fact-check.

et al., 2019). Deepfakes may further compound these vulnerabilities through targeted misinformation or manipulation in healthcare applications. Emerging research highlights that the integration of smart devices and IoT in healthcare, while transformative, also expands the attack surface for manipulative technologies like deepfakes (Jayatilleka & Halgamuge, 2020).

7.4.4 Why *Resilience*, Not Just *Detection*, Must Be the Goal

- **Detection Lag**: Algorithms flag fakes *after* the first viral spike; cue correction rarely overtakes initial exposure.
- **Cost Asymmetry**: Creating a believable fake is cheaper than reliably debunking it.
- **"Liar's Dividend"**: Once the public knows deepfakes exist, *real* footage can be dismissed as fake, eroding accountability.
- **Human-factor target**—Deepfakes hijack confirmation bias, emotional arousal, and heuristic trust in audio-visual cues; purely technical filters do not patch those cognitive exploits.

Key Takeaway

Deepfake volume, realism, and cross-domain harms are soaring faster than detectors can keep up—making whole-of-society resilience an urgent priority.

7.5 COGNITIVE BIASES AND HEURISTICS EXPLOITED BY DEEPFAKES

7.5.1 Why "Fast-Thinking" Makes Us Easy Targets

As illustrated in Figure 7.3, deepfakes work because they bypass slow, analytic reasoning and tap directly into the *automatic shortcuts* we all use to make sense of information. Research across psychology and communication studies shows that at least a dozen well-documented biases are routinely activated when people encounter synthetic media. When a fake aligns

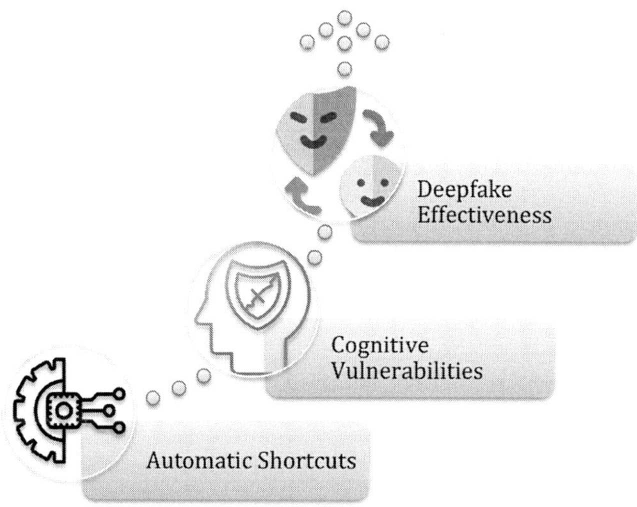

Figure 7.3 Reasons for deepfake effectiveness.

with a viewer's politics, identity, or momentary emotion, the brain's *default* is to accept rather than scrutinize (Taber & Lodge, 2006; Fazio et al., 2015).

7.5.2 Key Biases (with Deepfake Examples)

Table 7.7 outlines cognitive biases that contribute to increased susceptibility to deepfakes.

Each of these heuristics can be targeted by inoculation—for instance, *forewarning* people about the existence of AI voice cloning can counteract the *trust bias* by instilling healthy doubt about audio recordings (Mirza, 2024a, 2024b).

Table 7.7 Cognitive biases relevant to deepfake susceptibility

Bias/Heuristic	*Definition*	*Mechanism of Vulnerability*	*How a Deepfake Exploits It*	*Key References*
Confirmation Bias	Tendency to seek and believe information that confirms pre-existing beliefs	Reduces scrutiny of congruent misinformation.	Viewers more readily accept deepfakes that align with their ideology or emotions.	Taber and Lodge (2006); Meterko and Cooper (2022); Taylor (2025)
Illusory Truth Effect	Repetition of a statement increases its perceived accuracy	Familiarity is misinterpreted as truth.	Viral deepfakes repeated across platforms seem more credible over time.	Fazio et al. (2015)
Source Misattribution	Inability to recall the origin of a memory or claim	Memory retains content but loses source.	Viewers forget if content came from reliable or suspect sources, increasing susceptibility to decontextualized deepfakes.	Johnson et al. (1993); Mitchell (2000); Lindsay and Johnson (2020)
Perceptual Realism	Visual and auditory stimuli are instinctively trusted as reality	Visual input overrides analytical reasoning.	Deepfakes mimic authentic video/audio formats to trigger belief before critical thinking engages.	Reeves and Nass (1996); Europol (2022); Entrust (2023)
Authority Heuristic	Tendency to accept claims from perceived authority figures	Authority cues short-circuit critical evaluation.	Deepfakes simulate public figures or news anchors, which increases their persuasive power.	Cialdini (1993, 2007)
Familiarity Heuristic	Preference or trust for content that appears familiar	Familiarity enhances believability regardless of accuracy.	Deepfakes mimic familiar voices, phrases, or contexts (e.g., presidential speeches, breaking news formats).	Fazio et al. (2015)
Emotion-Driven Processing	Emotional arousal can bypass logical reasoning	Strong emotions impair rational evaluation.	Deepfakes often use outrage or fear (e.g., a faked scandal) to trigger viral sharing and reduce fact-checking.	Lerner et al. (2015); Regan (2025)

Table 7.7 (Continued) Cognitive biases relevant to deepfake susceptibility

Bias/Heuristic	*Definition*	*Mechanism of Vulnerability*	*How a Deepfake Exploits It*	*Key References*
Social Proof/ Bandwagon	Belief increases when many others believe or share the same information	Perceived consensus increases acceptance.	Popular or trending deepfakes gain legitimacy through likes, shares, and viral spread.	Cialdini (2007); Westling (2019)
Anchoring Bias	The tendency to rely too heavily on the first piece of information encountered	Initial false impression shapes lasting perception.	Initial exposure to deepfake biases future interpretations.	Englich and Frantz (2023)
Framing Effect	People's decisions influenced more by how information is presented than the content itself	Presentation format alters perceived credibility.	Deepfakes framed as credible news are more persuasive.	Nikolopoulou (2022)
Availability Heuristic	Judging probability/ truth by ease of recall	Recent exposure increases believability.	Deepfakes aligned with recent news/events feel more plausible.	Nikolopoulou (2022)
Overconfidence Bias	Overestimating one's own knowledge or detection ability	False confidence leads to lowered skepticism.	Assuming one can easily spot deepfakes increases vulnerability.	Nikolopoulou (2023); Entrust (2023)
Hindsight Bias	Belief that past events were predictable after they happen	Overestimation of prior knowledge, poor learning.	Victims of deepfakes falsely believe they were never fooled.	Guarnera (2024)
Trust Bias (Truth-Default)	Assuming audio-visual content is true unless clearly disproved	Default trust delays skepticism.	Deepfakes exploit initial trust to spread rapidly.	Europol (2022); Entrust (2023)

7.5.3 Behavioral Pathways Online

A decision-tree study of social media users shows three dominant paths when facing suspect content (Geeng et al., 2020).

1. **Instant Acceptance → Share** (trust + confirmation + overconfidence)
2. **Skeptical Investigation** (triggered by "something feels off")
3. **Scroll-Past/Ignore** (information overload, burnout)

Deepfake designers optimize for *Path 1*: short clips, emotional hooks, high social-proof counters. Our resilience programs must therefore (a) slow Path 1 and (b) make Path 2 easy and habitual.

7.5.4 Biases Can Misfire Both Ways

When awareness of deepfakes rises, the same shortcuts can flip: real footage may be dismissed as fake—the "liar's dividend" (Chesney & Citron, 2019). Large-N surveys find detection accuracy varies by demographic in-group; diverse networks enable "herd correction," dampening spread as dissenting friends supply counter-evidence (Lovato et al., 2024).

7.5.5 Implications for Defense

- **Prebunking Messages** should explicitly *name the bias* they counter (e.g., warn about audio-cloning to tackle truth-default).
- **Media-Literacy Drills** must rehearse the *pause-verify-share* reflex until it becomes automatic, offsetting emotional hijack.
- **Platform Nudges**—delayed autoplay, "double-check" prompts—insert cognitive friction to disrupt fast-thinking routes.

In short, *knowing* the neurological back-doors deepfakes use is the first inoculation dose; subsequent sections show how to harden them.

Key Takeaway

Mapping specific biases to deepfake tactics lets educators, platforms, and designers create targeted frictions (pause prompts, bias-named prebunks) that neutralize them.

7.6 INOCULATION THEORY—PREBUNKING DEEPFAKES WITH PSYCHOLOGICAL "VACCINES"

7.6.1 How Inoculation Works

Think of inoculation as a *cognitive vaccine* (see Figure 7.4): expose people to a "micro-dose" of misinformation *plus* a clear refutation, and their mental immune system learns to fend off stronger attacks later (van der Linden et al., 2020). First outlined by McGuire in the 1960s, the approach now has robust, modern evidence: dozens of studies from 2019–2023 show significant, lasting resistance to fake news, conspiracy theories, and AI-generated deepfakes (Maertens et al., 2021; Roozenbeek et al., 2022a, 2022b).

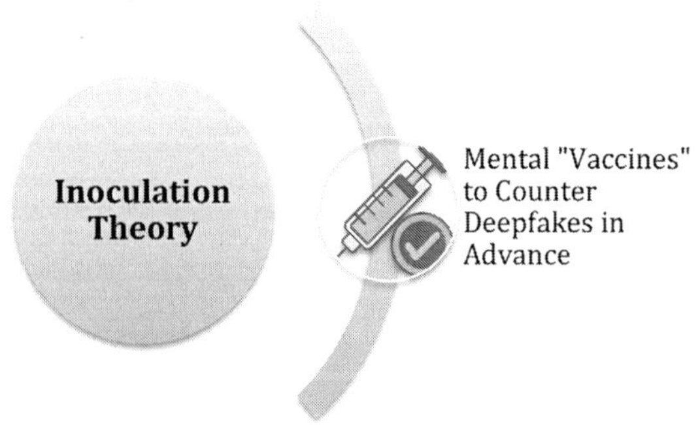

Figure 7.4 Cognitive vaccine.

7.6.2 Scalable Tools: Prebunk Videos and Games

- **Animated "Prebunk" Clips:** Five 90-second videos warning viewers about emotional language, scapegoating, false dichotomies, ad hominem attacks, and so on boosted recognition of those tactics and cut sharing of misinfo in a 5,000-person RCT (Roozenbeek et al., 2022).
- **Bad News/Go Viral! Games:** Short browser games let users *create* fake headlines, revealing the tricks from the inside; players show immediate drops in susceptibility, though effects begin to fade after ~8 weeks (Basol et al., 2020).
- **Platform Roll-Outs:** Google-Jigsaw pushed the animated clips as YouTube ads, reaching millions and replicating lab gains at scale (Roozenbeek et al., 2022). NATO and several EU states have since adopted similar prebunk packages (StratCom COE, 2022).

7.6.3 Known Limits

Table 7.8 summarizes the limitations of inoculation strategies against misinformation and highlights their corresponding design implications.

7.6.4 Putting Inoculation to Work

1. **Layer Boosters:** Integrate periodic reminders (memes, quizzes) into social feeds to keep immunity fresh.
2. **Target High-Risk Moments:** Run intensive prebunk ad-blasts weeks before elections or during crises.
3. **Blend with Literacy Programs:** Use inoculation as the "*hook*"; follow up with deeper Media Literacy 2.0 modules (see Chapter 7.3.2).
4. **Measure and Iterate:** Track belief-change and sharing-rates to refine content; discard one-off campaigns that don't move the metrics.

Table 7.8 Limitations of inoculation strategies against misinformation and their design implications

Issue	*Evidence of the Problem*	*Design Implications*
Decay over time	Inoculation effects drop markedly after 6–10 weeks without reinforcement (Basol et al., 2020).	Schedule booster videos, in-app pop-ups, or repeat game rounds.
Narrow coverage	Classic, claim-specific inoculation struggles with brand-new hoaxes.	Shift toward technique-based or "broad-spectrum" prebunks that teach the tactics, not the claim (Lewandowsky & van der Linden, 2021).
Uneven cultural reach	Most RCTs come from Western, high-literacy contexts; effectiveness in low-connectivity or authoritarian settings is unclear (Maertens et al., 2021).	Localize language, humor, and platform choice; co-design with regional NGOs.
Skepticism versus cynicism	Over-inoculation can raise doubt without improving truth-discernment (Cook et al., 2023).	Pair prebunks with verification tools and fact-checking tutorials.

7.6.5 Bottom Line

Inoculation is *not* a silver bullet, but it *is* a proven, low-cost first line of defense. When delivered through engaging media, refreshed regularly, and combined with verification skills, it can raise society's baseline resistance to deepfake manipulation—buying precious time for platforms and fact-checkers to act (van der Linden et al., 2020; Roozenbeek et al., 2022; StratCom COE, 2022).

Key Takeaway

Prebunk videos and games are a low-cost first line of defense; when refreshed and paired with verification tools, they buy critical time for fact-checkers.

7.7 MEDIA LITERACY AND EDUCATION AS VACCINE: TEACHING DEEPFAKE DETECTION

Media-literacy programs are the *long-term booster shot* that keeps inoculation effects alive. Their goal is two-fold: (a) give people the technical eye to spot synthetic media, and (b) normalize slow, critical reasoning whenever sensational video or audio appears. Figure 7.5 illustrates how media literacy and education can be used to combat deepfakes.

7.7.1 Global Momentum (2022–2025)

Table 7.9 presents policy and educational responses to deepfakes and media literacy across different regions and sectors.

Educating the public—especially students and young digital users—is a cornerstone of building resilience to deepfakes. Media literacy initiatives teach individuals to critically analyze media messages, verify sources, and recognize manipulation, directly addressing the cognitive biases and gaps discussed earlier. In recent years (2022–2025), there has been a

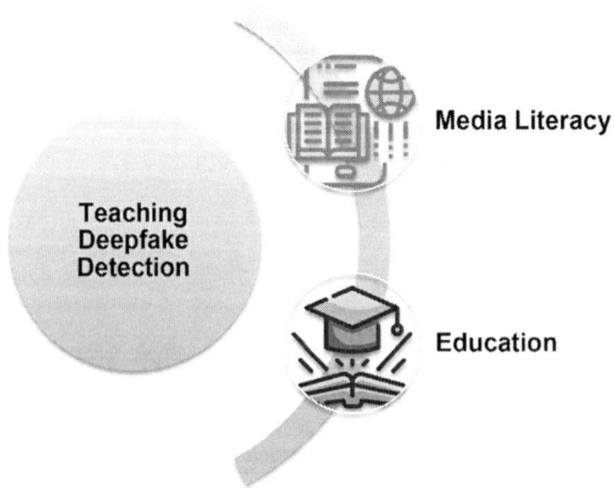

Figure 7.5 Combating deepfakes through media literacy and education.

Table 7.9 Policy and educational responses to deepfakes and media literacy by region and sector

Region/Policy Lever	*What Changed?*	*Why It Matters*
United States	- 18 states now mandate K–12 media-literacy instruction; >25 legislatures have debated new bills (Shapiro, 2023).	Bipartisan recognition that AI-driven rumors threaten elections and public health.
European Union	Digital Services Act obliges large platforms to "support media-literacy actions" and surface reliable context (European Commission, 2022).	Makes literacy a platform responsibility, not just a classroom topic.
Finland	Updated national curriculum embeds deepfake forensics from primary school onward (Sotkasiira & Salminen, 2022).	Finland tops the EU Media-Literacy Index six years running.
Global NGOs/Press	Surge of "deepfake days" and curricula showcased in The Week's 2023 roundup (The Week, 2023).	Civil society actors fill gaps where schools are slow to adapt.

surge in global efforts to integrate deepfake awareness into media literacy curricula (The Week, 2023). Policymakers are increasingly viewing digital and media literacy as a necessary form of "societal inoculation."

In the United States, at least 18 states have passed laws mandating media literacy education in schools as of early 2024—a significant increase driven by concerns about AI-generated misinformation and viral conspiracies (Shapiro, 2023). Over half of U.S. state legislatures have debated such bills, reflecting bipartisan consensus—albeit with some partisan variations—that teaching citizens to navigate digital misinformation is essential (Shapiro, 2023). Similar momentum is evident internationally: the European Commission's 2022 Digital Services Act includes mandates for platforms to support media literacy, while countries like Finland have updated their robust national curricula to address emerging threats like deepfakes (European Commission, 2022).

7.7.2 What *Effective* Deepfake Literacy Looks Like

What does deepfake-focused media literacy look like in practice?

Interactive Forensics: Educational programs now go beyond lessons on identifying fake news articles. They often use interactive exercises and real deepfake examples to train students' visual and auditory discernment. For example, the nonprofit-led **MisinfoDay** events in Washington State expose high school students to doctored images and deepfake videos in guided workshops (Shapiro, 2023). Students are asked to "spot the deepfake" through side-by-side comparisons, learn about AI image generation, and explore the realism of manipulated content. Evaluations suggest that students report increased confidence in assessing online content after participating in these sessions.

Public Micro-Courses: Beyond high schools, free public education is expanding. In 2022, MIT's Center for Advanced Virtuality launched a publicly accessible course titled *Fostering Media Literacy in the Age of Deepfakes*, which covers technical production methods, detection techniques (e.g., irregular blinking, audio mismatches), and ethical issues (MIT News, 2022). PBS also created a classroom lesson plan—*How to Detect Deepfakes and Avoid Being Fooled*—tailored to middle and high school students (PBS, 2023).

Critically, research is beginning to evaluate how effective these interventions are. A quasi-experimental study by El Mokadem (2023a, 2023b, 2023c) compared groups of students receiving a general misinformation literacy lecture, a deepfake-specific lesson, or no training. The deepfake-trained group rated a synthetic video significantly lower in perceived truthfulness and persuasiveness and were less inclined to share it. Even the general misinformation group showed some improvement, but the deepfake-specific training produced the greatest effect. However, the study noted that effects began fading after two weeks, reinforcing the need for recurring exposure—similar to booster shots in medical immunization.

Mnemonic Toolkits: Public awareness efforts also support adult media literacy. In late 2023, New Jersey state officials released a public fact sheet titled *Voter Alert: Don't Be Fooled by Deepfakes*, distributed both online and at community centers (New Jersey Division of Elections, 2023a, 2023b). It used accessible language to define deepfakes, shared election-related examples, and introduced the WATCH mnemonic: **Wait** before sharing, **Ask** questions, **Trace** the source, **Check** with fact-checkers, and **Help** others by reporting fakes. Such tools simplify core media literacy habits, improving public uptake.

Game-Based Prebunking: Public libraries and NGOs have also circulated infographics and held workshops aimed at older adults—who, research shows, can be particularly vulnerable to online deception (Shapiro, 2023). A 2023 survey by Boston University found that over 70% of adults view misinformation as a major societal problem, yet awareness of deepfakes remains limited (Shapiro, 2023). This education gap underscores the urgency of accessible, lifelong digital literacy initiatives.

7.7.3 Does It Work? Evidence so Far

Table 7.10 evaluates the efficacy of media literacy and educational interventions.

Collectively, these examples support the notion that media literacy education—especially when interactive, age-appropriate, and reinforced—can serve as a cognitive "vaccine" against deepfake manipulation. However, just like medical immunity, the effects must be refreshed and institutionalized to remain effective.

Table 7.10 Efficacy of media literacy and educational interventions

Study/Program	*Population*	*Intervention*	*Outcome*
El Mokadem (2023)—Deepfake Literacy Lecture	University students (Egypt)	Lecture-based media literacy session focused on deepfake awareness and detection techniques.	Improved deepfake detection accuracy and skepticism toward manipulated media; participants who received the deepfake-focused lecture rated deepfake video content as significantly less credible (roughly 30% lower credibility rating) compared to a control group. However, without ongoing practice, the gains diminished over time (the one-off training effect was not permanent).

Table 7.9 (Continued) Efficacy of media literacy and educational interventions

Study/Program	*Population*	*Intervention*	*Outcome*
"MisinfoDay" High School Events (2019–2024) MisinfoDay (2024)	High school students (USA)	Annual hands-on workshops (on university campuses and in classrooms) teaching media literacy through interactive activities and games	Increased self-reported fact-checking skills and confidence in spotting misinformation among participating students. Post-event surveys indicated that students felt more equipped to critically evaluate online content and recognized misinformation as a serious problem more than they did before the event.
Statewide Infographic Campaigns (e.g., NJ 2023, New Jersey Division of Elections, 2023)	General public (statewide outreach, New Jersey as an example)	Public awareness campaign using posters, infographics, and online PDFs to educate about deepfakes and misinformation	Qualitative reports of heightened public caution and awareness. For example, New Jersey's 2023 deepfake awareness initiative distributed "Don't be Fooled by Deepfakes" infographics; officials noted the campaign raised voters' alertness to deepfake tactics and provided "critical tools" for discerning manipulated media. (No formal quantitative impact measured, but anecdotal feedback suggested more skeptical engagement with suspect content.)
Curriculum Integration (Finland, 2022)	National student population (Finland)	Media literacy is integrated across K–12 national curriculum (critical thinking and digital literacy taught from early education through high school)	Finland consistently achieves top scores in European resilience-to disinformation studies. Media literacy is treated as a core competence; consequently, Finnish students exhibit a high ability to discern misinformation, and Finland has ranked first in the EU's Media Literacy Index (measuring fake news resilience) every year since 2017. This comprehensive, mandatory curriculum correlates with a highly deepfake-resilient society.
Online "Prebunking" Games (Bad News, Harmony Square) (Basol et al., Roozenbeek et al.)	Global users (open online participation)	15–20-minute browser games that "inoculate" players by exposing them to weakened doses of misinformation techniques (players actively create or witness fake news tactics)	Approximately 15–20% improvement in players' ability to recognize misinformation techniques and discern fake news content after gameplay. Players also reported increased confidence in spotting disinformation. Some resilience persisted weeks later; however, studies found the effect diminishes after about two to three months without reinforcement, suggesting the need for periodic "boosters" to maintain the inoculation effect.

7.7.4 Key Lessons for Scaling Deepfake Literacy

- **Go beyond "Spot the Fake":** Teach *why* people share: emotion regulation and social-proof awareness blunt virality triggers.
- **Treat Adults as Learners Too:** Older citizens, not digital natives, were most susceptible in a 2023 Boston University survey Shapiro (2023).
- **Bake in Refresh Cycles:** Knowledge decays; semesterly refreshers or game replays act as boosters—mirroring medical practice.
- **Measure, Then Iterate:** Few programs collect longitudinal metrics; adopting simple pre-/post-tests (credibility ratings, share intention) will reveal staying power.

7.7.5 Bottom Line

Interactive, recurring media-literacy efforts—spanning classrooms, public libraries, MOOCs, and mobile games—function as a *societal vaccine* against deepfakes. They are most potent when (a) tightly linked to real examples, (b) refreshed on a schedule, and (c) paired with broader inoculation tactics described in Chapter 7.6. Done well, they shift citizens from passive consumers to active *fact-check nodes* in the information ecosystem.

Key Takeaway

Interactive, recurring programs—from K–12 to community workshops—act as long-term boosters, sustaining vigilance long after one-off campaigns fade.

7.8 PUBLIC PREBUNKING CAMPAIGNS AND SOCIAL INTERVENTIONS

Formal schooling reaches the young, but *whole-of-society* immunity demands fast, broad "prebunks" that meet citizens where they scroll. From 2022 to 2025, governments, NGOs, and the platforms themselves have experimented with short, *just-in-time* messages that warn people before deepfakes land in their feeds.

7.8.1 How Prebunking Works at the Population Scale

While formal education targets students and structured learning, broader public campaigns aim to inoculate the population at large—including adults outside of school settings. Between 2022 and 2025, we have witnessed a diverse set of public-facing efforts designed to "prebunk" deepfake narratives before they spread. These include governmental information campaigns, civil society initiatives, and strategic interventions by social media platforms.

One of the most empirically studied examples is the YouTube prebunking campaign initiated by Google's Jigsaw in collaboration with academic researchers. These interventions presented short videos (typically under 90 seconds) that warned viewers about manipulation tactics like scapegoating, emotional appeals, or visual deception. Experimental studies found that viewers who watched these clips were significantly better at recognizing such tactics in later media content, even amid noisy environments like YouTube (Roozenbeek et al., 2022). By 2023, the campaign had been localized into multiple languages—such as Polish, French, Spanish, and Hindi—tailoring examples to regional misinformation patterns.

Field data indicate that localized prebunking still yields measurable improvements in media discernment, although cultural context may influence effectiveness (Lewandowsky & van der Linden, 2023).

The scalability of such short videos makes them ideal for rapid deployment during crises or electoral periods. For instance, prior to national elections, platforms can deliver prebunking messages via paid ad slots, illustrating how AI can generate fake political speeches and providing tips to spot tell-tale signs like lip-sync mismatches or low-quality dubbing. Parallel efforts on Facebook (Meta) have introduced "AI-generated" labels for synthetic content—a form of ambient prebunking that alerts users before they interact (Journalist's Resource, 2023a, 2023b, 2023c). Although the effectiveness of such labeling remains debated, some early evidence suggests it increases user skepticism in a constructive way (Lewandowsky & van der Linden, 2023).

Influencers and community leaders have also been mobilized as "trust brokers" in prebunking efforts. During the COVID-19 infodemic, public health agencies worked with social media influencers to counter false claims. The same principle applies to deepfakes: trusted journalists, celebrities, or technologists can create educational content that exposes how a deepfake is constructed and how to recognize it. Research suggests that such messages—especially those infused with humor or relatability—can increase engagement without diluting the cautionary message (Basol et al., 2020). However, communicators must tread carefully: excessive exposure to deepfakes might provoke generalized distrust or the dismissal of real footage. So far, studies like those associated with the *Bad News* game have found that inoculated participants become more critically discerning, not cynically disbelieving (Roozenbeek & van der Linden, 2019).

In terms of real-world impact, Table 7.11 outlines several successful examples. In Ukraine, a coalition of NGOs launched the "Verify Before You Amplify" campaign during the 2022 war, distributing infographics and social media alerts warning against cheap fake videos portraying false official statements. Surveys later revealed increased skepticism among citizens toward unverified war footage (Freedom House, 2023). Meanwhile, in Taiwan, the government supports neighborhood "fake news vaccine" workshops and has integrated fact-checking bots into the LINE messaging app—allowing users to submit suspicious videos for real-time verification. Taiwan attributes part of its resilience to coordinated grassroots and digital prebunking efforts, especially against foreign influence campaigns (Chen et al., 2023).

In sum, public prebunking campaigns offer a versatile and fast-acting countermeasure to deepfakes. They are particularly effective when trusted messengers, accessible formats (e.g., short videos), and interactive tools are combined. For instance, the state of New Jersey established public hotlines for reporting fake election content, distributed physical posters at polling places, and published downloadable fact sheets like the "Don't Be Fooled by Deepfakes" campaign (New Jersey Division of Elections, 2023). These strategies form a multi-layered, population-wide defense system against manipulative media—moving societies closer to collective inoculation against AI-driven deception.

7.8.2 What the Research Says

- **Platform Studies**: The Jigsaw/YouTube ads—90s animations on scapegoating, ad hominem, and so on—improved later detection accuracy across ideologies; localization to Hindi, Polish, and French preserved effect sizes (Roozenbeek et al., 2022; Lewandowsky & van der Linden, 2023).
- **Field Campaigns**: New Jersey's "WATCH" mnemonic triggered a spike in voter calls questioning dubious robocalls and videos (New Jersey DoS, 2023).

Table 7.11 Examples of public inoculation campaigns and outcomes

Campaign/Study	*Intervention Description*	*Outcome*
YouTube Prebunk Ads (2022, U.S./Europe)	Short video ads showing common misinformation tactics (ad hominem, false dichotomies, scapegoating, etc.). Roozenbeek et al., 2022; Google, 2023	Viewers improved recognition of misinformation techniques by 5–10 percentage points in controlled trials. Program expanded to multiple languages in 2023.
New Jersey "WATCH" Voter Awareness (2023, U.S.)	Infographics and PSAs distributed across voting offices and libraries with the acronym "WATCH" (Wait, Ask, Trace, Check, Help). (New Jersey Department of State, 2023)	Officials noted increased public inquiries about the authenticity of videos, indicating higher vigilance.
Ukraine Information Resilience (2022)	Government + NGOs launched wartime campaigns to debunk fake videos and coach citizens to verify footage during conflict. (Pomerantsev, 2022; Martsenyuk, 2023)	Anecdotal reports show early debunking of Russian deepfake attempts. Public trust in verified channels remained strong during the initial phases of the invasion.
"Psychological-Vaccine" Billboards (2024, EU)	Posters in public places warning about deepfakes, with QR codes linking to media literacy websites. (Lovato et al., 2024)	Surveyed cities showed slightly higher awareness of "deepfake" as a term and how to report suspicious media compared to control sites.

- **Conflict Zones:** Ukrainian NGOs' rapid debunk posts clipped the reach of a forged *Zelenskyy surrender* video; follow-up surveys show higher baseline skepticism toward unverified war footage (Freedom House, 2023).
- **Outdoor Media:** "Psychological-vaccine" billboards in EU cities nudged awareness of the *term* "deepfake" and increased QR-code scans to literacy sites (Lovato et al., 2024).

7.8.3 Design Principles That Matter

1. **Speed > Polish:** Short, lightweight assets can be localized and pushed as ads within hours of a new misinformation vector.
2. **Credible Voices:** People trust content from *their* community—local journalists, clergy, or niche influencers—more than distant authorities.
3. **Repetition without Fatigue:** Rotate creative styles (humor, narrative, infographic) to maintain attention without normalizing the fake.
4. **Easy Hand-offs:** QR codes, "report deepfake" hotlines, or in-platform buttons let users act immediately, converting skepticism into containment.

7.8.4 Illustrative Outcomes

Collectively, these cases show that **campaigns can raise baseline awareness and create a more discerning public**, especially when they precede known waves of disinformation. Timing, credibility, and repetition are crucial for success.

Prebunking is most potent when *timely, brief, and contextualized.* Deployed ahead of elections, crises, or foreseeable disinformation waves, it raises society's "skepticism baseline" without breeding nihilism. Coupled with the deeper literacy efforts of Chapter 7.7, these campaigns form the outer ring of a *layered resilience architecture*—arming citizens *before* bad actors hit "upload."

Key Takeaway

Timely, localized messages delivered via trusted voices can raise a population's "skepticism baseline" just before disinformation waves hit.

7.9 PLATFORM ACCOUNTABILITY AND POLICY MEASURES

Deepfake resilience depends as much on *where* content spreads as on *what* it contains. Social media giants are the primary vectors, so their rules—and the laws that frame them—constitute society's next line of defense.

Platform-based defenses must also contend with security and privacy limitations inherent to distributed IoT and fog computing environments (Ekanayake et al., 2018), as deepfake media can exploit these systemic weaknesses to propagate rapidly.

7.9.1 Current Platform Rules (2024 Snapshot)

Table 7.12 presents platform policies on deepfakes, highlighting core rules and key limitations.

Overall trend: shift from **removal → transparency** (labels, disclaimers) between 2023 and 2024.

7.9.2 Does Labeling Work?

Early research is mixed:

- Labels raise skepticism modestly, but the effect is the *smallest* among low-literacy or fast-scrolling users Mirza (2023).
- Impact doubles when the label links to an explanation or fact-check, suggesting "explain-plus-warn" beats a bare tag.

Table 7.12 Platform policies on deepfakes: core rules and key limitations

Platform	*Core Deepfake Rule Set*	*Notable Gaps/Criticisms*
Meta (Facebook, Instagram)	Bans synthetic media that could cause "real-world harm" or mislead about a speaker's words; applies AI-generated labels and forces political advertisers to disclose edits.	"Harm" threshold subjective; enforcement uneven across languages (Journalist's Resource, 2023; BBC, 2024).
YouTube	Removes deceptive AI-altered content on elections, public health, and so on; pilots provenance metadata in uploads.	Relies heavily on user flags → viral clips often spread before review.
TikTok	Outright ban on deepfakes of private individuals; public-figure fakes allowed only if satirical or artistic (Heath, 2023).	Policy clarity is high, but detection tech is still immature.
X (Twitter)	Requires labels on "synthetic & manipulated media."	Post-2022 ownership change → enforcement inconsistent (Journalist's Resource, 2023).

7.9.3 The Detection Arms Race

Creating convincing fakes is still cheaper and faster than detecting them.

- **Automated filters** catch many first-generation videos but struggle with high-resolution, multimodal fabrications.
- **C2PA** provenance standard adds tamper-evident signatures at capture time, with major supporters including Adobe, Microsoft, and Intel among backers (Adobe, 2023). If widely adopted, it could shift expectations such that unsigned media becomes "guilty until proven authentic."

7.9.4 Emerging Legislation

Table 7.13 summarizes regional legislative and regulatory actions on deepfakes during 2023–2024.

Even blockchain-based provenance solutions, while promising for content authentication, are not immune to sophisticated adversarial attacks (Halgamuge, 2022). This underscores the need for continual risk assessment and adaptive security models.

7.9.5 Balancing Safety and Speech

Experts recommend a *tiered response*:

1. *Remove* clearly unlawful or high-harm fakes (fraud, harassment, incitement).
2. *Label* borderline or satirical synthetics instead of blanket bans.
3. *Provenance-first*: incentivize camera-to-cloud signing so authenticity is the default, not the exception.
4. *Due-process hooks* for appeals to avoid over-blocking legitimate parody or art.

Crucially, even perfect rules fail without *alert users*—hence the linkage to literacy (Chapter 7.7) and prebunking (Chapter 7.8).

7.9.6 Bottom Line

Platforms and lawmakers now supply the *structural scaffolding* of deepfake defense, but loopholes, enforcement lags, and detection limits persist. The safest architecture pairs

Table 7.13 Regional legislative and regulatory actions on deepfakes (2023–2024)

Region	*2023–24 Action*	*Key Provision*
United States	Patchwork of state laws (CA, TX) criminalizing election-interference and non-consensual sexual deepfakes; DEEPFAKES Accountability Act & DEFIANCE Act pending (Thomson Reuters, 2024).	Disclosure requirements; civil remedies for victims
European Union	AI Act mandates labeling of synthetic content; Code of Practice on Disinformation pushes platforms to curb deepfake campaigns (European Commission, 2022).	Fines for non-compliance; risk audits
China	2023 rules require prominent AI-altered disclosures and make platforms jointly liable for harms.	Strictest "prior review" regime to date

the "safe car" (robust policy, provenance tech) with the "safe driver" (informed, skeptical citizens). Only by integrating technical, regulatory, and educational layers can societies keep the next wave of synthetic deception in check.

Key Takeaway

Labels, provenance tech, and smarter takedown rules form the structural scaffold—but they only work when consistently enforced and paired with user literacy.

7.10 TOWARD A RESILIENCE ARCHITECTURE: DEFENSE-IN-DEPTH FOR THE DEEPFAKE ERA

Deepfake mitigation is most effective when multiple protective layers overlap rather than relying on any single "silver bullet." Drawing on the preceding sections, we sketch a *defense-in-depth* architecture with four mutually reinforcing rings.

7.10.1 Layer 1—The Individual

- **Skill-Set:** Critical thinking, lateral reading, reverse-image/voice searches.
- **Delivery:** Classroom media-literacy 2.0 (Chapter 7.7), prebunking games/videos (Chapter 7.6).
- **Outcome:** Citizens who instinctively *pause, verify, ignore*—the habit NPR calls "critical ignoring" (NPR 2023).

Metric: Decline in self-reported belief in verified falsehoods after exposure to training modules (Basol et al., 2021; Roozenbeek et al., 2022).

7.10.2 Layer 2—The Community

Journalists, educators, fact checkers, and local influencers act as *trust hubs* that:

1. Amplify corrections ("herd correction" cascades)
2. Model transparent verification workflows (source docs, watermarked originals)
3. Provide *cultural translation* of technical alerts for non-expert audiences

Case study: Ukrainian media collectives that crowd-debunked a fake "Zelenskyy surrender" video in 2022, limiting reach within hours (Lovato et al., 2024).

7.10.3 Layer 3—The Institutional/Platform Perimeter

- **Technical Shields:** AI detectors and cryptographic provenance (C2PA) at upload time (Adobe, 2023a, 2023b).
- **Policy Shields:** Label or remove rule-breaking content; surface fact-checks (Journalist's Resource, 2023).
- **Dynamic Updates:** Detectors retrained as new synthesis models emerge; periodic red-team audits (Microsoft, 2023).

The deployment of scalable blockchain-based provenance in large-scale content platforms must also balance security with efficiency, as highlighted in studies of sharding-based blockchain network vulnerabilities (Aiyar et al., 2021).

When one shield misses a clip, the others buy time for human review and community debunking.

7.10.4 Layer 4—The Governance Envelope

- **Statutes and Standards:** U.S. state bans on election deepfakes, EU AI Act disclosure rules, China's mandatory watermarking—providing back-stop deterrence (European Commission, 2022; Thomson Reuters, 2024).
- **Public Dashboards:** Annual *transparency reports* on takedowns and detector accuracy build trust.
- **Misinformation Resilience Index:** Composite score (belief prevalence + correction latency + literacy coverage) tracked by researchers at Harvard Kennedy School, 2023.

7.10.5 Keeping the System Adaptive

Table 7.14 outlines emerging deepfake challenges and the adaptive countermeasures being developed to address them.

Regular *curriculum refreshes* and *booster prebunks* ensure the individual layer evolves alongside threats.

7.10.6 Limits and Fail-Safes

Resilience ≠ immunity; some fakes will slip through. Success is measured by:

- **Reach**—fewer impressions before debunk
- **Duration**—shorter viral half-life
- **Damage**—reduced real-world consequences

When detection fails, legal recourse (civil remedies, criminal prosecutions) and rapid official clarification contain fallout.

7.10.7 Outlook

Between 2022 and 2025, societies moved from *reactive debunking* toward *preventive hardening*. Continued progress hinges on:

- Integrating provenance tech into consumer devices
- Funding longitudinal evaluations of literacy and prebunking
- Institutionalizing voluntary "*no-AI-manipulation*" pledges in politics and newsrooms

Layered, adaptive defenses—technological, social, educational, legal—can downgrade deepfakes from existential threat to *manageable risk*, ensuring misinformation finds ever fewer hosts in an increasingly resilient public sphere.

Table 7.14 Emerging deepfake challenges and adaptive countermeasures

Challenge	*Adaptive Response*
Real-time voice-cloning surge (Adobe, 2023)	Push detector updates to messaging apps; add audio provenance metadata
Closed-platform spread (encrypted chats)	Outreach via community champions; lightweight on-device verifier bots
Detection evasion	Rotate signature-based + content authentication approaches; bounty programs for new attacks

Key Takeaway

A defense-in-depth model—individual, community, platform, governance—turns inevitable detection lapses into contained, short-lived events.

7.11 CONCLUSION—FROM VULNERABILITY TO VIGILANCE

Deepfakes are not a passing fad; each new model raises the ceiling of realism and lowers the barrier to abuse. The through-line of this chapter is that *no single countermeasure is sufficient.* Instead, durable protection rests on civic resilience: a public that can recognize manipulation, institutions that respond quickly and transparently, and technologies that reinforce rather than erode trust.

7.11.1 What We Have Learned

Table 7.15 highlights the key pillars and strategic insights for combating deepfake misinformation.

7.11.2 The Synergy Principle

Detection algorithms (explored in earlier chapters) *flag* suspect media; societal measures taught here *decide what happens next*. When an alert appears, a literate, skeptical public is far less likely to share the clip, and journalists have workflow standards to verify or debunk it. *Technical and human layers are complementary, not interchangeable.*

Table 7.15 Key pillars and insights for combating deepfake misinformation

Pillar	*Key Takeaway*
Cognitive science	Understanding biases (confirmation, illusory truth, trust-default) lets us design "mental antibodies."
Inoculation	Short, gamified "prebunks" measurably reduce later susceptibility across ideologies (Roozenbeek et al., 2022; Basol et al., 2021).
Media literacy 2.0	From primary school to senior centers, curricula must cover AI generation, forensic cues, and emotion regulation (Shapiro, 2023; European Commission, 2022).
Platform and policy	Labels, provenance tags, and targeted bans are improving but need consistent enforcement and global norms (BBC, 2024; Thomson Reuters, 2024).
Layered architecture	Defense-in-depth—individual, community, platform, governance—contains outbreaks before they scale.

7.11.3 Priorities for the Next Wave

1. **Rigorous Impact Evaluation**
   Every prebunk video, curriculum module, or policy label should ship with a measurement plan—did it actually reduce false belief, and for how long? Cross-cultural replication is essential.
2. **Reaching the "Information-Hesitant"**
   Highly polarized or low-trust groups are prime targets for weaponized deepfakes yet are least likely to engage with mainstream corrections. Peer-led messaging, local influencers, and encrypted-chat fact-bots warrant experimentation.
3. **Preparing for "Hyper-Real" Fakes**
   As synthesis quality outpaces forensic cues, norms may need to flip: *extraordinary footage is untrusted until proven authentic.* Cryptographic provenance and multi-source verification become default expectations.
4. **Sustainable Boosters**
   Psychological immunity fades. Annual refresher games, updated classroom modules, and recurrent public-service ads should be budgeted like vaccination campaigns.

7.11.4 A Shared Responsibility

Like herd immunity, *resilience is collective*:

- *Platforms* provide safety belts (detection, labeling, takedowns).
  Governments set guardrails and deterrents.
- *Educators and media* cultivate critical habits.
- *Citizens* practice "pause, verify, ignore" in daily feeds.

When each actor does its part, deepfakes shift from existential threat to *manageable nuisance.*

Deepfake technology, with all its troubling implications for deception and trust, is likely here to stay and grow more sophisticated. This chapter has argued that our best defense is not a single tool but *societal resilience*: an informed, vigilant public and a responsive, accountable information ecosystem. We have seen how cognitive biases make us targets, but also how understanding those biases can empower "mental antibodies." We have discussed inoculation—both metaphorical and literal (in games and videos)—which shows great promise in preemptively debunking the fakes before they strike. We examined how media literacy, starting from a young age and extending to lifelong learning, can raise the baseline of skepticism and analytical skills across society. We looked at the crucial role of platforms and policies in shaping an environment where truth has a fighting chance—through labeling, content moderation, and legal deterrence of malicious actors. And we synthesized these elements into a vision of a multi-layered resilience architecture that can adapt to new threats.

To ensure narrative consistency with the book's broader themes, it's worth highlighting the synergy between *technological solutions* (addressed in previous chapters) and *societal solutions* (our focus here). Even the best deepfake detection algorithm will fail if people ignore its warnings or if a lie is more appealing than the truth. Conversely, an educated public can sometimes compensate for a lack of tech detection by using human judgment and collective verification. Therefore, investment in societal resilience is as important as investment in AI detection research. As one analyst put it, "The deepest fakes ultimately target the mind—so that's where the strongest firewall must be." The concept of *civic inoculation* encapsulates this idea: treating citizens not as passive consumers of whatever the internet feeds them but as active defenders of their own informational integrity. This aligns with broader efforts in democracy to foster critical thinking and engaged citizenship in the digital age.

Looking forward, several areas deserve further attention to keep resilience strong. One is *evaluation and iteration*: programs and campaigns should be rigorously evaluated for impact (did a given prebunk video actually reduce belief in a subsequent fake?). What works in one cultural context might need tweaking in another. Sharing best practices internationally will be key, since deepfake disinformation often flows across borders. Another area is *reaching the "hard-to-reach"*—individuals or communities deeply polarized or distrustful of mainstream information sources. These groups might be both most at risk of targeted deepfake campaigns and least receptive to inoculation messages from authorities. Creative strategies, possibly involving peer messengers or alternative channels, will be needed to extend resilience to these segments. Additionally, *resilience against "hyper-real" deepfakes* (the inevitable next generation that may defeat current detection and even fool experts) will require doubling down on principles over technical tells. It may be that, in the future, any sensational video must be treated with initial skepticism until verified by multiple reliable parties; the social norm could shift such that the *absence of provenance* is taken as a warning sign by default.

The conversation around deepfakes often swings between alarm and complacency. This chapter takes a balanced, proactive stance: yes, deepfakes pose serious challenges—they can manipulate opinions, inflict personal harm, and erode the fabric of reality—but we are not helpless. Through scientific understanding of human cognition, through education and smart policy, we can *inoculate our society* to a significant degree. The process is akin to inoculating against a disease: it requires foresight, widespread application, boosters, and monitoring, and even then it's not perfect—but it dramatically reduces the damage. And just as public health measures rely on collective action (herd immunity), building deepfake resilience is a shared responsibility. Tech companies, educators, policymakers, journalists, and individual citizens all have roles to play in this inoculation ecosystem.

7.11.5 Closing Reflection

The rise of deepfakes is a stress test for democratic information systems. It forces us to modernize habits built for a time when "seeing was believing." Yet the same technologies that fabricate evidence also enable rapid detection, wide-scale education, and global fact-sharing. *If we invest in those capabilities—and in the people who use them—future historians may record that the 2020s were not the decade truth died, but the decade society learned to defend it.*

Key Takeaway

The surest antidote to synthetic deception is civic inoculation: layered, adaptive systems that unite technology, education, policy, and everyday citizen skepticism.

REFERENCES

Adobe. (2023a). *Content Authenticity Initiative*. https://contentauthenticity.org
Adobe. (2023b). *Content Authenticity Initiative: Fighting Misinformation with Provenance*. https://contentauthenticity.org

Aiyar, K., Halgamuge, M. N., & Mohammad, A. (2021). *Probability distribution model to analyze the trade-off between scalability and security of sharding-based blockchain networks. 2021 IEEE 18th Annual Consumer Communications & Networking Conference (CCNC)*. IEEE.

Basol, M., Roozenbeek, J., & van der Linden, S. (2021). Good news about Bad News: Gamified inoculation boosts confidence and cognitive resistance against misinformation. *Journal of Cognition* 4(1), 1–14. https://doi.org/10.5334/joc.148

BBC. (2024). *Meta to Label All AI-generated Images, Including Political Ads*. https://www.bbc.com/news/technology-68684532

Cialdini, R. B. (1993). *Influence: The Psychology of Persuasion*. HarperCollins.

Cialdini, R. B. (2007). *Influence: The Psychology of Persuasion* (Rev. ed.). Harper Business.

Chen, Y., Lin, T., & Wu, H. (2023). Civic engagement and platform design: How Taiwan built digital resilience against disinformation. *Journal of Digital Citizenship* 5(2), 88–102.

Chesney, R., & Citron, D. K. (2019). Deep fakes: A looming challenge for privacy, democracy, and national security. *California Law Review* 107(6), 1753–1819.

Citron, D. K., & Chesney, R. (2020). *Deep fakes and the new disinformation war: The coming age of post-reality. Foreign Affairs* 99(5), 147–155.

Cook, J., Lewandowsky, S., & Ecker, U. K. H. (2023). The science of prebunking: A psychological toolkit to reduce susceptibility to misinformation. *Current Opinion in Psychology* 49, 101554. https://doi.org/10.1016/j.copsyc.2022.101554

Ekanayake, B. N. B., Halgamuge, M. N., & Syed, A. (2018). Security and privacy issues of fog computing for the Internet of Things (IoT). *Cognitive Computing for Big Data Systems Over IoT: Frameworks, Tools and Applications*, 139–174.

El Mokadem, A. (2023a). Deepfake literacy training among university students: A quasi-experimental approach. *Journal of Digital Media Education* 9(1), 23–35.

El Mokadem, A. (2023b). Deepfake literacy training enhances skepticism and detection among Egyptian university students: A quasi-experimental study. *Journal of Media Psychology and Education* 45(2), 132–146.

El Mokadem, S. S. (2023c). The effect of media literacy on misinformation and deep fake video detection. *Arab Media & Society* 35.

Englich, B., & Frantz, R. (2023). Anchoring effects in public opinion formation: Experimental evidence. *Journal of Behavioral Public Policy* 7(2), 145–162.

Entrust. (2023, December 15). The psychology of deepfakes: Why we fall for them. *Entrust Blog*. Retrieved from https://www.entrust.com/blog/2023/12/the-psychology-of-deepfakes-why-we-fall-for-them

European Commission. (2022). *The Digital Services Act (DSA): Ensuring a Safe and Accountable Online Environment. Publications Office of the European Union*. https://digital-strategy.ec.europa.eu/en/policies/digital-services-act-package

European Commission. (2022a). *Digital Services Act: A New Framework for Digital Platforms*. https://ec.europa.eu/commission/presscorner/detail/en/ip_22_1978

European Commission. (2022b). *Strengthened Code of Practice on Disinformation*. https://digital-strategy.ec.europa.eu/en/policies/code-practice-disinformation

Europol. (2022). *Facing Reality? Law Enforcement and the Challenge of Deepfakes, an Observatory Report from the Europol Innovation Lab*. Publications Office of the European Union, Luxembourg.

Fazio, L. K., Brashier, N. M., Payne, B. K., & Marsh, E. J. (2015). Knowledge does not protect against illusory truth. *Journal of Experimental Psychology: General* 144(5), 993–1002.

Freedom House. (2023). *Ukraine: Information Resilience in Wartime*. https://freedomhouse.org/report/ukraine-resilience

Geeng, C., Yee, S., & Roesner, F. (2020). *Fake news on Facebook and Twitter: Investigating how people (don't) investigate*. In *Proceedings of the 2020 CHI Conference on Human Factors in Computing Systems (CHI '20)*. Association for Computing Machinery (ACM), 1–14. https://doi.org/10.1145/3313831.3376784

Halgamuge, M. N. (2022). Estimation of the success probability of a malicious attacker on blockchain-based edge network. *Computer Networks* 219, 109402.
Harvard Kennedy School. (2023). *Misinformation Review: Resilience Metrics.* https://misinforeview.hks.harvard.edu
Heath, A. (2023, April 4). TikTok updates rules to restrict AI-generated content. *The Verge.* https://www.theverge.com/2023/4/4/23668272/tiktok-ai-generated-content-policy-updated-deepfakes
Hwang, T., & Solis, J. (2022). *Deepfakes in Wartime: The Ukraine Conflict and the Evolution of Information Warfare. Atlantic Council – Digital Forensic Research Lab (DFRLab).* https://www.atlanticcouncil.org
Jayatilleka, I., & Halgamuge, M. N. (2020). *Internet of Things in healthcare: Smart devices, sensors, and systems related to diseases and health conditions.* In *Real-Time Data Analytics for Large Scale Sensor Data.* Academic Press, 1–35.
Johnson, M. K., Hashtroudi, S., & Lindsay, D. S. (1993). Source monitoring. *Psychological Bulletin* 114(1), 3–28. https://doi.org/10.1037/0033-2909.114.1.3
Journalist's Resource. (2023a). *How Platforms Are Responding to Deepfakes.* https://journalistsresource.org
Journalist's Resource. (2023b). *How Tech Platforms Are Handling AI-Generated Content.* https://journalistsresource.org
Journalist's Resource. (2023c). *How Tech Platforms Label AI-Generated Content—And Does It Help?* https://journalistsresource.org
Kahneman, D. (2011). *Thinking, Fast and Slow. Farrar,* Straus and Giroux.
Lerner, J. S., Li, Y., Valdesolo, P., & Kassam, K. S. (2015). Emotion and decision making. *Annual Review of Psychology* 66, 799–823. https://doi.org/10.1146/annurev-psych-010213-115043
Lewandowsky, S., Ecker, U. K. H., & Cook, J. (2017). Beyond misinformation: Understanding and coping with the "post-truth" era. *Journal of Applied Research in Memory and Cognition* 6(4), 353–369.
Lewandowsky, S., & van der Linden, S. (2021). Countering misinformation and fake news through inoculation and prebunking. *European Review of Social Psychology* 32(1), 348–384. https://doi.org/10.1080/10463283.2021.1876983
Lewandowsky, S., & van der Linden, S. (2023). Debunking and prebunking in the age of misinformation. *Nature Human Behaviour* 7, 677–687. https://doi.org/10.1038/s41562-023-01501-w
Lovato, C., Petrovic, V., & van der Linden, S. (2024). Network-based correction of misinformation: Social inoculation and herd resilience. *Social Cognitive and Affective Neuroscience* 19(2), 112–124. https://doi.org/10.1093/scan/nsac110
Lovato, J., et al. (2024). Diverse misinformation: Impacts of human biases on detection of deepfakes on networks. *NPJ Complexity* 1(5).
Maertens, R., Roozenbeek, J., Basol, M., & van der Linden, S. (2021). Long-term effectiveness of inoculation against misinformation: Three longitudinal experiments. *Journal of Experimental Psychology: Applied* 27(1), 1–16. https://doi.org/10.1037/xap0000315
Marwick, A., & Boyd, d. (2018). *Media Manipulation and Disinformation Online.* Data & Society Research Institute.
Meterko, V., & Cooper, G. (2022). Cognitive biases in criminal case evaluation: A review of the research. *Journal of Police and Criminal Psychology* 37, 101–122.
Microsoft. (2023). *C2PA: Coalition for Content Provenance and Authenticity.* https://www.microsoft.com/en-us/security/blog
Mirza, R. (2023). Labeling AI-generated content: A digital literacy challenge. *Internet Policy Review* 12(1). https://policyreview.info/articles/news/ai-labeling-mirza
Mirza, R. (2024a). Additional commentary. *Harvard Kennedy School Misinformation Review* (anticipated).
Mirza, R. (2024b, February 16). How AI deepfakes threaten the 2024 elections. *The Journalist's Resource* (Shorenstein Center, Harvard Kennedy School). Retrieved from https://journalistsresource.org

Mitchell, K. J. (2000). *Memory source monitoring: Implications for eyewitness testimony. Applied Cognitive Psychology* 14(7), 49–61.

MIT News. (2022). MIT launches media literacy course on detecting deepfakes. *Massachusetts Institute of Technology News*. https://news.mit.edu/2022/media-literacy-deepfakes-course-0926

Molins, L. (2025, February 26). The rise of deepfakes: What digital platforms and technology organizations should know. *Deloitte UK*. Retrieved from https://www.deloitte.com/uk/en/Industries/tmt/analysis/the-rise-of-deepfakes-what-digital-platforms-and-technology-organizations-should-know.html

Nanayakkara, N., Halgamuge, M., & Syed, A. (2019). *Security and privacy of internet of medical things (IoMT) based healthcare applications: A review. 2019 IIER 750th International Conference on Advances in Business Management and Information Technology (ICABMIT)*. Institute for Technology and Research.

New Jersey Division of Elections. (2023a). *Don't Be Fooled By Deepfakes* [Infographic campaign]. https://nj.gov/state/elections/voting-info-deepfakes.shtml

New Jersey Division of Elections. (2023b). *Voter Alert: Don't Be Fooled by Deepfakes* [Public fact sheet]. https://nj.gov/state/elections/

Nikolopoulou, K. (2022, December 7). What is the framing effect? Definition & examples. *Scribbr*. Revised June 25, 2023, from https://www.scribbr.com/research-bias/framing-effect/

Nikolopoulou, K. (2023, March 18). What is overconfidence bias? Definition & examples. *Scribbr*. Revised February 6, 2025, from https://www.scribbr.com/research-bias/overconfidence-bias

NPR. (2023). *How to Resist Misinformation Without Becoming Cynical*. https://www.npr.org/2023/11/09/misinformation-resistance

PBS. (2023). *How to Detect Deepfakes and Avoid Being Fooled* [Lesson plan]. https://www.pbs.org/education/

Pham, D. V., et al. (2010). *Optimizing windows security features to block malware and hack tools on USB storage devices*. In *Progress in Electromagnetics Research Symposium*. The Electromagnetics Academy.

Regan, G. (2025, January 22). The psychology of deepfakes in social engineering. *Reality Defender Insights*. Retrieved from https://www.realitydefender.com/insights/the-psychology-of-deepfakes-in-social-engineering

Reeves, B., & Nass, C. (1996). *The Media Equation: How People Treat Computers, Television, and New Media Like Real People and Places*. Cambridge University Press.

Roesner, F. (n.d.). Misinformation flow chart. *EurekAlert!*. Retrieved June 14, 2025, from https://www.eurekalert.org/multimedia/867697.

Roozenbeek, J., Maertens, R., McClanahan, W. P., & van der Linden, S. (2022a). Psychological inoculation improves resilience against misinformation: Evidence from a field experiment with YouTube ads. *Science Advances* 8(33), eabo6254. https://doi.org/10.1126/sciadv.abo6254

Roozenbeek, J., Maertens, R., McClanahan, W., & van der Linden, S. (2022b). Psychological inoculation improves resilience against misinformation on social media. *Science Advances* 8(36), eabo6254. https://doi.org/10.1126/sciadv.abo6254

Roozenbeek, J., & van der Linden, S. (2019). The fake news game: Actively inoculating against the risk of misinformation. *Journal of Risk Research* 22(5), 570–580. https://doi.org/10.1080/13669877.2018.1443491

Roozenbeek, J., van der Linden, S., & Nygren, T. (2022c). Prebunking misinformation with short videos: Evidence from a field experiment. *PNAS* 119(32), e2114480119. https://doi.org/10.1073/pnas.2114480119

Roozenbeek, J., van der Linden, S., Lewandowsky, S., et al. (2022d). Psychological inoculation improves resilience against misinformation across cultures. *Science Advances* 8(25), eabo6254.

Shapiro, D. (2023, October 12). U.S. schools try to prepare students for an AI-powered world of misinformation. *NPR*. https://www.npr.org/2023/10/12/media-literacy-deepfakes-education

Sotkasiira, T., & Salminen, M. (2022). Critical media literacy in Finland's national core curriculum: Building digital resilience in secondary education. *Nordic Journal of Comparative and International Education (NJCIE)* 6(2), 24–41. https://doi.org/10.7577/njcie.4707

StratCom Centre of Excellence. (2022). *Operationalising "Prebunking": NATO Resilience Strategy Updates. NATO Strategic Communications COE.* https://stratcomcoe.org

Stroud, N. J. (2021). Nurturing a healthy news ecosystem. *Political Communication* 38(3), 289–298.

Taber, C. S., & Lodge, M. (2006). Motivated skepticism in the evaluation of political beliefs. *American Journal of Political Science* 50(3), 755–769. https://doi.org/10.1111/j.1540-5907.2006.00214.x

Tandoc, E. C., Lim, Z. W., & Ling, R. (2018). Defining "fake news": A typology of scholarly definitions. *Digital Journalism* 6(2), 137–153.

Taylor, M. (2025, January 28). *How Understanding Cognitive Biases Protects Us Against Deepfakes.* University of Arkansas. *Retrieved from* https://walton.uark.edu/insights/posts/how-understanding-cognitive-biases-protects-us-against-deepfakes.php

Thomson Reuters. (2024a). *Deepfakes and the Law: State and Federal Responses.* https://www.thomsonreuters.com/en/legal

Thomson Reuters. (2024b). *Deepfakes and U.S. Legal Responses: A State-Level Overview.* https://www.thomsonreuters.com/en/legal

TikTok (ByteDance). (2023, February). *TikTok's New Rules on Deepfakes and Synthetic Media.*

van der Linden, S., Roozenbeek, J., *& Compton, J.* (2020). Inoculating against fake news about COVID-19. *Frontiers in Psychology* 11, 566790. https://doi.org/10.3389/fpsyg.2020.566790

The Week. (2023, August 9). Why media literacy is becoming a global priority. *The Week.* https://www.theweek.com/media-literacy-global-efforts

Westling, J. (2019, February 28). Deception & trust: A deep look at deep fakes. *Techdirt.* Retrieved from https://www.techdirt.com/2019/02/28/deception-trust-deep-look-deep-fakes/

Chapter 8

Combating Deepfake Videos

A Comprehensive Detection and Analysis System Using Advanced Machine Learning Techniques

K.A. Varunkumar, K. Annapurani, T. Balachander, K.A. Vinodhini, and T. Anstey Vathani

8.1 INTRODUCTION TO DEEPFAKES

The rapid progress of machine learning (ML) algorithms and deep neural networks has also driven an explosion in highly realistic deepfake videos. Deepfakes, a form of manipulated media that is the product of advanced deep learning, have proliferated across popular social media networks. These are troubling videos because they are spreading unchallenged and could be making fat people sick. Deepfakes have implications far beyond simply amusing ourselves; they can also spread inaccurate information, sway public opinion, and potentially defame people or companies [1]. In light of these threats, there is an acute and ubiquitous demand for reliable tools to detect, demonstrate, and monitor the spread of deepfake content to safeguard individuals, organizations, and society at large.

The deepfake threat has been recognized by researchers and technology companies and is receiving serious attention in the form of the development of more sophisticated deepfake detection algorithms. These algorithms employ elaborate strategies like reverse engineering, facial recognition, or complex pattern analysis to detect irregularities in deepfake videos. The algorithms can help differentiate between real and insincere content by looking at subtle signposts such as facial expressions, blinking patterns, and inconsistencies in how things are lit. Also, the recent progress in ML is such that these algorithms are constantly learning and updating themselves in terms of discriminatory power, to the point of keeping up with emerging deepfake techniques [2].

But addressing the deepfake threat in full will require an all-hands-on-deck approach, with governments, technology platforms, and researchers working together. The government can contribute by laying down a regulatory framework and guidelines for synthetic media production and dissemination [3]. It also means that the tech companies themselves have a duty to build strong detection methods into their platforms that can block deep fake material. Research organizations also play a role in creating new technologies and techniques to accurately confirm and engage with deepfakes. Post-processing by these stakeholders enables knowledge, resource, and expertise sharing that helps make society more resistant to unsavory impacts from adversarial deepfake manipulation. In conclusion, the spread of deepfakes is a multifaceted problem that should be systematically addressed by a wide spectrum of efforts. Using cutting-edge ML techniques and sophisticated detection algorithms while encouraging cooperation, we can stifle the threat of deepfakes and protect the authenticity of the digital content and conversation. It's this joined-up thinking that's essential to retain the trust and authenticity that today's world so desperately needs.

Work to thwart deepfakes has made progress in a few critical areas. Face expression, head movement difference, lip synchronization, and audio-visual correlation are utilized by

 DOI: 10.1201/9781003539032-8

detection algorithms to detect fake media. In addition, ML approaches of counter GANs and capsule networks are being researched for higher detection accuracy [4]. The development of large datasets such as the DeepFake Detection Challenge (DFDC) and forensic tools also helps with the algorithm training and the manual verification sides. Methods such as challenges and international workshops are proposed to support the sharing of knowledge. Regulation and automatic detection by social media platforms are also working. Educational and awareness campaigns are key to the public's understanding and resistance against deepfake manipulation.

But the subject is not closed, and further investigations and discussions are necessary. Key to our detector design is a behavioral analysis of human deepfake detection for guiding the design of detectors [5]. The progress of deep learning architectures allows efficient detection models. Sustained contributions from tech companies, governments, and research organizations will be necessary to keep pace with evolving deepfake methods. Ethical guidelines and defense mechanisms in social media systems are among the means to alleviate the detrimental effects of deepfakes. Together, society can prepare more effectively to guard against the threats of manipulative synthetic media.

8.2 MOTIVATION AND PURPOSE

In the modern age of technology, the widespread distribution of misinformation content and fake news is an act that can threaten the foundation of society, creating uncertainty in terms of credibility as well as disrupting public discourse. The manipulation goes well beyond just spreading misinformation; these tactics are often used for social and political manipulation, taking advantage of the public's weakness in decision-making. Such manipulation can not only play with perceptions of individuals but also spread toxicity and create divisions between sectors and also diminish trust in established institutions. Now, let us take the misleading content floating all around on online platforms, like YouTube, Facebook, and Twitter, which is spreading false information. It is a major area of privacy concern, as it takes a few minutes to adapt an individual based upon the data collected from them and force them to act in a way by exploiting their personal data [6].

The doors of information security are blown wide open toward cybersecurity threats as malicious Internet users leverage information security gaps, committing fraud against systems. This presents a dual challenge as human and cyber protectors have to navigate a maze of mega data-trains that focus on keeping personal and sensitive information secure and private while managing hordes of beefy contradictions [7]. Trust has shrunk not just in the media but also in the institutions, as we all become selective consumers and question the quality of information being served to us. But this crisis of confidence reaches beyond digital platforms, undermining the foundations of reliable information sharing from traditional media sources upon which democratic societies depend.

In spite of these challenges, technological progress creates both opportunities and threats. Some advances in technology and algorithms can be used to preserve the integrity of the media and to improve the authenticity of the communication. Examples include automated fact-checking systems that are useful in spotting and flagging misinformation at scale. Nevertheless, these advances also create new opportunities for deception, as deepfakes and AI-generated text provide extra challenges to the political misinformation environment [8]. While we must search for technology-driven interventions, we must balance that with ethical considerations, because protecting the truth and integrity is our first priority. This means that the problem of misinformation and fake news is multifaceted and requires rethinking our response. The approach must be broad, consisting of technological innovation for detection and mitigation, regulatory action that creates guidelines and mechanisms for enforcement, and the space to engage in ethical reflection so as to protect the pillars of our democracy in a more digital world [9]. Through this digital maze, collaborative initiatives like the latter are really what is needed. In that context, working with different stakeholders such as tech companies, governments, NGOs, and educational institutions will be key to establishing a coordinated approach to counter misinformation. Such collaborations can contribute to more standardized practices and protocols that improve the collective capacity to identify and respond to misinformation in a timely and effective manner.

Technology companies, for that matter, can do their bit by updating algorithms that give precedence to verified fast facts and genuine sources over others, consequently making it tough for fake news to flourish on social media platforms. Moreover, these companies can enforce stricter verification requirements on news content creators, allowing only reputable sources to publish news content [10]. On the other hand, the government agencies could work on the legislative side, writing laws that would criminalize the intentional creation or distribution of fake news, while protecting freedom of speech. As the communication infrastructure was international, this framework must not only promote national cooperation to confront misinformation that travels through borders but also enforce an international regulation for such communication. And finally media literacy non-profits can also be very beneficial to society by showing the public how to recognize and evaluate the legitimacy of information. Such programs are essential in developing an astute citizenry capable of traversing an intricate media environment without being ensnared by misinformation [11]. Along with this, it is necessary to make the public aware of misinformation and the verification of sources via campaigns that make the public aware of the danger of misinformation and checking sources before advancing content.

Along with these cooperative efforts, the building of enhanced technological tools has to go on. By having artificial intelligence (AI) operate in the background, more advanced fact-checking services can not only expose overt misinformation but also identify more nuanced biases and exaggeration in reporting. These could come in the form of browser extensions or social media tools that will notify users of the trustworthiness of the content they consume in real-time. Equally important, however, is that we construct these technological solutions to be ethical to avoid future misuse. New tools designed for combating misinformation should integrate privacy-preserving techniques to avoid increasing situations of surveillance or privacy violations of users [12]. In addition, a certain level of transparency regarding the functioning of these technologies is essential to ensure users trust them and avoid misuse of them by operators of the platform or other entities.

In conclusion, combating the so-called plague of misinformation and fake news would need holistic measures combining all possible technological innovation; collaborative regulation of the tech industry; educational initiatives; and an ethical system of governance. Only through collaboration across the varied stakeholders can society hope to safeguard the information environment and uphold the pillars of democratic discussion in the digital era. The challenge of misinformation and fake news is a huge, multifaceted, broadly defined project with any number of paths forward, which is a problem because the digital landscape is just as complex as the information it contains. Now, such a project would entail the creation and deployment of high-tech solutions, such as complex algorithms to identify misinformation and fight against it. That would mean automating the fact-checking processes that could scavenge on a whole range of data to find false information or recognize when new trends were emerging in deceptive content creation using AI and ML.

Additionally, the project scope would include the creation of regulatory frameworks for the spread of information on the Internet. This will mean working with legislators and legal authorities to quote and enact rules to tackle the dissemination of false information, without sacrificing tenets of free speech. It would also include education and awareness—teaching the public critical thinking skills and media literacy skills to help them navigate the media landscape and separate credible from illegitimate sources [13]. In the end, it would not be the enhancements of that project that would be cited as its success: It would be the ability of society to withstand the assault of disinformation that ensures that the content of information is protected, and the theatre of democratic discussion remains intact.

This juxtaposition makes the misinformation and fake news problem more complex, given the nature of speed digital media works on and the global aspect of information dissemination. Thus, any project to address these issues needs to be both strong and flexible to respond rapidly to the new developments and new techniques of misinformation strategies. Within technological solutions, although developing sophisticated algorithms and automated systems for fact-checking will be undertaken, this project will also need to address the integration of these technologies into existing digital platforms. Such as social media networks, news outlets, and search engines, where misinformation usually spreads the quickest. Such technological integrations should be easy to integrate, so they do not impede the natural utilization of these platforms while being successful at reducing the spread of fake news [14].

In addition, a digital literacy toolkit appropriate for different demographics would be a helpful tool for the project going forward. This toolkit would consist of tutorials, webinars, and interactive modules to further the public's capacity to critically assess the credibility of information. It'd further encourage engagement with the algorithms and the operations that sit behind the scenes of content curation and targeted advertising, both of which tend to be influential components behind misinformation and ways of spreading it.

Perhaps even more importantly, the project would also include a worldwide network of fact-checkers and information verifiers. The network would connect different fact-checkers around the world to share data and tactics to combat misinformation more effectively globally. So, integrating blockchain technology might make sense to ensure the integrity and transparency of the fact-checking process in a way in which the data and its verifications are tamper-proof.

Lastly, the success of the project will be heavily reliant on continued assessments and feedback systems. Frequent assessments would use surveys, focus groups, and data analytics to assess how well the strategies and technologies are working [15]. This feedback will orient incremental enhancements, as a way to make certain that the venture stays at the leading edge of the battle against misinformation. Each of these backstops, whether it be through the technological range of mitigations, work toward supportive regulatory frameworks, education efforts, or international cooperation and competition, is all part of the foundation necessary to build a society resistant to the challenge of misinformation and, ultimately, protective of the integrity of its own democratic processes. The project would seek to minimize the prevalence of fake news while promoting a more informed, engaged, and critical thinking society.

8.3 ML AND DEEP LEARNING

In video and image analysis using deep learning, there are two types of models that are applied, which are VGG16–long short-term memory (LSTM) fusions and ResNet–LSTM fusions. These models are a combination of a convolutional neural network (CNN) and recurrent neural network (RNN), which is one of the highest levels to capture the synergistic benefits of CNNs and RNNs for global and local visual content. The VGG16 + LSTM model is the first one that takes advantage of VGG16, which is a powerful model for image feature extraction and LSTM, which should be used for sequential data. The combination of the two allows the model to process visual information but also to learn about temporal dependencies present within video data, making it useful for tasks like video classification and action recognition. In contrast, the second model (ResNet + LSTM) combines the residual neural network (ResNet) architecture (which is designed to train very deep networks) with LSTM. By employing both of them, the model is able to memorize complex visual information and temporal correlations, and this makes it one of the most useful and significant models for video captioning and anomaly detection tasks as well. These models represent the new frontier in deep learning architecture by providing a powerful combination of CNNs and LSTMs capable of addressing challenging video and image analysis problems.

These are clearly promising models, and the deep learning community is constantly using these types of successes to push the community forward by devising new ways of refining hybrid architectures [16]. Optimizing the parameters of the network and training techniques is a common active research area of improving these models to a higher efficiency level, logical in real-life usage contexts. For example, researchers are exploring ways to decrease the computational cost of training and deploying these deep networks, while still achieving optimal performance. Methods like pruning, quantization, and knowledge distillation are becoming popular as effective approaches for reducing such models to be more efficient and faster, which are critical for deploying on mobiles and low-resource scenarios.

Further, transfer learning has been proven beneficial to improve the performance of VGG16+LSTM and ResNet+LSTM models. This enables developers to achieve higher accuracy and improved generalization by using the features from pre-trained networks on large datasets and then fine-tuning them for a particular task. Besides making training faster, this strategy helps with the fact that in very specialized domains, we can have limited annotated data.

A schematic diagram of a Convolutional Neural Network (CNN) architecture, in Figure 8.1, showing input image layers, convolutional layers, pooling layers, and fully connected layers used for deepfake detection.

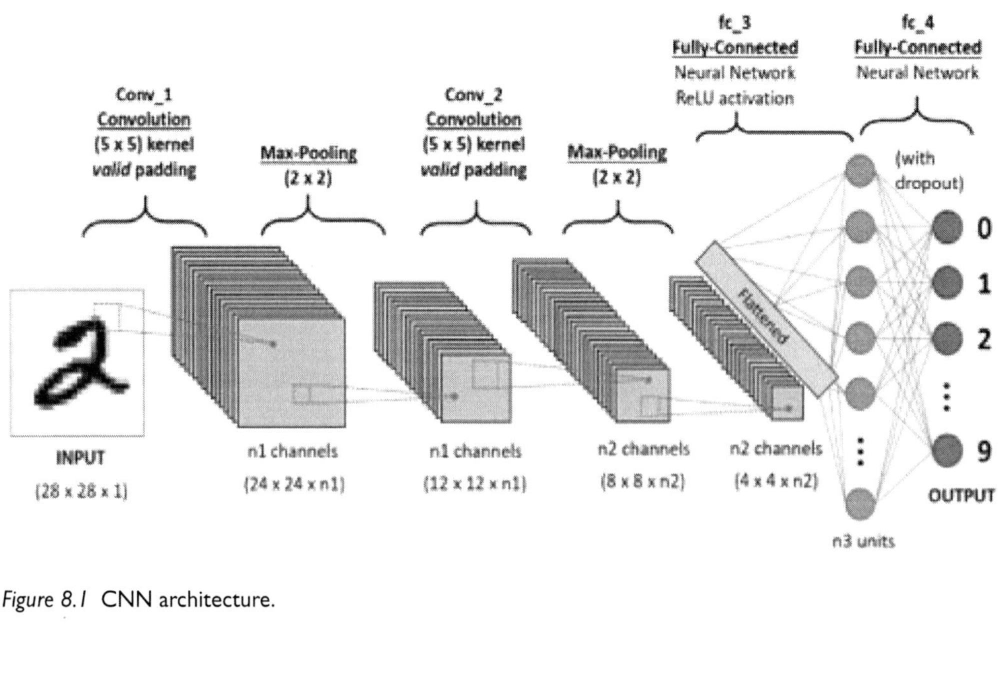

Figure 8.1 CNN architecture.

Another exciting area of research is the combination of these models with attention mechanisms. By incorporating attention mechanisms, the network may be able to hone in on more salient aspects of the video frames, which could help with interpretability and general model performance in several contexts, especially where understanding context is paramount (e.g., complex scene recognition or lighting and environmental dynamics).

Future work to apply such hybrid models will require academia and industry to work together closely [17]. These partnerships enable the creation of customized solutions to unique problems, ranging from real-time sports video analytics to automatic video content tagging for a media library. These models, when combined together, can significantly improve outcomes in multiple sectors such as entertainment, healthcare, and public safety. These models will be key to further understanding deep learning's ability to analyze video and images at scale as we continue to make breakthroughs in this area. VGG16 + LSTM, a hybrid deep learning architecture like the VGG16 Architecture, integrates the VGG16 CNN with LSTM recurrent neural networks. Using VGG16, a very well-performing model for image classification, to extract visual features from an image allows us to obtain deep convolutional feature representations that capture texture, shape, and semantic information. The LSTM network takes these features and is very efficient in temporal data operations, for example, due to its ability to learn temporal dependencies between time steps [18]. By combining both of these aspects, the model is able to efficiently learn both sequence data and the visual contents of images, which makes it fit for tasks like video classification, action recognition, and image captioning. This is the CNN used, VGG16, used with LSTMs, which combines the advantages of both convolutional networks and LSTMs and hence serves as a strong base to handle visual data having both spatial and temporal nature.

Diagram of the VGG16 deep learning architecture given in Figure 8.2, illustrating stacked convolutional layers followed by pooling and fully connected layers for image feature extraction and classification.

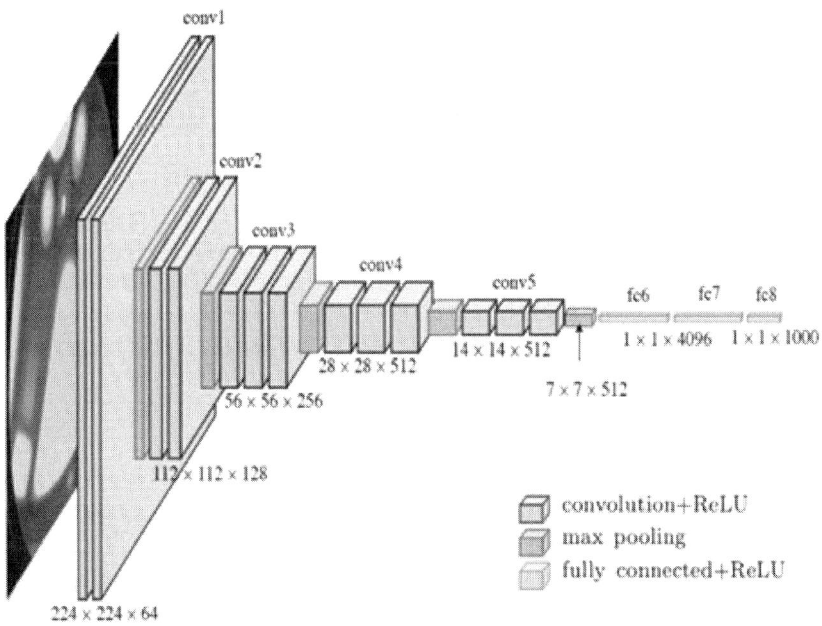

Figure 8.2 VGG16 architecture.

ResNet architecture is combined with LSTM recurrent neural networks to obtain a unified, generic framework suitable for various video and image analysis tasks [19]. Based on the work of ResNet, which was widely adopted due to its strong performance on very deep networks and its ability to address the vanishing gradient problem, the model was used as a backbone for feature extraction from the images. The extracted features are then fed into the LSTM network, which is great to capture temporal dependencies from sequential data. This helps the model to represent not only complex visual features but also the temporal dynamics of visual information, which makes it most fitting for video captioning, activity recognition, and anomaly detection tasks. After the ResNet, they have implemented an LSTM architecture that draws upon the utility of LSTM as a method to incorporate both spatial and temporal information and create an architectural framework that handles the visual data in a powerful and effective manner, ideal for various computer vision and video analysis needs. With these additional capabilities, the ResNet + LSTM architecture can address complex problems in practice, including some where the perception of dynamic contexts is required [20]. In the example of using it in an autonomous vehicle, this architecture can be used to process continuous video footage and determine how to track and anticipate pedestrians or the behavior of other vehicles over time. This allows CS-ARE to utilize spatial knowledge from ResNet and temporal wisdom from LSTM to predict and drive in an accurate and real-time manner, both of which are crucial for the safety and effectiveness of autonomous driving tasks.

Similarly, in healthcare, ResNet + LSTM can be applied in patient monitoring systems utilizing a continuous video for monitoring patient activities and identifying behavioral abnormalities or emergencies. The model can, for instance, evaluate time series of movements to determine if there are indications of distress or sudden movements that require emergency medical attention. This application is not just for ensuring patient safety, but it also assists healthcare providers in providing timely treatment. In addition, the entertainment industry can use this architecture to develop powerful video editing tools and content creation. By understanding the semantics of video sequences, content, and context, AI can automate time-consuming editing processes like scene detection and summarization, improving post-production workflows and enabling automatic scenarios with better sport strategies and viewer-oriented content. Additionally, combining ResNet + LSTM is emerging as a powerful tool in the surveillance and security domain. It helps with constant tracking and anomaly detection with alerts on any abnormal activity or behavior over a long duration. It is an essential capability for monitoring public spaces, safeguarding airports, or securing critical infrastructure, as analyzing both situational and historical context can quickly identify potential risks or incidents.

So there are a couple of potential implications of research moving forward, including little optimizations around trying to improve the efficiency of the model; trying to reduce latency for real-time processing; improving the model's generalizability from limited data; and implementing advanced techniques, for example, few-shot learning. Such developments will surely create new opportunities to use deep learning more efficiently in a wide variety of fields, making smart systems even more important for the success of our digital society.

Block diagram of the Residual Neural Network (ResNet) architecture given in Figure 8.3, highlighting residual blocks with skip connections that enable training of very deep neural networks.

This is a worrying societal threat, specifically the deepfakes—the so-called synthetic media that use AI/ML to manipulate images and/or videos toward putting words in someone's mouth they never spoke, seriously undermining the very foundations of the trust-based society that we have built since the dawn of modern civility. The use of deepfake technology is evolving rapidly, as is the work done against these malicious creations, which makes this field critically important.

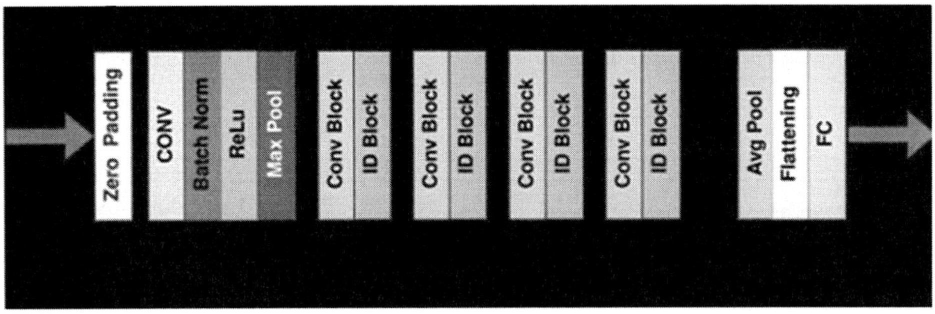

Figure 8.3 ResNet architecture.

Advanced detection algorithms that are underpinning the technical fight against deepfakes. These systems examine various features of videos to identify incongruities that suggest alterations. The facial expression analysis is especially useful because, on a lot of occasions, the deepfakes cannot mimic the expression subtleties of the human characters. Likewise, scrutiny of head gyrations as efficiently as lip-syncing can expose an unnatural simulator, as gear presently cannot imitate completely fluid hand–eye coordination. In addition, the inclusion of checks for audio-visual correlation further strengthens the resilience of detection systems. When there is a mismatch between the words being spoken and the movement of the lips and the flow of the speech, deepfakes that change the video without changing the audio tracks (or vice versa) can be automatically detected. In addition to these, there are ML styles that provide new mechanisms to learn detection, and counter GANs and capsule networks also fall into this category. Besides tech solutions, large datasets like the DFDC are essential resources for testing and training detection algorithms. Such datasets, comprising both authentic and fake content examples, are essential to creating effective detection tools that can learn to spot the difference between real and fake media. These technical efforts are complemented by collaborative initiatives among academia, industry, and government. Competitions and global big events focused on detecting deepfakes encourage the trade of information and new ideas. This approach standardizes methodologies and shares solutions that can be utilized to improve the effectiveness of detection tools across platforms and media types.

We have already seen steps toward regulation, as governments wake up to the risks of a deepfake world. However, legislation criminalizing malicious deepfake creation and distribution is in the works, raising free speech and enforcement issues. At the same time, social media platforms are putting more and more automated systems in place to detect and block deepfake content before it has a chance to go viral.

The deepfake-fighting playbook also emphasizes the need for public education and awareness, as noted by the executive director of the gun-violence prevention advocacy group during the interview (09:02). Raising public awareness of how to identify and report deepfakes, alongside the ethical issues of creating and sharing them, will help society counter the use and manipulation of these technologies. Ready access to the technology can help open it up and allow people to better judge whether what they see in the media is accurate. There will always be room for further research into human behaviors toward deepfakes, and further development should ensure there is space for ongoing evolution. The relationships between perceptions, susceptibility, and deepfakes are likely to inform means to generate advances in deepfake detection and education. In addition, as deep learning architectures develop, we can build more complex and faster detection models. Such advancements are required to ensure we are not left behind, considering deepfakes quality keeps improving.

Tech firms and governments, as well as universities, should keep their collaboration and resource allocation in place. Additionally, it is necessary to create ethical guidelines on synthetic media usage while adapting detection systems into large digital platforms early on and as often as possible to protect public debate and trust. To sum up, deepfakes pose significant challenges, but this is where technology and law should work hand-in-hand. A strategy that involves technological innovation, sensible regulatory frameworks, public education, and international cooperation may provide a comprehensive solution to the threats posed by this disruptive technology. And all of these actions together will allow our society to be much better defended against the risks of artificial, misleading media. However, the article offers a literature review on the three research strands within deepfake detection: learning how deepfakes are generated, how to detect them using ML methods, and the ethical and legal issues involved in deepfake creation. Understanding how the technology works, such as GANs and neural networks. Detection techniques use ML, image forensics, and behavioral cues to differentiate real from fake content, although adversarial training makes it challenging, for example, with deepfakes creation. Focus turns to the auditory aspect, such as voice analysis and speaker identification, and applications in the real world of cybersecurity, journalism, and social media appear. A recurring theme includes ethical considerations addressing regulatory requirements and the trade-off between the right to free speech and the right to privacy. In addition, the literature emphasizes the provision of public awareness and media literacy programs that enable people to critically engage with the digital media ecosystem. Collectively, these studies illustrate the multidimensional complexity of deepfake detections, highlighting technological, ethical, and implementation aspects with topical relevance for the future of verification in maintaining the integrity of digital media and preventing deepfake abuse, and other research exploring the challenges, advancements, and methods in adapting to the real-world prowess of deepfake technology.

In this era of AI, deepfakes' synthetic media, in particular, generated by generative adversarial networks (GANs) models, have surfaced as one of the most menacing digital hazards. Although deepfakes were originally created for non-combative, creative, and benign purposes, these tools are now capable of accurately imitating human likeness for fundamental purposes. This chapter unpacks the deepfake threat ecosystem, providing a deep insight into how these technologies are built, disseminated, weaponized, and defended against. Deepfake creation involves using deep learning algorithms trained on large datasets of images, videos, or voice samples. Key technologies include:

- GANs: A pair of neural networks, a generator and a discriminator, compete to generate media that looks progressively more real.
- Autoencoders and VQ-VAEs: For face swapping, voice synthesis.
- Diffusion: Another newish category that can produce even more photorealistic generation.

Some of the popular tools are DeepFaceLab, Zao, Reface App, MyHeritage AI Time Machine, and Descript (Voice Cloning). The availability of these tools makes deepfakes easy for novices and sophisticated actors alike to create.

Here is a brief overview of the key findings and developments in this field.

8.4 DEEPFAKE GENERATION TECHNIQUES

Various studies have reported on the underlying components behind deepfake generation, such as GANs, autoencoders, and neural network architectures. Researchers have begun to examine how these tools time-shift and re-process these audio-visual materials.

8.4.1 Detection Methods

Much of the literature is focused on creating and augmenting the process of deepfake identification. Several approaches have been suggested, such as ML models, image forensics, and behavioral cues. Others have pointed out the flaws of existing detection methods, for example, through adversarial training of deepfake models to avoid being detected.

8.4.1.1 Deepfake Detection for Human Face Images and Videos

The authors provide a comprehensive overview of existing methodologies, dataset trends, and prevailing challenges, and they emphasize the recent advancements in deep neural network (DNN)-based approaches for detecting and classifying DeepFakes. They further note that this technology continues to evolve rapidly, bringing forth both promising opportunities and significant risks. This survey intends to understand the complexities of the field by categorizing detection methods and reviewing the techniques for creating deepfakes. The authors also review the history of deepfake datasets and generate insight into detection models that can be trained to detect a wide range of data. They hope this survey will be useful to both researchers and practitioners who are interested in applying deep learning methods to fight the rapidly growing deepfake content, providing them with state-of-the-art detection methods and valuable resources to effectively reduce the associated problems.

8.4.1.2 Optimizing Deepfake Video Detection Using Image Preprocessing

The growing issues surrounding the possible dangers of deepfake technology to cybersecurity, privacy, and national security. Using novel, near-proximity image enhancement techniques alongside local dataset cleansing, the authors propose an optimization scheme for an already-existing Xception-based deepfake detection method. They show an impressive performance working in their own experiment with the Xception Binary Classifier-Inference model, while recognition increased from 94% to 96%. Such research works toward reinforcing the ability to combat deepfake attacks by bolstering defense mechanisms for deepfake content detection.

8.4.1.3 Deep Learning for Deepfakes Creation and Detection

The ResNet-50 model, etc., and how effective it is in manipulating the content of media, demonstrates the growing sophistication of deep learning architectures in generating highly realistic synthetic imagery. His work highlights the role of the ResNet-50 architecture, with its many deep layers and use of residual connections, in effectively capturing the subtle differences and irregularities that are often present in manipulated video frames. This usage is essential because it showcases the ability of ResNet-50 to improve deepfake detection capabilities, providing a solid foundation to identify and mitigate the growing threat of manipulated media content. Such a capability is an essential requirement of many applications to ensure the integrity and trustworthiness of digital content.

8.4.1.4 Deepfakes Detection Using Human Eye-Blinking Pattern

A new method for detecting GAN-based deepfake generators, DeepVision takes advantage of the measurement of this gaze by analyzing the eye-blinking pattern in humans, which can be affected by a great number of factors, including gender, age, emotional state, and cognitive works. Deepfakes can then be detected by monitoring these alterations through integrity verification, which are heuristic methods based on research in medicine, biology, and brain engineering, and using ML and statistical methods. DeepVision—Anomaly Detection in Blinking Patterns: Based on the blinking time, number of times repeated, and time lag that elapsed when blinks appear quickly within a short period of time, this method is aimed at detecting anomalies. The effectiveness of DeepVision is supported by experimental results, which show a data augmentation of 87.5% on seven of the eight types of videos used for deepfake detection. This indicates an opportunity to utilize eye-blinking patterns as a more reliable reference to overcome the shortcomings that pixel-based integrity verification algorithms have, thereby eliminating any need for facial attribute re-synthesis.

8.4.1.5 Deep Convolutional Neural Network Architecture

With the rise of deepfakes using adversarial networks to warp the concepts of social integrity and trust, robust detection methods are more essential than ever. Although beneficial, as CNNs cannot grasp inter-frame dissimilarity, the authors propose that a better deep convolutional neural network (D-CNN) model can be developed. Their approach, trained with diverse kinds of image sources and optimized with binary cross-entropy and Adam optimizer, shows excellent accuracy on seven datasets ranging from deepfake to real images. The D-CNN architecture with accuracies of 94.67–99.33%, which shows in Table 8.1, have great promise in overcoming the threat of an uncontrolled proliferation of deepfakes, thus helping to protect the authenticity of digital content and trust in society.

Modality: The kind of input used for detection, that is, images, video frames, or audio.

It is then tested based on different datasets, and the training size is also adjusted for comparison purposes; the accuracy will differ based on the previous parameters.

Assessing the efficiency with respect to computational time and hardware resource consumption.

New Directions → There are some new techniques which have multimodal detection (e.g., video + audio cues).

Figure 8.4 shows an example of detecting scams based on deepfakes, which gives us the scenario of how voice scams in UK are being carried out. We explain the chart in the following text.

The CEO of a UK energy firm was, in March 2019, tricked into believing he was getting a phone call on his mobile from his boss, the CEO of the parent company in Germany. The voice, tone, and mannerisms were one and the same. Due to a need for secrecy and immediacy, the German "CEO" demanded that €220,000 ($243,000) be transferred to a Hungarian supplier.

Table 8.1 Comparison of deepfake detection techniques

Technique	*Modality*	*Approach*	*Detection Features*	*Accuracy*	*Efficiency*	*Strengths*	*Limitations*
Eye-Blinking Analysis	Video	Heuristic/ Biological cues	Involuntary blink patterns, eye movement	~65–80%	High (real-time possible)	Lightweight; doesn't require training	Fails on non-face videos or high-quality fakes
XceptionNet	Image/Video	Deep Learning (CNN)	Spatial-temporal inconsistencies	~90–95%	Moderate (GPU preferred)	High accuracy; pre-trained models available	Computationally intensive
ResNet-50	Image/Video	Residual CNN	Facial region discrepancies, artifacts	~85–93%	Moderate	Versatile, robust to noise and compression	May need fine-tuning on specific datasets
DeepVision	Image/Video	Hybrid AI + Forensic Techniques	Frame-level artifacts, texture analysis	~92–96%	High (optimized pipeline)	High precision; interpretable outputs	Requires quality input; limited to visuals
Audio Deepfake Detection (e.g., DeFakeNet)	Audio	Deep Learning + Spectrograms	Frequency modulation, voice clone patterns	~88–94%	Moderate	Effective for voice-based attacks	Less mature than visual deepfake detectors
Lip-Sync Discrepancy Detection	Video	ML + Audio-Visual Sync	Mismatch in lip movement and speech audio	~80–90%	Moderate	Good for talking head fakes	Ineffective without sound

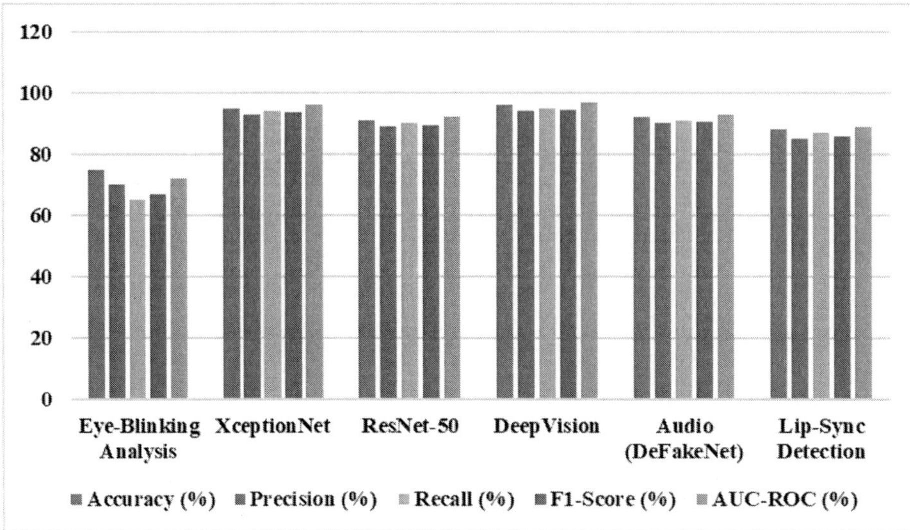

Figure 8.4 Deepfake CEO voice scam—$243,000 fraud in the UK (2019).

Modus Operandi

Little did the UK CEO know then or there that the voice on the other end of the phone was a deepfake voice. Using AI voice synthesis trained on the speeches and recreational online recordings of the victim, cybercriminals made an almost real voice clone. It was one of the first reported instances of corporate fraud using deepfake audio.

The attackers

- Employed voice-cloning software to replicate the German CEO's voice
- Made the VoIP-based call to hide the origin
- Emailed them afterward to give it an air of legitimacy

Outcome

- The funds were sent per the instructions.
- The fraud came to light only after having failed the second try and raised suspicions.
- The funds were first routed via accounts in Hungary and Mexico, thus no possibility of recovery.

Impact

- Exposed executives to social engineering via audio deepfake
- Drew international concerns over the AI-based impersonation menace
- Made companies reconsider how they do voice authentication and internal transfer protocols

8.5 CONCLUSION

Deepfake technology poses new and unprecedented challenges to the integrity of digital media, fueling concerns over the propagation of information, the absence of trust, and privacy and security issues. To counter these challenges, our research initiated work into creating high-tech deepfake detection software using the ResNet, LSTM, and CNN models. By studying the fundamentals of each of the paradigms along with a combination of these methods in a single detection framework, we hope to further contribute toward the detection of harmful synthetic media. Our strategic choice behind our deepfake detection software that employs the ResNet, LSTM, and CNN Models to handle the different aspects of deepfakes, as there is a range of manipulation techniques used. Those models have some special characteristics, which can represent temporal dependencies, capture sequential information, and extract powerful features (most of the time to prevent an overfitting problem) essential for accurate prediction. We combined the strengths of these different approaches and are doing well to classify and differentiate between real and fake deepfake media. Based on our research, we know that detection performance should be evaluated using detailed performance metrics (i.e., precision, recall, F1 score, etc.). Having tested the software exhaustively within each of these approaches, we had a reasonable understanding of the advantages and disadvantages of each, which in turn could inform the eventual optimization of our detection software for accuracy and reliability.

In addition, the continued focus on improvement has motivated us to perform our research. As always with emergent threats, we must continue to be flexible and invest in a robust response to synthetic media manipulation. That's why we are committed to continuous R&D to improve our models, implement the latest advancements in deep learning technology, and stay one step ahead of bad actors looking to capitalize on areas of weakness in digital media. Together, our deepfake detection software, powered by ResNet, LSTM, and CNN models, takes an important step in the battle against manipulation by synthetic media. After conducting careful research, running extensive tests, and adhering to the core beliefs of our founding team, we have created a solid, valid tool to identify and lessen the destructive impact of Deepfake content. We will continue to advance the detection of deepfakes, partnering with academic, industrial, and government partners, but, most importantly, we look forward to a safer and more reliable online world for everyone. Using this as a basis, we have several initiatives to develop in the future to complement our deepfake detection technology. First, we would like to increase and diversify our datasets, training our model with more sources and scenarios of deepfakes. This expansion will include not only more diverse imagery but also languages and cultures, to ensure that our technology works effectively around the world. Our goal is to increase the robustness of our models against ever more sophisticated deepfake techniques that could potentially pass undetected due to the absence of sufficient amounts of data in our training datasets. The second thing is more related to the inclusion of more neural network architectures, promising in similar fields, such as GANs and transformer architectures. These technologies have shown great promise in learning and generating complex patterns and sequences, which could be key in detecting the subtle artifacts of deepfakes. These advanced techniques can be harnessed to improve our detection systems' understanding of the nuances of deepfake manipulations, thus making our detection more effective. Additionally, we acknowledge the necessity of real-time detection capability as an essential component of limiting the impacts of deepfakes, in particular for social media channels and news media. In this regard, we will be focusing on making our models more computationally efficient, ensuring that they operate in real-time environment without compromising on accuracy. Reducing processing needs and increasing the speed of our algorithms will be a key point for deployment in applications requiring instantaneous detection. Continued partnership has always been a key part of our model. We will further build partnerships with tech companies, educational firms, and regulators to continue sharing insights, tools, and best practices. Not only will these collaborations support the advancement of our detection software, but they will also further the establishment of standards and protocols for addressing synthetic media within the wider community. Our ethical focus will also be on transparency and privacy issues involved with deploying AI when addressing sensitive applications. We must respect user privacy and data integrity in our solutions and clearly outline how our technology works or where it might fail. In conclusion, we are continuing our research and development activities to build a secure system for the future, anticipating what can only be perceived today and future predicted scenarios, and providing the freshest technology, battling the growing challenges of deepfakes. When pursuing this, we are committed to the highest standards of scientific rigor and ethical responsibility.

8.6 FUTURE ENHANCEMENT

Although our ResNet-, LSTM-, and CNN-based deepfake detection tool is an important step toward mitigating the threats of synthetic media manipulation, there are a number of more effective and robust directions for continued work. Some possible directions include the combined utilization of multimodal data. For example, exploring the integration of video and audio features could enhance the accuracy of our detection system. Adding other elements will contribute to a wider feature space and increase the distinction between real and fake content. Adversarial Training: Adversarial training methods should be examined to enhance our detection software against adversarial attacks. Training with adversarial examples makes our models more robust and ensures that they will reliably perform on the real data. Real-Time Detection: Research approaches for real-time deepfake detection allow timely response against illicit synthetic media manipulation. Low-latency detection for real-time applications will rely on efficient algorithms and require optimization. Collection of Large-Scale Datasets: To accommodate various types of deepfakes and variations, we can broaden our dataset collection process. We can design broader datasets with more content and manipulation methods and train better models that can generalize to a broader range of deepfake content. Explainability and Interpretability: Explainability and interpretability should be added to our detection software in some way to provide insight into what our models are doing to come to a decision. Integrating interpretability methods, for instance, attention mechanisms or saliency maps, can help provide the users with indication on why a specific media content is flagged as a deepfake. Create a user-friendly interface for our deepfake detection software to ease use and adoption to non-expert users. By adding intuitive visualization tools and interaction patterns, users will be able to interact with the software more efficiently and be able to understand the detection results with trust. Extensive Validation/Deployment: Deploy our detection software extensively/validate extensively in real-world settings (e.g., social media or content moderation systems). To assess the practicality and scalability of our software, we will need to work with the appropriate industry partners and stakeholders. Continuous Monitoring and Updating: We should have a framework to continuously monitor and update our detection software to keep pace with new deepfake methods and new threats. Having automated update mechanisms and proactive monitoring will help our software stay relevant in identifying new forms of synthetic media manipulation. With these future work directions, we can advance the deepfake detection area and contribute to a safer and more trustworthy digital environment for everyone. Overall, to drive progress and counter the persistent threat of synthetic media manipulation, we will need to maintain the collaboration with actors in academia, industry, and the government.

REFERENCES

1. Afchar, Darius, Vincent Nozick, Junichi Yamagishi, and Isao Echizen. "Mesonet: A compact facial video forgery detection network." In *2018 IEEE International Workshop on Information Forensics and Security (WIFS)*, pp. 1–7. IEEE, 2018.
2. Afzal, Shehzad, Sohaib Ghani, Mohamad Mazen Hittawe, Sheikh Faisal Rashid, Omar M. Knio, Markus Hadwiger, and Ibrahim Hoteit. "Visualization and visual analytics approaches for image and video datasets: A survey." *ACM Transactions on Interactive Intelligent Systems* 13, no. 1 (2023): 1–41.
3. Agarwal, Sakshi, and Lav R. Varshney. "Limits of deepfake detection: A robust estimation viewpoint." *arXiv preprint arXiv:1905.03493* (2019).
4. Ajao, Oluwaseun, Deepayan Bhowmik, and Shahrzad Zargari. "Sentiment aware fake news detection on online social networks." In *ICASSP 2019–2019 IEEE International Conference on Acoustics, Speech and Signal Processing (ICASSP)*, pp. 2507–2511. IEEE, 2019.
5. Akhtar, Zahid. "Deepfakes generation and detection: A short survey." *Journal of Imaging* 9, no. 1 (2023): 18.
6. Dolhansky, B. "The dee pfake detection challenge (DFDC) pre view dataset." *arXiv preprint arXiv:1910.08854* (2019).
7. Eelmaa, Simone. "Sexualization of children in Deepfakes and hentai." *Trames* 26, no. 2 (2022): 229–248.
8. Hinton, Geoffrey E., Alex Krizhevsky, and Sida D. Wang. "Transforming auto-encoders." In *Artificial Neural Networks and Machine Learning–ICANN 2011: 21st International Conference on Artificial Neural Networks, Espoo, Finland, June 14–17, 2011, Proceedings, Part I 21*, pp. 44–51. Springer Berlin Heidelberg, 2011.
9. Korshunov, Pavel, and Sébastien Marcel. "Vulnerability assessment and detection of deepfake videos." In *2019 International Conference on Biometrics (ICB)*, pp. 1–6. IEEE, 2019.
10. Kumar, Akash, Arnav Bhavsar, and Rajesh Verma. "Detecting deepfakes with metric learning." In *2020 8th International Workshop on Biometrics and Forensics (IWBF)*, pp. 1–6. IEEE, 2020.
11. Li, Yuezun, Ming-Ching Chang, and Siwei Lyu. "In ictu oculi: Exposing ai created fake videos by detecting eye blinking." In *2018 IEEE International Workshop on Information Forensics and Security (WIFS)*, pp. 1–7. IEEE, 2018.
12. Lyu, Siwei. "Deepfake detection: Current challenges and next steps." In *2020 IEEE International Conference on Multimedia & Expo Workshops (ICMEW)*, pp. 1–6. IEEE, 2020.
13. Mittal, Trisha, Uttaran Bhattacharya, Rohan Chandra, Aniket Bera, and Dinesh Manocha. "Emotions don't lie: An audio-visual deepfake detection method using affective cues." In *Proceedings of the 28th ACM International Conference on Multimedia*, pp. 2823–2832. 2020.
14. Narayan, Kartik, Harsh Agarwal, Kartik Thakral, Surbhi Mittal, Mayank Vatsa, and Richa Singh. "Df-platter: Multi-face heterogeneous deepfake dataset." In *Proceedings of the IEEE/CVF Conference on Computer Vision and Pattern Recognition*, pp. 9739–9748. 2023.

15. Nguyen, Huy H., Junichi Yamagishi, and Isao Echizen. "Capsule-forensics: Using capsule networks to detect forged images and videos." In *ICASSP 2019–2019 IEEE International Conference on Acoustics, Speech and Signal Processing (ICASSP)*, pp. 2307–2311. IEEE, 2019.
16. Nguyen, Thanh Thi, Quoc Viet Hung Nguyen, Dung Tien Nguyen, Duc Thanh Nguyen, Thien Huynh-The, Saeid Nahavandi, Thanh Tam Nguyen, Quoc-Viet Pham, and Cuong M. Nguyen. "Deep learning for deepfakes creation and detection: A survey." *Computer Vision and Image Understanding* 223 (2022): 103525.
17. Rossler, A., D. Cozzolino, L. Verdoliva, C. Riess, J. Thies, and M. Nießner. FaceForensics++: Learning to detect manipulated facial images. In *Proceedings of the IEEE/CVF International Conference on Computer Vision (ICCV)*, pp. 1–11. IEEE, 2019. https://arxiv.org/abs/1901.08971.
18. Tariq, Shahroz, Sangyup Lee, and Simon S. Woo. "A convolutional lstm based residual network for deepfake video detection." *arXiv preprint arXiv:2009.07480* (2020).
19. Vaccari, Cristian, and Andrew Chadwick. "Deepfakes and disinformation: Exploring the impact of synthetic political video on deception, uncertainty, and trust in news." *Social Media+ Society* 6, no. 1 (2020): 2056305120903408.
20. Yu, Peipeng, Zhihua Xia, Jianwei Fei, and Yujiang Lu. "A survey on deepfake video detection." *Iet Biometrics* 10, no. 6 (2021): 607–624.

Chapter 9

Cloud AI

Data Breach Detection

M. Fatima, Kalpana Rai, Alfiya Jahan, Amit Jatav, and Harshita Yadav

9.1 INTRODUCTION

In 2023, a massive data leak rocked Microsoft when an improperly configured Azure Blob Storage account exposed a staggering 38 terabytes of confidential information. This breach occurred because an overly permissive Shared Access Signature (SAS) token granted unrestricted access to sensitive files, including internal emails, passwords, and development documents. The fallout highlighted a critical truth that cloud storage security is only as strong as its weakest configuration [1].

As cloud platforms like Sky Vault—a user-friendly storage solution similar to Google Drive and Dropbox—continue to grow, there is a risk of unauthorized access and data exposure. To meet this challenge, **Cloud Guard AI: Data Breach Detection** employs cutting-edge machine learning and behavioral analytics to monitor activity in real-time. It detects suspicious logins, abnormal file transfers, and unusual access patterns, alerting users instantly to potential threats.

With Cloud Guard AI, Sky Vault users gain a powerful line of defense against cloud breaches, ensuring their data remains secure, private, and protected in an ever-evolving digital landscape.

9.2 HISTORY

9.2.1 Evolution of Cloud Computing

Cloud computing has revolutionized to manage and access data, offering unprecedented convenience, scalability, and efficiency. Emerging from the foundation principles of early computer networking, it has evolved into highly advanced and sophisticated systems that power today's digital world [2].

Figure 9.1 demonstrates a timeline of the evolution of cloud computing.

- **1990s—The Rise of Virtualization and Networking**
  The 1990s marked a significant leap in the evolution of cloud computing, with mainstream adoption of virtualization technology companies like VMware, software solutions that enable multiple operating systems to run simultaneously on a single physical machine, maximizing hardware efficiency and resource utilization.
- **Early 2000s—The Emergence of Modern Cloud Services**
  The early 2000s marked the rise of modern cloud computing as major platforms began to receive the technological landscape in 2016 Amazon Web Services (AWS).

DOI: 10.1201/9781003539032-9

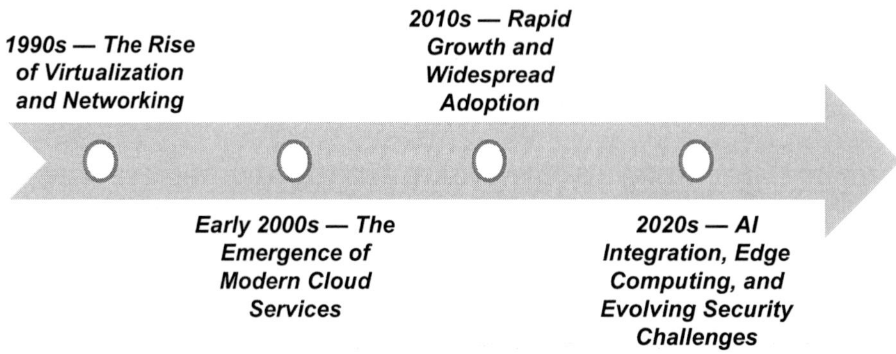

Figure 9.1 Timeline of evolution of cloud computing.

AWS launched groundbreaking services like S3 (simple storage service) and EC2 (elastic cloud computing), offering scalable storage and on-demand computing power, revolutionizing how businesses manage infrastructure. Around the same time, Google introduced Google Docs and spreadsheets with the potential of cloud-based software for real-time collaboration and accessibility.

- **2010s—Rapid Growth and Widespread Adoption**
  The 2010s saw a surge in the adoption of cloud computing as companies around the world started to embrace cloud services for operational cost savings, scalability, and innovation. Major participants entered the market during this time, such as Microsoft Azure and Google Cloud Platform, which offered robust Infrastructure as a Service and Platform as a Service options that allowed organizations to build, deploy, and manage applications seamlessly. Adoption of the cloud rapidly entered across other sectors like finance, healthcare, and education and fundamentally changed how data was stored, secured, and accessed. This period marked the beginning of a cloud-first strategy, whereby organizations sought to enhance agility, collaboration, and productivity globally with cloud technologies.
- **2020s—AI Integration, Edge Computing, and Evolving Security Challenges**
  The incorporation of AI, machine learning, and edge computing into cloud technology in the 2020s enables closer proximity data processing to the user, hence real-time data processing and minimized latency. The global COVID-19 pandemic acted as an accelerant for cloud technology due to the shift to remote work; companies worldwide adopted virtual collaboration and cloud technology to continue operations. However, with rapid growth comes equally heightened cybersecurity challenges, including data breaches, ransomware attacks, and increased cyber threats. Concerns regarding the protection and resiliency of vital information have highlighted the increasing reliance on advanced security solutions such as AI-based anomaly detection and proactive threat monitoring for cloud infrastructures.

9.2.2 The Rise of Cloud Security Challenges

The advent of cloud computing has transformed data storage and management for organizations, offering unprecedented scalability, accessibility, and cost-effectiveness. This transition has also made cloud systems vulnerable to cyberattacks and data breaches. In recent times, several high-profile security incidents have exposed critical weaknesses, highlighting the pressing need for strong and anticipatory security protocols to safeguard sensitive information and preserve confidence in cloud-based environments. Recent major data breaches have highlighted the increasing issues and security gaps in cloud computing systems [3].

9.2.2.1 *Data Breaches in Cloud Storage Systems*

Figure 9.2 shows a timeline of some of the data breaches.

Microsoft Azure Data Leak (2023)

Incident: An improperly configured Azure Blob storage account led to the exposure of 38 TB of confidential data, allowing unauthorized individuals to access internal company information.
Cause of Breach: The security lapse occurred due to an excessively permissive SAS token that granted unrestricted access to cloud-stored files.
Impact of Breach: The compromised data included internal emails, passwords, and development files, potentially jeopardizing Microsoft's security and intellectual property.
Lesson Learned: This incident necessitates rigorous cloud storage policies regarding the use of SAS tokens and the importance of limiting access to sensitive data.

Uber Cloud Infrastructure Breach (2022)

Event: Hackers exploited stolen staff credentials and gained access to sensitive data such as source code and internal communication by infiltrating Uber's cloud-based infrastructure.
Causes of Breach: Uber's internal credential management system enabled hackers to gain admission through weaknesses and inadequate identification and access management policies.
Effect of Breach: The attack exposed the ride details, the potentially compromised internal systems, and the sensitive customer information.
Learned Lessons: This violation emphasized the importance of multi-factor authentication (MFA), increased credit management policies, and more effective employee safety training to prevent unauthorized access.

Facebook Data Breach (2021)

Event: Personal information of more than 530 million Facebook users, including phone numbers, email addresses, and other account details, was available and found on a

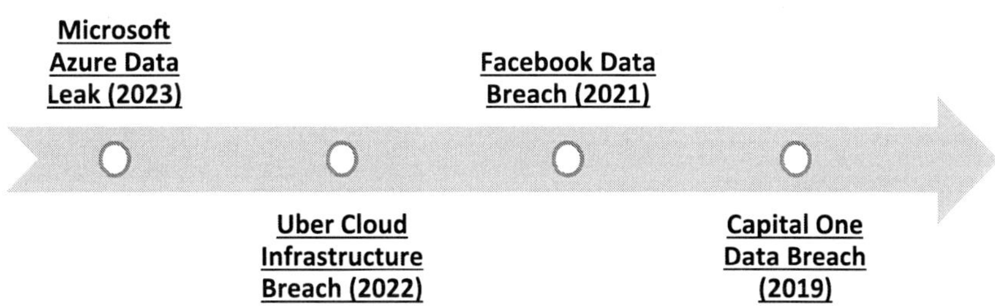

Figure 9.2 Timeline of data breaches.

public hacker forum.

Causes of Breach: The vulnerability in Facebook's cloud system caused data leakage, where data scraping tools were able to collect personal information from publicly accessible profiles.

Effect of Breach: The privacy of millions of users was compromised, leading to important concerns.

Learned Lessons: This phenomenon highlighted the need for strong data access control, better encryption practices, and ongoing vulnerability testing for cloud-based data storage.

Capital One Data Breach (2019)

Event: A major safety violation in the records of 100 million Capital One Customers after a firewall misunderstanding in their cloud service hosted on AWS allowed hackers to reach sensitive financial data.

Causes of Breach: The vulnerability stems from improperly configured cloud firewalls that allow unauthorized access to the data of Capital Forest stored in AWS.

Effect of Breach: The data compromised included personal information such as social security numbers, bank account details, and credit card applications.

Learned Lessons: This incident underlined the importance of regular cloud configuration audit, an appropriate access control mechanism, and real-time monitoring to detect unauthorized access.

9.2.2.2 *Key Takeaways from Cloud Data Breaches*

Recent examples of cloud data violations highlight the significant weaknesses in the cloud storage system, which include misconceptions and weak access controls to targeted cyberattacks. These incidents outline the immediate requirement of active safety measures, such as real-time monitoring, discrepancy detection, and strong access management [4].

By learning from these violations, organizations can apply smart solutions such as an AI-based discrepancy detection system to identify suspicious activities and prevent unauthorized access. Technologies such as Cloud Guard AI play an important role in ensuring data security, protecting sensitive information, and creating a more secure cloud infrastructure for the future [5].

9.2.3 Cloud Guard AI: A Proactive Approach to Cloud Security

In light of the increasing number of cloud data violations, traditional security methods often decrease in detecting and reducing sophisticated threats. Cloud Guard AI provides an innovative, AI-managed solution that enhances cloud storage security through real-time monitoring and discrepancy detection. By analyzing frequent user behavioral patterns—such as login space, access time, and file transfer activities—Cloud Guard AI can quickly identify unusual or suspicious tasks. For example, unauthorized login, unusually large file transfer, or access from unexpected places can be immediately flagged, which helps prevent potential violations [6].

Cloud Guard uses behavioral analysis to establish a baseline of normal user activity. The active risk mitigation is another standout feature, where Cloud Guard AI not only identifies suspicious activities but also takes preventive action such as sending immediate alerts or restricting access to sensitive files [7].

Additionally, Cloud Guard AI is designed to handle the environment on a large scale, which is suitable for scalable and diverse use cases. From real-time monitoring, intelligent behavior analysis, and a combination of automated response mechanisms, Cloud Guard addresses AI key weaknesses in cloud storage systems. It provides a reliable and active solution to protect users against protecting sensitive data, reducing risks, and developing cyber threats.

9.3 CLOUD GUARD AI

9.3.1 Methodological Approach

The approach adopted in this book chapter focuses on detecting discrepancies through behavioral analysis of user activities. Behavior analysis involves monitoring, understanding, and analysis of user interaction with systems to identify patterns of general behavior. By identifying deviations from these installed patterns, the system can detect potentially suspected or malicious activities that may indicate misuse or safety threats. Figure 9.3 refers to the reaction of components and threats in the cloud environment, detecting discrepancies.

9.3.1.1 *Sky Vault*

To apply and display this concept, we developed a dummy application called Sky Vault, which serves as a simulated cloud storage platform. Sky Vault will be designed to perform

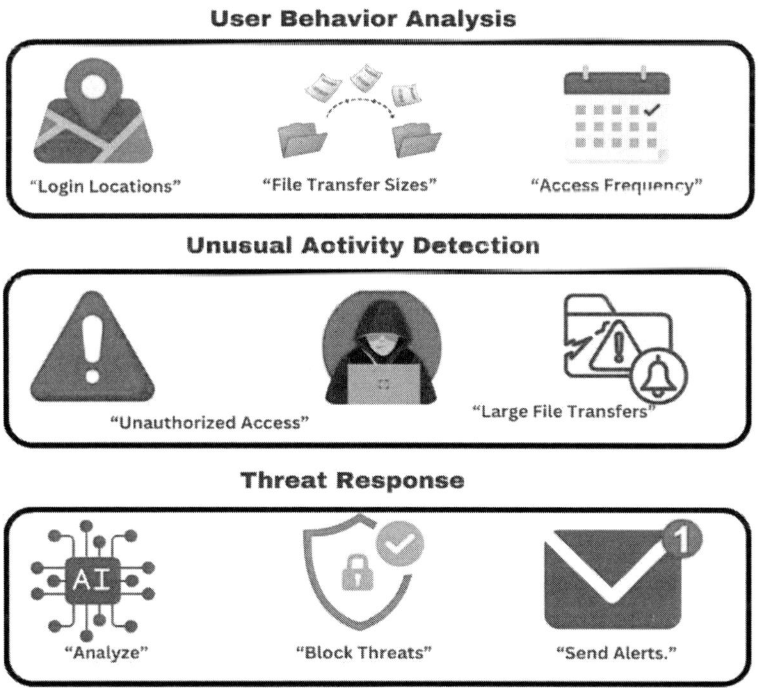

Figure 9.3 Smart threat detection and rapid response.

similar storage solutions such as Google Drive, Dropbox, or Google Cloud. The application allows the user to conduct major operations such as:

- **Uploading Files:** Users can securely store files in the Sky Vault environment.
- **Download Files:** Files can be accessed and recovered by users if needed.
- **Delete Files:** User can remove unnecessary or old files from storage.

The Sky Vault application mimics the functionality of the real-world cloud storage platform, which provides a controlled environment to monitor user behavior. Each user action within the system—such as upload, download, and deletion—can be analyzed to identify the pattern of general activity. Over time, it enables the system to install the baseline of the expected behavior for each user.

By analyzing these behavioral patterns, the system can explore asymmetric activities effectively distracting from general use. Examples of such anomalies include:

- **Unusual File Access Pattern:** For example, a user suddenly in a short period to download or remove a large number of files.
- **Suspected Upload Activities:** Uploading files with unexpected formats, unusually large size, or prohibited materials.
- **Irregular Access Timing:** Accessing the storage system in odd hours or from unusual places.

The behavior analysis approach ensures that discrepancies are constantly detected and flag activities that otherwise do not get attention by traditional rules-based systems. Sky Walt Dummy Apps serves as a test to apply this approach, a realistic yet controlled landscape.

9.3.1.1.1 Sky Vault Login Interface

Figure 9.4 shows the login screen of the SkyVault app. This is how we present a secure and simple method for users to access their cloud storage accounts. Users need to input their email and password in the given fields for authentication to keep it secure. A user can click on the Login button to start managing their files once he has logged into their account. If someone is new and does not have an account already, there is a link just below the login button saying "Create an account" that leads to registration, which is quick and easy.

9.3.1.2 Sky Vault Upload Files Section

Figure 9.5 depicts the "Upload Files" interface of the Sky Vault application, which is a cloud storage platform. The general area permits users to upload files through drag-and-drop or by using the "Choose File" button followed by the "Upload" option.

The sidebar offers key navigation options:

- **+ New:** Create new folders or content.
- **Home:** Main dashboard.
- **Upload Files:** Current upload screen.
- **All Files:** View all stored files.
- **Shared with Me:** Files shared by others.
- **Recent:** Recently accessed files.
- **Starred:** Favorite files.
- **Spam:** Unwanted files.

Figure 9.4 Secure login Hub.

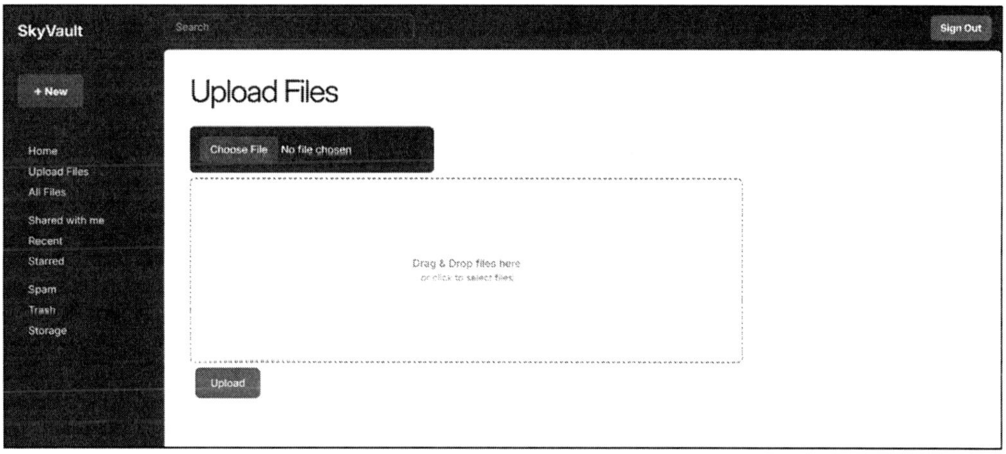

Figure 9.5 Sky vault drag-and-drop file upload screen.

- **Trash:** Deleted files.
- **Storage:** Storage usage details.

The "Sign Out" button ensures secure logout. The interface is clean, intuitive, and efficient for file management.

9.3.1.3 Sky Vault Files Section

Figure 9.6 shows the "All Files" screen of the Sky Vault app, listing all uploaded files. Each file shows its name, size, and time of upload. Users can see, manage, or remove files using available choices.

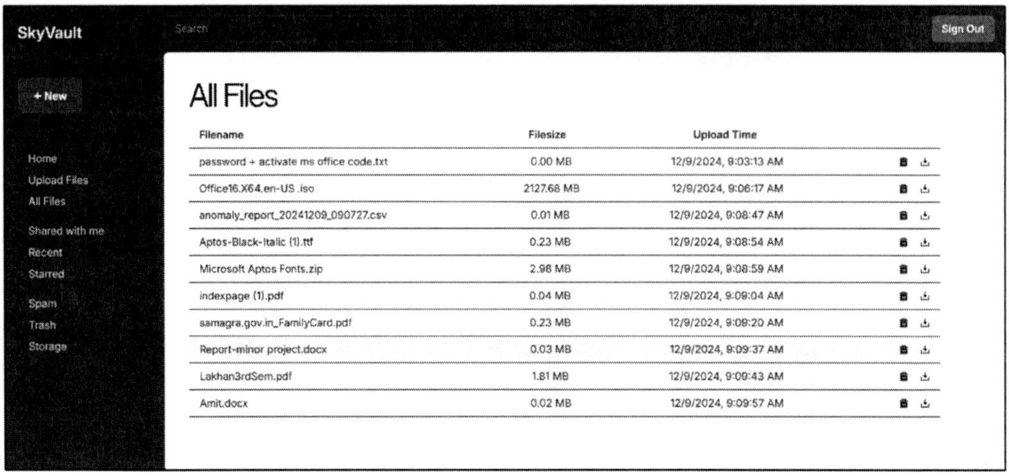

Figure 9.6 "All files" dashboard in sky vault.

9.3.2 Cloud Guard AI

Sky Vault handles files in an efficient manner, making sure they are safe, though keeping out bad effects is key to protecting the information. Cloud Guard AI is a top-cloud safe plan made to watch over data, files, and apps kept in the clouds. It uses smart technology to spot risks, stop wrong entry, and make sure the file job is safe, giving users a trustworthy and automatic defense way for their cloud keep.

9.3.2.1 *Cloud Guard AI Login Interface*

In Figure 9.7, the login panel of Cloud Guard AI provides users with a fast, easy, and highly secure entry point into its advanced Data Breach Detection system. User authentication involves logging in using the same email address used on the Sky Vault Account. This allows Cloud Guard AI to recognize and track behaviors related to the Sky Vault account, helping to provide enhanced security information and a seamless experience across programs. Figure 9.8 shows a flow diagram describing the interaction between Sky Vault and Cloud Guard AI.

9.3.2.2 *Cloud Guard AI Dashboard Section*

Figure 9.9 is designed to provide a centralized platform for monitoring, analyzing, and managing user activities and file interactions in a cloud environment. It offers a clean, user-friendly interface with key metrics, recent activity tracking, and anomaly detection capabilities, ensuring robust oversight and enhanced security.

Figure 9.8 illustrates the flow chart of the interaction between SkyVault and Cloud Guard AI. It outlines the process beginning with a user logging into SkyVault and performing activities such as uploading or deleting files. These actions are monitored by Cloud Guard AI, which collects and preprocesses user activity data. The data is then analyzed using a machine learning model to detect any suspicious activity. If no anomalies are found, the system continues monitoring; otherwise, suspicious actions are flagged. Alerts are sent, corrective measures are taken, and feedback is used to update the AI model for improved accuracy. This flow ensures continuous protection and proactive detection of unauthorized activities.

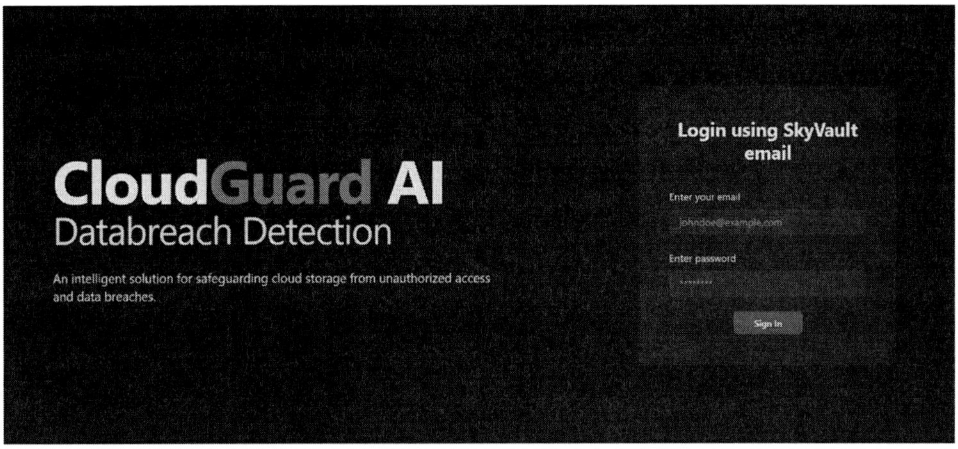

Figure 9.7 Cloud guard AI login dashboard.

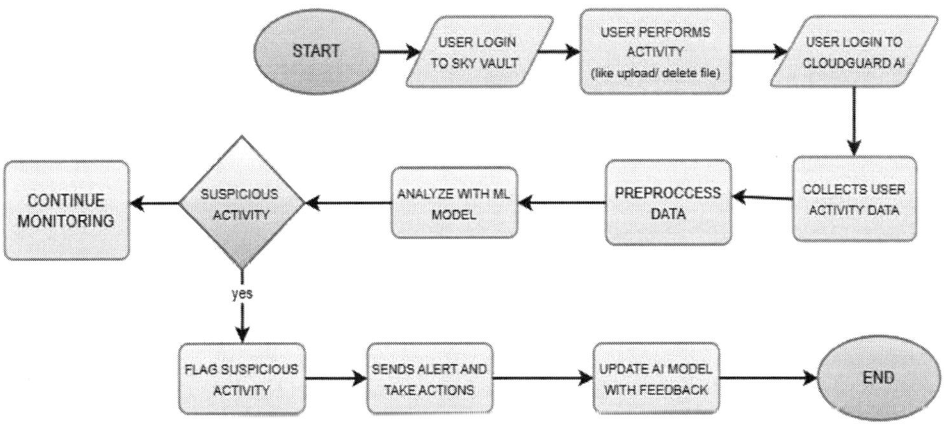

Figure 9.8 Flow chart of interaction between sky vault & cloud guard AI.

The **Analytics Overview** section presents critical metrics for quick insights into system performance:

- **Total Files:** Displays the total number of files monitored (currently 8)
- **Total Activities:** Reflects the number of recorded actions or interactions (currently 75)
- **Anomalies Detected:** Highlights the number of unusual or suspicious activities flagged (currently 9)

The **Recent Activities** section provides a chronological list of the most recently monitored files and actions. Each entry includes:

- **File Name:** For example, chess (1).png, anomaly_report_20241209_091009.csv, and jdk-23_windows-x64_bin.exe
- **Timestamps:** Indicating the exact date and time of the activity (e.g., 2024-12-10 04:35)

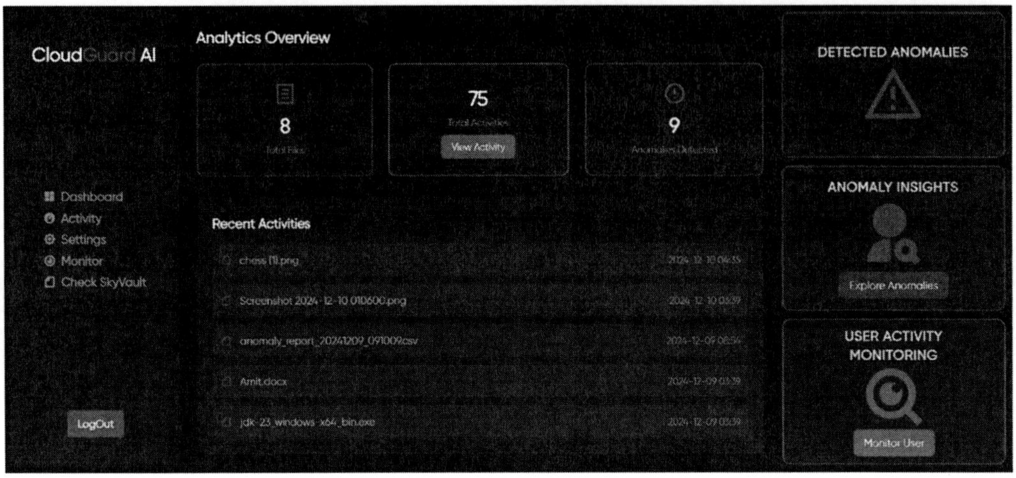

Figure 9.9 Cloud guard AI homepage.

This feature enables users to track recent actions, identify any unusual files, and ensure system transparency.

1. **Detected Anomalies:** It displays the total count of flagged anomalies and emphasizes their importance for investigation.
2. **Anomaly Insights:** It provides deeper insights into detected anomalies, their nature, and potential risks.
3. **Monitor User:** It enables real-time tracking of user activities to identify suspicious or irregular behavior.

9.3.2.3 Cloud Guard AI Activity Section

Figure 9.10 presents a vibrant, meticulous display of a user's recent actions within the Sky Vault app. Specifically, this interface details file operations such as upload, update, and deletion. As a result, Figure 9.10 serves as a longitudinal log, capturing and representing critical data points related to every transaction where a file was used. Cloud Guard AI takes activity logging a step further by using AI/ML functionality to assess user behaviors along with file operations. This consists of identifying specific features such as file size, file extension, and the status of the action (e.g., success, failure). For example, when a user uploads a file in Sky Vault, Cloud Guard AI captures the timestamp, the type and size of the file, and whether or not the user successfully uploaded the file. This same logging takes place for all user actions and stays true for update or delete actions, where previous versions are logged for accountability.

AI/ML will allow Cloud Guard AI to take file logging past a one-dimensional action log, to an analysis of the user pattern and behavior in terms of file operations. Continuous activity logging would also allow Cloud Guard AI to monitor file operations that were out of the ordinary, such as abnormal file sizes (e.g., 7GB), suspicious file extensions (e.g., .vbs), or a sudden increase in deletions, which may suggest security risk/unauthorized exfiltration.

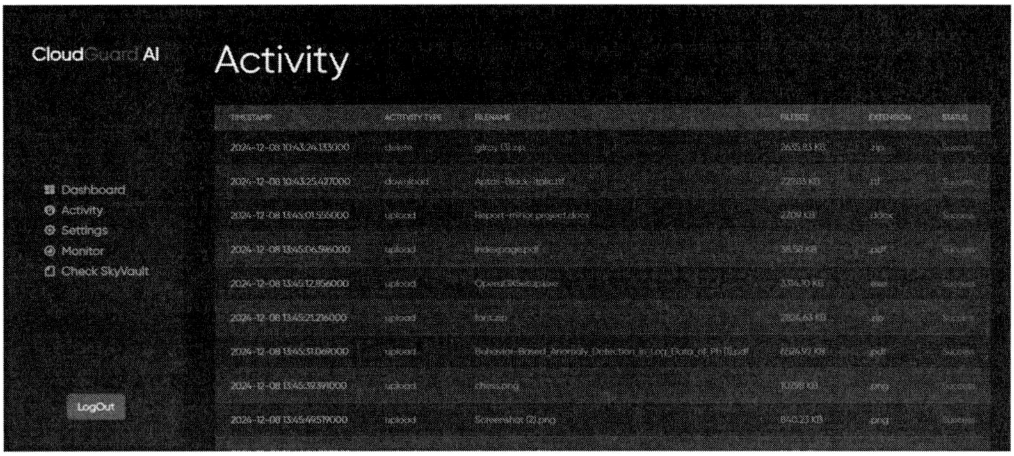

Figure 9.10 Cloud guard AI activity section.

Doing so should allow organizations to mitigate risk proactively from potential threats related to a data breach or insider risks and promptly take corrective action in real-time. It is about ensuring data integrity, ensuring accountability, and ensuring that organizations utilize AI intelligence to protect against unauthorized or malevolent activities against cloud-based files. This makes Cloud Guard AI a critical safeguard and security product in ensuring transparent access to the management of files.

9.3.2.4 *Cloud Guard AI Settings Section*

Figure 9.11 is designed to provide users with a highly customizable interface, offering complete control over their personal and system preferences to ensure optimal security and

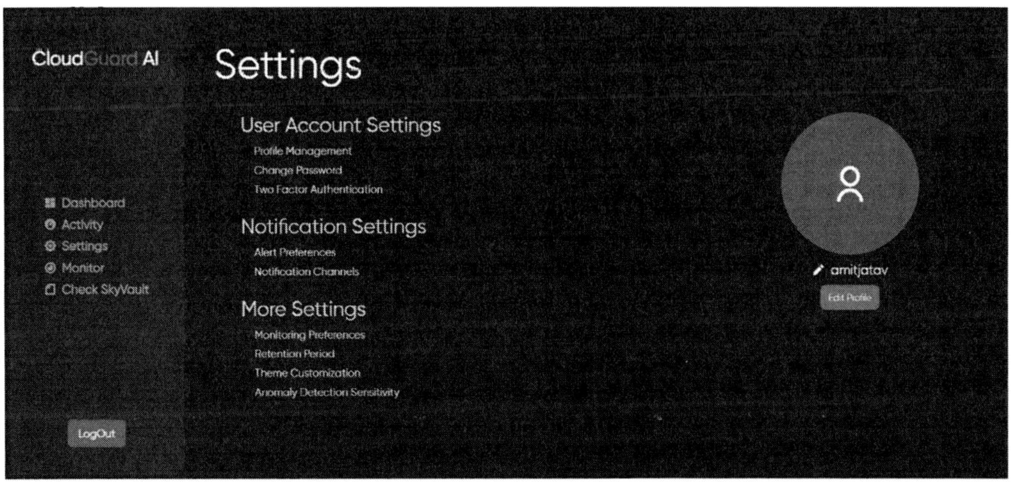

Figure 9.11 Cloud guard AI settings section.

user experience. This page is organized into three primary sections: User Account Settings, Notification Settings, and More Settings, each tailored to enhance the overall functionality and security of the platform.

1. **User Account Settings:**
   User Account Settings allows users to manage their personal user account and secure it within Cloud Guard AI.
   - **Profile:** Users can edit their personal information, like their name, email address, or profile picture. The ability to edit personal details lets users keep their account information current, which is an added convenience for identifying and managing accounts in larger teams or organizations.
   - **Change Password:** This secure part of the program allows users to reset or change their account password. By implementing a strong password policy and requiring that accounts don't use predictable passwords, users will be protected against unauthorized access.
   - **Two-Factor Authentication (2FA):** 2FA is an important security feature that can help add greater protection by providing a second layer of protection when users access Cloud Guard AI. Users can enable 2FA to complete a second verification step, by using either an OTP/one-time password/token for verification via an email or text message (SMS) or an authentication application. This significantly improves the platform's defenses against unauthorized access and vulnerabilities to data exposure and loss.
2. **Notification Settings:**
   The Notification Settings allow users to choose how to receive alerts from the system and devices when they need to be informed of updates, alerts, or potential security threats.
   - **Alert Preferences:** The Alert Preferences allow users to decide what notifications they want to receive alerts for. Some may be critical, like potential downtime or performance issues, or anomaly detection for suspicious file activity in Sky Vault. By customizing Alerts Preferences for notifications, users are alerted to activities that are pertinent to them, rather than being overloaded with unnecessary notifications.
   - **Notification Channels:** The notification settings give users options on how they would like to receive notifications, for example, externally via email, text messages, or SMS.

1. **User Account Settings**
   These settings allow users to manage and secure their personal accounts within Cloud Guard AI.
   - **Profile Management:** This feature enables users to update essential personal information such as their name, email address, or profile picture. The ability to modify these details ensures users can keep their account data up-to-date, which is particularly useful for account identification and management in larger teams or organizations.
   - **Change Password:** In this secure section, users can reset or change their account passwords. A robust password policy, alongside prompts for complex password creation, ensures high security against unauthorized access.
   - **Two-Factor Authentication (2FA):** This important security feature enhances protection by adding another layer. By enabling 2FA, users are required to complete

a second verification step, such as an OTP sent via email or SMS, or through an authentication app. This significantly enhances the platform's defense against unauthorized logins and potential data breaches.

2. **Notification Settings**
   These settings empower users to tailor how they receive system alerts, ensuring they stay informed about important updates and potential security threats.
   - **Alert Preferences:** Users can specify the types of notifications they want to receive. These might include critical alerts about potential downtime, performance issues, or anomaly detection related to unusual file activities within Sky Vault. Customizing these preferences ensures that users are only alerted to relevant events, avoiding notification overload.
   - **Notification Channels:** Users have the flexibility to choose their preferred method of receiving notifications. Available options include email, text messages (SMS), and app-based push notifications.
3. **More Settings**
   Advanced users can access extended customization and configuration settings to optimize their Cloud Guard AI experience in this section.
   - **Monitoring Preferences:** Users can toggle monitoring functionality for specific file types while employing customizable filters to either exclude or include particular file extensions (e.g., exclude.jpg files or allow.txt files). The system allows real-time updates to file type configurations for increased monitoring efficiency.
   - **Retention Period:** Users can establish retention policies for both file activity logs and anomaly records to define custom timeframes such as keeping logs for 30 days. Optimize storage space and maintain data protection standards through automatic archival or secure record deletion once they reach their retention deadline.
   - **Theme Customization:** Users who desire a customized visual interface can choose between dark mode and light mode, along with other UI adjustments. This functionality provides improved user comfort, particularly for individuals who spend extensive time using the platform.
   - **Anomaly Detection Sensitivity:** Users can adjust the sensitivity of anomaly detection by selecting different settings that range from strict to low. Users receive immediate feedback and visual representation about sensitivity settings, which helps them balance detection accuracy against false positive rates for customized performance across various applications.

The Cloud Guard AI platform offers users a customized experience through integrated settings which balance security aspects with personalization and user-friendly operation. Cloud Guard AI gives users full control over their cloud storage through strong privacy settings and adjustable notifications, as well as precise security monitoring, which enables them to detect potential threats and activities.

9.3.2.5 *Cloud Guard AI Monitor Section*

Figure 9.12 provides a detailed visual representation of generally perceived anomalies over time, providing users with clear insight into unusual activity in a cloud environment. The central graphic shows outliers that apply to a particular stamp, with each point being monitored. Anomalies are highlighted with a big dot. This indicates that an abnormal rating

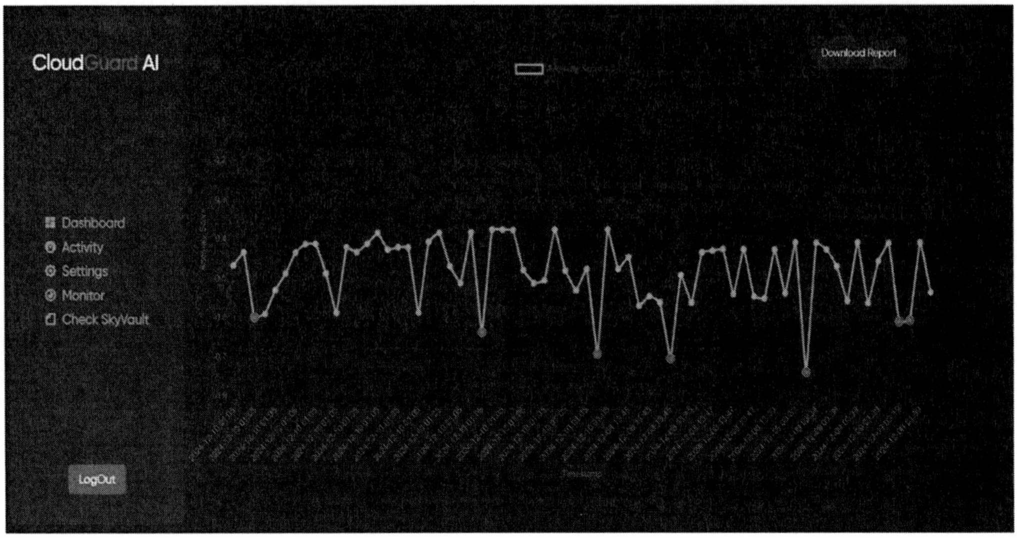

Figure 9.12 Cloud guard AI monitor section.

exceeds a predefined threshold, signal potential, or suspicious behavior. Anomaly analysis is based on several factors, including file size, file extensions, operational status (such as uploads, downloads, deletions), frequency of activity, and user behavior patterns such as deviations from general usage. These factors are monitored and processed using AI and ML algorithms to identify unusual patterns that differ from basic activity. Additionally, the Download Report button allows for anomaly data and allows further analysis to provide a comprehensive understanding of anomalies and their effectiveness. Cloud Guard AI companies combine real-time anomaly awareness with an intuitive user interface to help them effectively monitor cloud activity, identify risks, and ensure data integrity.

Figure 9.13 illustrates the **end-to-end workflow of SkyVault and CloudGuard** interaction. It shows how the user logs in through the SkyVault app, which collects and verifies credentials from the database. User activities like upload, delete, or download are logged and analyzed by CloudGuard with the help of the AI engine. If suspicious behavior is detected, alerts are sent by CloudGuard, and high-impact threats are blocked, while normal activities continue smoothly.

9.4 SOFTWARE REQUIREMENTS

9.4.1 AI/ML Frameworks

TensorFlow, scikit-learn: Implemented Isolation Forest for anomaly detection.
NumPy, Pandas: Data preprocessing and analysis.

Backend Technologies

Node.js, Express.js: Backend server for handling API requests and database interactions.

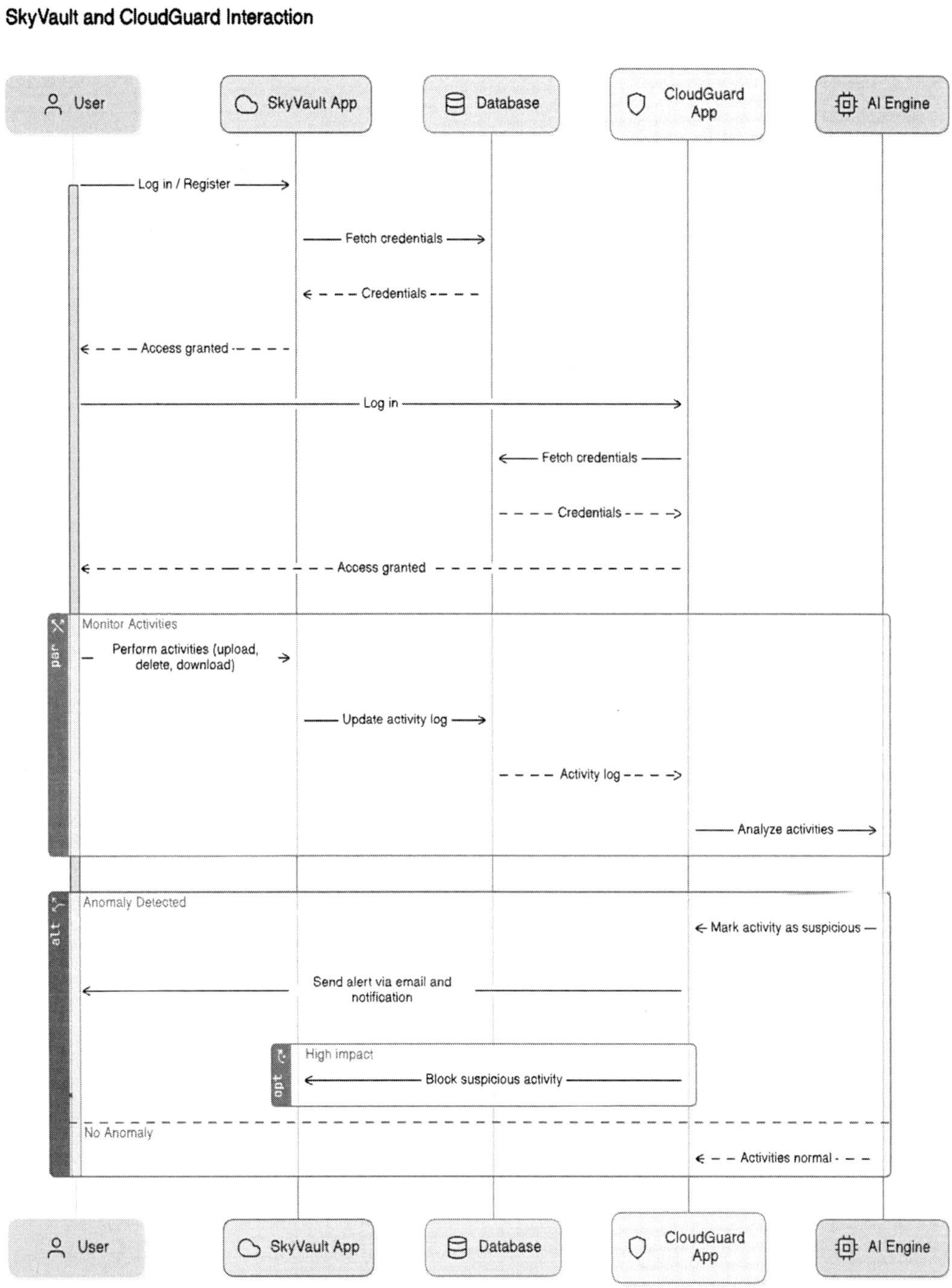

Figure 9.13 End-to-end workflow of sky vault and cloud guard.

Frontend Technologies

HTML, CSS, JavaScript: UI/UX development for Cloud Guard AI interfaces.

Data Storage and Processing

MongoDB: Centralized database for storing user activity logs, shared between Sky Vault and Cloud Guard AI.

Cloud Storage

Sky Vault: Cloud activity monitoring and data sourcing.

Anomaly Detection Algorithms

Isolation Forest: Used to detect anomalies in user activity and file operations.

9.4.2 Development

VS Code: Code development and optimization.

9.4.2.1 Data Collection and Processing

As the data procurement and processing phase of this chapter does not allow existing datasets to be available, a systematic approach was applied to simulate user activity and set up a robust database infrastructure. A detailed explanation of the methodology is given below.

9.4.2.2 Creating a Dummy User in the Sky Vault App

To generate realistic data for the book chapters, I created a Dummy User in the Sky Vault Platform. Each dummy user was assigned a clear profile and various activities for file management. This includes the following:

File Upload: Simulated file uploads with various file sizes and extensions.
Update Files: Changed previously uploaded files to follow changes and versions.
Deleting Files: Simulated deletion activities to test file removal operations and log entries.

This process ensured the generation of diverse and representative data, capturing real-world scenarios that users would typically perform within a file management system.

9.4.2.3 Database Infrastructure Using MongoDB

The database is structured into four collections: User, Profile, Activity, and File. These collections are defined using Mongoose schemas, which describe the structure and relationships of the data stored in the MongoDB database, as shown in Figure 9.14.

User Collection

The User collection holds essential user information such as their full name, username, phone, email, password, and timestamps like loggedInAt and loggedOutAt. This collection also contains references to the other collections (like Profile, Activity, and File).

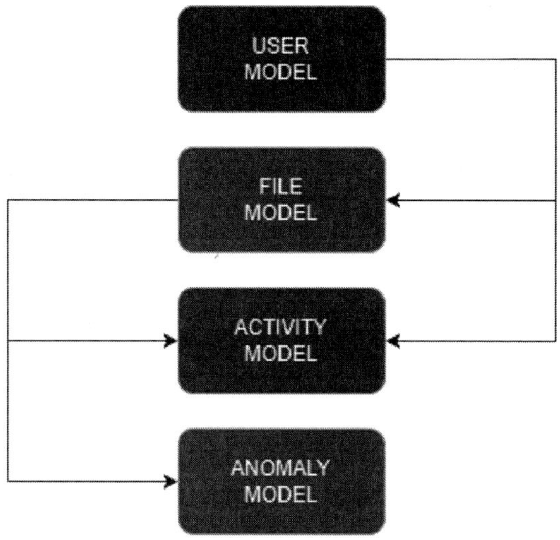

Figure 9.14 Hierarchical data models for comprehensive monitoring.

Usage

The Profile collection is referenced in the User collection via an ObjectId field (e.g., profile), allowing a user to have one associated profile.

Profile Collection

The Profile collection stores additional user information, such as their profile name, email, and picture. It maintains a one-to-one relationship with the User collection by storing the user's object ID, where the user field references the corresponding User document. This setup makes it easy to manage user-specific data while keeping the primary User collection optimized for essential information like authentication and session tracking.

Activity Collection

The Activity collection is used to track various activities performed by the user. This could include login history, actions performed, or any other interactions within the application. Multiple activities can be associated with a single user, creating a one-to-many relationship. It is designed to log the various actions that users perform on files within the system. This collection captures key actions such as uploading, downloading, and deleting files and stores important metadata about each action. It stores critical details such as the user who performed the action by storing the object ID, the file involved, timestamps for each action, and metadata about the file (like its name, size, and extension). This model helps to monitor, audit, and manage file-related actions within the system efficiently.

Usage

- This model helps track and audit the various actions users perform on files within the system. By storing the time and details of each file-related activity (upload, download, delete), the system can monitor user interactions, provide logs for security and compliance, and offer insight into how files are managed.
- The timestamps (fileUploadedAt, fileDownloadedAt, and fileDeletedAt) allow for a precise history of actions, helping administrators or system maintainers monitor and troubleshoot file management activities.
- The fields filename, filesize, and fileExtension allow for easy identification of the file involved in the action, even when the specific file is not immediately accessible.

File Collection

The File collection stores files related to the user, such as profile pictures, uploaded documents, or other media. The User collection contains an array of references to the File collection, allowing multiple files to be associated with each user.

It is responsible for managing and storing information related to files that have been uploaded by users. It captures key metadata about the files, such as their names, sizes, types, and relationships to users and activities. This model also tracks the activities associated with each file, such as upload events.

Usage

- **User and File Association:** The user field helps associate each file with a specific user, making it clear who owns or uploaded the file.
- **File Metadata:** The filename, uploaded filename, filetype, fileExtension, and file-size fields store important metadata about each file. These fields help identify, categorize, and manage the file in the system.
- **File Tracking:** The upload time field allows the system to know when each file was uploaded. This can help sort files by upload time or for audits.
- **Activity Tracking:** The activity field provides a way to track all actions (uploads, downloads, deletions) associated with each file. The file's interactions with the system are linked through the Activity collection, providing a comprehensive history of the file's lifecycle.

9.5 MACHINE LEARNING MODEL

9.5.1 The Role of Isolation Forest in Cloud Guard AI for Anomaly Detection

We have established a common MongoDB database that serves as the data repository for both Sky Vault and Cloud Guard AI. This allows both systems to share the same set of user activity logs, which are then analyzed by Cloud Guard AI to detect abnormal or potentially malicious actions. **Isolation Forest** plays a critical role by helping identify unusual patterns in user activities that could indicate a data breach, unauthorized access, or other security threats.

9.5.2 Isolation Forest Work

Data Collection G Preprocessing

- Sky Vault records detailed logs of user activities, which include key information such as:
- **User ID**: Identifies the person performing the activity
- **File Name**: The designated name of the file associated with the current action or operation
- **File Size**: The size of the file being uploaded, downloaded, or deleted
- **File Extension**: Type of file (e.g., .txt, .exe).
- **Operation Type**: What action was performed (upload, update, delete).
- **Status of Operation**: Specifies the outcome of the action, indicating whether it was successful or encountered a failure.
- **Timestamp**: The exact time when the action took place.

Feature Development

The activity logs are then pre-processed, where meaningful features are extracted that will be fed into the Isolation Forest algorithm. Some of these features include:

- **File Size:** Large files might indicate data exfiltration or unauthorized uploads, which are typically irregular actions.
- **File Extension:** Certain file extensions might be unusual or unexpected in the system. For example, executable files (e.g., .exe, .bat) might be a red flag.
- **Operation Type:** Multiple operations like failed login attempts or repeated uploads in a short period may signal suspicious behavior.
- **Timestamps:** If activities occur during off-hours or at unusual frequencies, they may indicate an attempt to avoid detection.

User Behavior Patterns: These could include a combination of how often a user interacts with the system, types of files accessed, and consistency in actions over time.

9.5.3 Isolation Forest for Anomaly Detection

An unsupervised machine learning algorithm specifically designed to detect anomalies in high-dimensional datasets by isolating data points that deviate significantly from the norm. Isolation Forest will learn the patterns of normal behavior of the user by observing the activities logged in Sky Vault.

The algorithm functions by recursively and randomly partitioning the data into smaller subsets, making it easier to isolate anomalies that require fewer splits compared to normal data points. For each data point (i.e., a user's action), the algorithm isolates it by randomly choosing features and splitting the data. Normal behavior, which occurs frequently, will be partitioned into several splits. However, anomalies—rare or abnormal behaviors like an unusual file upload or failed login attempt require fewer splits to be isolated. Figure 9.15 demonstrates the Isolation Forest Process flow diagram. Figure 9.16 demonstrates anomaly detection score interpretation.

Key Steps of the Isolation Forest Process

- **Data Isolation:** The algorithm isolates data points by randomly selecting a feature and making binary splits. If a data point (such as a suspicious user activity) is different from the rest of the data, it will be isolated more quickly.
- **Anomaly Scoring:** Once trained, each data point receives an anomaly score based on how easy it was to isolate. Higher anomaly scores indicate that the behavior is rare and abnormal. These can be flagged as potentially suspicious or malicious.

Anomaly Detection in Real-Time

Once trained, the Isolation Forest model will analyze the incoming activity logs in real-time. For every user action performed on Sky Vault, the model will:

- Score the activity based on its degree of anomaly.
- Flag any activity that surpasses the threshold as suspicious.

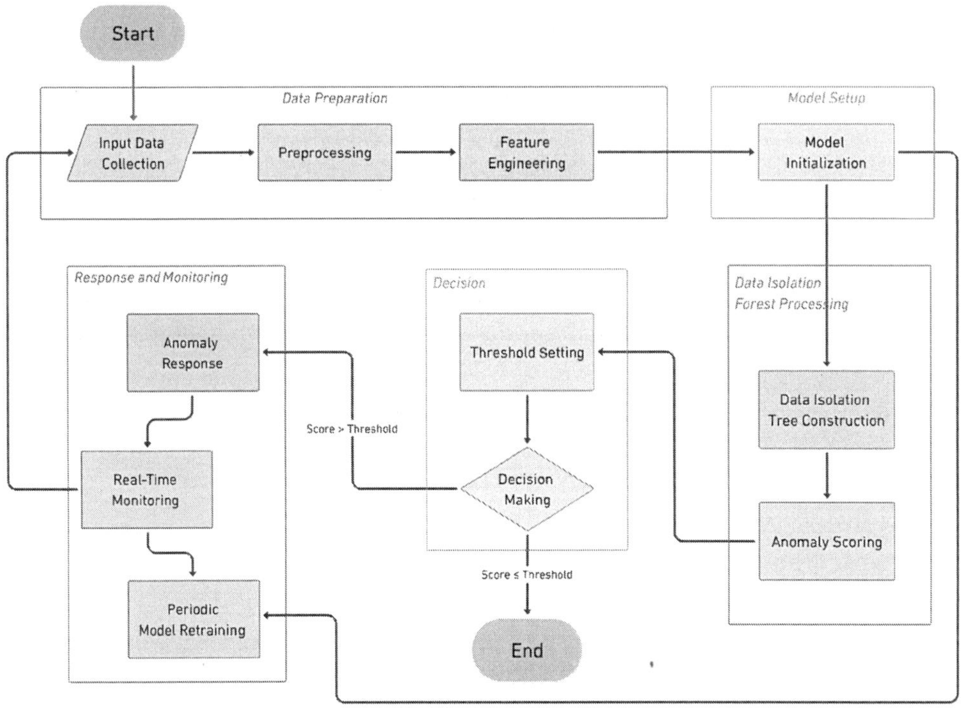

Figure 9.15 Flowchart depicting isolation forest process.

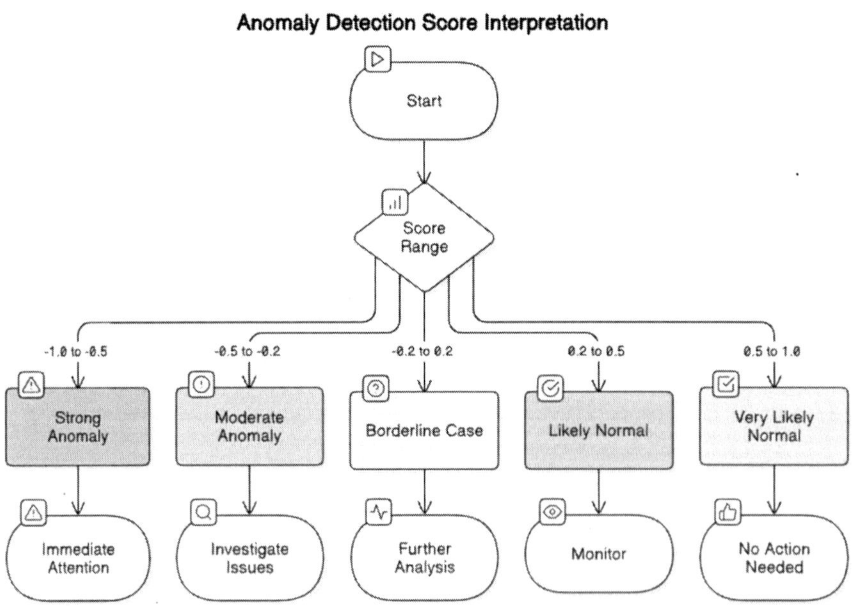

Figure 9.16 Anomaly detection score interpretation.

Example of suspicious behaviors that would be flagged:

- Unusual File Uploads: A user uploading an unusually large file that doesn't match their usual activity pattern.
- Rare File Types: Files with rare extensions (e.g., .exe) are being uploaded, which are typically outside the scope of the platform's normal file types.
- Multiple Failed Login Attempts: A sudden surge in failed login attempts could indicate a brute-force attack or unauthorized access attempt.

Key Parameters Monitored in Isolation Forest Implementation

1. **Temporal Features**
   - **fileUploadedAt:** Tracks the exact timestamp of file uploads, helping identify unusual upload patterns.
   - **Time-Based Activity Patterns:** Analyzes trends in user activities over time, such as frequency, time of day, and irregular gaps, to detect deviations.
2. **File-Related Features**
   - filename: Assesses file types, naming conventions, and extensions to uncover patterns or anomalies (e.g., suspicious file names or uncommon formats).
   - **File Operations:** Monitors activities like uploads, downloads, and deletions to detect abnormal actions.
   - **File Characteristics:** Examines file size, type, and frequency of operations for consistency across user behavior.
3. **User Behavior Features**
   - User ID (via user field in activities): Links activities to specific users, allowing the system to monitor behavioral trends and flag unusual actions.
   - **Activity Patterns:** Tracks user-specific patterns, such as file operations or access frequency, identifying behaviors that deviate from their established norms.
4. **Siordia Logic**
   - **Anomaly Score:** The model computes an anomaly score for each activity, quantifying how likely an action is to be anomalous.
   - **Anomaly Flag:** Returns a Boolean as an anomaly indicator for quick classification, marking activities as normal or suspicious.

9.6 TRAINING AND OPTIMIZATION

In the development of Cloud Guard AI, the training and optimization phase played a critical role in ensuring accurate anomaly detection and efficient system performance. Figure 9.17 demonstrates a summary chart showing the performance overview.

9.6.1 Training Phase

1. **Data Preparation:**
   - A dataset was created using simulated user activities performed on the Sky Vault app, as no predefined dataset was available.
   - These activities included file uploads, downloads, and user actions, which were stored in a MongoDB database. The common database allowed seamless connectivity between Sky Vault and Cloud Guard AI for consistent data sourcing.

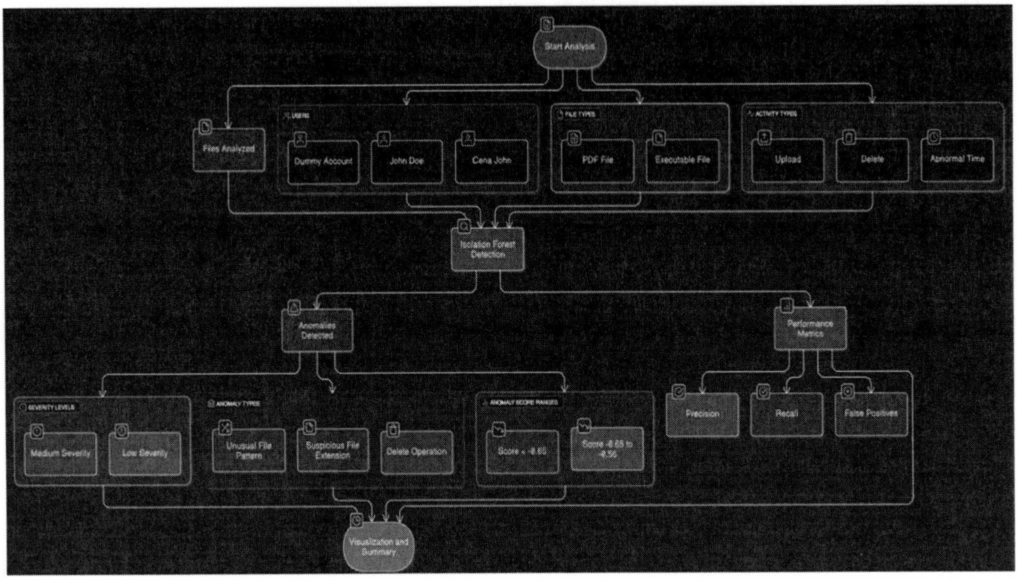

Figure 9.17 Summary chart showing performance overview.

2. **Data Preprocessing:**
    - Raw data was cleaned to remove inconsistencies, duplicates, and irrelevant information.
    - Relevant features such as file access patterns, timestamps, and user actions were extracted to form a structured dataset.
3. **Model Selection and Training:**
    - The Isolation Forest algorithm was selected for anomaly detection due to its ability to handle high-dimensional data and efficiently detect outliers.
    - The model was trained on the prepared dataset to learn normal user behaviors and identify deviations or anomalies.
    - Key parameters like contamination rate (to balance normal vs. abnormal data) were fine-tuned during the training phase.

9.6.2 Optimization Phase

1. **Hyperparameter Tuning:**
   The parameters of the Isolation Forest model, such as the number of trees and maximum sample size, were optimized to improve detection accuracy and efficiency.
2. **False Positive/Negative Reduction:**
   Threshold values for anomaly detection were carefully adjusted to reduce false positives (normal activities flagged as anomalies) and false negatives (actual anomalies missed).
3. **Performance Enhancement:**
    - Real-time performance was optimized by improving the computational efficiency of the model.
    - The system was configured to process incoming data in near real-time, ensuring timely anomaly detection without delays.

4. **Model Retraining:**
   - The model was designed for periodic retraining with new data to adapt to evolving user behavior patterns.
   - Continuous feedback from detected anomalies was used to further enhance model accuracy.
5. **System Scalability:**
   - Optimization techniques ensured that the system could scale effectively to handle large datasets and high volumes of activity logs.
   - MongoDB's ability to manage large, structured data played a key role in maintaining smooth system operations.

9.6.3 Test and Validation Phase

During the development of Cloud Guard AI, the Test and Validation phase aimed to evaluate the performance, accuracy, and reliability of the anomaly detection model, specifically focusing on the Isolation Forest algorithm. This phase was crucial to confirm the system's capability to promptly identify abnormal user activity and provide valuable cybersecurity insights.

9.6.4 Model Testing Strategy

The testing process aimed to validate the model's capacity to detect anomalous activities and differentiate them from regular user behavior within file access and usage patterns. The testing involved the following steps:

- **Data Splitting:**
  - The dataset underwent splitting into training and testing sets to ensure the model was tested on unseen data. The training set facilitated training the Isolation Forest algorithm, while the testing set assessed how well the model adapted to new data. A standard split ratio (e.g., 80% training and 20% testing) ensured a thorough evaluation.
- **Simulated User Activity:**
  - The testing dataset included simulated user actions like file uploads, downloads, and system interactions on the Sky Vault app. These activities were purposely crafted to encompass both normal and abnormal behavioral patterns. Abnormal activities consisted of:
    - Suspicious file uploads/downloads (e.g., from unrecognized IPs or at unusual timestamps).
    - Unusual login times or logins from unverified devices.
    - Excessive file access or unauthorized file attempts. These activities were introduced to assess the model's sensitivity and accuracy in detecting deviations from typical user behavior.

9.7 VALIDATION AGAINST REAL-WORLD DATA

Although the data used in testing was simulated, the next step in the validation process involved comparing model predictions against a set of real-world scenarios. This was done by running the model on logs from actual user activities in the Sky Vault app, which had been captured over a period of time. The validation against real-world data helped ensure that the model would perform effectively in a live environment.

Real-World Data Simulation
The test set included synthetic and real-world user behavior patterns, like login and file-sharing activities. By inputting these into the model, we verified its ability to detect true anomalies without triggering false alarms for regular activities.
Model Calibration
The model was fine-tuned based on test feedback, focusing on adjusting the anomaly threshold. Cloud Guard AI aimed to avoid misidentifying users' daily activities while accurately flagging genuine anomalies like abnormal logins or suspicious file access.
Continuous Model Improvement
Cloud Guard AI was designed for ongoing enhancement through model retraining. As user behaviors change, the system updates the model with new data periodically to adapt to evolving trends and potential threats. This iterative process ensures effectiveness, especially against previously unseen anomalies.

Advantages

The integration of Cloud Guard AI with the Sky Vault app delivers various benefits, improving security and user experience:

- **Improved Data Security:** AI-driven anomaly detection enables real-time identification of suspicious activities, enhancing overall cloud storage security and safeguarding user data from unauthorized access, breaches, and malware attacks.
- **Real-Time Monitoring:** Continuous monitoring within Sky Vault helps prevent security incidents by detecting anomalous behavior promptly, reinforcing proactive cybersecurity measures.
- **Reduction in False Positives:** The system minimizes false alerts, reducing unnecessary flags on normal user behavior. This streamlines operations, allowing the security team to focus on genuine threats.
- **Automated Threat Detection:** AI-powered anomaly detection automates the identification of unusual patterns, freeing up security personnel from constant manual monitoring to concentrate on complex tasks.
- **Scalability:** The system's scalable architecture ensures it can handle increased demands effectively.
- **Improved Efficiency in Threat Detection:** The system's precision in classifying and isolating anomalous behavior enhances its efficiency over traditional methods. This leads to quicker detection and more accurate threat identification, crucial for minimizing damage during a security breach.
- **Enhanced User Experience:** Sky Vault platform users benefit from automated threat detection with minimal false alarms, ensuring a seamless experience without constant interruptions from irrelevant security alerts. The system's precise malicious activity detection preserves the user experience by safeguarding legitimate users.
- **Customizable and Adaptive Solution:** Cloud Guard AI adapts to various user behaviors and patterns, allowing customization to align with different security policies or needs. This adaptability caters to diverse industries and user requirements, making it a versatile solution for various cloud security scenarios.

- **Proactive Security Approach:** Cloud Guard AI's real-time anomaly detection offers proactive security measures instead of reactive responses. This proactive stance enables businesses to anticipate threats, maintaining continuous data protection from the outset.
- **Cost-Efficient Security Solution:** The AI-driven anomaly detection system reduces reliance on costly manual monitoring and intervention. By automating cybersecurity processes, it not only enhances security but also delivers a cost-effective alternative to traditional security measures.
- **Seamless Integration with Sky Vault and Cloud Guard AI:** Integrating Sky Vault with Cloud Guard AI establishes a unified system where both platforms collaborate seamlessly. This smooth data flow between applications boosts overall system efficiency and user satisfaction, ensuring operational continuity and robust security.
- **Future-Proof Growth and Adaptation:** Cloud Guard AI's ability to learn and enhance itself over time allows it to evolve alongside emerging security threats. As new risks emerge, the system can be updated and optimized to remain effective, guaranteeing long-term security readiness.

Applications and Future Scope

- **Anomaly Detection in Cloud Environments:** Identifies unauthorized activities like file uploads, downloads, or deletions to enhance security.
- **Data Breach Prevention:** Proactively detects potential breaches and suspicious activities to reduce the risk of data leaks and cyber threats.
- **User Behavior Monitoring:** Monitors user interactions with files, ensuring accountability and transparency by tracking file size, type, and activity status.
- **Integration with Cloud Storage Platforms:** Seamlessly integrates with platforms like Sky Vault for real-time monitoring and analysis of cloud-stored data.
- **Automated Alerts for Anomalies:** Triggers notifications when anomalies are detected, enabling timely intervention to safeguard critical data.
- **Audit Trail Management:** Maintains detailed logs of user activities for compliance and forensic investigations.
- **Enhanced Cloud Security:** Improves cloud-based system security through AI-driven monitoring and anomaly detection.
- **Optimization of System Performance:** Processes large data volumes efficiently using MongoDB and AI/ML algorithms for real-time insights without performance bottlenecks.
- **Customizable Detection Sensitivity:** Allows administrators to adjust anomaly detection thresholds for better accuracy without increasing false positives.
- **Support for Multi-User Environments:** Tracks activities for multiple users, making it suitable for enterprise-level cloud security monitoring.

Future Goals

1. **Cardinal to Major Cloud Storage Platforms**
   Applications are extended to seamlessly integrate into critical cloud storage platforms, including Google Drive, Dropbox, and a wide range of other services. This integration allows users to monitor activity and identify anomalies in several cloud environments via a single interface. The most important features include actual tracking of important events, such as uploading files, downloading, extinguishing fires, and changing

them. By providing a uniform and detailed view of cloud activity, users can ensure proactive monitoring and enhanced data security with external storage solutions.

2. **Proofing Advanced Abnormalities through Severity Classification**
The abnormality evidence algorithm has been upgraded, and a severity classification has been introduced to classify the demonstrated abnormalities as low, moderate, or high risk. Severity is determined based on factors such as activity type, frequency, location, and possible effects. For example, a large sudden deletion can trigger a high-quality alarm, while an abnormal upload with a single file can be identified as low markings. This detailed approach allows the system to effectively prioritize risks. This minimizes false alarms but allows for quick and appropriate responses to critical threats at the same time.
3. **Automatic Blocking of Suspicious or Unauthorized Users**
To enhance security, applications have an automatic blocking mechanism for applications to quickly restrict unauthorized users when they recognize suspicious activity. Examples include abnormal attempts to log on, irregular file access patterns, or abnormal behavior such as massage files. The system responds in real-time by obtaining access or blocking accounts, reducing potential risks before escalating. This positive measure quickly addresses weaknesses and protects the integrity of sensitive data and systems.
4. **Real-Time Monitoring and Immediate Updates**
The introduction of real-time monitoring provides users and administrators with insight into cloud storage activity. Events like file uploads, downloads, fire extinguishing, changes, and more will be updated immediately in the dashboard. In the event of an abnormality, the system will immediately trigger notifications to relevant stakeholders, ensuring timely corrective actions. This continuous monitoring ability promotes aggressive security, reduces reaction times, and improves overall threat management.
5. **MFA System (Rugged Multi-Factor Authentication)**
To improve account security, the application includes a robust MFA system (Rugged Multi-Factor Authentication) during user registration. Supports security levels such as OTPs via SMS or email, as well as authentication tools from third-party providers such as Captcha Challenge, Biometric Review, or Google Authenticator. Due to the requirements of several review procedures, MFA allows only certified users to access sensitive data and carry out high-risk activities.
6. **Monitoring Dashboards for Organizational Oversight**
A comprehensive management dashboard has been developed that allows organizations to oversee real-time oversight for employee cloud activities. Administrators receive detailed visibility into actions such as file upload, download, access patterns, and deletion. The dashboard contains a severity base to identify tailormade warning messages, anomaly speeches, and suspicious behavior. Administrators can respond quickly by restricting user access, publishing accounts, and limiting investigation implementation. This feature improves organizational control and actively tackles potential safety threats.
7. **Improved User Alert System and Activity Limit Control**
The User Alert System is updated to deliver real-time notifications via several channels, including email, SMS, and in-app messages. Users will receive immediate warnings about suspicious activities such as unauthorized registrations, data changes, and potential violations. Additionally, the intuitive user interface directly controls suspicious activity and activates actions such as restricting files. This allows users to take crucial action to protect their data and get complete control of their cloud environment.

Results

Username	*Filename*	*Description*	*Anomaly Score*	*Severity*	*Detected At*
dummyaccount	Markseet3rd.pdf	Unusual pattern detected based on historical activity	−0.668940741	medium	2024-12-12T10:44:53.045Z
dummyaccount	Anaconda3-2024.10-1-Windows-x86_64.exe	Unusual file size: 973.34 MB | Unusual activity time: 03:00 | Suspicious file extension: .exe	−0.682374224	medium	2024-12-12T10:44:53.064Z
dummyaccount	PersonalDocuments.pdf	Delete operation detected	−0.561835538	low	2024-12-16T13:16:00.563Z
dummyaccount	Marksheet.pdf	Unusual pattern detected based on historical activity	−0.631586879	medium	2024-12-16T13:16:00.571Z
dummyaccount	pycharm-community-2024.2.4.exe	Unusual file size: 478.27 MB | Unusual activity time: 01:07 | Suspicious file extension: .exe	−0.565380036	low	2024-12-16T13:16:00.580Z
johndoe	Antivirus-2024-Windows-x86_64.exe	Unusual file size: 1972.84 MB | Unusual activity time: 05:10 | Suspicious file extension: .exe	−0.652311355	medium	2024-12-16T13:16:00.604Z
johndoe	Nifty-Blockchain.pdf	Unusual pattern detected based on historical activity	−0.673838396	medium	2024-12-16T13:16:00.673Z
johndoe	Exploring the Universe A Compreh.pdf	Delete operation detected	−0.676189019	medium	2024-12-16T13:16:00.678Z
johndoe	Integration of AI with Neuroscience Presentation.pdf	Unusual pattern detected based on historical activity	−0.64659012	medium	2024-12-18T16:42:43.200Z

Glossary of Terms

- **Anomaly Score**
  An anomaly score is a quantitative metric generated by an AI model to represent the degree of deviation a given data point or activity exhibits from established normal patterns. In the context of CloudGuard AI, this score is used to assess whether a user action within the Sky Vault cloud storage platform is potentially suspicious or unauthorized. A higher score indicates a greater likelihood of anomalous behavior.
- **False Positive Rate**
  The false positive rate is a statistical measure that indicates the proportion of normal (non-malicious) instances that are incorrectly identified as threats by an anomaly detection system. Within CloudGuard AI, maintaining a low false positive rate is critical to ensuring that legitimate user activities on the Sky Vault platform are not erroneously flagged, thereby minimizing alert fatigue and optimizing system reliability.
- **Real-Time Inference**
  Real-time inference refers to the capability of a machine learning model to analyze incoming data and generate predictions or classifications instantaneously as events occur. For CloudGuard AI, real-time inference enables immediate detection and response to abnormal user behavior within the Sky Vault cloud environment, thereby enhancing the platform's ability to proactively mitigate potential security threats.

9.8 CONCLUSION

Cloud Guard AAI demonstrates its ability to effectively identify anomalies on the Sky Vault Cloud memory platform. The results confirm that the model accurately identifies suspicious activities and can significantly contribute to the safety and integrity of user data in cloud storage systems. Continuous learning and real-world data integration are extremely important to further improve performance, especially when adapting to user behavior and emerging cybersecurity threats. With additional finer and regular updates, Cloud Guard could potentially evolve into a highly reliable and efficient tool for protecting cloud storage systems from new threats and unauthorized activities.

REFERENCES

[1] R. Karri, J. Rajendran, K. Rosenfeld, M. Tehranipoor, Trustworthy hardware: Identifying and classifying hardware trojans, *IEEE Comput.*, 43 (10) (2010), pp. 39–46.
[2] H. Mouratidis, Secure by design: Developing secure software systems from the group up Intern, *J. Secure Software Eng.*, 2 (3) (2011), pp. 23–41.
[3] Internet Security Threats Report. Symantec. http://www.symantec.com/threatreport/
[4] R.C. Newman, *Computer Security: Protecting Digital Resources*, first edition, Jones & Bartlett Publishers (February 20, 2009).
[5] Bloomberg, *The AI Effect: Amazon Sees Nearly 1 Billion Cyber Threats a Day,* (2024).
[6] J. Jang-Jaccard, S. Nepal, A survey of emerging threats in cybersecurity. *J. Comput. Syst. Sci.*, 80 (5) (2014), pp. 973–993.
[7] J. Chang, K.K. Venkatasubramanian, A.G. West, I. Lee, Analyzing and defending against web-based malware. *ACM Comput. Surv. (CSUR)*, 45 (4) (2013), pp. 1–35.

Chapter 10

Developing SHDO

A Case Study on Vehicle Insurance Fraud Detection

Zainab Saad Rubaidi, Boulbaba Ben Ammar, Khalil Masmoudi, Mohamed Ben Aouicha, and Afif Masmoudi

10.1 INTRODUCTION

Recent machine learning (ML) research has begun to pay more and more attention to unbalanced learning in problems with classification tasks [1, 2]. Minority positive instances from disciplines include credit scores in the financial domain [3], mechanical flaw identification [4], crowd behavior detection [5], disease diagnosis [6], and other medicinal disciplines play a key role in datasets with imbalanced classes [7]. The conventional classifiers or ML algorithms, nevertheless, frequently give the highest priority to negative majority examples [8]. To tackle this issue, scholars have proposed solutions on two distinct levels: namely, the algorithmic level and the data level.

The issue of collaborative classifiers learning has increased in popularity at the algorithmic level. A strong classifier is created by combining weak classifiers created by methods like Random Forest (RF) [9], XGboost [10], and AdaBoost [11] using two strategies, including averaging and voting. This enhances classification precision and makes up for the shortcomings of a single classifier on unbalanced samples. Deep learning models or algorithms like CNN [12] and DBN [13] are frequently used in several research works to process unbalanced datasets. Deep network training, however, frequently takes a long time for data processing.

Undersampling and oversampling, or a combination of both, are called hybrid sampling techniques and are also widely applied through the data level scenario. The key point of using this approach is to equalize the encumbrances of the negative and positive classes while training the ML classifier by aggregating the importance of positive examples or reducing the impact of negative samples.

By generating completely new and varied instances to train the models on, data augmentation is the strategy used to overcome an unbalanced class problem in classification problems and enhance the effectiveness and results of supervised ML models [14]. To improve the amount, accuracy, and variation of data training, data augmentation can be used [15]. In recent years, research on data augmentation methods has gained significant popularity, with a focus on establishing a taxonomy and distinguishing the different types of data augmentation methods [16]. This paper proposes an intelligent approach called Sequential Hybrid Data Oversampling (SHDO) for data resampling, comprising mixing contributions of various data oversampling methods such as random oversampling, synthetic minority oversampling technique (SMOTE), SVMSMOTE, BorderLine SMOTE, and SMOTEN. In addition, statistical tests and validation are applied to analyze the results of the proposed approach with ML algorithms for handling the imbalance class problem for binary

DOI: 10.1201/9781003539032-10

classification datasets. The primary advantage of the proposed approach is that it achieves results comparable to the best possible outcomes without requiring a technique-selection step. This aspect offers significant benefits by saving valuable time and resources.

10.1.1 Contribution

We introduce the SHDO data oversampling approach, which combines multiple oversampling techniques to address class imbalance more effectively. SHDO enhances model performance by generating diverse synthetic samples, overcoming limitations of existing methods such as overfitting and poor handling of class boundaries. It demonstrates superior F1-scores and AUC values compared to several established techniques and improves recall for minority class instances. SHDO was evaluated across RF and XGBoost classifiers on three datasets, including two real vehicle insurance fraud, predictive maintenance, and one synthetic dataset. SHDO proves to be a versatile and effective approach. The method's performance is validated through rigorous statistical analysis, ensuring its robustness and reliability.

10.2 RELATED WORK

Data oversampling is a method utilized in the ML context to mitigate class imbalance, where there are fewer examples from the potential dataset minority class than from the dominant samples present in the majority class. This imbalance class problem can result in biased algorithms that fail to accurately classify minority class samples. Oversampling techniques are employed to address this issue by artificially increasing the number of samples in the minority class. Replication is one such approach where existing minority samples are replicated to attain a well-adjusted class representation.

A prevalent oversampling method called the SMOTE is widely applied for solving the unbalance class problem [17], but it has three major flaws: it oversamples noisy [18] and uninformative [18] data, and choosing the right number of nearest neighbors can be difficult to determine. While RCSMOTE [19] manages the range of synthetic examples, borderline-SMOTE [19] also generates synthetic samples in the minority class close to the choice border that separates the minority and majority classes and concentrates on strengthening class boundary information within a chosen region.

To handle overlapped samples of various classes, a K-means SMOTE [20] integrates clustering with SMOTE, while the G-SMOTE [21] produces artificial examples in a given symmetrical region space of the dataset points. Maldonado et al. [22] presented a solution for high-dimensional datasets using the LNSMOTE [23], which takes into account the local neighborhood information of samples, and the DBSMOTE [24] approach that employs the density-based DBSCAN algorithm. A Gaussian distribution of data is combined with SMOTE in Gaussian-SMOTE [25], which is based on the dataset's probability densities. While these algorithms improve the SMOTE approach to varying degrees, they do not extract or fully utilize sample distribution information or modify the random choice of adjacent neighbors. Adaptive synthetic (ADASYN) oversampling [26] makes artificial instances in the minority class with a higher compactness in regions of the feature space where the minority class is underrepresented.

When dealing with imbalanced datasets, a hybrid strategy combines two or more oversampling methods to produce a more potent outcome. To solve the overfitting issue brought on by random oversampling while enhancing the balance of the class distribution, for instance, random oversampling and SMOTE might be combined [27]. The balance of the class distribution can also be improved while taking into account the cost of misclassifying certain classes through the combination of random oversampling and cost-sensitive learning [28].

Innovative hybrid techniques, such as the Hybrid Sampling Method based on Data Partition, have been developed in a recent study. This technique oversamples boundary minority samples by selectively removing noisy minority samples from the data samples in different places. The production of synthetic samples inside the same cluster as the oversampling seed is taken into account when using weighted oversampling. According to reference [29], this strategy attempts to increase the efficiency of the oversampling technique and enhance its addressing of imbalances between classes.

Other hybrid methods for dealing with imbalanced data include "SMOTE-ENN" [30], which incorporates the SMOTE oversampling method with the edited nearest neighbor (ENN) technique and "SMOTE-Tomek links" [31], which mixes the SMOTE oversampling technique with the Tomek links method. These mixed methods outperform existing oversampling methods like random oversampling and SMOTE alone, according to findings from experiments on a variety of datasets. The optimal method to solve the imbalance class problem when using a major dataset, such as the credit card dataset [32] for fraud classification, must be chosen by comparing various oversampling methodologies. In [33], the authors introduced data distribution and spectral clustering-based SMOTE (DDSC-SMOTE), an enhanced oversampling algorithm designed to overcome the limitations of traditional SMOTE methods. DDSC-SMOTE improves upon SMOTE by incorporating adaptive strategies for sample allocation, seed sample selection, and synthesis. It uses spectral clustering to better allocate synthetic samples and prioritize important minority class instances. Evaluations on UCI datasets show DDSC-SMOTE significantly outperforms existing oversampling techniques in G-mean and F1-score, providing a more effective solution for handling imbalanced data.

Hybrid data oversampling methods, which combine several oversampling techniques, have a lot of potential solutions to solve the issue of undisturbed class samples in the ML domain. These techniques can overcome the drawbacks of utilizing just one oversampling strategy, enhancing the effectiveness of ML algorithms. However, more research work is required to confirm the results of these hybrid methods and to identify the most efficient mix of oversampling strategies for particular cases.

10.3 OVERALL METHODOLOGY

The methodology described in this paper normally includes a number of phases and techniques, such as a binary imbalance dataset, data splitting, data resampling, ML algorithms, assessment metrics, and the findings obtained. The general methodology provided in this research article is presented in Figure 10.1.

10.3.1 Binary Imbalance Dataset

Obtaining a dataset with a binary classification challenge is the first step in the proposed methodology. This dataset has one class, called the majority class, having more examples compared to the other minority class.

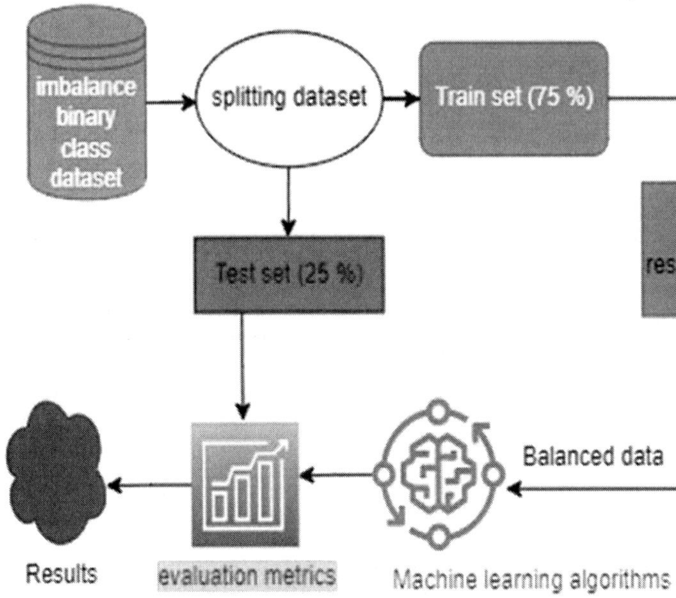

Figure 10.1 A framework for the proposed methodology.

10.3.2 Data Split

In this phase, the dataset is separated into training and testing sets. The testing set is utilized to assess the success of the ML algorithm, while the training set is utilized for training the model.

10.3.3 SHDO Resampling Methodology

To weigh, the amount of examples in each class, this step seeks to resample the data classes to be evenly distributed. Our suggested (SHDO) technique, which is detailed in more depth in the following section, can be used to accomplish the task of resampling.

10.3.3.1 SHDO Approach

This subsection provides an in-depth explanation of the structure and components used to describe our proposed new SHDO approach, which can be employed for resampling any potential binary class dataset. Figure 10.2 shows the framework for the proposed approach's structure.

As shown in Figure 10.2, the structure of this approach consists of a combination of five data oversampling methods, namely, SVMSMOTE, BorderLine SMOTE, Random oversampling, SMOTE, and SMOTEN. We begin by applying the first technique, followed by the implementation of the second technique to the results obtained from the previous application. We repeat this process for all five techniques until a balanced dataset is achieved through their successive application. The pseudocode for the algorithm of the planned

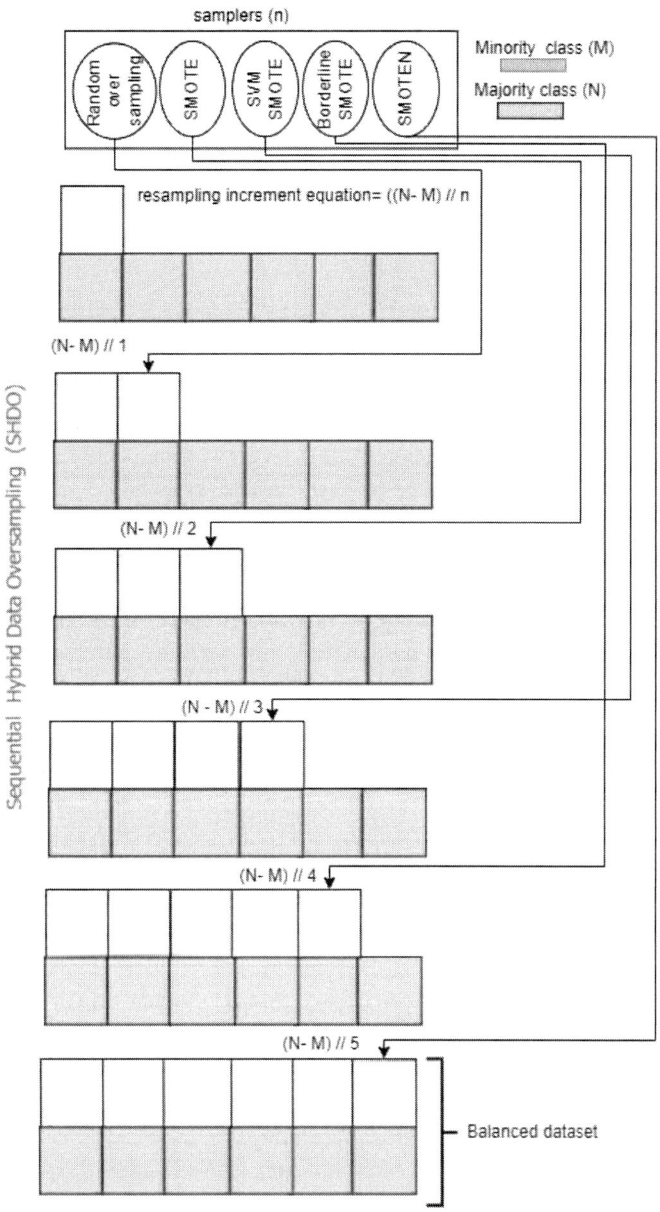

Figure 10.2 The structure of proposal SHDO approach.

SHDO approach is summarized in Algorithm 1. We implemented the following Algorithm 1 for the proposed method, which integrates various oversampling techniques to generate diverse synthetic samples. This implementation is designed to address class imbalance more effectively and improve model performance across different datasets.

Algorithm 1 A working flow of the proposed SHDO algorithm.

1: start
2: Compute the number of the new data to generate.
  a. Compute the quantity of instances in the majority class (N)
  b. **Compute the quantity of instances in the minority class (M)**
  c. The number of instances in the minority class to be generated is equal to (N−M)
3: Generate new data using different oversampling techniques and in a specific order for each chosen technique. This step will generate (N−M)/5 new instances.
  d. **Apply the randomOverSampler to generate (N−M)//5 new instances to obtain M+(N−M)//5 instances in the minority class.**
  e. **Apply the SMOTE to generate (N−M)//5 new instances to obtain M+2*((N−M)//5) instances in the minority class.**
  f. **Apply the SMOTEN to generate (N−M)//5 new instances to obtain M+3*((N−M)//5) instances in the minority class.**
  g. **Apply the BorderlineSMOTE to generate (N−M)//5 new instances to obtain M+4*((N−M)//5) instances in the minority class.**
  h. **Apply the SVM SMOTE to generate (N−M)//5 new instances to obtain M+5*((N−M)//5) = M+N−M=N instances in the minority class (which is equivalent to the number of instances in the majority class.**
4: stop

The proposed SHDO algorithm starts by defining a class that takes in data, label, and an optional sampler parameter. The data, label, and sampler parameters are assigned to instance variables. A method named "resampling" is defined to perform the resampling algorithm.

The algorithm starts to select the samples present in the majority and minority classes from the input binary classification data. The number of samples to be added to the minority class data using the majority class data is computed, and the number of data over resampling techniques to be created, n, is defined. Equation (10.1) is used to calculate the scale of the resampling increment.

$$S = \frac{(N - M)}{n} \tag{10.1}$$

where S represents the resampling increment and denotes the number of samples that are required to be added to the minority class data to balance the class distribution. Here, the total samples in the majority class are denoted as "N," the total samples in the minority class are denoted as "M," and the number of resampling techniques is denoted as "n." The whole number of instances in the minority class must be subtracted from the total number of instances in the majority class to calculate the resampling increment. The number of resampling techniques is then multiplied by the outcome. The number of instances further is added to the minority class data and is shared among the various resampling strategies in an equal amount, thanks to the division by the number of resampling approaches. The class distribution can be balanced by adding the estimated resampling increment to the minority class data using the majority class data.

The algorithm iterates through each resampling technique, and for each iteration of the loop, it concatenates the majority and minority class data into a single data frame X. The labels are extracted from X into y, and the label column is removed from X. The i-th data oversampling resampling algorithm in self.sampler is used to resample X and y, and the resampled data is assigned to X_resample and y_resample. X_resample and y_resample are concatenated to create a new oversampled data frame. The loop ends, and the final oversampled balanced data frame is returned. The pseudocode summary box for the SHDO algorithm, incorporating the flow logic and structure, is presented in Table 10.1.

10.3.4 ML Algorithms

The next stage is to select an ML classifier to be used for the task after the data has been prepared. We employ well-known ML techniques like RF and XGBoost.

10.3.5 Assessment Metrics

The next stage is to assess the model's performance using the unseen set, which is the testing dataset, once it has been trained. This step is used to evaluate the ML classification model on the testing set and to contrast the expected results with the actual results. Accuracy, F1-score, and AUC–ROC curve are examples of evaluation measures that can be used to gauge the effectiveness of the model.

Table 10.1 Pseudocode summary box for the SHDO algorithm

1: Start

2: Compute the number of new data instances to generate:
 a. Let N = number of instances in the majority class
 b. Let M = number of instances in the minority class
 c. Compute Δ = N−M (number of instances to generate)

3: Sequential Oversampling Process (generate Δ / 5 instances per technique):
 d. Apply RandomOverSampler to generate Δ / 5 instances
  → Minority class size becomes M + (Δ / 5)
 e. Apply SMOTE to generate Δ / 5 instances
  → Minority class size becomes M + 2 * (Δ / 5)
 f. Apply SMOTEN to generate Δ / 5 instances
  → Minority class size becomes M + 3 * (Δ / 5)
 g. Apply BorderlineSMOTE to generate Δ / 5 instances
  → Minority class size becomes M + 4 * (Δ / 5)
 h. Apply SVM SMOTE to generate Δ / 5 instances
  → Minority class size becomes M + 5 * (Δ / 5) = N

4: Stop

10.4 EXPERIMENTAL RESULTS

10.4.1 Datasets Description

This study compared the effectiveness of various data oversampling methods, including the SHDO methodology we proposed, on three datasets with class imbalance problems. The section is likely to cover the experimental methodology, evaluation metrics, statistical analysis, and our suggested SHDO strategy with two ML classifiers (RF and XGBoost), which compare the performance of various data oversampling strategies listed previously. It also discusses the outcomes, using metrics like the F1-score. These datasets include those for synthetic datasets, predictive maintenance, and automobile insurance fraud.

10.4.1.1 Vehicle Insurance Fraud Dataset

This dataset is one of the datasets that were used for conducting our experimental work and has been collected from the Kaggle platform [34]. It consists of vehicle insurance claim information obtained through the Angoss Knowledge Seeker Software. The data encompasses 15,420 claims from January 1994 to December 1996, with 32 predictor variables and one target variable, which indicates whether a claim is Fraud or No Fraud. The data set contains 14,497 genuine claims, which are equal to 94% and 923 fraud instances, which indicate 6%, with an average of 430 claims per month. Additionally, the dataset has 6 numeric features and 25 alphanumeric features, with a total of 33 features per instance, including:

- Personal information of the insured (e.g., age, gender, and marital status)
- Insurance contract details (e.g., policy type, vehicle category, deductible insurance payments, number of supplements, agent type, and insurance coverage)
- Circumstances surrounding the accident (e.g., the date and location of the accident, policy report filed, presence of witnesses, and fault liability)
- Other information related to the insurance (e.g., the number of cars, previous claims, and driver rating)
- The target feature indicating whether fraud was found (yes or no)

10.4.1.2 Predictive Maintenance Dataset

The 10,000 data points in this dataset [35] are organized into rows with 14 attributes and a unique identifier ranging from 1 to 10,000. The product ID feature includes a variant-specific serial number and the letters L, M, or H, which stand for poor product quality variants (which account for 50% of all products), medium product quality variants (30%), and high product quality variants (20%). A random walk procedure is used to generate the air temperature [K] feature, which is then normalized to a standard deviation of 2 K about 300 K. The air temperature + 10 K is added to a random walk process that has been adjusted to a 1 K standard deviation to produce the process temperature [K] feature. A regularly distributed noise is added on top of a power of 2860 W to determine the rotational speed [rpm] characteristic. With a sigma value of 10 Nm and no negative values, the torque [Nm] characteristic reflects torque values that are generally dispersed around 40 Nm. The tool wear [min] feature indicates how much extra time the utilized tool takes during the procedure; the quality variants

H/M/L add 5/3/2 minutes, respectively. Finally, the machine failure label specifies which of the following categories the machine has failed in this specific data point. The machine failure label also specifies which of the following failure modes the machine experienced during this specific data point. The imbalance ratio in this dataset is approximately 28.5:1, indicating a more significant imbalance between the two classes (failure or non-failure).

10.4.1.3 Synthetic Dataset

Scikit-learn is a popular ML library in Python [36]. It provides several built-in datasets for practice and experimentation. This dataset has been generated randomly in a subset form for a performance comparison of the proposed oversampling techniques for solving imbalanced class problems. The imbalance ratio of this dataset is approximately 7.13:1 between 0 and 1 classes.

10.4.2 Application of Different ML Algorithms for Binary Classification

In this subsection, a comparative analysis of the results attained using data oversampling techniques previously employed and our proposed approach is presented. We used three different datasets for binary classification evaluation, with a 75% training and 25% testing split. The oversampling techniques were applied only to the training data, and two ML classifiers, RF and XGBoost, were employed for the classification process. The classifiers were tested 83 times with various hyperparameter settings on different datasets. However, we reported the parameters that delivered the best classifier's performance. For example, on the Vehicle Insurance Fraud dataset, we used 50 maximum splits, 5 minimum splits, and 30 n_estimators for RF. In this case, the n_estimators factor regulates the number of decision trees in the RF, while both the maximum splits and minimum splits parameters regulate the extreme depth of the decision tree and the number of samples needed to divide a node, respectively. We utilized 50 n_estimators and 10 maximum splits for XGBoost. The n_estimators option determines the number of decision trees in the XGBoost ensemble, while the maximum splits parameter regulates the decision tree's maximum depth. For the Predictive Maintenance dataset, we used 50 maximum splits, 5 minimum splits, and 130 n_estimators for RF, and 10 maximum splits and 130 n_estimators for XGBoost. Finally, for the synthetic dataset, we set RF with 50 maximum splits, 2 minimum splits, and 130 n_estimators. Table 10.2 summarizes the testing results of all three unbalanced datasets used (original data).

Table 10.2 Testing results of all three unbalance datasets used

Dataset	*Model*	*F1-Score*	*Accuracy*	*Precision*	*Recall*	*AUC*
Predictive Maintenance	XGBoost	0.7792	0.9864	0.8696	0.7059	0.8511
	RF	0.6466	0.9812	0.8958	0.5059	0.7519
Synthetic	XGBoost	0.7797	0.9480	0.8214	0.7419	0.8596
	RF	0.8276	0.9600	0.8889	0.7742	0.8802
Fraud Vehicle Insurance	XGBoost	0.1099	0.9370	0.3571	0.0649	0.5287
	RF	0.0086	0.9403	1.0000	0.0043	0.5022

As shown in Table 10.2, the XGBoost and RF exhibit strong performance on predictive maintenance and synthetic datasets, with XGBoost slightly better at balancing recall and precision. However, both models struggle on the highly imbalanced fraud vehicle insurance dataset, particularly in recall, resulting in poor F1-scores and AUC values that can be improved using our proposed SHDO. The graphical representation of the models' comparison is presented in Figure 10.3.

Data augmentation is a popular approach used to address the problem of unbalanced classes in classification tasks by creating new and diverse examples to enhance the classification accuracy of ML models. This paper proposes an intelligent approach called SHDO for data augmentation, which combines various data oversampling methods such as SMOTE, Random Oversampling (RO), SVMSMOTE, BorderLine SMOTE (BLS), and SMOTEN. Table 10.3 summarizes the testing results using the vehicle insurance fraud dataset.

Table 10.3 presents the testing results for the vehicle insurance fraud dataset, applying various oversampling techniques to RF and XGBoost classifiers and showing inconsistent performances. The XGBoost model using the proposed SHDO achieved the highest F1-score (0.563), reflecting a balanced trade-off between precision and recall. However, its AUC score of 0.576 indicates only a moderate capacity to distinguish between fraudulent and non-fraudulent claims. The RF classifier with Random OverSampler showed similar moderate performance (F1-score 0.486; AUC 0.591). In contrast, combinations like RF with SMOTEN (F1-score 0.377; AUC 0.510) and XGBoost with ADASYN (F1-score 0.469; AUC 0.559) performed poorly, with low AUC values close to random guessing. These low results emphasize that certain oversampling techniques may not substantially enhance the classifiers' ability to detect fraudulent claims, and there is considerable scope for improving the overall performance of the detection system. Despite not achieving the highest scores, SHDO provides distinct advantages by addressing limitations such as bias toward the majority class, overfitting

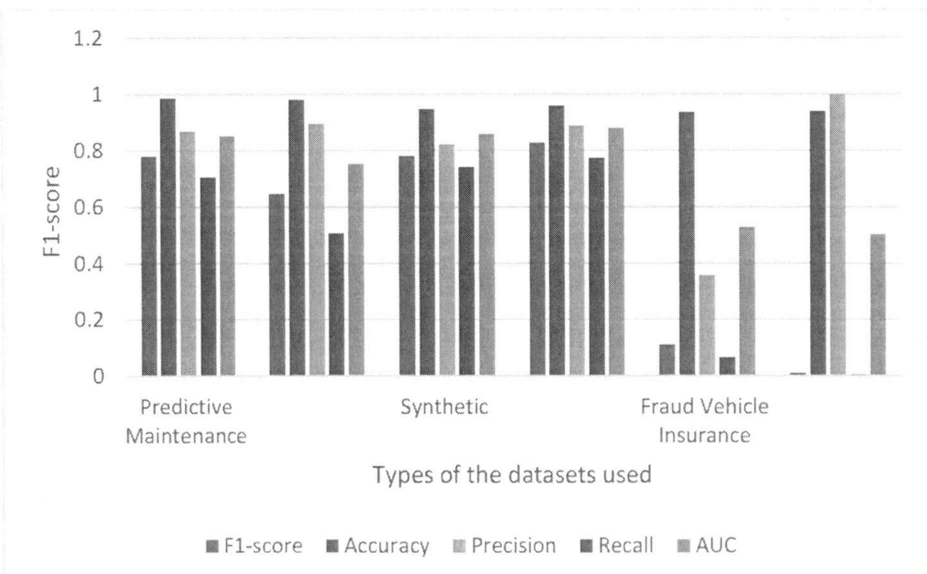

Figure 10.3 Machine learning models' performance comparison using imbalance datasets.

Table 10.3 Testing results of the used ML classifiers using vehicle insurance fraud dataset

Classifier	*Oversampling Technique*	*F1-Score*	*AUC*
RF	Random OverSampler	0.486297	0.591615
	Proposed SHDO	**0.517722**	**0.516764**
	ADASYN	0.432742	0.538816
	SVMSMOTE	0.513933	0.569855
	BorderlineSMOTE	0.497041	0.588139
	SMOTEN	0.376962	0.510025
	SMOTE	0.500074	0.575229
XGBoost	Random OverSampler	0.375315	0.632153
	Proposed SHDO	**0.562996**	**0.575739**
	ADASYN	0.468853	0.558838
	BorderlineSMOTE	0.471549	0.557035
	SVMSMOTE	0.552220	0.536616
	SMOTE	0.469420	0.556440
	SMOTEN	0.480617	0.546372

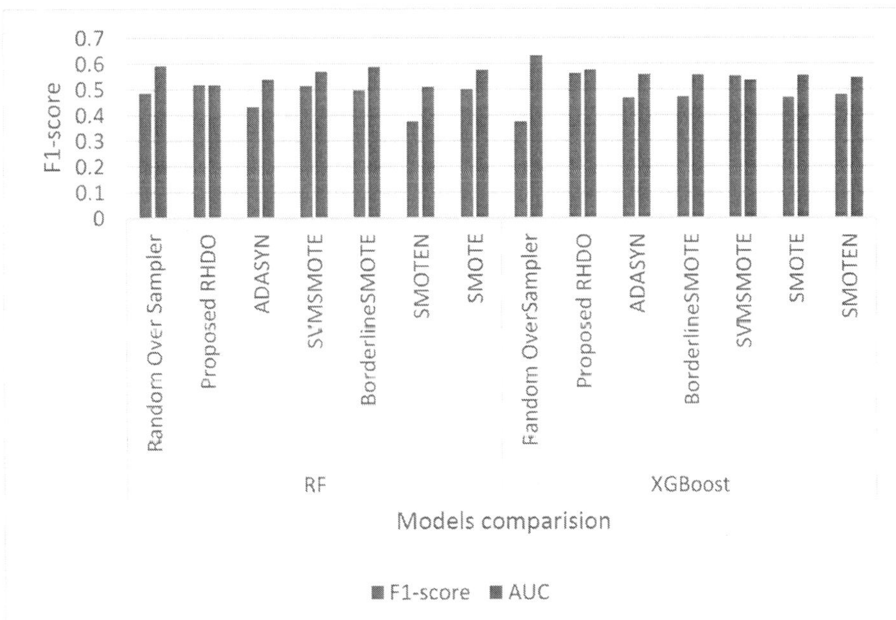

Figure 10.4 Machine learning models' performance comparison using vehicle insurance fraud dataset.

due to sample duplication, and ineffective handling of class boundaries. SHDO's effective generation of synthetic samples and balanced dataset suggests it is a promising method for improving performance in binary classification tasks with class imbalance. Figure 10.4 shows the ML models' performance comparison using the vehicle insurance fraud dataset.

Table 10.4 summarizes the testing findings using the predictive maintenance dataset.

Table 10.4 Testing results of the used ML classifiers based on predictive maintenance dataset

Classifier	*Oversampling Technique*	*F1-Score*	*AUC*
RF	**Proposed SHDO**	**0.887326**	**0.845610**
	Random Over Sampler	0.583293	0.806784
	SVMSMOTE	0.638643	0.792644
	Borderline SMOTE	0.521182	0.754646
	SMOTE	0.536138	0.766240
	SMOTEN	0.597383	0.732042
	ADASYN	0.538742	0.772951
XGBoost	Random OverSampler	0.599529	0.830228
	Proposed SHDO	**0.889132**	**0.884716**
	SVMSMOTE	0.608583	0.814980
	SMOTEN	0.619941	0.830057
	Borderline SMOTE	0.570982	0.814079
	SMOTE	0.573681	0.815735
	ADASYN	0.560293	0.812094

In a binary classification task on a predictive maintenance dataset, the performance of various oversampling techniques applied to RF and XGBoost classifiers was evaluated, as detailed in Table 10.4. The testing results for the predictive maintenance dataset demonstrate significant variations in classifier performance with different oversampling techniques. The RF classifier using the proposed SHDO method achieved the best results, with an F1-score of 0.887 and an AUC of 0.846, reflecting both strong predictive accuracy and good class discrimination. Similarly, XGBoost paired with the proposed SHDO also showed robust performance, achieving an F1-score of 0.889 and an AUC of 0.885, suggesting it is effective in handling class imbalance and predicting failures in maintenance.

On the other hand, techniques like RF with Borderline SMOTE (F1-score 0.521, AUC 0.755) and XGBoost with ADASYN (F1-score 0.560, AUC 0.812) performed less effectively, especially in terms of recall and precision. These results indicate that while the proposed SHDO oversampling technique leads to superior predictive performance, other oversampling methods yield more moderate outcomes, leaving room for optimization in class imbalance handling for predictive maintenance tasks. Figure 10.5 demonstrates the ML classifiers' performance comparison using the predictive maintenance dataset.

Table 10.5 shows the testing outcomes on the synthetic dataset show a broad variation in performance across different oversampling techniques for both RF and XGBoost classifiers. The RF and XGBoost models paired with the proposed SHDO method achieved the same highest performance, with an F1-score of 0.975 and an AUC of 0.960, reflecting excellent precision, recall, and a strong ability to differentiate between classes. Similarly, XGBoost with SVMSMOTE delivered solid results, attaining an F1-score of 0.778 and an AUC of 0.814, indicating a well-balanced predictive capacity.

On the other hand, combinations like XGBoost with SMOTEN performed poorly, with an F1-score of 0.530 and an AUC of 0.532, suggesting a performance close to random chance in distinguishing between classes. Other techniques, such as RF with ADASYN

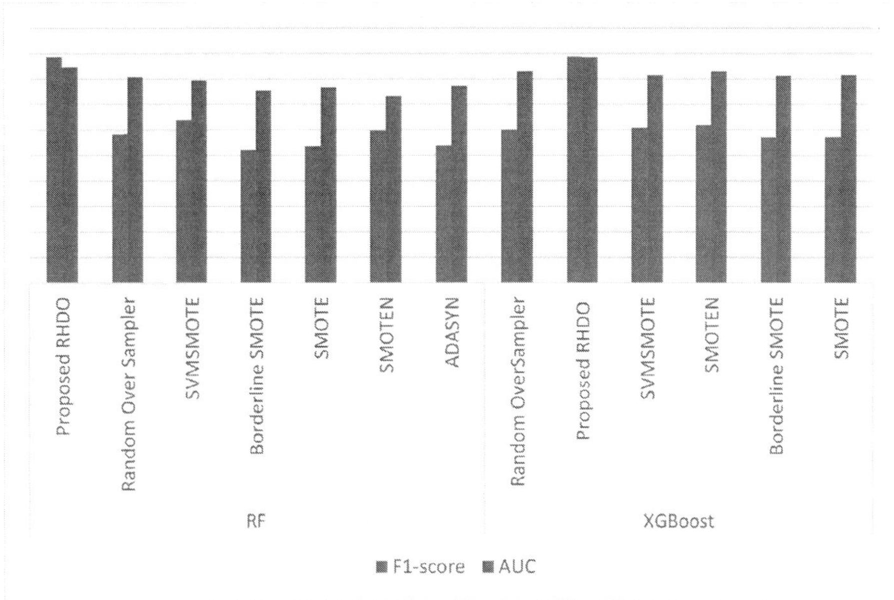

Figure 10.5 Machine learning classifiers' performance comparison using predictive maintenance dataset.

Table 10.5 Testing results of the used ML classifiers using the synthetic dataset

Classifier	*Oversampling Technique*	*F1-Score*	*AUC*
RF	SMOTE	0.750582	0.883267
	Proposed SHDO	**0.975939**	**0.960526**
	Random Over Sampler	0.763373	0.901679
	ADASYN	0.716697	0.865002
	Borderline SMOTE	0.830578	0.919797
	SMOTEN	0.768010	0.707394
	SVMSMOTE	0.841391	0.898954
XGBoost	SMOTE	0.709804	0.749374
	Proposed SHDO	**0.975939**	**0.960526**
	Random Over Sampler	0.707944	0.737811
	SMOTEN	0.529557	0.532258
	SVMSMOTE	0.778391	0.813743
	Borderline SMOTE	0.674156	0.710267
	ADASYN	0.678777	0.754235

(F1-score 0.717, AUC 0.865), showed moderate results. Inclusively, the proposed SHDO method consistently enhanced performance, particularly for RF, while the effectiveness of other oversampling techniques varied and, in some cases, led to suboptimal results. Figure 10.6 shows the ML models' performance comparison using the synthetic dataset.

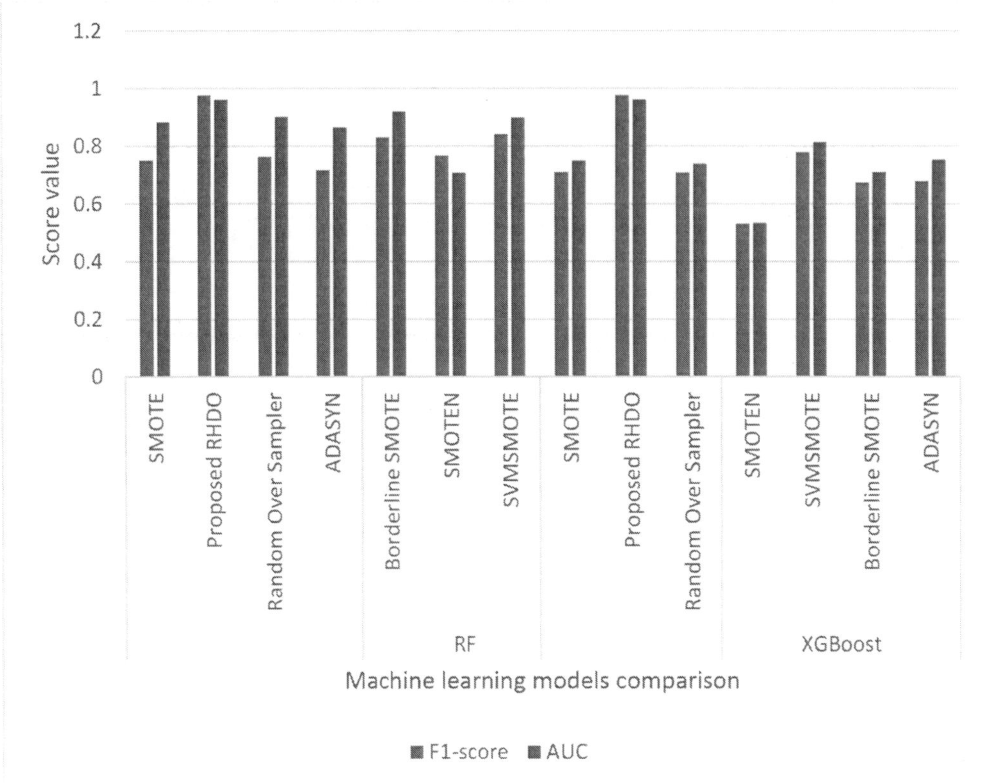

Figure 10.6 Machine learning models' performance comparison using the synthetic dataset.

In general, the proposed SHDO approach showed that it can handle the imbalance class problem in binary classification tasks, outperforming some of the top oversampling methods in terms of performance. The method is best suited for circumstances where there is a substantial class imbalance and other approaches might not work.

10.5 VALIDATION OF THE PROPOSED METHOD

10.5.1 Error Analysis

Using data oversampling methods to balance datasets that have unequal class distribution, in which one class is underrepresented in comparison to the other, might help supervised ML models perform better. To determine how the proposed oversampling approaches would affect the outcomes of the models, it is crucial to conduct a statistical error analysis. The results obtained by the ML models trained on the original imbalanced dataset and the oversampled dataset are compared using various statistical metrics, such as recall, precision, accuracy, and F1-score. These measurement metrics provide an estimate of the quality of the predictions made by the model and assist in determining which oversampling technique is most appropriate for the given problem. The F1-score metric, however, was employed as an acceptable measure for the imbalance dataset in the tests conducted for this work. Figure 10.7 shows the performance error analysis for the oversampling approaches that have been suggested.

The performance of several data oversampling and resampling methods, including our proposed SHDO approach (hybrid), was assessed using the F1-score metric, represented on the X-axis, and the number of evaluations for parameter selection in ML classifiers, as shown in Figure 10.3. This assessment was conducted through numerous trials with two different ML classifiers across three datasets. The red line depicts the lowest F1-score number, and the blue line shows the highest. The findings unequivocally show that the suggested SHDO approach, illustrated by the green line plot in Figure 10.7, consistently outperformed the other data oversampling approaches while only occasionally underperforming them. All things considered, our method outperformed the majority of the procedures assessed and delivered close to the ideal results and even superior ones in more than 20% of the experiments run.

In terms of context, the explanation describes the results of an experiment comparing different data oversampling and resampling techniques for ML using the F1-score metric. The graph in Figure 10.4 shows the performance of each technique, with the green line representing the results of the proposal SHDO approach. The conclusion is that the proposed approach performed well compared to other techniques, although it was not the top performer overall. Figure 10.8 shows the results after the relative enhancement rate of the proposed method with respect to the best obtained result using the other methods. Hence, the relative improvement rate (RIR) is computed in equation (10.2) as follows:

$$\mathrm{RIR} - \frac{(\mathrm{score} - \mathrm{best\,score})}{\mathrm{best\,score}} \tag{10.2}$$

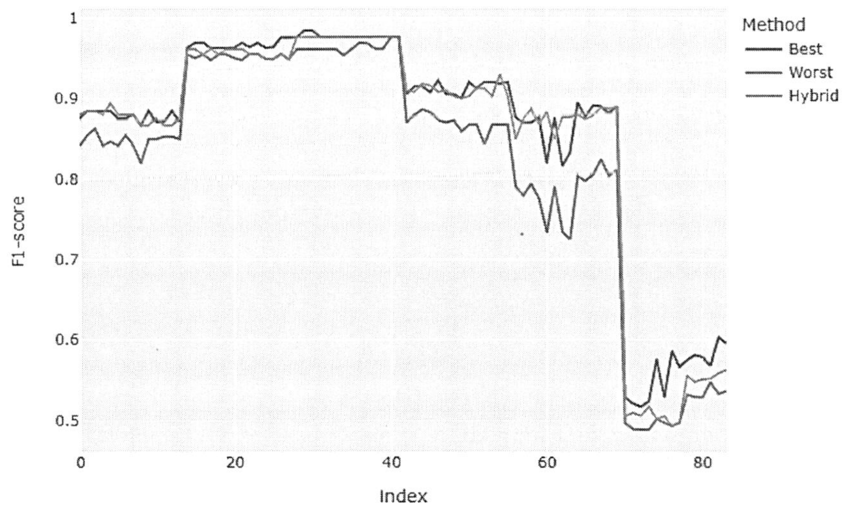

Figure 10.7 The performance error analysis for the proposed SHDO (hybrid) compared to the best and the worst results obtained using the other data oversampling techniques.

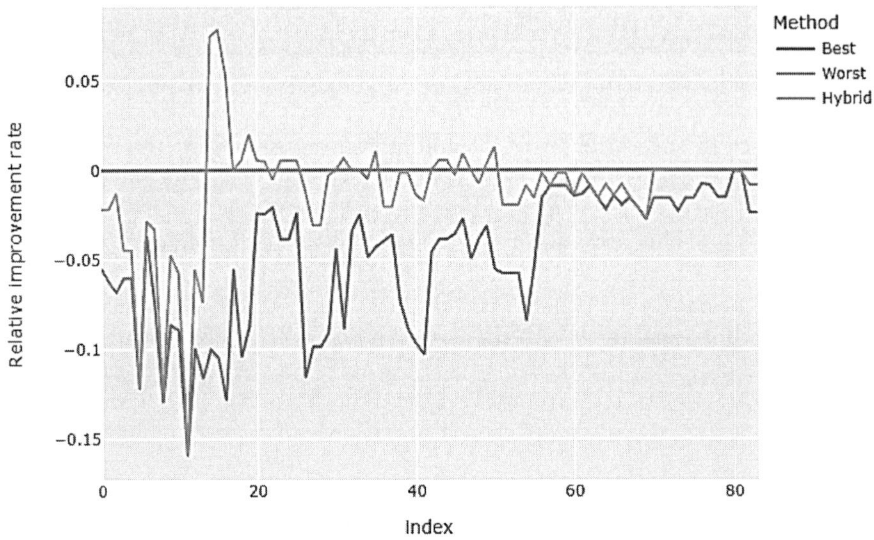

Figure 10.8 The relative improvement rate induced by the proposed SHDO approach (hybrid) in terms of F1-score with respect to the best score obtained by the other oversampling techniques.

10.5.2 Statistical Validation

An analysis of variance was performed to statistically validate the earlier results. The performance of the stated SHDO approach in comparison to the employed data oversampling procedures is therefore evaluated using a statistical *t*-test to compare the means of the F1-score outcomes. Best denotes the highest F1-score results from the experiments we ran for this study. Hybrid is the F1-score value produced by our suggested SHDO method. The *p*-value that was achieved for this test is 0.75. This finding suggests that the variation within each group is very minor compared to the difference in the means between the two groups, and the *p*-value is significantly higher than the usually accepted significance level of 0.05. This indicates that, at the 0.05 significance level, there is not enough proof for rejecting the null hypothesis that states there is no significant difference between the means of the two groups. Hence, the F1-scores obtained through the proposed method are statistically equivalent to the best one provided using the other sampling techniques.

Moreover, to confirm the latter results, the histogram of the proposed method's RIR and the quantiles were plotted. The obtained results that are displayed in Figure 10.5 show, for example, that the RIR is positive in more than 20% of the experiments performed. They also show that the potential underperformance compared to the best performing technique is less than 5% in 93% of the experiments. The histogram and quintiles of the RIR of the F1-score for the proposed sampling technique are presented in Figure 10.9.

Figure 10.10 shows a mini-info graphic for the proposed SHDO's applications.

Table 10.6 displays an executive summary of the SHDO approach.

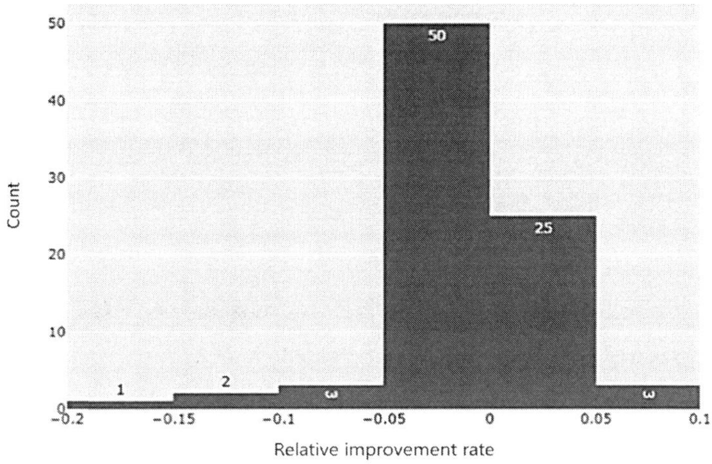

(a)

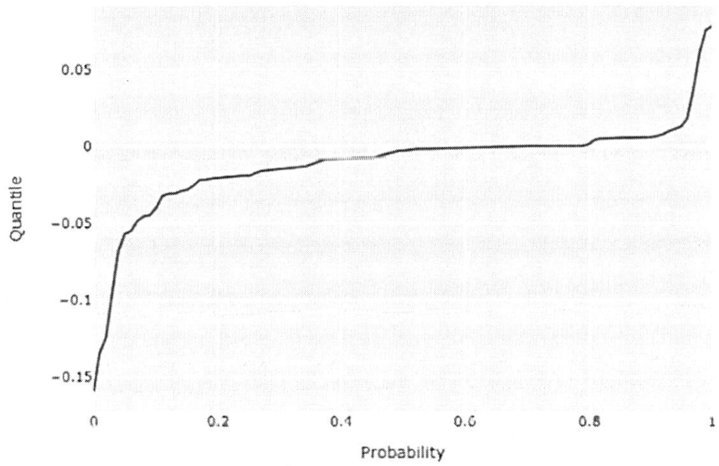

(b)

Figure 10.9 Histogram (a) and quantiles (b) of the relative improvement rate of the F1-score for the proposed SHDO resampling technique with respect to one giving the highest score among the others' sampling techniques.

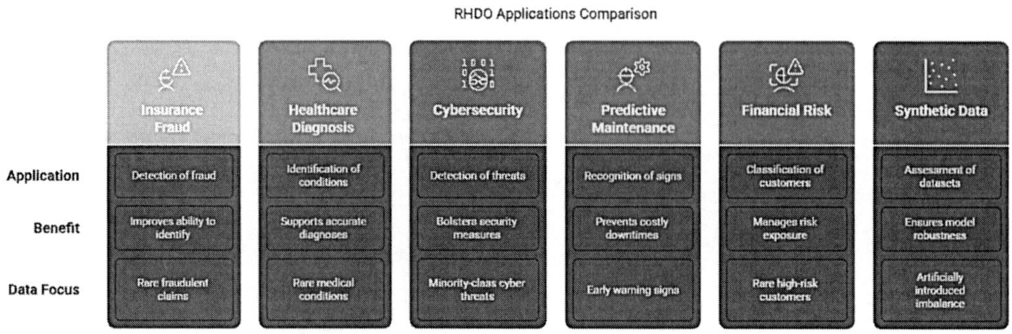

Figure 10.10 Mini-info graphic of the SHDO's applications.

Table 10.6 An executive summary of the SHDO approach

Aspect	*Details*
Proposed Method	Sequential Hybrid Data Oversampling (SHDO)
Key Advantages	– Balanced class distribution—improved F1-score and AUC—adaptable to various datasets—integration of five oversampling methods
Oversampling Techniques	RandomOverSampler, SMOTE, SMOTEN, BorderlineSMOTE, SVMSMOTE
Datasets Used	1. Predictive Maintenance; 2. Synthetic; 3. Fraud Vehicle Insurance
Comparison Models	Random Forest (RF), XGBoost
Best Results (F1-Score)	– Synthetic: RF (0.8276)—Maintenance: XGBoost (0.7792)—Fraud: XGBoost (0.1099)
Best Results (AUC)	– Synthetic: RF (0.8802)—Maintenance: XGBoost (0.8511)—Fraud: XGBoost (0.5287)

10.6 CONCLUSIONS AND PERSPECTIVES

This research presents the SHDO approach for binary classification tasks. It has been tested and evaluated on three binary class datasets and provided the highest performance across all datasets used in this study, consistently outperforming other oversampling techniques in terms of F1-score and AUC. SVMSMOTE ranked second in terms of performance, yielding strong results across datasets, further highlighting its reliability. On the synthetic dataset, while Random Over Sampler and SMOTE also performed well, SHDO's ability to adapt to various data complexities solidified its superior performance. Both RF and XGBoost classifiers demonstrated robust performance, reaching high scores on all datasets.

For future work, further studies should assess the scalability of SHDO on larger, more complex datasets with hundreds of features to validate its broader applicability. Evaluating SHDO's performance with state-of-the-art learners and ensemble classifiers on diverse imbalanced binary classification problems will help confirm its versatility. Additionally, expanding the evaluation to include metrics like precision, recall, and specificity will offer a more nuanced view of oversampling strategy effectiveness. Finally, the development of novel oversampling methods and more advanced classifiers could lead to even greater improvements in detecting fraudulent activities and other rare occurrences in various domains.

REFERENCES

1. Kovács, G. (2019). Smote-variants: A python implementation of 85 minority oversampling techniques. *Neuro Computing*, 366, 352–354.
2. Kumar, V., Lalotra, G. S., Sasikala, P., Rajput, D. S., Kaluri, R., Lakshmanna, K., . . . & Uddin, M. (2022, July). Addressing binary classification over class imbalanced clinical datasets using computationally intelligent techniques. In *Healthcare* (Vol. 10, No. 7, p. 1293). MDPI.
3. Brown, I., & Mues, C. (2012). An experimental comparison of classification algorithms for imbalanced credit scoring data sets. *Expert Systems with Applications*, 39(3), 3446–3453.
4. Samanta, B. I. S. W. A. J. I. T., Al-Balushi, K. R., & Al-Araimi, S. A. (2003). Artificial neural networks and support vector machines with genetic algorithm for bearing fault detection. *Engineering Applications of Artificial Intelligence*, 16(7–8), 657–665.
5. Xie, S., Zhang, X., & Cai, J. (2019). Video crowd detection and abnormal behavior model detection based on machine learning method. *Neural Computing and Applications*, 31, 175–184.
6. Ahsan, M. M., Luna, S. A., & Siddique, Z. (2022, March). Machine-learning-based disease diagnosis: A comprehensive review. In *Healthcare* (Vol. 10, No. 3, p. 541). MDPI.
7. Kalwa, U., Legner, C., Kong, T., & Pandey, S. (2019). Skin cancer diagnostics with an all-inclusive smartphone application. *Symmetry*, 11(6), 790.
8. Kang, Q., Fan, Q., & Zurada, J. M. (2021). Deterministic convergence analysis via smoothing group Lasso regularization and adaptive momentum for Sigma-Pi-Sigma neural network. *Information Sciences*, 553, 66–82.
9. Díaz-Uriarte, R., & Alvarez de Andrés, S. (2006). Gene selection and classification of microarray data using RF. *BMC Bioinformatics*, 7, 1–13.
10. Wang, C., Deng, C., & Wang, S. (2020). Imbalance-XGBoost: Leveraging weighted and focal losses for binary label-imbalanced classification with XGBoost. *Pattern Recognition Letters*, 136, 190–197.
11. Thanathamathee, P., & Lursinsap, C. (2013). Handling imbalanced data sets with synthetic boundary data generation using bootstrap re-sampling and AdaBoost techniques. *Pattern Recognition Letters*, 34(12), 1339–1347.
12. Kvamme, H., Sellereite, N., Aas, K., & Sjursen, S. (2018). Predicting mortgage default using convolutional neural networks. *Expert Systems with Applications*, 102, 207–217.
13. Yu, L., Zhou, R., Tang, L., & Chen, R. (2018). A DBN-based resampling SVM ensemble learning paradigm for credit classification with imbalanced data. *Applied Soft Computing*, 69, 192–202.
14. Van Dyk, D. A., & Meng, X. L. (2001). The art of data augmentation. *Journal of Computational and Graphical Statistics*, 10(1), 1–50.
15. Mumuni, A., & Mumuni, F. (2022). Data augmentation: A comprehensive survey of modern approaches. *Array*, 100258.
16. Fonseca, J., & Bacao, F. (2022). Research trends and applications of data augmentation algorithms. *arXiv preprint arXiv:2207.08817*.
17. Chawla, N. V., Bowyer, K. W., Hall, L. O., & Kegelmeyer, W. P. (2002). SMOTE: Synthetic minority over-sampling technique. *Journal of Artificial Intelligence Research*, 16, 321–357.
18. Soltanzadeh, P., & Hashemzadeh, M. (2020). RCSMOTE: Range-controlled synthetic minority over-sampling technique for handling the class imbalance problem. *Information Sciences*, 542, 92–111.
19. Han, H., Wang, W. Y., & Mao, B. H. (2005, August 23–26). Borderline-SMOTE: A new over-sampling method in imbalanced datasets learning. In *Proceedings of the International Conference on Intelligent Computing (ICIC)*, Hefei, China, pp. 878–887.
20. Douzas, G., Bacao, F., & Last, F. (2018). Improving imbalanced learning through a heuristic oversampling method based on k-means and SMOTE. *Information Sciences*, 465, 1–20.
21. Douzas, G., & Bacao, F. (2019). Geometric SMOTE a geometrically enhanced drop-in replacement for SMOTE. *Information Sciences*, 501, 118–135.

22. Maldonado, S., López, J., & Vairetti, C. (2019). An alternative SMOTE oversampling strategy for high-dimensional datasets. *Applied Soft Computing*, 76, 380–389.
23. Maciejewski, T., & Stefanowski, J. (2011, April 11–15). Local neighbourhood extension of SMOTE for mining imbalanced data. In *Proceedings of the IEEE Symposium on Computational Intelligence and Data Mining (CIDM)*, Paris, France, pp. 104–111.
24. Bunkhumpornpat, C., Sinapiromsaran, K., & Lursinsap, C. (2012). DBSMOTE: Density-based synthetic minority over-sampling technique. *Applied Intelligence*, 36, 664–684.
25. Pan, T., Zhao, J., Wu, W., & Yang, J. (2020). Learning imbalanced datasets based on SMOTE and Gaussian distribution. *Information Sciences*, 512, 1214–1233.
26. He, H., Bai, Y., Garcia, E. A., Li, S. (2008, June 1–8). ADASYN: Adaptive synthetic sampling approach for imbalanced learning. In *Proceedings of the IEEE International Joint Conference on Neural Networks (IJCNN)*, Hong Kong, China, pp. 1322–1328.
27. Turaba, M. Y., Hasan, M., Khan, N. I., & Rahman, H. A. (2022). Fraud detection during financial transactions using machine learning and deep learning techniques. In *2022 International Conference on Communications, Computing, Cybersecurity, and Informatics (CCCI)*. IEEE, pp. 1–8.
28. Le, T., Vo, M. T., Vo, B., Lee, M. Y., & Baik, S. W. (2019). A hybrid approach using oversampling technique and cost-sensitive learning for bankruptcy prediction. *Complexity*, 2019.
29. Chen, L., Jiang, J., & Zhang, Y. (2021). HSDP: A hybrid sampling method for imbalanced big data based on data partition. *Complexity*, 2021, 1–9.
30. Kovács, G. (2019). An empirical comparison and evaluation of minority oversampling techniques on a large number of imbalanced datasets. *Applied Soft Computing*, 83, 105662.
31. Batista, G. E. A. P. A., Prati, R. C., & Monard, M. C. (2004). A study of the behavior of several methods for balancing machine learning training data. *ACM SIGKDD Explorations Newsletter*, 6(1), 20–29.
32. Saad Rubaidi, Z., Ben Ammar, B., & Ben Aouicha, M. (2023, May). Comparative data oversampling techniques with deep learning algorithms for credit card fraud detection. In *Intelligent Systems Design and Applications: 22nd International Conference on Intelligent Systems Design and Applications (ISDA 2022) Held December 12–14, 2022-Volume 1*. Springer Nature Switzerland, pp. 286–296.
33. Li, X., & Liu, Q. (2024). DDSC-SMOTE: An imbalanced data oversampling algorithm based on data distribution and spectral clustering. *The Journal of Supercomputing*, 1–30.
34. Vehicle Claim Fraud Detection Dataset. Retrieved from: https://www.kaggle.com/datasets/shivamb/vehicle-claim-fraud-detection (accessed February 20, 2023).
35. Machine Predictive Maintenance Classification Dataset. Retrieved from: https://www.kaggle.com/datasets/shivamb/machine-predictive-maintenance-classification (accessed February 20, 2023).
36. Scikit-learn. Make classification. Retrieved from: https://scikitlearn.org/stable/modules/generated/sklearn.datasets.make_classification.html (accessed February 20, 2023).

Chapter 11

Securing Our Shared Future

Recommendations for Healthy Technology Progress

Samar Bouazizi and Hela Ltifi

11.1 INTRODUCTION

The advancements witnessed in the rapidly changing technological environment are redefining industries and the way we interact with the world. Technologies like artificial intelligence (AI), machine learning (ML), cloud computing, and the Internet of Things (IoT) (Eguia et al. 2024; Yuvashree 2023) are improving operational efficiencies and, at the same time, streamlining a shift in decision-making processes in various industries. As organizations adopt these technologies, they experience advantages such as improved productivity and elevated customer experiences, as well as more efficient resource management, among various other benefits. Nonetheless, the integration of technology also presents challenges, including vulnerabilities in cybersecurity and ethical quandaries, alongside the necessity for robust frameworks to ensure equitable access to these advancements.

Recent incidents underscore these challenges with alarming clarity. The 2020 algorithm failure in a widely used US hospital risk-prediction system—which systematically underestimated the needs of black patients due to biased training data (Bajwa et al. 2021) (Alowais et al. 2023)—reveals how even well-intentioned AI deployments can perpetuate harm when ethical considerations are secondary. Similarly, the 2021 ransomware attack on Ireland's Health Service Executive, which paralyzed healthcare delivery for weeks (Aslan et al. 2023), demonstrates the catastrophic consequences of inadequate cybersecurity in critical infrastructure

The purpose of this chapter is to describe key trends in technologies that have major importance in fields such as healthcare, education, and manufacturing today, and also to highlight the beneficial effects and factors that contribute to key success. Such organizations face challenges and obstacles pertinent to interoperability problems, scalability issues, along ethical concerns regarding data privacy and algorithmic bias (Umayal 2024; Cucciniello et al. 2024; Wolff et al. 2021; Zaidi et al. 2024).

The aim of this chapter is to provide a holistic understanding of the revolutionary potential of technology through a detailed review of case studies and literature, with emphasis on responsible practices for implementation. This study outlines potential directions for development and provides pragmatic recommendations that augment the ongoing debate on how to address the complexities involved in technological advancement in a manner that emphasizes security, equity, and innovation. Knowing these dynamics is central to positioning oneself at the heart of the Fourth Industrial Revolution and championing an inclusive and sustainable technological future.

This chapter methodically reviews the wide-ranging impacts of emerging technologies on industries through seven thematic sections. It begins by analyzing ongoing technology

DOI: 10.1201/9781003539032-11

trends—AI, cloud computing, the IoT, and data analytics—prior to examining next-generation innovations like blockchain and big data analytics. Subsequent sections cover implementation concerns, such as security vulnerabilities and ethical concerns over data privacy and algorithmic bias, while proposing attendant cybersecurity measures and governance frameworks. Case studies demonstrate real-world use in healthcare, education, and manufacturing, with both efficacy and limits. The discussion culminates with policy recommendations for fostering secure, equitable innovation, followed by an in-depth examination of deepfakes as a critical convergence point for emerging technology governance. The chapter concludes by exploring future trends and their societal implications.

11.2 TRANSFORMATIVE TECHNOLOGIES: AI, CLOUD, AND IOT-DRIVEN INDUSTRY SHIFTS

11.2.1 Key Technology Trends

Current technology trends (i.e., AI/ML, IoT, cloud computing, blockchain, and data analytics) are significantly reshaping industries and the digital landscape. To visualize the intersection of these trends, Figure 11.1 illustrates how they interact and influence various sectors, including healthcare, education, and manufacturing.

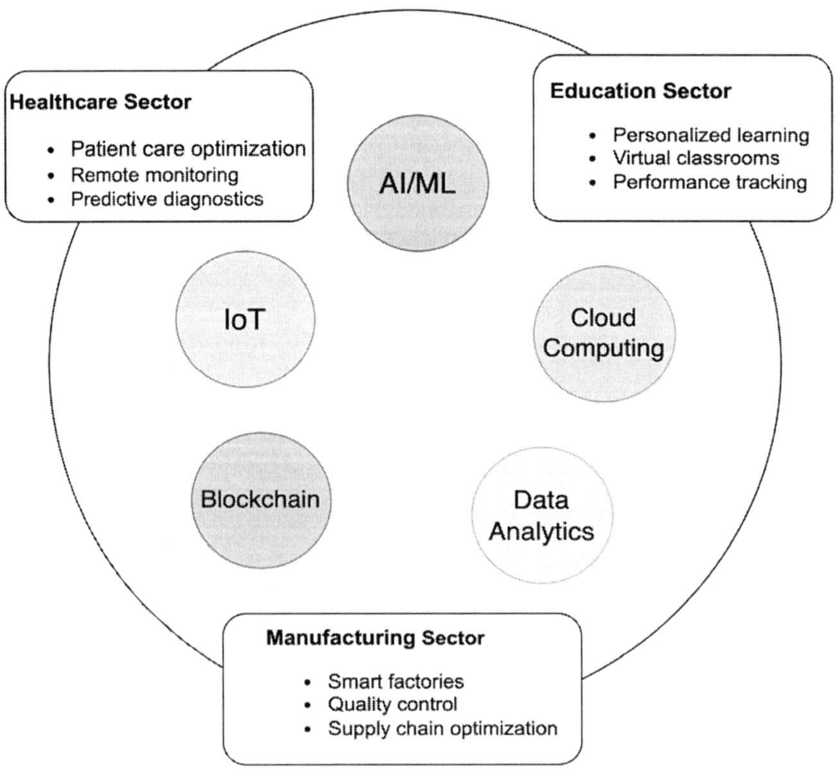

Figure 11.1 Technology ecosystem and sector impact.

11.2.1.1 AI and ML

AI has become a transformative force in many industries, particularly ML, which is changing how tasks are executed and decisions made internally; as such, AI systems understand natural language, recognize patterns, and execute analyses that no human could (Davenport 2018). It has significantly advanced healthcare, financial, and manufacturing industries:

11.2.1.1.1 Natural Language Processing

Natural language processing (NLP), a branch of AI, now allows computers to understand and generate human language. In healthcare, this means doctors can quickly access and interpret patient records, leading to faster diagnoses and better care. However, as these systems handle sensitive data, it is crucial to address concerns around privacy and transparency to maintain patient trust. Its applications extend well into various domains. AI-powered systems are making huge strides across a wide array of sectors, especially in healthcare, finance, and manufacturing. For example, in healthcare, such systems can go through a large volume of medical literature and patient records to aid diagnosis and treatment planning, as noted by Eguia et al. (2024). Furthermore, with regard to extraction and analysis in electronic health records, NLP contributes significantly to the clinical decision-making support system and thereby improves outcomes in patient care. Applications are common in the financial industry, where they are used for sentiment analysis of financial news, and even include social media data that can help inform investment decisions. Furthermore, chatbots and virtual assistants based on NLP are revolutionizing customer service in banking and other financial institutions, providing personalized guidance and support around the clock. In manufacturing, NLP assists in analyzing customer reviews about products and evaluating reviews to help manufacturers enhance product quality and increase customer satisfaction. The use of AI and NLP in different industries indicates the increasing relevance of the technologies in optimizing processes and improving outcomes in different fields (Badrinarayanan 2024).

11.2.1.1.2 Pattern Recognition Revolution: Efficiency Gains and Human Consequences

While AI-based pattern recognition has indubitably revolutionized industries, its social footprint is equally profound. Consider a 95%-accurate-on-average lung cancer screening AI that fails to detect tumors in Black patients 40% more often due to having been trained on biased data (Bajwa et al. 2021; Albaroudi et al. 2024)—a somber reminder that technical success is no assurance of equitable outcomes.

Technical Advancements With Human Context

- **Healthcare:** ML models now predict disease progression (Fakoor et al. 2013) and analyze medical images with superhuman precision (Lee et al. 2018), but when deployed without diverse datasets, they risk exacerbating healthcare disparities.
- **Finance:** Algorithmic trading systems process market trends in microseconds (Badrinarayanan 2024), yet their opaque decision-making can trigger flash crashes that wipe out retirement savings.
- **Manufacturing:** Predictive maintenance AI reduces equipment downtime by 30% (Badrinarayanan 2024), while simultaneously displacing workers who lack retraining programs.

The Double-Edged Sword of Efficiency: These applications demonstrate AI's transformative potential, but the findings of Section 3.2 about algorithmic bias are a reality check: technical solutions must be paired with ethical guardrails. In either AI healthcare diagnostic systems or antifraud screening technologies, the patterns AI learns don't just exist in the abstract—they have consequences for who gets loans, medical care, and job opportunities.

11.2.1.1.3 Enhanced Decision-Making Processes

AI technologies are making many decision-making processes much better in a variety of industries. In healthcare, AI-driven clinical decision support systems provide real-time support for health professionals to realize quality improvement in care with reduced medical errors, according to Alowais et al. (2023). Equally, AI makes the delivery of personalized medicine possible through analyzing data of individual patients to suggest treatment plans, as mentioned by Bajwa et al. (2021). AI-based credit-scoring models in the finance sector analyze voluminous datasets to speed up lending decisions. Let the robo-advisors recommend investments that best fit the financial goals and risk tolerance of the users. Manufacturing: In manufacturing, AI optimizes supply chain management through improved insights on inventory levels and demand forecasts with improvements in logistics, hence enhancing decision-making for better production and distribution. These developments indeed represent the transformational power of AI in decision-making within different sectors.

11.2.1.1.4 Operational Efficiency Improvements

AI technologies have improved operational efficiencies across diverse industry sectors. Some examples include the automation of routine tasks in appointment scheduling and billing, which releases health personnel's time for care. Virtual nursing solutions powered by AI alleviate the shortages and improve the efficiency of care provided. AI automates mundane tasks involved in the finance sector, such as data entry and report generation, which in turn increases efficiency and reduces human error. AI streamlines complicated financial processes like invoice processing and accounts payable for quicker transactions at lower costs. Manufacturing: With AI-driven automation, the repetition of tasks decreases human intervention and minimizes the chance of error, thus enhancing productivity. Besides, AI improves quality control with its precise identification of product defects and inconsistencies, which helps in efficient product quality and waste reduction. All these put together prove the magic of AI in changing the face of operational efficiency across industries (Elete et al. 2024).

Conclusively, AI technologies have revolutionized many of the very important sectors: natural language understanding and processing, pattern recognition, healthcare, financial institutions, and manufacturing. Accomplishing those jobs that, generally speaking, call for human intelligence, AI therefore enhances the process of making vital decisions while increasing the pace at which all other operations occur, by enormous proportions. Such will be their continuing development to broaden their reach into these areas where efficiency, accuracy, and innovation are key to greater achievement.

11.2.1.2 Cloud Computing: Revolutionizing IT Infrastructure

Cloud computing has rapidly emerged as the transformational technology that changes fundamentally how organizations deal with their resources in IT. This shift of paradigm from the traditional on-premise infrastructure to cloud-based services offers several advantages, particularly concerning resource accessibility, flexibility, scalability, and cost-effectiveness.

11.2.1.2.1 *Accessing Powerful Computing Resources*

Cloud computing enables organizations to access a wide range of computing resources over the internet, therefore eliminating the need for an extensive physical infrastructure. This paradigm shift has several key implications. First, there is no longer a need for on-site physical hardware since an organization can store and process data without relying on local servers and data centers. Instead, these resources are remotely hosted by cloud service providers, a factor that has considerably reduced the physical footprint of IT operations. Second, cloud services offer on-demand resource provisioning that enables users to automatically create computing resources as needed without human interaction with service providers. The self-service model ensures that organizations get the resources they need precisely when they need them. Last but not least, cloud services enable broad network access that allows service access using standard mechanisms by any type of client platform. Accessibility in this manner promotes collaboration and, therefore, facilitates remote work capabilities among teams irrespective of the physical location (Hossain et al. 2022).

11.2.1.2.2 *Promoting Flexibility*

This may be especially suitable for periodic workloads with variably scaling in response to shifts in demand on the market: Cloud computing could offer an alternative that allowed fast adaptation in step with such requirements, not fettered as organizations would have traditionally been by in-house hardware infrastructure. Second, cloud computing's added advantage relates to services having access anywhere—easy, convenient, and remote working, hence from any place. This level of flexibility has become increasingly fundamental in the modern business landscape, particularly due to global developments such as the COVID-19 pandemic.

Besides, in cloud computing, resources can be dynamically allocated or reallocated by demand, whereby organizations can efficiently manage their IT resources and optimize all aspects of their performance and related costs (Bhattacharyya et al. 2022).

11.2.1.2.3 *Enhancing Scalability*

One of the most significant advantages of cloud computing is scalability. The cloud systems can elastically provision and release resources, thus enabling organizations to scale capabilities up or down fast in response to fluctuating demands. This elasticity allows businesses to efficiently manage resources by scaling up or down depending on the needs. Especially for those companies that face demand fluctuations, it is very important not to suffer from great investments in hardware up-front, with the purpose of serving sudden bursts of increased activity. This cloud computing promotes high performance at the top during peak times of use and optimizes cost during periods of low use, making the IT solution effective and cost-efficient (Selvan Chenni Chetty et al. 2023).

11.2.1.2.4 *Cost-Effectiveness*

Cloud computing has major cost advantages over a traditional IT setup. Among many of the substantial benefits is a decline in capital investment, as an organization will no longer invest in hardware and software. Most importantly, the key advantage of many cloud services have on-demand types of payment structures where an organization pays only for the usage; hence, it reduces the cost, which will further provide alignment to its IT cost usage. Additionally, most cloud services include in their package maintenance and updates, hence diminishing the need for organizations to invest in the continuous upkeep of hardware infrastructure. This shift also leads to increased operational efficiency due to the reduced need for in-house IT staff focused on managing hardware, therefore translating to huge cost savings within the organization (Sujatha & Ambia 2024). It shows, therefore, a paradigm shift in the management of IT infrastructures. This field opens access to great computing power without extensive physical infrastructure. The result is unequalled flexibility, scalability, and affordability. As long as the technology continues to evolve, it will keep influencing business operations and innovations. This further cements its place as the bedrock of modern IT strategy (Stoica & Nitu 2024).

11.2.1.3 IoT: Connecting Devices and Enabling Data Exchange

IoT's network of connected devices—from hospital monitors to smart thermostats—runs on wisely chosen protocols that balance efficiency with human safety. Think about how a compromised insulin pump (Chataut et al. 2023) illustrates the risks of these technical trade-offs: Wi-Fi provides immediate patient data transmission but leaves medical devices vulnerable to cyberattacks, whereas Zigbee's low-energy profile (well-suited to elderly fall-sensing sensors) values battery longevity over extended range connectivity (Elgazzar et al. 2022; Reddy 2023). Such trade-offs are life-critical when buggy implementations cause emergency warnings to be delayed or privacy is breached in smart cities. Proper communication between IoT devices isn't a technical problem—it's a social imperative.

IoT devices are essentially fitted with sensors that keep collecting data from the environment on parameters like temperature, humidity, and motion. All such data is communicated to other devices or a central system using communication protocols like MQTT, HTTP, and CoAP. The collection of data would comprise gathering information, processing it either locally through edge computing or sending it to the cloud platform for analysis, and then transmitting the processed data for further action. Advanced analytics are performed on such information collected, always seasoned with a little touch of AI and ML (Chataut et al. 2023).

IoT hugely automates the process in many industries, hence improving efficiency, reducing costs, and increasing productivity. In manufacturing, IoT sensors monitor machine performance and allow for predictive maintenance, thus reducing equipment downtimes (Niu et al. 2022). IoT-enabled tracking devices improve visibility and efficiency in supply chain management (Zhang & Liu 2021). In agriculture, IoT devices monitor soil conditions and crop health, thus enabling data-driven farming practices (Chataut et al. 2023).

IoT in smart homes works to further convenience, efficiency, and security. It helps to automate the house and therefore controls systems pertaining to lighting, heating, and security for entertainment with much more ease, in line with occupants' preferences. Devices like thermostats and lighting systems leverage the energy to optimum levels to minimize bills, ultimately contributing toward going green. Besides, the advent of smartphone applications has been furthering remote observations and the ability to manage several devices with real-time alerts in security linked to enhanced video feeds in home safety (Chataut et al. 2023).

The healthcare sector is transforming patient care and operational efficiency. Devices automatically collect health metrics, such as heart rate and blood pressure, making it possible to monitor patients from a distance without physical visits. Real-time monitoring of health provides alerts to health providers when abnormalities occur from normal parameters (Kelly et al. 2020). The IoT facilitates the realization of smart healthcare facilities by allowing real-time information sharing among devices, patients, and healthcare personnel, which in turn improves the quality of services. Through the analysis of patients' records, healthcare providers are able to design tailored treatment strategies and predict potential health complications prior to their aggravation (Chataut et al. 2023).

11.2.1.4 Data Analytics

Data analysis refers to a systematic computational assessment of information aimed at revealing trends, patterns, and knowledge that can inform the decision-making process. With the current data-centered environment, companies are more than ever depending on sophisticated analytic techniques for extracting useful knowledge from large amounts of data. The process has a pivotal role in opportunity identification, function optimization, and enhancing the overall company performance (Abdul-Azeez et al. 2024).

11.2.1.4.1 Advanced Analytics Techniques

Advanced analytics entails an extensive variety of complex methods that surpass traditional data analysis methods. Some of the most significant methods in this scope encompass ML, which entails algorithms capable of learning from data and making predictions. ML models have the capability to identify intricate patterns and associations in big datasets, hence allowing organizations to predict trends and behaviors with great precision (Nguyen et al. 2021). This allows organizations to revise their strategies based on predictive knowledge, making them more adaptive organizations with respect to changing markets. The other most important technique includes data mining, which basically focuses on the patterns and extracting useful information out of large data (Bharara et al. 2018). Data mining allows organizations to sift through massive volumes of information in record time and provide insights for making timely and informed decisions. Data mining helps businesses uncover hidden opportunities and avoid risks that may not be apparent through traditional techniques of analysis.

Statistical analysis is also at the heart of advanced analytics (Lalanne 2016). It is a methodology where, through the use of statistical methods, data is analyzed. It helps summarize complex data sets and interpret them. Through statistical analysis, an organization can find correlation and causation, which are key components of strategic planning. Such insight allows evidence-based decision-making to help businesses efficiently allocate resources and create targeted initiatives.

11.2.1.4.2 Importance of Data Analytics

With the Fourth Industrial Revolution, the volume and variety of data have become unprecedented. The organizations are confronted with structured, semi-structured, and unstructured data emanating from diverse sources such as the IoT, operations, and social media. Advanced analytics techniques are required to change this raw data into actionable insights that businesses can leverage to add more value by finding better ways to optimize operations and ultimately maximize profits.

The advanced techniques of big data analytics will provide organizations with the ability to make much better decisions, outpacing the competition in their respective markets. In fact, the capability of analyzing and interpreting big datasets effectively has started to become one of the main competencies that will determine business survival in an increasingly complex, data-rich environment. By embracing data analytics, organizations position themselves not only to respond to today's market demands but also to forecast future trends that will drive continuous growth and innovation (Abdul-Azeez et al. 2024; Dika-Krluku 2024).

11.2.2 Emerging Trends

In addition to the current key trends mentioned earlier, several emerging technologies are expected to play a crucial role in shaping the future. Following, we present these emergent trends.

11.2.2.1 Blockchain: Balancing Innovation and Societal Impact

Blockchain's decentralized architecture creates immutable transaction records through distributed consensus (Zheng et al. 2018), offering transformative potential across industries while presenting critical societal trade-offs. As indicated in Table 11.1, uses of the technology reveal conflicts between technical possibility and human effect. The cryptographic underpinning of blockchain yields tamper-proof information in the form of chained blocks of transactions, while decentralized peer-to-peer networks eliminate single points of failure (Zheng et al. 2017). This enables revolutionary uses like cryptocurrency transfers and smart contract automation (Achmad Bagraff et al. 2024), while supply chain uses enable real-time product provenance. However, such benefits come with significant drawbacks like enormous energy consumption (Nofer et al. 2020), scalability limitations under high-transaction contexts, and regulatory fragmentation across jurisdictions. Proof-of-work protocols' ecological footprint, discussed later in Section 3.1, is a particularly urgent problem in need of balanced solutions that maintain blockchain's security advantages while addressing sustainability imperatives.

Blockchain's transparency builds trust by allowing all participants to authenticate transactions independently, and its elimination of intermediaries reduces costs and friction in processes ranging from insurance claims to cross-border payments. In supply chain applications, the technology helps combat counterfeiting in such sensitive industries as pharmaceuticals and luxury goods. Yet realizing blockchain's complete potential to create a more secure and transparent future will mean going beyond its current limitations through

Table 11.1 Societal implications of blockchain adoption

Application Domain	*Technical Benefit*	*Human Impact*	*Key Challenge*
Financial Systems	Tamper-proof transaction records	Reduces fraud in remittances for migrant workers	High energy consumption (Nofer et al. 2020)
Healthcare Data	Secure patient record sharing	Enables refugee medical history portability (Achmad Bagraff et al. 2024)	Requires digital infrastructure in developing regions
Supply Chains	Real-time product provenance tracking	Verifies ethical sourcing for consumers	Potential vendor privacy concerns

technological advances and responsible models of implementation that consider both operational efficiency and social fairness.

11.2.2.2 *Big Data Analytics*

Big Data Analytics refers to the process of studying large amounts and varied types of data—called "big data"—to uncover hidden patterns, connections, and other insights that can enable better-informed decision-making. As the volume, velocity, and variety of data being generated continue to grow exponentially, organizations are increasingly applying advanced analytical techniques to extract useful information from these data sets (Prakash et al. 2024).

Trend analysis is quite important in business for understanding market dynamics. It can analyze trends and changes in historical data from markets, based on which businesses take strategic action through price readjustments, product introductions, or geographical expansions. Big data analytics helps facilitate competitor analysis; thus, one is enabled to monitor the movements of a competitor or key metrics performance. Analyzing competitors' data with respect to their own would enable any firm to see gaps in the marketplace and create points of difference (Marasu & Arathi 2023).

Big data analytics also has a strong impact on consumer preferences. Businesses can make offerings based on individual preferences by analyzing consumer behavior data. For example, e-commerce platforms use big data to recommend products based on past purchases and browsing history, which enhances customer experience and improves sales. Moreover, sentiment analysis enables firms to comprehend consumer feelings toward their brands or products by analyzing social media interactions, reviews, and feedback. This will provide real-time insight into customer needs and concerns that a company can immediately act upon, thus enhancing brand loyalty.

Some of the key techniques in big data analytics include data mining, ML, and NLP (Prakash et al. 2024). Data mining is a method of exploration in large datasets to find patterns and relationships within. Some techniques to segment customers or forecast future trends include clustering, classification, and regression. The algorithms of ML analyze a huge amount of data and learn with time and new inputs. Therefore, companies can automate decision-making processes and improve predictive analytics. NLP can analyze unstructured data sources like customer reviews or social media posts, extracting useful insights from texts to understand consumer sentiment and preferences.

Big data analytics has a lot of advantages. Access to deep insights into data lets organizations make strategic decisions with reduced reliance on intuition. Data analysis helps businesses identify inefficiencies, streamline operations, and cut costs. Further, the understanding of consumer preferences leads to effective marketing strategies and improvement in customer experience through personalization. Big data analytics will help an organization understand the dynamics of the market and consumer preferences, thus enabling it to make informed decisions for growth and customer satisfaction. However, privacy, data quality, and skill shortages are some key challenges that need to be addressed if the full potential of big data analytics is to be realized within business contexts (Lee & Mangalaraj 2022).

11.2.2.3 *Virtual and Augmented Reality*

Virtual reality (VR) and augmented reality (AR) have indeed been considered two of the most immersive technologies, which will further enhance user experience by adding digital information into the physical world or by providing a completely virtual environment. Although both these technologies aim to upgrade user interaction, they do that in fundamentally disparate ways (Baragash et al. 2022).

Through VR technology, the user will be engaged in an utterly virtual environment, detached from the real world. These typically include headsets that are worn by the user and show a 360-degree view of a digitally created space; using controllers or hand-tracking devices, users can interact with this virtual environment in a way that is remarkably interactive—a truly emotive and realistic simulation. VR finds its applications across different domains, the most popular being in the gaming industry, which creates interactive and enjoyable experiences when players are able to adventure through worlds that are fantastical. In education and training, it serves to simulate real-life situations, such as medical training or flight simulations, allowing learners hands-on experience without the obvious risks (Zhao et al. 2023). Further, VR finds its application in healthcare therapeutically to conduct exposure to phobias and pain management techniques (Bruno et al. 2022).

Opposed to it, AR overlays digital information on the real world with an aim to enrich the user's perception of their environment. That's commonly delivered through a user's smartphone, tablet, or AR headset. While VR transports the user into a completely new environment, AR enhances the present physical world by inserting more virtual objects into it, thereby allowing users to interact with both real and virtual things at the same time. AR has some pretty neat applications in gaming, with games like Pokémon Go integrating gameplay with real-world locations, turning players into outdoor enthusiasts. These applications of AR enhance learning through interaction by adding context or visualizations to educational content, in this case, showing complex scientific concepts through the use of interactive 3D models. Retail lets consumers have a view of products in their own spaces prior to purchase by enabling customers to virtually try on clothes or see how furniture would appear in their homes (Baragash et al. 2022).

Key differences between VR and AR are presented in Table 11.2.

The core benefits of VR and AR encompass a number of key points: increasing the level of engagement by creating immersive experiences that are superior in holding user attention compared with many types of traditional media; improving learning outcomes through interactive, experiential learning opportunities which can enhance understanding and retention; and being more accessible, as AR applications can be easily accessed via widely available devices such as smartphones, and hence are far more user-friendly than VR systems, which do often require more specialized equipment (Salama 2024). Nevertheless, all these technologies bear a set of challenges. High-quality VR systems are extremely expensive to establish; they involve both special hardware and software development. Furthermore, a lot of users experience much discomfort or even motion sickness in using VR

Table 11.2 Key differences between VR and AR

Characteristic	*Virtual Reality (VR)*	*Augmented Reality (AR)*
Immersion	Completely immerses users in a simulated environment	Enhances the real world with digital information
Interaction	Interaction is limited to the virtual environment	Users engage with both virtual and physical objects
Hardware Requirements	Requires dedicated VR headsets and controllers	Can be accessed via smartphones, tablets, or AR glasses

headsets, which discourages many from putting them on. Furthermore, both VR and AR entail huge expenses in time and resources to develop captivating content (Salama 2024).

Finally, VR and AR technologies are changing user experiences in all industries by overlaying digital information on the physical world or completely immersing users in a virtual environment. Examples in gaming, education, and training suggest their potential for increasing engagement and learning outcomes. As these technologies continue to evolve, reducing cost, user comfort, and content creation challenges are essential to ensuring these technologies can have a broad impact on society.

11.2.2.4 5G Networks

5G technology ushers in a new frontier in wireless communication characterized by faster speeds, lower latency, and better reliability than all predecessors. It is the next-generation network that will enable the support of various devices and applications in a manner that fundamentally changes how we connect and interact with technology. Probably, the most noticeable advantage of 5G is that it offers incredibly high data transfer rates, much higher than what 4G networks can provide. Whereas downloading a movie using a 4G network could take several minutes, 5G networks can do this in just a few seconds. This increased speed will not only improve user experiences but also enable the transfer of volumes of data required by advanced applications (Wei et al. 2023).

5G technology has more stable, reliable connections that drop fewer calls and are less frequently interrupted in the transmission of data. This will be crucial for applications needing a constant connection, such as in autonomous cars or remote healthcare. Advanced network architecture improves how signals are managed and decreases congestion, hence assuring better quality in the connected world. 5G is especially important for IoT, given that the interconnectedness of a large number of devices should not fail. Besides that, compared to 4G, 5G allows raising the number of possibly connected devices per square kilometer from about 100,000 to 1 million. This increased capacity will enable smart cities, industrial automation, and extensive sensor networks to work smoothly and efficiently; thus, innovation in many industries will be driven ahead (Paolino et al. 2019).

5G also enables new applications that become possible with its unique features. The ultra-low latency of 5G-in as little as 1 millisecond allows autonomous vehicles to process, in real-time, data from the surrounding environment, data critical to on-board safety features such as collision avoidance systems. Further, 5G provides for V2X-a more effective management of traffic flow and greater safety due to increased interconnectedness among vehicles and infrastructure (Molina-Masegosa & Gozálvez 2017).

5G's speed and reliability in healthcare make telemedicine possible, with real-time consultations and remote surgeries that reduce delays in patient care. Wearable health devices also send large amounts of data at fast speeds, continuously monitoring patient metrics and sending updates in real-time to health professionals (Ghadi et al. 2024).

In the case of smart cities, 5G can improve the flow of traffic, enhance public safety through surveillance systems, and increase energy efficiency through smart grids. Besides, sensors connected by 5G can provide real-time data on air quality, noise levels, and other environmental factors, and thus, a city could act proactively about emerging issues (Paolino et al. 2019).

In all, 5G technology is not just about faster internet and more reliable connections; it is also about catalyzing the power of IoT and innovative applications in areas like autonomous vehicles and telemedicine. As this technology continues to be deployed across the world, it is expected to reshape industries and make life easier by facilitating seamless connectivity among an ever-increasing number of devices (Shafique et al. 2020).

11.3 CYBERSECURITY VULNERABILITIES IN EMERGING TECH: FROM IOT EXPLOITS TO ALGORITHMIC BIAS

In this section, existing security vulnerabilities and ethical concerns associated with technology are discussed.

11.3.1 Security Vulnerabilities

Security vulnerabilities can stem from software, human behaviors, network configurations, and endpoint devices-especially with the IoT (Aslan et al. 2023). One of the major issues is **unpatched software** (Groš et al. 2021). Too many organizations simply do not patch their software, operating systems, and applications on a regular schedule, which means known vulnerabilities remain open for attackers to use. Good patch management will close these gaps and help avoid certain types of attacks, including ransomware or malware infections. Furthermore, newly discovered vulnerabilities known as **zero-day exploits** (Mohamed et al. 2024), which have not yet been fixed by vendors, are a serious risk because attackers will be able to leverage these in advance of defenses being implemented. This calls for real-time scanning of vulnerabilities and patching on time.

Weak access controls (Berliner 2017) significantly contribute to the security threat. Inadequately implemented identity and access management solutions grant unauthorized users access to confidential data. As a countermeasure to this threat, the usage of multi-factor authentication (MFA) and role-based access control is essential to minimize privilege escalation and unauthorized access. Furthermore, vulnerabilities are major contributors to instigating cybersecurity breaches. **Phishing attacks**, according to Asiri et al. (2023), employ social engineering to compel users to divulge sensitive information or click on harmful links and continue to be a significant source of cybersecurity attacks. Routine security awareness training is instrumental in equipping workers with the skills necessary to recognize such threats and understand how to act accordingly. Additionally, insider threats, as Villarreal-Vasquez et al. (2023) have found, can endanger systems via personnel, be they employees or contractors, with malicious intentions or who unknowingly compromise data. The impact of such insider threats can be largely reduced by adopting measures like network segmentation and user activity monitoring.

For network weakness, issues tend to happen due to insecure configurations (Thomas et al. 2025), for example, poorly configured firewalls, open ports, or default passwords that offer potential entry points for the attacker. Regular audits and penetration testing can identify and remedy these weaknesses. **Lack of network segmentation** (Wang et al. 2024) means that an attacker, upon gaining access to part of a network, is able to laterally move around and access sensitive assets. This risk can be considerably reduced by segregating high-value assets such as financial servers.

The openness and resource-constrained nature of IoT systems make them particularly vulnerable to threats such as DDoS attacks, malware, and intrusion. To meet these challenges, AI methods, especially ML and deep learning, have been found very effective in enabling real-time anomaly detection and predictive security. Integration of blockchain technology can enhance IoT security by providing decentralized, tamper-proof infrastructures for secure device identity management and data integrity (Xu et al. 2021).

Of course, the last would be **endpoint vulnerabilities** (Noor & Mustafa 2024), since most of the attack vectors predominantly target laptops, smartphones, and IoT devices. These need to be protected with endpoint protection solutions that contain antivirus, anti-malware, and real-time threat detection capabilities. By mitigating each of these different types of vulnerabilities, organizations can make significant strides toward improving overall security posture (Alshammari 2023).

11.3.2 Ethical Concerns

Ethical concerns surrounding technology primarily revolve around data privacy, surveillance, algorithmic bias, responsibility in cybersecurity breaches, and the impact on employment. The concern of **data privacy**, brought to the forefront by Ehimuan et al. (2024), is of critical importance because of the vast accumulation of personal information, which raises vital questions about the methods used for data storage, sharing, and use. Organizations must follow privacy laws, such as the General Data Protection Regulation (GDPR), while also being transparent in their data management processes. There are ethical concerns when businesses utilize personal information for advertising or surveillance without seeking explicit consent from users and thus potentially infringing on individuals' rights to privacy.

In addition, **monitoring and surveillance technologies** (Hussain et al. 2023), such as facial recognition and staff monitoring equipment, have the potential to invade individual privacy if used improperly. Care must be taken to balance valid security requirements with ethical concerns, not to slip into overreach or misuse of such technologies. Another important concern relates to **algorithmic bias** (Albaroudi et al. 2024), in which ML algorithms, when trained on biased data, can perpetuate discrimination in critical domains like hiring, lending, or policing. To foster the ethical development of AI, it is important to build fairness tests, use diverse data sets, and conduct regular audits to detect and minimize bias.

Organizations are also held accountable in the event of **cybersecurity breaches** (Tran et al. 2024). They have ethical dilemmas in their role to safeguard user data and are responsible for prioritizing clear communication about incidents. Preemptive measures, such as employing secure encryption methods, are paramount in ensuring the trust of users. Finally, the growing automation of tasks using AI raises ethical questions about job displacement. Organizations have to think about launching reskilling programs or identifying alternative opportunities for affected employees to deliver equal outcomes. Collectively, these ethical concerns highlight the need for a careful and responsible approach to technology implementation, balancing innovation with the protection of individual rights and societal welfare.

Table 11.3 summarizes key ethical concerns associated with emerging technologies, identifies the primary stakeholders affected by each issue, and outlines recommended safeguards to mitigate potential risks.

To better understand and visualize the various cybersecurity vulnerabilities and ethical issues discussed, a risk assessment matrix has been developed (cf. Figure 11.2). This matrix categorizes risks based on their likelihood of occurrence and potential impact on organizations and stakeholders. The quadrant representing high impact and high likelihood highlights the most critical risks that require immediate attention. Among these are cybersecurity threats, such as phishing attacks, which remain prevalent, and ethical concerns, including

Table 11.3 Ethical considerations in emerging technologies: concerns, stakeholders, and safeguards

Ethical Concern	*Affected Stakeholders*	*Recommended Safeguards*
Privacy	Individuals, Organizations	• Data encryption • Informed consent • Transparent data policies
Bias	Marginalized groups, Developers	• Diverse and representative datasets • Fairness audits • Inclusive design processes
Accountability	Regulators, AI Developers, Users	• Clear governance frameworks • Explainability and transparency standards • Legal and ethical compliance
Job Displacement	Workers, Communities	• Workforce reskilling and upskilling programs • Social safety nets • Inclusive economic policies

privacy violations and algorithmic discrimination. Medium-impact threats consist of insider threats, vulnerabilities in IoT devices, and issues caused by the digital divide, while low-impact threats comprise minor configuration errors and minimal data access. The matrix utilizes a color-coding system—red for high impact, yellow for medium impact, and green for low impact—to convey at a glance the severity of risk. Furthermore, it distinguishes between cybersecurity vulnerabilities, designated by blue labels, and ethical concerns, designated by purple labels, thereby assisting organizations in determining their risk mitigation priorities. The risk model proposed allows organizations to efficiently target their security expenditures and resources, formulate effective mitigation strategies, channel compliance efforts to areas of risk, and inform policy design and implementation.

11.3.3 Cybersecurity Measures to Address Vulnerabilities and Ethical Concerns

To efficiently reduce vulnerabilities while at the same time tackling ethical issues, it is crucial for organizations to have a far-reaching set of cybersecurity best practices that enhance security and protect user rights. The implementation of strong authentication mechanisms, including MFA, must be adopted along with strict password policies to significantly reduce the risk of unauthorized access (Berliner 2017). Ongoing monitoring and recording are also crucial; through the use of Security Information and Event Management tools (Granadillo et al. 2021), organizations are able to attain real-time threat identification and response, thus allowing them to act swiftly in case of possible cybersecurity intrusions.

In addition, data encryption is critical in the protection of sensitive data. Deployment of data-at-rest and data-in-transit encryption ensures that such data remains protected from unwanted access or interception, thus minimizing threats associated with data breaches. Moreover, organizations should conduct periodic security audits to identify vulnerabilities within their system, network, and user behavior; such audits are an integral part of maintaining an active security posture and correcting possible weaknesses before they are exploited.

The use of a zero-trust architecture (Sedjelmaci & Ansari 2024) is an extremely effective approach, where each user or device must constantly authenticate its validity before being allowed access to any resource. This model significantly minimizes the risk of insider threats

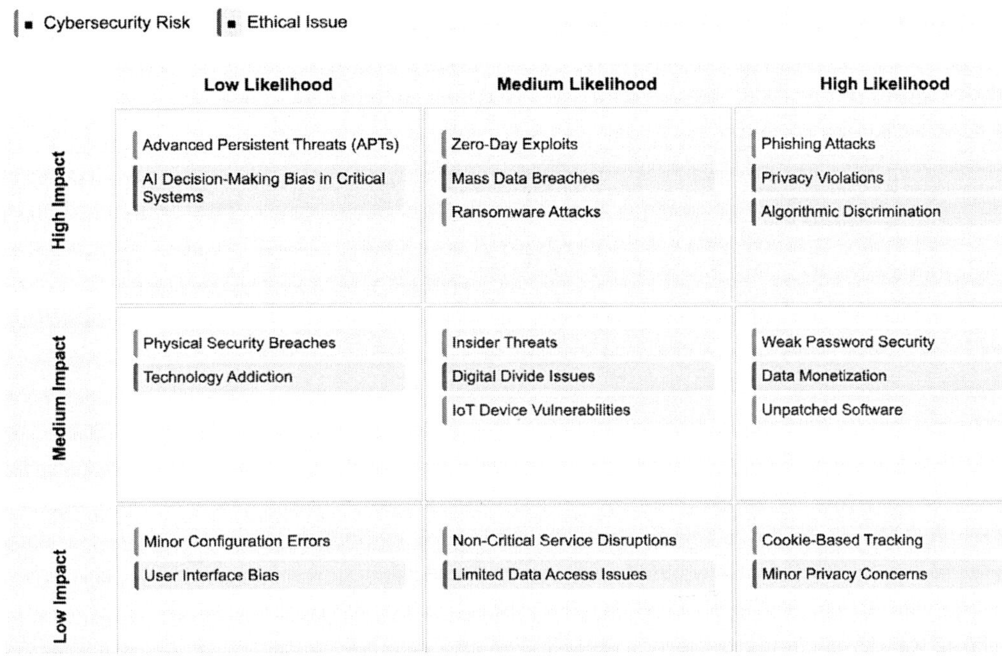

Figure 11.2 Risk matrix: cybersecurity vulnerabilities and ethical issues.

and lateral movement across the network. Finally, security awareness training for employees is crucial; teaching staff how to recognize phishing, how to securely deal with sensitive information, and how to adhere to cybersecurity policies inculcates security awareness and vigilance in the organization. By taking these measures, organizations can not only enhance their cybersecurity profile but also address the ethical challenges of data privacy and protection of users, thereby ensuring a safer digital environment.

11.4 SECTOR-SPECIFIC TECH ADOPTION: HEALTHCARE, EDUCATION, AND MANUFACTURING CASE EVIDENCE

Case studies of technology adoption in healthcare, education, and manufacturing (Umayal 2024; Cucciniello et al. 2024; Wolff et al. 2021; Zaidi et al. 2024) show significant positive impacts on operational efficiency, patient, and student outcomes. Stakeholder involvement, organization readiness, and system ease of use are the most critical success factors. However, challenges such as scalability, interoperability, and context-dependent barriers persist. Table 11.4 provides a structured overview of these case studies, highlighting the specific technologies implemented, critical success factors, implementation barriers, and measured impacts.

As demonstrated later in Table 11.5, healthcare, education, and manufacturing each face distinct technological adoption barriers requiring sector-specific mitigation strategies (Umayal 2024; Qing 2024; Zaidi et al. 2024).

Based on the studies presented in Table 11.3, we have developed the following discussion:

Table 11.4 Examples of technology implementations

Paper	*Technology*	*Sector*	*Success Factors*	*Barriers/Challenges*	*Measured Impact*
Umayal (2024)	HR, Telemedicine, AI	Healthcare	Implementation, ethical alignment	Not specified	Operational efficiency, communication, and care outcomes
Bizimana Rukundo (2024)	Telemedicine, Wearables, Mobile Apps	Healthcare (chronic disease)	Not explicit	Privacy, digital adoption	Patient outcomes, chronic disease management
Al Zulayq et al. (2024)	eHealth, Telemedicine, EHR, Mobile Health	Healthcare	Not explicit	Adoption, privacy	Diagnostics, personalization, patient satisfaction
Alawiye (2024)	Telemedicine, EHRs, Mobile Health	Healthcare	Improved access, efficiency	Data privacy	Healthcare delivery, diagnostics
Alnasser et al. (2024)	AI	Healthcare workplaces	Stakeholder acceptance, data privacy	Not explicit	No explicit measurable outcomes
Qing (2024)	AI, DSS, LMS	Higher education	Self-efficacy	Not specified	Learning outcomes, satisfaction, tool usage
Alajlan et al. (2024)	EMR	Healthcare	Not explicit (implementation inferred)	Not direct	Interdisciplinary collaboration, diagnostics, efficiency
Zaidi et al. (2024)	IoT	Healthcare	Not explicit (focus on impact)	Not specified	Productivity gains, digital transformation
Limna (2023)	Digital health transformation	Healthcare	Not explicit; synthesizes evidence	Privacy, provider resistance, regulatory barriers	No original case studies; focuses on impacts (efficiency, costs, outcomes)
Alanazi et al. (2023)	EHR	Healthcare	Not explicit; links to system quality, training	No empirical assessment, mixed evidence	No explicit measurement of success factors
Memon et al. (2022)	Interactive, self-regulated learning tech	Education	Not explicit; relates to student satisfaction, academic/ functional performance	Lacks detailed case studies	Measures satisfaction, academic outcomes
Salih et al. (2022)	ERP	Manufacturing SMEs	Top management, vendor support	Limited to manufacturing, not healthcare	Analyzes satisfaction, functional performance
Wolff et al. (2021)	AI	Healthcare	Policy, technology, impact measurement	Barriers identified in real-life cases	Focuses on measurable outcomes and success factors
Badr et al. (2021)	Digital health	Healthcare (Lebanon)	Stakeholder engagement, technical readiness, satisfaction	Not explicit	Measures satisfaction, engagement
Petitgand et al. (2020)	AI	Healthcare	Not explicit; reviews implementation factors	Lacks quantified measurement	Focuses on implementation factors, not outcomes
Cucciniello et al. (2016)	Electronic Medical Records (EMRs)	Healthcare	Organizational conditions, adoption processes, implementation strategies	Not explicitly detailed	Lacks explicit measurement of impact; discusses impact on outcomes in health

11.4.1 Key Findings: Impact of Technology in Specific Sectors

The impact of technology across specific sectors has been one of great improvements, complemented by challenges. The digital health tools—EHRs, AI, telemedicine, and IoT medical wearables—in healthcare have been instrumental in improving operational efficiency, quality of care, and patient outcomes. However, several studies highlight certain pitfalls in each of these aspects: privacy issues, user resistance, and inconsistent clinical outcomes. Various enablers for successful AI implementation in healthcare are needed, such as policy frameworks, technical integration, and economic impact measures. The second are participation design practices that would contribute significantly to technology adoption where the end-user participated in active involvement during development.

Industry 4.0 technologies are being adopted increasingly in manufacturing—IoT, robotics, and predictive maintenance—to enhance productivity, reduce downtime, and optimize the value chain, which are only hindered by more significant challenges, including upskilling the workforce and addressing cybersecurity risk and integration concerns with legacy systems.

The education sector has also benefited from the use of technology in learning management systems, AI-driven platforms, and decision support systems for performance improvement in learning, engagement, and satisfaction. However, these gaps exist with regard to scalability and developing appropriate, robust evaluation methods for understanding the long-term impacts.

A number of **critical success factors (CSFs)** emerge across these sectors. Universal themes include stakeholder engagement, which emphasizes the importance of end-users in design and deployment, and the need for training and digital literacy to ensure better adoption. Organizational readiness, defined by leadership commitment, investment in infrastructure, and effective workflow integration, is considered very important for successful technology implementation. The sector-specific CSFs are data interoperability and clinician satisfaction in healthcare; IoT system maturity and predictive analytics capabilities in manufacturing; and customizability to diverse classrooms, along with support for self-regulated learning in education.

Barriers and Challenges: Still, a variety of obstacles and challenges stand in the way. General interoperability issues contribute to a higher risk of failed integrations across the fragmented systems in the industries of healthcare, manufacturing, and educational technology. With regard to costs and scalability, the initial costs were very high, and scaling up pilot projects was quite difficult. Besides, ethical and privacy concerns associated with AI-based tools pose risks such as bias, data misuse, and violation of privacy, most especially in a health setting.

Frameworks and Methodologies: These have, in turn, led to the development of several frameworks and methodologies to address such issues. Generalized frameworks include the Technology Acceptance Model and Information Systems Success Models that provide orderly ways of assessing technology use. Quantitative approaches such as SEM and regression analyses, along with mixed-methods approaches, are resorted to in recent literature to explore issues relating to technology implementation and its effects. On the whole, these reflect both the highly transformative potential of technology in this or other spheres and the cautious consideration that it requires due to challenges and ethical implications.

While all sectors face shared challenges like data privacy and interoperability, Table 11.5 highlights how these manifest uniquely across domains, requiring tailored technological and policy responses.

Table 11.5 Sector-specific challenges and tailored mitigations

Sector	*Unique Challenge*	*Technology Leveraged*	*Policy Requirement*
Healthcare	Patient data silos	Federated learning for AI	General Data Protection Regulation (GDPR)-like patient consent protocols
Education	Digital divide in rural schools	Cloud-based LMS (Learning Management Systems) platforms	Universal broadband initiatives
Manufacturing	Predictive maintenance costs	IoT + 5G sensor networks	Tax incentives for SME (small and medium enterprises) adoption

These sector-specific considerations inform the targeted recommendations in Section 11.5, where mitigation strategies are mapped to organizational contexts.

11.5 POLICY AND IMPLEMENTATION ROADMAPS: SECURE, EQUITABLE TECH ADOPTION

Based on the findings of this chapter, we make a set of recommendations that are aimed at securing healthy technology progress, with security, equity, and innovation. These recommendations are organized according to policy frameworks, implementation best practices, and collaboration models.

11.5.1 Policy Frameworks

Policies for policymakers to ensure technology use equitably are as follows:

Universal Access Initiatives: Policymakers are to create policies that will be of great help in achieving universal access to technology, especially in less privileged communities. This could include subsidies for internet access, funding for digital literacy programs, support for infrastructure development, among others, in rural areas.

Regulatory Standards for Accessibility: Establish regulatory standards to ensure that technology firms design products and services that are accessible for use by any individual, particularly people with disabilities. This can be done through guidelines that highlight best practices in inclusive design.

Data Privacy and Protection Laws: Enact comprehensive data protection laws that ensure the protection of personal information for individuals while also holding organizations responsible in case of data breaches. Such laws shall include provisions about transparency regarding the collection and use of data.

Support of Research and Development: Ensure that the government provide finances for research and development in technologies emerging, be it for health tech innovation, social good, or sustainable energy solutions that level the playing field to bridge inequalities in access and create a fair playground for the use of technology.

Australia's technology governance landscape provides a concrete implementation model for these policy frameworks. As shown in Figure 11.3, key recommendations align with active

Australian Technology Governance Applications

Cybersecurity

- Aligns with ACSC's Essential Eight strategies for critical infrastructure protection
- Complements Australia's 2023-2030 Cyber Security Strategy on IoT device security (see Section 3.1)

AI Governance

- Support for astralla's AI Ethics Principles and ongoing parliamentary consultations on generative AI
- Case study finding affirm National AI Centre priorities in healthcare diagnostics (Bajwa et al., 2021)

Digital Safety

- Reinforces eSafety Commissioner initiatives on deepfake detection tools
- Education sector guidance (Section 4.2) aligns with Be Connected digital literacy programs

Policy Innovation

- Cross border models (Section 5.3) reflecting

"Australla's proactive stance on tech governance – from mandatory ransomware reporting to responsible AI trials – provides a testbed for this chapter's recommendations."

Figure 11.3 Call-out box-Australian technology governance applications.

Australian initiatives—from ACSC cybersecurity standards to eSafety's deepfake mitigation programs—demonstrating their real-world applicability.

11.5.2 Best Practices for Implementation

Strategies for the adoption of secure technology solutions by organizations are as follows:

Adopting a Security-First Approach: gives the premise on which an organization should consider how to embed mechanisms for cybersecurity as they develop the technology. This approach promotes periodic risk assessment and the adoption of secure code writing practices.

Employee Training: regular employee training on good cybersecurity practices: how to identify phishing emails, password management, and insider data protection regulations.

Regular Software Update and Patch Management: are standard best practices that seek to reduce vulnerabilities, requiring prompt application of security patches. The organization also needs to closely monitor any zero-day vulnerabilities and react swiftly.

Incident Response Plans: develop detailed incident response plans that outline procedures applicable to the detection, response, and recovery following cybersecurity incidents. Continuous testing through mock exercises should be conducted in order to validate readiness.

Data Encryption: effective encryption policies must be employed to secure sensitive information both in transit and at rest to avert unauthorized access and potential data breaches.

11.5.3 Collaboration Models

Fostering partnerships among governments, private sector leaders, and communities is essential for sustainable technological progress. Several collaborative models can facilitate this:

Public–Private Partnerships (PPPs): Incentivize partnerships among all levels of government and private sector organizations to share resources and expertise to develop secure technology solutions. These can provide a platform to share knowledge and evoke innovation to help solve societal challenges.

Community Engagement Initiatives: Engage local communities in decision-making processes related to technology deployment and usage. The engagement of community stakeholders ensures that technological solutions respond to particular local needs and concerns.

Cross-Sector Innovation Hubs: Create innovation hubs that bring together academia, industry leaders, non-profits, and government agencies in collaborative research projects aimed at developing safe and equitable technologies.

As mapped in Figure 11.4, civil society's role in monitoring industry complements academic research—a dynamic exemplified by our education case studies (Section 4.2).

Global Cooperation on Cybersecurity Standards: International cooperation toward establishing standardized cybersecurity practices on a global basis would improve those best practices cross-border. Collective efforts are paid off as most cyber threats expand across the country's boundary.

Platforms: Provide sharing on best practices and case studies between organizations in pursuit of the same technological advancements and/or with like challenges within their cybersecurity area of operations.

These recommendations, addressing policy frameworks, best practices in implementing secure technologies, and collaborative models, will allow stakeholders to work toward a healthier technological landscape: one that places security, equity, and innovation front and center. These strategies will enhance the resilience not just of organizations but also ensure that technology serves the broader interests of society as a whole.

Figure 11.5 visually summarizes the key policy recommendations and their implementation stages, as outlined in this section. The flowchart is designed to guide governments

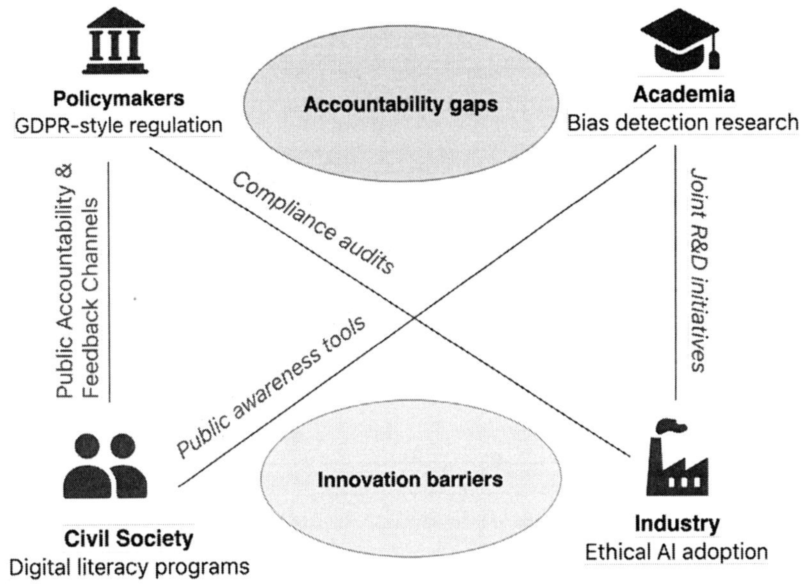

Figure 11.4 Stakeholder interdependencies in tech governance.

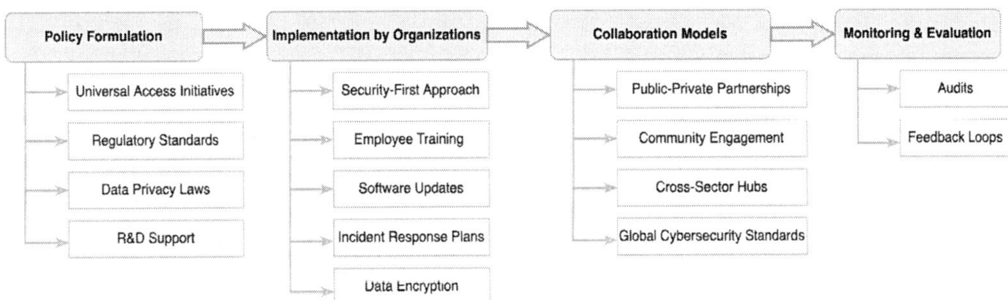

Figure 11.5 Policy framework flowchart for governments and organizations.

and organizations in adopting a structured approach to equitable, secure, and innovative technology progress.

11.6 DEEPFAKES AS A CONVERGENCE POINT FOR EMERGING TECH GOVERNANCE

The risks and policy frameworks discussed throughout this chapter find urgent, tangible expression in the challenge of AI-generated deepfakes. As synthetic media powered by the very advancements in generative AI, cloud computing, and data analytics examined in Sections 11.2 and 11.3, deepfakes crystallize three critical threats: (a) **systemic misinformation** through hyper-realistic impersonation, (b) **privacy erosion** via non-consensual synthetic content, and (c) **cybersecurity breaches** employing engineered audio/video for social engineering (Albaroudi et al. 2024; Ehimuan et al. 2024).

The chapter's recommended frameworks provide direct pathways for mitigation:

- **Cross-Sector Collaboration** (cf. Section 5.3) becomes essential when deepfakes simultaneously impact electoral processes (government), corporate reputations (industry), and public trust (civil society).
- **Ethical AI Development** (cf. Section 2.1.1) must prioritize detection capabilities and provenance standards to counter synthetic media at scale.
- **Regulatory Mechanisms** like those proposed for data privacy (cf. Section 5.1) require adaptation to mandate watermarking and establish liability frameworks for malicious deepfake creation.

Critically, deepfakes exemplify why the chapter's emphasis on **adaptive governance** is paramount: as detection technologies evolve, so too do generation methods. This arms race mirrors the IoT security challenges in Section 3.1, demanding the same dynamic policy responses. By viewing deepfakes not as an isolated phenomenon but as a convergence point for broader technological risks, this analysis underscores the necessity of the proactive, multi-stakeholder approaches championed throughout the chapter.

11.7 FUTURE DIRECTIONS

With technology still at a very rapid evolution rate, there are some future directions that can be expected in terms of development and integration within different sectors. First is the development in the field of AI and ML, which will probably be focused on improving governance frameworks and governance structures that ensure the responsible usage of AI. It also involves the development of algorithms that are fair, transparent, and accountable to address questions of algorithmic bias, ensuring AI applications equitably serve the needs of all users (cf. Figure 11.6).

Whereas current cloud computing complementarity is targeting integration with edge computing, in the future, emphases that will allow organizations to cut latency and do more real-time decision-making are due to data processing having been brought closer to its point of origin (cf. Figure 11.6). Further, with several organizations embracing hybrid or multi-cloud approaches, emphasis is also starting to shift toward interoperability solutions that can work seamlessly across multiple platforms and simplify data migration between them.

The IoT will continue to expand; most of the effort, however, will be related to security since devices in general can't help but be vulnerable due to their key characteristic: being connected. Some future evolutions could be blockchain-based node identity management and integrity of data for privacy concerns and eventually build trust in IoT ecosystems. Furthermore, 5G technology development will be a further boost to IoT applications, enabling better and more reliable connectivity, which is essential for smart cities and autonomous systems (cf. Figure 11.6).

Data analytics will continue to evolve in the future, with more sophisticated techniques driven by the use of AI to automate interpretative and decision-making processes (cf. Figure 11.6). As organizations increasingly rely on data-driven decisions, focus shall shift toward improving data quality, ensuring that data usage is done in an ethical manner, and increasing the use of advanced analytical models that can handle the complexity of big data.

Further, increasing applications in education, training, and other related fields are expected. Possible future directions include the development of user-friendly low-cost solutions in VR/AR that will increase ease of access and user experience (cf. Figure 11.6), thus promoting wider mainstream diffusion across diverse demographics.

It is also important to establish robust cybersecurity frameworks as emerging technologies introduce new vulnerabilities. Building on this in the future will require collaboration across governments, the private sector, and communities for comprehensive approaches toward cybersecurity that keep pace with threats. This same spirit of collaboration will be called upon in building standardized practices for addressing the global nature of cyber threats. In other words, the future of technology will be characterized by ethical considerations, increased security, and collaborative frameworks that ensure equity in access and benefits throughout society (cf. Figure 11.6). By prioritizing these aspects, stakeholders can harness the transformative potential of technology while mitigating associated risks.

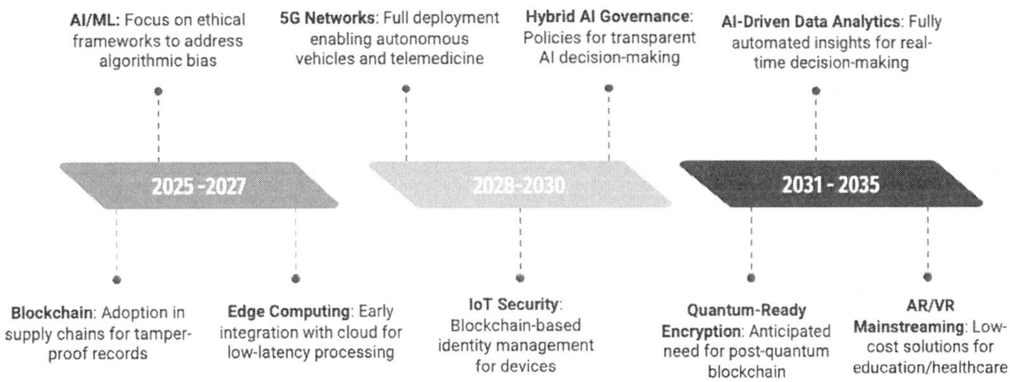

Figure 11.6 Anticipated timeline for emerging technology developments (2025–2035).

Table 11.6 Tech governance executive summary

Domain	*Major Challenges*	*Success Factors*	*Recommended Interventions*	*Linked Sections*
Cybersecurity	IoT vulnerabilities (Chataut et al. 2023)	Zero-trust adoption (Sedjelmaci & Ansari 2024)	Mandatory penetration testing for critical infrastructure	3.1, 5.2
Policy	Cross-border regulatory fragmentation	Stakeholder working groups (Wolff et al. 2021)	Model laws for AI/blockchain governance	5.1, 5.3
Innovation	Bias in training datasets (Albaroudi et al. 2024)	Diverse development teams (Bajwa et al. 2021)	Public-private R&D funding for ethical AI tools	2.1.1, 4.2
Community	Digital literacy gaps (Qing 2024)	Localized training programs	School curricula co-created with tech firms	4.2, 5.3

The complex challenges of governing emerging technologies require coordinated action across multiple domains. Table 11.6 synthesizes key findings from this chapter, mapping major challenges to evidence-based solutions in cybersecurity, policy, innovation, and community engagement. Drawing on case studies from healthcare, education, and manufacturing, this executive summary highlights how success factors like stakeholder collaboration (Section 5.3) and ethical frameworks (Section 3.2) can mitigate risks while fostering equitable progress.

11.8 CONCLUSION

The conclusion could be that, with rapid development in technology, it is a thing of pace that is changing many industries fast by improving their operations and decision-making for better output. The AI, cloud computing, IoT, and data analytics are some of the trends that are revolutionizing industries yet place new demands and ethical considerations. This, in turn, means that cybersecurity will have to be equally strong to safeguard sensitive data and user privacy. The case studies reviewed here have shown considerable positive impacts of technology implementation in healthcare, education, and manufacturing; at the same time, they have also indicated some persistent challenges related to scalability, interoperability, and ethical considerations. The CSFs, including stakeholder engagement and organizational readiness, have emerged as essential elements for successful technology adoption. Moving forward, the need is for convergence-developing inclusive frameworks that advance the cause of technology access with policymakers, industry leaders, and communities coming together. It is through partnership and sharing of best practices that stakeholders will be able to clear their way through the maze of challenges in the digital landscape and fully realize the benefits of technological innovation.

Ultimately, with the future moving to become increasingly interconnected and technologized, that focus needs to be on the bottom line, ensuring such an advancement serves larger social interests of operational performance enhancement, transparency, inclusivity, and ethical responsibility. The future is bright, full of huge opportunities; a thoughtful approach in addressing the resulting challenges will bring us closer to a more secure and equitable technological environment for everybody.

Key Takeaways

- **AI and IoT Dualities:** While AI-driven diagnostics (Bajwa et al. 2021) and IoT-enabled automation (Zaidi et al. 2024) boost efficiency, they require robust governance to address bias (Albaroudi et al. 2024) and cybersecurity risks (Aslan et al. 2023).
- **Sector-Specific Success Factors:** Stakeholder engagement and organizational readiness emerged as universal CSFs across healthcare (Umayal 2024), education (Qing 2024), and manufacturing (Zaidi et al. 2024) case studies.
- **Policy Imperatives:** Cross-border collaboration (cf. Section 5.3) and adaptive regulatory frameworks (cf. Section 5.1) are essential to balance innovation with equity in 5G, cloud, and blockchain adoption.
- **Implementation Roadmap:** Organizations must adopt security-first approaches (cf. Section 5.2), including employee training and zero-trust architectures (Sedjelmaci & Ansari 2024), to mitigate vulnerabilities.

By prioritizing these dimensions, stakeholders can harness technology's transformative potential while safeguarding against its risks—ensuring progress benefits society as a whole.

REFERENCES

Abdul-Azeez, O., Ihechere, A. O., & Idemudia, C. (2024). Enhancing business performance: The role of data-driven analytics in strategic decision-making. *International Journal of Management & Entrepreneurship Research*, 6(7), 2066–2081.

Achmad Bagraff, H., Kholis, N., Mugiyati, & Ghofi Nabila, F. (2024). Implementing blockchain technology for optimized supply chain and enhanced sustainability. *International Journal of Innovative Science and Research Technology (IJISRT)*, 9(8).

Alajlan, A. A. M., Alanazi, A. A. A., Al Fahad, A. I. A., Alnughaymishi, A. A. S., & Al Harbi, S. H. (2024). The role of electronic medical records (EMRs) and health informatic technician in enhancing interdisciplinary collaboration. *International Journal of Health Sciences*, 8(S1), 1860–1869.

Alanazi, F. M., Almohesen, S. A., Alharbi, M. B., Alharbi, K. J., Alharbi, T. M., Alruwaydhan, N. A., Alharbi, M. S., & Almutairi, O. M. (2023). Using electronic health records to improve patient health care. *Saudi Journal of Medicine*, 8(9): 514–518.

Alawiye, T. (2024). The impact of digital technology on healthcare delivery and patient outcomes. *E-Health Telecommunication Systems and Networks*. https://doi.org/10.4236/etsn.2024.132002

Albaroudi, E., Mansouri, T., & Alameer, A. (2024). A comprehensive review of AI techniques for addressing algorithmic bias in job hiring. *AI*, 5(1), 383–404.

Alnasser, A. H., Hassanain, M. A., Alnasser, M. A., & Alnasser, A. H. (2024). Critical factors challenging the integration of AI technologies in healthcare workplaces: A stakeholder assessment. *Journal of Health Organization and Management*. https://doi.org/10.1108/JHOM-04-2024-0135

Alowais, S. A., Alghamdi, S. S., Alsuhebany, N., et al. (2023). Revolutionizing healthcare: The role of artificial intelligence in clinical practice. *BMC Medical Education*, 23, 689.

Alshammari, B. M. (2023). AIBPSF-IoMT: Artificial intelligence and blockchain-based predictive security framework for IoMT technologies. *Electronics*, 12(23), 4806.

Al Zulayq, A. A. S., Al-Zulaiq, S. A. S., et al. (2024). Transforming patient care: A systematic review of the impact of eHealth on healthcare delivery. *Journal of Ecohumanism*, 3(8), 1685–1689.

Asiri, S. A., Xiao, Y., Alzahrani, S., Li, S., & Li, T. (2023). A survey of intelligent detection designs of HTML URL phishing attacks. *IEEE Access*, 11, 6421–6443.

Aslan, Ö., Aktuğ, S. S., Ozkan-Okay, M., Yilmaz, A. A., & Akin, E. (2023). A comprehensive review of cyber security vulnerabilities, threats, attacks, and solutions. *Electronics*, 12(6), 1333.

Badr, N., Chami, E., & Asmar, M. (2021). e-Health implementation in lebanese teaching hospitals: What can we learn from their successes and imminent challenges. In *Proceedings of the 14th International Joint Conference on Biomedical Engineering Systems and Technologies (BIOSTEC 2021)—Volume 5: HEALTHINF*. ISBN 978-989-758-490-9, SciTePress, 304–311.

Badrinarayanan, A. (2024). AI in manufacturing: Driving operational excellence. *International Journal of Scientific Research in Computer Science, Engineering and Information Technology*, 10(6), 585–594.

Bajwa, J., Munir, U., Nori, A., & Williams, B. (2021). Artificial intelligence in healthcare: Transforming the practice of medicine. *Future Healthcare Journal*, 8(2), e188–e194.

Baragash, R. S., Aldowah, H., & Ghazal, S. (2022). Virtual and augmented reality applications to improve older adults' quality of life: A systematic mapping review and future directions. *Digital Health*, 8.

Berliner, D. (2017). Sunlight or window dressing? Local government compliance with South Africa's promotion of access to information act. *Governance*, 30, 641–661.

Bharara, S., Sabitha, S., & Bansal, A. (2018). Application of learning analytics using clustering data Mining for Students' disposition analysis. *Education and Information Technologies*, 23, 957–984.

Bhattacharyya, L., Purohit, S. G., Fatmawati, E., Sunil, D. M., Toktakynovna, Z., & Sriramakrishnan, G. V. (2022, October). Cloud computing for suitable data management and security within organisations. In *2022 3rd International Conference on Smart Electronics and Communication (ICOSEC)* (pp. 912-916). IEEE.

Bizimana, R. T. (2024). The impact of digital health on improving patient outcomes. *Newport International Journal of Research in Medical Sciences*, 5(3), 38–41.

Bruno, R. R., Wolff, G., Wernly, B., Masyuk, M., Piayda, K., Leaver, S., Erkens, R., Oehler, D., Afzal, S., Heidari, H., Kelm, M., & Jung, C. (2022). Virtual and augmented reality in critical care medicine: The patient's, clinician's, and researcher's perspective. *Critical Care*, 26.

Chataut, R., Phoummalayvane, A., & Akl, R. (2023). Unleashing the power of IoT: A comprehensive review of IoT applications and future prospects in healthcare, agriculture, smart homes, smart cities, and Industry 4.0. *Sensors*, 23(16), 7194.

Cucciniello, M., Lapsley, I., & Nasi, G. (2016). Managing health care in the digital world: A comparative analysis. *Health Services Management Research*, 29(4), 132–142.

Davenport, T. H. (2018). *The AI Advantage*. Cambridge, MA: MIT Press.

Dika-Krluku, N. (2025). Importance of data analytics in business. *Science International Journal*, 3(3), 111–115.

Eguia, H., Sánchez-Bocanegra, C. L., Vinciarelli, F., Alvarez-Lopez, F., & Saigí-Rubió, F. (2024). Clinical decision support and natural language processing in medicine: Systematic literature review. *Journal of Medical Internet Research*, 26, e55315.

Ehimuan, B., Chimezie, O., Ob, Akagha, O. V., Reis, O., & Oguejiofor, B. B. (2024). Global data privacy laws: A critical review of technology's impact on user rights. *World Journal of Advanced Research and Reviews*, 21(2), 1058–1070.

Elete, T. Y., Nwulu, E. O., Erhueh, O. V., Akano, O. A., & Aderamo, A. T. (2024). Digital transformation in the oil and gas industry: A comprehensive review of operational efficiencies and case studies. *International Journal of Applied Research in Social Sciences*, 6(11), 2611–2643.

Elgazzar, K., Khalil, H., Alghamdi, T., Badr, A., Abdelkader, G. R., Elewah, A., & Buyya, R. (2022). Revisiting the internet of things: New trends, opportunities and grand challenges. *Frontiers in the Internet of Things*, 1, Article 2022.

Fakoor, R., Ladhak, F., Nazi, A., & Huber, M. (2013). Using deep learning to enhance cancer diagnosis and classification. In *Proceedings of the ICML Workshop on the Role of Machine Learning in Transforming Healthcare*.

Ghadi, Y. Y., Shah, S. F., Mazhar, T., Shahzad, T., Ouahada, K., & Hamam, H. (2024). Enhancing patient healthcare with mobile edge computing and 5G: Challenges and solutions for secure online health tools. *Journal of Cloud Computing*, 13, 93.

Granadillo, G. G., Zarzosa, S. G., & Díaz, R. (2021). Security information and event management (SIEM): Analysis, trends, and usage in critical infrastructures. *Sensors* (Basel, Switzerland), 21.

Groš, S., Kovačević, I., Dujmi'c, I., & Petrinovic, M. (2021). Controlled update of software components using concurrent exection of patched and unpatched versions. *ArXiv, abs/2106.01154*.

Hossain, M. A., Hwang, S., & Kim, J. (2022). Resource profiling and performance modeling for distributed scientific computing environments. *Applied Sciences*, 12(9), 4797.

Hussain, N. M., O'Halloran, M., Mcdermott, B., & Elahi, M. A. (2023). Fetal monitoring technologies for the detection of intrapartum hypoxia—challenges and opportunities. *Biomedical Physics & Engineering Express*, 10.

Kelly, J. T., Campbell, K. L., Gong, E., & Scuffham, P. (2020). The Internet of Things: Impact and implications for health care delivery. *Journal of Medical Internet Research*, 22(11), e20135.

Lalanne, C. (2016). Statistical data analytics. Foundations for data mining, informatics, and knowledge discovery. *Journal of Statistical Software*, 69, 1–2.

Lee, I., & Mangalaraj, G. (2022). Big data analytics in supply chain management: A systematic literature review and research directions. *Big Data and Cognitive Computing*, 6, 17.

Lee, S. I., Celik, S., Logsdon, B. A., et al. (2018). A machine learning approach to integrate big data for precision medicine in acute myeloid leukemia. *Nature Communications*, 9, 42.

Limna, P. (2023). The digital transformation of healthcare in the digital economy: A systematic review. *International Journal of Advanced Health Science and Technology*, 3(2), 127–132.

Marasu, N., & Arathi, D. M. (2023). Big data analytics and mining for effective visualization and trends forecasting of crime data. *International Journal for Research in Applied Science and Engineering Technology*, 11(12), 529–534.

Memon, M. Q., Lu, Y., Memon, A. R., Memon, A., Munshi, P., & Shah, S. F. A. (2022). Does the impact of technology sustain students' satisfaction, academic and functional performance: An analysis via interactive and self-regulated learning? *Sustainability*, 14(12), 7226.

Mohamed, N., Taherdoost, H., & Madanchian, M. (2024). Comprehensive review of advanced machine learning techniques for detecting and mitigating zero-day exploits. *EAI Endorsed Transactions on Scalable Information Systems*, 11(6).

Molina-Masegosa, R., & Gozálvez, J. (2017). LTE-V for sidelink 5G V2X vehicular communications: A new 5G technology for short-range vehicle-to-everything communications. *IEEE Vehicular Technology Magazine*, 12, 30–39.

Nguyen, H. X., Vu, T. T., Vo, T. P., & Thai, H. (2021). Efficient machine learning models for prediction of concrete strengths. *Construction and Building Materials*, 266, 120950.

Niu, B., Zhang, J., & Mu, Z. (2022). IoT-enabled delivery time guarantee in logistics outsourcing and efficiency improvement. *International Journal of Production Research*, 61(12), 4135–4156.

Nofer, M., Gomber, P., Hinz, O., & Schiereck, D. (2020). Blockchain. *Business & Information Systems Engineering*, 59, 183–187.

Noor, M. A., & Mustafa, K. (2024). A taxonomy of endpoint vulnerabilities and affected blockchain architecture layers. *Concurrency and Computation: Practice and Experience*, 36.

Paolino, M., Carrozzo, G., Betzler, A., Meixner, C. C., Khalili, H., Siddiqui, S., Sechkova, T., & Simeonidou, D. (2019). *Compute and Network Virtualization at the Edge for 5G Smart Cities Neutral Host Infrastructures*. 2019 IEEE 2nd 5G World Forum (5GWF), 560–565.

Petitgand, C., Motulsky, A., Denis, J. L., & Régis, C. (2020). Investigating the barriers to physician adoption of an artificial intelligence-based decision support system in emergency care: An interpretative qualitative study. In *Digital Personalized Health and Medicine* (pp. 1001–1005). IOS Press.

Prakash, S., Kumbhar, U. T., Kakade, S. V., Anitha, G., & Mittal, A. (2024). Integration of data mining and big data analytics in healthcare. In *2024 International Conference on Healthcare Innovations, Software and Engineering Technologies (HISET)*, 230–233.

Qing, G. (2024). Decision support systems for lifelong learning: Leveraging information systems to enhance learning quality in higher education. *Journal of Internet Services and Information Security*, 14, 121–143.

Reddy, B. (2023). Unleashing the power of the Internet of Things: Enabling technologies, protocols, and applications for a connected world. In *2023 3rd International Conference on Advancement in Electronics & Communication Engineering (AECE)*. GHAZIABAD, India, 2023, pp. 739–743.

Salama, A. F. (2024). The impact of AI applications (virtual reality and augmented reality) in the hospitality industry: Opportunities and challenges. *Journal of Association of Arab Universities for Tourism and Hospitality*, 27(1), 109–124.

Salih, S. H., et al. (2022). Critical success factors for ERP systems' post-implementations of SMEs in Saudi Arabia: A top management and vendors' perspective. *IEEE Access*, 10, 108004–108020.

Sedjelmaci, H., & Ansari, N. (2024). Zero trust architecture empowered attack detection framework to secure 6G edge computing. *IEEE Network*, 38, 196–202.

Selvan Chenni Chetty, T., Bolshev, V., Shankar Subramanian, S., Chakrabarti, T., Chakrabarti, P., Panchenko, V., Yudaev, I., & Daus, Y. (2023). Optimized hierarchical tree deep convolutional neural network of a tree-based workload prediction scheme for enhancing power efficiency in cloud computing. *Energies*, 16(6), 2900.

Shafique, K., Khawaja, B. A., Sabir, F., Qazi, S., & Mustaqim, M. (2020). Internet of Things (IoT) for next-generation smart systems: A review of current challenges, future trends and prospects for emerging 5G-IoT scenarios. *IEEE Access*, 8, 23022–23040.

Stoica, M., & Nitu, A. (2024). Efficiency and cost-effectiveness in agile DevOps with cloud computing. *Proceedings of the International Conference on Business Excellence*, 18, 3543–3556.

Sujatha, S., & Ambia, D. G. (2024). Analyzing the cost-effectiveness of adopting cloud computing solutions in library. *International Journal of Advanced Research in Science, Communication and Technology*, 4(3), 2581–9429.

Thomas, B., Thampi, S. M., & Mukherjee, P. (2025). Identifying insecure network configurations through attack modeling and explainable AI. In *International Conference on Information Systems Security*, pp. 201–212. Cham: Springer.

Tran, T., Do, B. G., Ngo, A., Krishtipati, S., Dang, N. A., & Sarkar, S. (2024). The impacts of layoffs announcement on cybersecurity breaches. *Pacific Asia Conference on Information Systems*, 2024, 1–29.

Umayal, K. (2024). Strategic integration of digital health technologies for enhanced patient-centered care in modern healthcare management. *Shanlax International Journal of Management*, 11(iS1-Jan), 68–73.

Villarreal-Vasquez, M., Modelo-Howard, G., Dube, S., & Bhargava, B. K. (2023). Hunting for insider threats using LSTM-based anomaly detection. *IEEE Transactions on Dependable and Secure Computing*, 20, 451–462.

Wang, Z., Xia, M., Weng, L., Hu, K., & Lin, H. (2024). Dual encoder–decoder network for land cover segmentation of remote sensing image. *IEEE Journal of Selected Topics in Applied Earth Observations and Remote Sensing*, 17, 2372–2385.

Wei, Z., Qu, H., Wang, Y., Yuan, X., Wu, H., Du, Y., Han, K., Zhang, N., & Feng, Z. (2023). Integrated sensing and communication signals toward 5G-A and 6G: A survey. *IEEE Internet of Things Journal*, 10, 11068–11092.

Wolff, J., Pauling, J., Keck, A., & Baumbach, J. (2021). Success factors of artificial intelligence implementation in healthcare. *Frontiers in Digital Health*, 3. https://doi.org/10.3389/fdgth.2021.594971

Xu, L. D., Lu, Y., & Li, L. (2021). Embedding blockchain technology into IoT for security: A survey. *IEEE Internet of Things Journal*, 8(13), 10452–10473.

Yuvashree, S. (2023). Current trends and innovation in information. *International Journal of Trendy Research in Engineering and Technology*, 7(5), 1–3.

Zaidi, S. M. R., Alam, A., & Khan, M. Y. (2024). Enhancing efficiency in advanced manufacturing through IoT integration. In *Engineering Headway. 2nd International Conference on Recent Advancements in Materials, Design & Manufacturing*. Trans Tech Publications Ltd. https://doi.org/10.4028/p-4hbpgf

Zhang, Y., & Liu, N. (2021). Optimal Internet of Things technology adoption decisions and pricing strategies for high-traceability logistics services. *Sustainability*, 13(19), 10597.

Zhao, X., Ren, Y., & Cheah, K. S. (2023). Leading virtual reality (VR) and augmented reality (AR) in education: Bibliometric and content analysis from the Web of Science (2018–2022). *SAGE Open*, 13.

Zheng, Z., Xie, S., Dai, H., Chen, X., & Wang, H. (2017, June). An overview of blockchain technology: Architecture, consensus, and future trends. In *2017 IEEE International Congress on big Data (BigData Congress)*, pp. 557–564). IEEE.

Zheng, Z., Xie, S., Dai, H., Chen, X., & Wang, H. (2018). Blockchain challenges and opportunities: A survey. *International Journal of Web and Grid Services*, 14, 352–375.1

Index

For Product Safety Concerns and Information please contact our EU representative GPSR@taylorandfrancis.com Taylor & Francis Verlag GmbH, Kaufingerstraße 24, 80331 München, Germany